EXPLORING THE OLD TESTAMENT

Volume 4

The Prophets

OLD
TESTAMENT

Exploring the
Old Testament

A Guide to the Prophets

Volume
Four

GORDON MCCONVILLE

InterVarsity Press
Downers Grove, Illinois

InterVarsity Press
P.O. Box 1400, Downers Grove, IL 60515-1426
World Wide Web: www.ivpress.com
E-mail: mail@ivpress.com

InterVarsity Press® is the book-publishing division of InterVarsity Christian Fellowship/USA®, a student movement active on campus at hundreds of universities, colleges and schools of nursing in the United States of America, and a member movement of the International Fellowship of Evangelical Students. For information about local and regional activities, write Public Relations Dept., InterVarsity Christian Fellowship/USA, 6400 Schroeder Rd., P.O. Box 7895, Madison, WI 53707-7895, or visit the IVCF website at <www.intervarsity.org>.

Cover photograph: Josef Molar/Superstock

ISBN-10: 0-8308-2554-1
ISBN-13: 978-0-8308-2554-7

Printed in Great Britain ∞

Library of Congress Cataloging-in-Publication Data

McConville, J. G. (J. Gordon)
    Exploring the Old Testament/J. Gordon McConville.
        p. cm.
    Includes bibliographical references and index.
    Contents:—v. 4. The prophets
    ISBN 0-8308-2554-1 (v. 4: cloth: alk. paper)
    1. Bible. O.T.—Introductions. I. Title.

BS1140.3 .M33 2002
221.6'1—dc 21

                                                                                    2002032821

| **P** | 26 | 25 | 24 | 23 | 22 | 21 | 20 | 19 | 18 | 17 | 16 | 15 | 14 | 13 | 12 | 11 | 10 | 9 | 8 | 7 | 6 | 5 | 4 | 3 |
| **Y** | 28 | 27 | 26 | 25 | 24 | 23 | 22 | 21 | 20 | 19 | 18 | 17 | 16 | 15 | 14 | 13 | 12 | 11 | 10 | 09 | 08 | 07 |

Contents

THE PROPHETS

THE DATES OF KINGS AND PROPHETS

The dates of the kings of Israel and Judah are disputed. One view of the chronology is given in *IBD* I, pp. 268–77, in which the authors follow the concept of co-regencies proposed by E. R. Thiele, *The Mysterious Numbers of the Hebrew Kings* (Grand Rapids: Eerdmans, 1965). Not all scholars are convinced by this solution, and commentators on the prophetic books often accept that dates can only be approximate. The dates adopted in the present volume follow J. Bright, *A History of Israel* (London: SCM, 1972, second edition) which is largely based in turn on W. F. Albright in *BASOR* 100 (1945), pp. 20–22. In the table below, no account is taken of co-regencies, although these may be needed to solve some problems (for example, see Bright, p. 271, n. 8, on the twenty years given to Pekah in 2 Kgs 15:27).

For different versions of the chronology of the Kings of Judah from Uzziah to Hezekiah see F. I. Andersen and D. N. Freedman, *Micah* (AB; New York: Doubleday, 2000), p. xviii.

In the table below the prophets are aligned only approximately with the kings, for ready reference. The table should be used with reference to the discussions of the Date and Destination of the individual prophets. (Jonah and Daniel are put in brackets for reasons that will become clear in the chapters on those books.)

BEFORE THE EXILE

Kings of Israel		Kings of Judah		Prophets
Jeroboam II	786–746	Uzziah	783–742	Amos (Jonah)
Zechariah	746–745			
Shallum	745			Hosea
Menahem	745–738	Jotham	742–735	
Pekahiah	738–737			
Pekah	737–732	Ahaz	735–715	Isaiah, Micah
Hoshea	732–722			
		Hezekiah	715–687	
		Manasseh	687–642	
		Amon	642–640	
		Josiah	640–609	Habakkuk, Nahum Zephaniah
		Jehoahaz	609	Jeremiah
		Jehoiakim	609–597	Obadiah
		Jehoiachin	597	
		Zedekiah	597–587	Ezekiel Joel?

EXILE AND AFTER:
KINGS OF BABYLON AND PERSIA
(see also table at Daniel: Date and Destination)

Kings of Babylon and Persia		Prophets
605–562	Reign of Nebuchadn(r)ezzar	(Daniel)
562–560	Reign of Amel-marduk (Evil-Merodach)	
560–556	Reign of Neriglissar	
556–539	Reign of Nabonidus	Second Isaiah
549–539	Belshazzar co-regent	
539	Babylon captured by Cyrus the Persian	
539–530	Reign of Cyrus after capture of Babylon	
530–522	Reign of Cambyses	
522–486	Reign of Darius I Hystaspes	Haggai, Zechariah, Malachi

KEY TO PANELS

This key to the panels helps locate the special and suggested exercises that occur throughout the volume. It should be noted that the panels are not exhaustive treatments of topics, and are meant to be read and used in their contexts. Panels sometimes cross-refer to other parts of the book.

A number of themes may be picked up by looking carefully across the different kinds of boxes (for example: Israel, metaphor, prophecy/prophets, rhetoric).

'THINK ABOUT' PANELS

'DIGGING DEEPER' PANELS

OTHER PANELS

INTRODUCTION

WHAT THIS BOOK AIMS TO DO

This book aims to help students study the Prophets. Like other volumes in the *EOT* and *ENT* series, it is intended to give the student a primary resource to enable him or her to study the texts independently. It provides introductory material on each book, a basic commentary, and pointers to theological interpretation. It is also interactive. Interspersed in the interpretation are a number of panels, which invite the student to think about what has been learnt (Think about), or to take an aspect of the study further (Digging deeper). Some of the panels are simply background notes, supplying extra information to clarify difficult issues or points. Essay titles as such are not supplied, but can be constructed out of many of the panels. A key to the panels enables the reader to see at a glance what topics are dealt with in them.

The book is intended to open onto a range of critical and interpretative literature on the prophets. Each chapter is supplied with lists of commentaries and other works, most of which are referred to in the chapter in question. Items marked with * are considered suitable as first ports of call,

while others are more complex, or relate to specific issues.

Above all the book is written in the belief that the prophets have important things to say to modern people. They are sometimes misunderstood, and, in church life, often neglected. That is nothing new for the prophets, as it was neglect that they themselves typically challenged in their hearers, rather than offering them 'some new thing'. So I hope that this book will make a small contribution to their being heard clearly again.

STUDYING THE PROPHETIC BOOKS

PROPHETS AND BOOKS

The study of the prophets can be illustrated by two very different passages from the prophetic books, one near the beginning and the other right at the end. The first is Isa. 6:1–13. In this, Isaiah has his famous vision of God as the heavenly king. It is the most dramatic picture of the prophet's experience of God. Isaiah is overwhelmed by the vision of God's glory, so that he is deeply aware of his own sin. Yet apparently it is this vision that inspires and motivates his whole ministry. The vision leads to understanding, and to action. It is no surprise, then, that this passage has become the classic text for the idea of call itself. (It is one of the passages that are always read at ordination services in the Church of England.)

The second passage, much less famous, is Mal. 4:4–6. These words close the whole collection of the prophetic books. They exhort the people to remember the laws of Moses, and promises the return of 'Elijah' 'before the great and terrible day of the Lord comes'. The law and the prophets stand together in these verses. The prophets stand alongside a 'book' (Moses' law), and they have themselves become a book. The close of the prophetic section of the Old Testament announces the concept of 'the law and the prophets', a canon of Scripture.

Our study of 'the prophets' lies between these two moments: the conviction of individuals that they had words from God that were urgent, for people then and there; and the collection of the prophets' words for the benefit of new generations, well beyond their own time, right down to us who still read them and are challenged by them.

In studying the prophets we cannot avoid the 'book'. Indeed, 'The Prophets' in the title of this volume refers to a division of the canon of the Old Testament. When we look for Jeremiah, what we find is a book that tells us about Jeremiah and the things he did and said. The book was written (finally at least) by someone other than Jeremiah, for a time and place other than his own. And a number of the prophets are much more elusive than Jeremiah. (How often, when introducing one or other of the prophetic books, I have had to say: 'Very little is known about x'!)

Even so, we will not be wrong to look for the prophet. Isaiah's vision speaks of the central idea in the books: that God spoke to individuals and commissioned them to speak in turn.

The relationship between 'prophet' and 'book' could be stated as a kind of problem or dilemma. Are we being teased with the promise of introductions to real people who finally elude us? Some studies focus so much on the book – in the guise of 'the tradition', or the 'final form' – that we lose the prophet altogether. Some regard the prophetic figures as the fictitious creations of the writers or communities who created the books. In my view, the opposite poles of prophet and book need not be treated as a problem. They are simply an inevitable part of the study before us. Both poles must be respected: the book because it is part of the canonical literature, and the prophet because his God-given message is the controlling idea in the book.

What, then, are the key elements in studying the prophetic books? The following topics correspond to the headings we shall use in this volume when we come to each of them.

THE PROPHET

Each chapter that follows will begin with some notes on the Date and Destination of the prophecy. This will ask questions about who the prophet was, the time in which he worked, and whom he spoke to. But what may we know about the prophets? We have several lines on this.

Information in the individual books

A number of the books give information about the prophets in their introductory headings, or superscriptions (e.g. Amos 1:1; Jer. 1:1–3) and elsewhere (Amos 7:14; Jer.

THE PROPHETS AS A SECTION OF THE OLD TESTAMENT CANON

The books that bear the names of prophets form a distinct section of the Old Testament. This is true whether we are thinking of the Christian form of the Old Testament canon, or the Jewish form (the 'Hebrew Bible'). The Hebrew Bible is usually divided into three sections: the Law (that is, the Pentateuch, or the Five Books of Moses), the Prophets and the Writings. In that division, the Prophets section is further divided into the Former Prophets (the Historical Books from Joshua to Kings, without Ruth), and the Latter Prophets. These Latter Prophets are the books that carry the names of particular prophets.

Christian Bibles broadly follow the order of the Greek Old Testament (known as the Septuagint, or LXX), and put these prophetic books at the end of the Old Testament. They also include two books that are omitted from the Hebrew form of the canon, namely Lamentations and Daniel. In the Hebrew form, these two (along with Ruth, Chronicles, Nehemiah, Ezra and Esther) belong in the Writings section. However, Lamentations was linked from a very early period with Jeremiah, and so was attached to that book in the canonical tradition found in LXX. Daniel is different in important ways from the other books in the prophetic collection. In scholarship it is usually classified as 'apocalyptic' rather than prophecy. (This is explained in the chapter on Daniel.) However, as it is like the prophets in its idea of an individual who receives revelations from God, and as it also has

specific links with certain prophetic books (especially Jeremiah and Ezekiel), it too found its way into the prophets section of the canon as we have it in LXX, and so in Christian Bibles.

In *Exploring the Old Testament* we have adopted the divisions of the Christian Old Testament. This means, for example, that the volume on the Historical Books includes Ruth and Chronicles–Esther, and also that we deal with Lamentations and Daniel in the present volume. This choice has not been made for dogmatic reasons. But as we expect most of our readers to be using English Bibles, and the discussions presuppose no knowledge of Hebrew, it was the natural choice.

For the same reason we are using the term 'Old Testament'. Of course this is a loaded term, as is the alternative, the Hebrew Bible. Strictly speaking, each of these names implies a claim to 'own' the book in question, either on the part of the Christian Church or the Jewish synagogue. It is not our intention in *EOT* to enter a debate about this, or to be dogmatic about it. And we hope that a Jewish reader could use our volumes for his or her own study. Yet *EOT* is a companion series to *ENT*, and the primary target audience of both is students undertaking introductory courses on the Bible in broadly Christian contexts. In *EOT* this will emerge most clearly from those parts of our studies that reflect on the relationship between the Old and New Testaments.

25:1–3; Zech. 1:1, 7; 7:1). These point to historical situations, and sometimes give details about the prophet's family and his location in society (Jeremiah and Ezekiel were of priestly families). Some also tell about things they did (Amos 7:10–14; Isaiah 7—8). The Book of Jeremiah tells us a good deal about that prophet, including an incident that gives a clue about how his book came to be written (Jeremiah 36).

However, this kind of information varies

from book to book. Some of the headings give little away (Joel 1:1; Nah. 1:1; Hab. 1:1; Mal. 1:1), and the prophets can remain rather shadowy. Even where much information seems to be given, scholars scrutinize it severely to see what it really tells. Since the information is patchy, it probably means that it is not felt to be greatly important in itself. When books do tell us details about a prophet's life, it is likely that this is not for its own sake, but is part of the message of the book. This is certainly true of Jeremiah 36, for example. (See below, The prophets: Did they write? for more on Jeremiah 36. Some scholars used to talk of 'biographical' parts of Jeremiah, but that idea is no longer popular, because it is recognized that the writers did not have the same interest in people's lives for their own sake as a modern reader might have).

A broad Old Testament picture

Apart from details about individual prophets, we have some glimpses of 'the prophets' as a body. The stories of Elisha, for example, speak of a group of 'the sons of the prophets' (just another way of saying 'the prophets'), who live and work together (2 Kgs 4:1; 6:1). This suggests they were a recognizable group within society. A story of King Saul suggests that they engaged in ecstatic behaviour, under the influence of 'the spirit of God' (1 Sam. 10:9–13). King Ahab expected them to give him guidance when he was facing a big decision, such as whether to go to war (though Ahab was careful to choose which ones he listened to! 1 Kgs 22:6–8).

The prophets as a body come to be regarded as the ones who called Israel to repent. This is how they appear in 2 Kgs 17:13, and there are echoes of this in the prophetic books themselves (Hos. 6:1; Jer. 3:1—4:4). They do not always appear in a good light, however. The story of Ahab already illustrates this (1 Kgs 22:24). And the prophetic books themselves sometimes portray 'the prophets' as unfaithful time-servers (e.g. Hos. 4:5; Amos 7:12–13; Jer. 23:9–40). This raises the question of how people might know the difference between a 'true' prophet and a 'false' one. The book of Jeremiah faces this problem directly. (It raises a quite different point for some scholars, namely whether the Old Testament

has a unified view of 'the prophets'. See the panel: Digging deeper: Finding prophets.)

Sociology

The biblical picture has been viewed by some recent scholarship from a particular angle. If we have only limited knowledge about individual prophets, perhaps we can find out something about their 'social location', that is, their place as a group or class within society. Fundamental to this concept is that prophets have 'support groups', that is groups that recognize the prophet as speaking authoritatively.

To try to discover the prophets' social location, scholars have observed how intermediaries are placed in other societies: do they, and their support groups, belong within the 'establishment' or outside it? Do they support or disturb the *status quo*? Sociological studies have examined the different names used for prophets ('prophet', 'seer', 'man of God') and the ways in which they receive messages from God (especially in speech and vision). Variations in these respects have led some to find regional variations in the status and roles of prophets. Northern prophets, for example, have been thought to belong within a particular tradition in which the Mosaic covenant plays a significant governing role in their thought. Southern prophets like Isaiah, in contrast, are said to be influenced by 'vision', and this is related to a theology in which the temple, and the Davidic covenant, play an important role. (Wilson 1980, Petersen 1981 and Overholt 1996 are key studies on this topic.)

One gain of this approach is to give a way of thinking about how a prophet's words might originally have been preserved. If prophets had 'support groups' they will have wanted to preserve the authoritative words. One reason for this will have been to measure them against events, and have proof of their authenticity. It is clear that there was a great concern to know whether prophets' words were true or false (Deut. 13; 18:20–22).

The question of how prophets' words were preserved comes up differently with different prophets. See, for example, Isaiah: The composition of Isaiah 1—39.

The prophets: Did they write?

A special question in studying the prophets as individuals concerns how they gave their messages. Did they speak only, or did they also write? When they spoke, was it only in rather short poetic oracles, or could they also give more connected 'sermonic' speeches? (This last question comes up sharply in Jeremiah.) These questions are obviously related to the broader question of how accurate a picture of the prophet we are getting from the book.

This is a fundamental issue in the study of the prophets, but there is surprisingly little agreement about it. The classic critical view was that prophets spoke in poetry, and the prosaic sections of their books were written only afterwards by less gifted disciples (proposed by B. Duhm 1901; see L. Stulman 1986 e.g. pp. 8–9). This view has been greatly contested in Jeremiah studies, where a number of scholars have argued that Jeremiah himself uttered the sermonic speeches (e.g. J. Bright; see on Jeremiah: Critical Interpretation). (The debate now seems to have reached an opposite extreme, with some saying the prophets were *not* prophets but *poets*; see Finding prophets.) The idea that prophets were really poetic speakers went hand in hand with the idea that there was a gradual transition from authentic prophetic speech to written book.

While some modern studies play down the connection between the prophet and the written word, others are finding evidence that points in the opposite direction. Referring to Ancient Near Eastern evidence, as well as evidence from writing in pre-exilic Israel and Judah, H. Barstad writes: 'it is probable that prophecies were written down at a very early stage and later collected' (1996, p. 124). Indeed, it is likely that prophecies, when uttered, would have been written down straight away. This may have been because it was regarded as important to record the message from God in the most accurate way possible, or to ensure it reached the right hearer (Barstad 1996, p. 123). (The same point has been made by A. R. Millard (1985) who also thinks the words would have remained unchanged when passed down from one generation to another. See also A. Malamat 1995, especially pp. 55–56.) R. P. Gordon also points to the significance of Ancient Near Eastern evidence in encouraging the search for the forms of prophecy that lie behind the books as we have them (1995, p. 602).

One passage in our books throws light on this question. In Jeremiah 36 we read of how Jeremiah wrote his oracles on a scroll and had it read to King Jehoiakim. The king, who found Jeremiah's words unwelcome, destroyed the scroll. Jeremiah responded by making another, with yet more of his words written on it. Does this episode tell us anything about how prophets *usually* had their words recorded? Or is this a unique incident, caused by the fact that Jeremiah was banned from going himself to the king at that time (Jer. 36:5–6)? It is impossible to be sure. What it does show is that the readers and hearers of Jeremiah would not have thought it strange that a prophet should write down his words

(Barstad 1996, pp. 125–26). We have one other instance of Jeremiah writing, in his letter to the exiles in Babylon (Jer. 29:4–28).

As we said a moment ago, the question of whether the prophets wrote is related to the question of how accurate a picture we have of them in their books. How much of what we read there actually came from them? Commentators vary greatly on this. Among those who attribute very little of the books to the prophets are O. Kaiser (see chapter 1), and R. P. Carroll (see chapter 2). At the other end of the scale are, for example, J. A. Motyer, J. H. Hayes and S. A. Irvine (see chapter 1) and J. Bright (see chapter 2).

As commentators disagree over these basic issues, it follows that there is no scholarly consensus on who the prophets were or what they said or thought. What was the message of Jeremiah? Well, it depends whom you read. What some think is the message of Jeremiah others will attribute to later editors. An example of this diversity is the question of whether prophets were essentially preachers of judgement and doom, or whether they also urged repentance and held out the hope of salvation. (See Isaiah: Is prophecy predictable? See also the panel: Prophetic tradition: How oracles got into books, in Critical Interpretation of Micah.)

THE BOOK

We have spent some time thinking about how to find the person behind the book. It is now time to think a little about the book. The prophetic books are not just raw collections of disjointed sayings, but carefully constructed pieces of literature. In each of them we meet immediately a voice that is not the same as the prophet's voice. This voice is heard in the superscriptions, the opening words of the book. Already here is a sign of organization, of someone who has set the prophet's words in context and is writing for an audience that may be different from the prophet's original audience.

In addition to superscriptions we also have narratives about the prophets and other characters (e.g. Hosea 1, 3; Isaiah 7—8; Jeremiah 32—44). The narratives and the sayings have been linked together, according to a sense of theme. For example, the story of Jeremiah redeeming the field of his cousin Hanamel is part of the 'Book of Consolation' (Jeremiah 30—33), which also contains Jeremiah's sayings about the New Covenant (Jer. 31:31–34). The sayings and the story are on the theme of salvation,

Digging deeper:
FINDING PROPHETS

For further discussion on the search for the prophet's own words, see the debate between A. G. Auld, R. P. Carroll, H. G. M. Williamson, H. Barstad and T. Overholt in *The Prophets: a Sheffield Reader* (P. R. Davies ed.). Auld thinks that even the idea of 'prophets' as we find it in the books is late (post-exilic). Carroll supports this, adding that the Old Testament disagrees with itself over whether the 'prophets' were a good thing or a bad thing (pp. 43–44); prophets were really 'poets', 'free spirits', only tamed by an orthodox tradition (pp. 46–48). Williamson, Barstad and Overholt all make responses to this view. One response is that prophetic behaviour was well known in contemporary societies (Overholt). And it is also argued that Auld and Carroll have paid too little attention to Ancient Near Eastern parallels (Barstad, p. 113).

which is predominant in this part of the book of Jeremiah. Similarly, sayings themselves have often been organized according to a definite structural plan. This is very clear in Isaiah 1—12, where sayings of judgement and salvation alternate. All these features show that someone has thought about what the message of the prophet adds up to, how it fits, not only into his own life, but into the life of the community in which he ministered.

There are further signs of how sayings have been gathered into a book. The two different forms of Jeremiah (Hebrew MT and Greek LXX) show two different attempts to shape the memory of Jeremiah's life and work into a book. The overlapping of material between books is another indicator: between prophetic books (Isa. 2:2–4; Mic. 4:1–4), and between prophetic books and other types of book (Isaiah 36—39 and 2 Kings 18—20; Jeremiah 52 and 2 Kings 25). This shows a conscious use of existing material. (Both Isaiah 36—39 and Jeremiah 52 present versions of the events in question that are adapted to the interests of the respective prophetic books.) Finally, there are editorial comments, additions, and linkages, e.g. Mal. 4:4–6 [3:19–24]; Isa. 2:5; Hos.14:9 (with the last of these compare Psalm 1 as a 'wisdom' superscription to the Book of Psalms).

The formation of the book

Can we discover the process by which the words of the prophet came to be collected in the book? A good deal of scholarship on the prophets has concerned itself with this question. The same means have been applied to it as to other parts of the Old Testament, especially literary criticism, form criticism, and redaction criticism. Examples of these will be given in the course of the present book. Here we will give some examples and definitions.

Literary criticism In Old Testament scholarship until recently, literary criticism meant noticing such things as inconsistency, incoherence, and differences of style, in order to separate the stages in a book's composition, and find its original form. This method of studying biblical books was at the forefront of scholarship in the modern period, that is, from the late nineteenth century on. In Pentateuchal studies, Julius Wellhausen formulated the well-known four-document theory (JEDP; see G. J. Wenham in *EOT: The Pentateuch*).

In the prophets, the leading name was Bernhard Duhm, whose commentary on Isaiah in 1892 was 'the first genuinely modern commentary on a prophetic book' (Blenkinsopp 1984, p. 28). Duhm wanted to separate out the genuine words of the prophet from later expansions, which he thought inferior. For Duhm, this was not a purely academic exercise, for he had a real religious interest in doing this. He thought that if he could find the true words of the prophet he would also uncover his religious experience, which he believed was a deep and true experience of God. This knowledge of God was bound up, in Duhm's view, with the poetic expression, which he thought marked true prophecy. Literary criticism in its heyday, therefore, had a profound religious motivation, at least for some of its advocates. (J. Skinner's study of Jeremiah (see chapter 2) is a good example of this in English.)

In our own study, the literary critical interest comes out most strongly in Jeremiah, where the prose-sermons were attributed to a different source from the poetic oracles.

Narratives about the prophet were assigned to yet another source. (See Jeremiah: Critical Interpretation.)

The problems with literary criticism are, first, that it made certain assumptions about the form of 'authentic' prophecy, which may not hold true, and second that it devalues much of what we find in the prophetic books.

Form criticism Form criticism is a study of forms of speech as used in specific settings. It was applied with great success to the Psalms, where a setting could be readily identified (Israel's worship), and where a number of recurring elements suggested that Psalms could be classified into a small number of types.

In the prophets, the search for typical forms took the study of prophetic speech much further than literary criticism had done. The pioneer of form criticism, H. Gunkel, thought prophets uttered 'vision-reports' (reports about their experiences of having visions), and spoke words of threat and promise (Tucker 1971, pp. 55–56). The most influential study of prophetic forms has been C. Westermann's (1991, pp. 90–98). He finds three types: accounts (including vision reports), speeches and prayers. The speeches are the most important. These divide mainly into announcements of judgement or salvation, and the underlying idea is of pronouncements by a messenger (Westermann 1991, pp. 93, 98–128). The effect of this is to claim that the prophetic speeches merely announce something that has already been decided. When the prophet announces God's judgement, not only is the judgement inevitable, but the announcement itself has a certain power to set it in motion (Westermann 1991, pp.

65–67). This is different from the idea of a 'threat', which could imply a chance to avoid the judgement by repenting.

The strength of form criticism in the prophets is in the 'messenger'-concept, which recognizes the force of the words spoken. Westermann rightly sees that no distinction can be made between the word of God and the word of the prophet (Westermann 1991, pp. 94–95). We will come back to this under 'Rhetorical Intention' below. The weakness is perhaps in its idea that classical forms of the announcements are brief (Westermann 1991, p. 105), which sets off again on a hunt for the 'original' and therefore (like literary criticism) thinks of some of the writing in the prophetic books as secondary and in a sense a degeneration.

Redaction criticism Redaction criticism is the prevailing type of criticism in modern scholarly writing on the prophets. It is different from literary and form criticism because it is interested in principle in the formation of the books up to their final form. It recognizes that the words of prophets have been recast into new contexts, and so given new meanings. And it assumes that these new contexts and meanings are as important and interesting as any original ones. Redaction criticism has two aspects, therefore: the study of the stages of a book's growth, and the study of the finished work itself, with all the inner relationships between its parts that have been produced by the process.

Most modern studies of prophetic books assume that the book has undergone a complicated process of growth. With a pre-exilic prophet this may mean that his prophecies were first collected together by people rather close to him in time, that the book was then formed into a shape resembling what we now have in the time of King Josiah or the exile, and finally was filled out by still more expansions (this is the account of Collins 1993, pp. 15–16). Another advocate of redaction criticism is R. E. Clements, who writes:

> Even so complex a composition as the book of Isaiah, which evidently took centuries to reach its final form, shows evidence that, through its many stages of growth, intentional connections and interrelationships between the parts were planned (Clements 1996, p. 204).

The growth of books, then, is not haphazard, but comes out of careful theological reflection. This means that there is an important connection between the process of growth and the interpretation of the book in its final form. Because the process of growth was governed by theological aims, the finished book offers possibilities for theological interpretation by the comparison of its various parts together (Clements 1996). We have already noticed some of the ways in which the raw materials of prophecy have been formed together into books, for example, the careful arrangement of the prophecies in Isaiah 1—12, where sayings of judgement and salvation alternate, making us think about how those two kinds of message might relate to each other.

Redaction criticism, therefore, is an important attempt to account for the 'book'-characteristics of prophecy that we noticed at the beginning of this section. If as readers of the prophetic books we think that they – especially the larger ones – are rambling and shapeless, redaction criticism encourages us to look beyond our first impressions to think about their message as a whole.

Redaction criticism leaves certain questions unanswered, such as the precise means by which smaller units were gradually enlarged into recognizable blocks and finally books. We will meet a number of theories about this in our study (such as W. McKane's 'rolling corpus' in Jeremiah; and H. G. M. Williamson's belief that Deutero-Isaiah shaped the whole block of Isaiah 2—55). Some think the cult (the institutions of Israel's worship life) was the vehicle in which the books were carried as they developed (Coggins 1996, p. 81). See also the panel: Was there an Ezekiel school? in Critical Interpretation of Ezekiel.

THEOLOGICAL THEMES

This section looks for the theological contribution made by the prophetic book in question. In thinking about prophetic theology, we are faced again with the question of prophet or book: are we looking for the theology of the prophet himself, or the theology of the book? The theological themes that we find are, of course, found in the *book*, or even in the books as a collection. R. E. Clements probably expresses the most common modern view when he says that this is where we should look for the theological contribution of the 'prophets':

> It is our contention, however, that it was not until a whole corpus of prophetic sayings came into being as a written record that it became possible and necessary to look for a larger degree of coherence and consistency in their implied disclosure of the divine nature and a genuine theology became possible (Clements 1986, p. 206).

However, the books give us a picture of prophets who were themselves theologically motivated. They believed they were commissioned by the God of Israel (not another god) to speak his word. And we saw that some scholars at least thought that the books preserve the prophets' words accurately. Prophets plainly had strong beliefs about God and were prepared to take enormous risks in order to declare them.

What were those ideas? If we were to identify the main thrusts of the prophets' theology, it would probably be twofold: an opposition to the worship of gods other than Yahweh; and a demand for justice and righteousness in the community that laid claim to being the chosen people.

Yet we do not have to suppose that their theology was unique. At one time it was thought that the prophets were the true founders of Israelite religion in its best form, or 'ethical monotheism', as some put it. When Wellhausen famously put the 'Law' after the Prophets, reversing the traditional order (Moses first, then prophets), he was promoting that kind of idea. The prophets spoke for a religion of the heart; the law debased this into a preoccupation with rituals and legalism. (See Gordon 1995, pp. 4–5 for a brief account of this.) But those days are long gone. Nowadays it is recognized that the relationships between the prophetic books and the theological traditions of Israel are complex.

If the prophets are distinctive, it will not be at the level of what they believed, in and of itself. In the following, we will notice briefly some relationships that prophetic theology has with other parts of the Old Testament.

The Prophets and other OT literature

Prophets and Wisdom For example, the prophets were once sharply distinguished from Israel's Wisdom traditions. Wisdom was universal, while the prophets were narrowly focused on Israel's own religion and special status. But it is clear that prophets and Wisdom share important

---

Digging deeper:
PROPHECY AND WISDOM

The comparison of prophecy and Wisdom is complicated by a number of factors. For example, is the picture of Wisdom as we have it in Proverbs true to Wisdom's origins, or has it been conformed to an 'orthodox', Yahwistic theology? Was there a distinct class of 'sages'? Jer. 18:18 suggests that the 'wise' were a group who could be easily distinguished from prophets and priests. If so, what did they believe? J. L. Crenshaw speaks of a sceptical Wisdom, which was at last 'wedded' to Yahwism (1981, p. 24). On the other hand there is the familiar problem of deciding what prophets actually said and thought.

One issue, which is sometimes said to put a difference between prophets and Wisdom, is 'epistemology', that is, how they 'knew' God's will. The 'wise' attached importance to teaching, learning, counsel, or what we might call working things out (see the range of vocabulary used for these things in Prov. 1:2–6). Prophets, on the other hand, had special revelations from God. This is an overstatement, however. The 'wise' knew that true knowledge began in knowing God (Prov. 1:7). And prophets, on the other hand, could rely on 'natural' intelligence and common sense (e.g. Isa. 28:23–39; Amos 3:3–8). See Williamson, 'Isaiah and the Wise', for his careful analysis of how Isaiah agrees and disagrees with the Wise on this subject. Compare this with the essays of A. Macintosh and W. McKane in the same volume. What do you conclude from these about the relation of prophets to the Wisdom traditions?

emphases. For example, prophets preach that people should seek justice and righteousness (Isa. 1:26–28; Amos 5:24); and this is also a concern of Proverbs (Prov. 16:8, 11–13). Moreover, this concern is based on very similar beliefs about the world. Prophets and Wisdom teachers alike believe that right behaviour is related to the created order of the world. This is well expressed by Barton (see chapter 1) (pp. 55–57).

Prophets and Law The idea that Law could simply be dated later than prophecy has also proved hard to maintain. Most critical scholarship allows that at least some Pentateuchal laws (e.g. Exod. 20:22—23:10) are relatively early. They share with the prophets a belief in the connection between worship and right behaviour, and also a concern for justice that goes beyond the letter of the law (e.g. Exod. 22:21–24 [20-23]). Furthermore, comparisons between the major blocks of the Old Testament (such as Law and Prophets) are now usually in the context of redaction criticism (which we have discussed above). This means that important links are often noticed across the blocks. For example, Jeremiah's metaphor of a 'circumcision of the heart' (Jer. 4:4) is also found twice in Deuteronomy (Deut. 10:16; 30:6). The idea of 'Deuteronomistic' editing of the prophetic books makes it impossible to think of a rigid division between the blocks. (For the theory of the Deuteronomistic editing of Jeremiah, see Critical Interpretation of Jeremiah.)

Prophets and Deuteronomy How the prophets relate to Deuteronomy is a special and complicated question. A critical view is expressed by J. Blenkinsopp, who sees an important difference between prophets and Deuteronomy. He thinks that Deut. 34:10–12 carefully places the revelation given to Moses on a higher level than all prophetic teaching that came after him:

> Never since has there arisen a prophet in Israel like Moses, whom the
> LORD knew face to face.

Balancing this text, however, is Deut. 18:15–18, which leads us to expect that there *will* be other prophets like Moses. Blenkinsopp thinks Deut. 34:10–12 intends to guard against a misunderstanding of that text (1984, pp. 189–90). However, it is not clear that this is the intention of Deut. 34:10–12. Other texts mark out individuals as greater than all others before or since, and they have an element of exaggeration in them (see 2 Kgs 18:5, about Hezekiah; then 2 Kgs 23:25 about Josiah – can both of these texts be literally true?). The canonical prophets may be viewed as being in continuity with Moses.

The issue pinpointed by Blenkinsopp, however, is the one with which we began: that the work of prophets is enshrined in books, and the prophetic legacy stands alongside that of Moses. Was this the work of the deuteronomists, as many think? It is an open question whether it was such a group, or if others were involved in carrying and finalizing the prophets' words. In any case, it is extraordinarily difficult to extricate deuteronomic theology from that of the prophets. Many have thought, indeed, that Deuteronomy was the work of prophets. (Hosea is often held to be the specific source of Deuteronomic theology; e.g. Nicholson 1986.) Others think, in contrast, that it was Deuteronomy that exerted influence on them (e.g. Andersen and Freedman in their commentaries on Hosea and Amos; and I have argued likewise in my commentary on Deuteronomy).

said there is more broadly relevant. However, it cannot be carried over wholesale to all the other prophets. For example, Hosea's 'story' differs because the Jerusalem traditions play no part there.)

To call this set of assumptions a 'story' is not to reduce its importance. On the contrary, it is to try to understand what made the prophets and their hearers tick. Why did Amos or Micah or Zechariah bother to do it? The answer is that they believed God had worked in Israel's life in the past and would do so again in the future. The greatest imaginable things were at stake. The people of Yahweh could either hear and obey him, and enter into the life that he held out for them, or they could look for their well-being elsewhere (in other gods, or in throwing in their lot with the 'superpowers' of the day), and lose their part in God's intention to bless them.

Patterns in the prophetic books: The shifting lens – the meaning of 'Israel'

One of the striking things is the subtle ways in which the story changes. In a sense this is a simple and natural shift of the lens. The later books (Haggai, Zechariah, Malachi) no longer look forward to judgement and exile, but back on it. Even so, they still believe in a greater salvation ahead, so the basic pattern does not change. More important is the way in which concepts such as 'covenant' and even 'Israel' change. As we have just noted, 'covenant' in Isaiah 40—55 changes to include other nations. The disturbing effect of that for Israelites was probably also felt by those who read Jonah, and heard of a repentance by the Ninevites, and how Yahweh decided not to judge them after all.

Similarly, when Israelites heard the name 'Israel', it would have brought to mind for them the memory of their election and salvation. 'Israel' was saved from slavery in Egypt, and brought into its own land. Other nations were driven out of Canaan to allow this to happen (Joshua). But what does 'Israel' mean when a large part of the nation has been taken away into exile in Assyria, to be mixed up hopelessly with other peoples of the Assyrian empire and never heard of again? This huge event in Israel's life meant the loss, not of a small part of the whole, but the ten tribes, out of twelve, that made up the northern kingdom. In the Books of Kings that part itself was simply called 'Israel' (the southern two tribes were called Judah).

The story of the prophetic books involves re-thinking who 'Israel' is. The prophets sometimes speak of a 'remnant' in order to show how the story of Israel is advancing (Isa. 10:20–23; Jer. 5:10; Joel 2:32 [3:5]). They also sometimes picture a reunion of Israel, north and south, in a way that cannot be meant in a plain historical sense (Ezek. 37: 15–17). In other words, 'Israel' is redefined in the prophets as a people that remains faithful to Yahweh. That people, however, is still heir to all the ancient promises that first called a people out of Egypt.

MORE ON 'ISRAEL'

The point just made has obvious implications for how we understand the term 'Israel' today. If the name 'Israel' can keep changing what it refers to, and is qualified in the way that we have seen, in what sense may it refer to modern 'Israel'? Do 'Israelite' and 'Israeli' mean the same thing?

The point is considered further in two panels: in chapter 1, How can the exiles be 'Israel'? and, in chapter 2, Israel's return to its land.

It is in this way, finally, that the prophetic books make their distinctive mark on the Old Testament. They project faithful Israel into a future that is still not realized at the end of the Old Testament period. In the prophets one can speak of 'eschatology', that is, a theology of the 'end'. This emerges in various ways in our books, as we shall see.

Eschatology is often thought to be the special province of 'apocalyptic'. However, eschatology is not confined to apocalyptic, nor is it the essential characteristic of it (see the panel on Apocalyptic in the chapter on Daniel). However, the fact that Daniel is included in the form of the canon in Christian Bibles shows that a concern with the future is a direction set by the prophetic books. Eschatology in the Prophets means looking forward to greater fulfilments of God's promises than the people experiences in the present.

RHETORICAL INTENTION: PROPHETIC 'ART'

The prophets may not have been original in their theology, but they are unparalleled in the Old Testament for their power to *persuade*. I have included the topic Rhetorical Intention in the treatment of each prophetic book because it helps us to think about how the prophets aimed to make an impact on their hearers, and also about how the books make an impact on their readers.

'Rhetorical criticism' is an important recent development, not only for the prophets, but for all the biblical literature. But it is perhaps especially important for the prophets. The type of rhetorical analysis I mean is more than just stylistic analysis (though the term was once used for this; Muilenburg 1969). Instead, it is the study of how language is used in order to persuade people to a point of view (see Patrick and Scult 1990, for an important application of the method to biblical studies).

Defined in this way, every aspect of prophetic language comes into the frame of our study. Why did the prophets so often speak in poetic forms? Part of the answer is no doubt that the sublime language of poetry was thought suitable to speak about God. (See the panel: The song of the vineyard as poetry, at Isa. 5:1–7.) But in addition, the prophets used their poetry to take hold of the hearer's attention, to challenge and surprise (Amos's turning of the Oracles Against the Nations form on Israel and Judah is a well known example of this; Amos 2:4–8). The prophets' *art* is not an optional extra to their message, but essential to it. We might say that it is not just for aesthetic purposes, but we must qualify this by saying that its aesthetic qualities – its rhythms, alliterations, onomatopoeias, symbolism – are part of its attractiveness. Unfortunately only some of these features can be represented in translation. But these techniques of communication are very important for an understanding of the prophets' mission. (In R. P. Gordon's collection of important essays on prophecy, by far the largest section is entitled 'The Art of Prophecy'; Gordon 1995.)

The art of the prophets is not just their poetry, but also their narrative, their use of metaphor, their rhetorical use of dialogue (Haggai, Malachi), their symbolic actions (see panel on Prophetic symbolic actions at Ezek. 4:1—7:27). That these were used for effect is clear because they were sometimes extreme and shocking (Hosea's marriage to a prostitute, Hosea 1; Jeremiah's metaphor of divorce to proclaim the end of the relationship between Yahweh and Israel; Jer. 3:1–5; Ezekiel's pushing of the prostitute image to lurid extremes, Ezekiel 16; 23). No holds were barred in the prophets' methods of persuasion.

Rhetorical criticism is concerned with speakers or writers and their 'audiences'. We have already discovered, however, that it is not easy to pin down the prophets and their original audiences. So we have to think more broadly about who is persuading whom. We have already seen that the form in which we now have the prophetic books is an important level of our study of the prophets. This is true for the rhetoric of the books as much for their theology. The book itself, as a record and memory of the prophet's words, has its own audience, which might be quite different from the prophet's. That is, the words of Amos take on a quite new significance when read by (or to) an audience in the exile in Babylon. Nor is there only one possible audience of the final form of the book, but many – including modern audiences and readers of the books. So the analysis of the book's rhetorical power is rather open-ended. Yet it will aim to show how the books can go on being effective in new situations.

Art and the divine word

The prophets' art in their speech can be explained at a deeper level. For it demonstrates effectively the central importance of the Word of God in their thought. I said a moment ago that the prophets used poetry because it was an appropriate way to speak about God. Of course, the biblical witness is not that poetry is the only appropriate means of speaking about God (since the Bible also includes laws, narratives, letters and other forms). But poetry has a capacity both to speak about things that are very familiar, and to lead the imagination on to new ways of

thinking and understanding. Poems do not give cut and dried meanings, but are often open to several interpretations. It is in this openness that the reader or hearer is invited to think about God.

Digging deeper:
POETRY, METAPHOR AND THEOLOGY

For more on poetry and theology see Miller (2000) and Sherwood (2001). Steiner (1989) is a sophisticated philosophical treatment of poetry and transcendence.

For definitions of metaphor and related terms, see Cotterell and Turner 1989, pp. 299–303; and on metaphor and theology, see Soskice 1995.

There is a further reflection on metaphor below at Joel: Rhetorical Intention.

To say that prophetic speech is rhetoric, then, is to make a theological point. Prophets speak the word of God, and they do so in ways that are appropriate to their subject (God and the heavenly realm). The same ways are also suitable for calling people back to God. At this point we may notice a connection with what we said above about prophetic speech as the speech of a messenger (when we discussed Westermann on form criticism). Rhetorical criticism applied to the prophets confirms that that idea is helpful. However, rhetorical criticism takes us further in thinking about how speech becomes effective. In contrast to Westermann's view, a pronouncement of judgement may well have the effect of turning people from their sin, and so avoiding the judgement that was pronounced. The best (perhaps only) example of this in the prophetic corpus is the book of Jonah, where the people of Nineveh repent. God's 'rhetorical intention' was presumably fulfilled in that repentance – even if Jonah's was not!

Think about
RHETORIC AND SPEECH-ACTS

Rhetorical criticism has much in common with 'speech-act theory', which analyses language in terms of its power to act or 'perform'. The classic is J. L. Austin's *How to Do Things With Words* (1962). It has been applied to the way in which God may be said to 'speak' in Wolterstorff's philosophical study, *Divine Discourse*. Wolterstorff also uses a form of the 'messenger' (or 'ambassador') metaphor. Further interesting reflections on the human and divine word are found in McKane 1995, e.g. pp. 14–22.

CANONICAL CONTEXT
This final division of our treatment of each prophetic book aims to say something about how the book in question stands in relation to the wider canon, both Old and New Testaments. For many readers, this may be the goal of their study of the books. It is important to consider what exactly might be meant by this idea.

The canonical dimension of the study of the Old Testament was put on the academic map by Brevard Childs in several publications, especially his *Introduction to the Old Testament as Scripture* (1979). Childs appeared to mean several different things by canonical interpretation. Foremost was a focus on the individual biblical book in the form in which it was 'canonized'. His concern in this was to get beyond historical criticism to theological

interpretation of the final text. He believed that the theological meaning of the book, as it was received by the believing community, was more important than other meanings that might be discovered at different stages in the book's composition.

In my treatment of the individual books in this volume, I have placed most emphasis on the final form. For example, the book of Isaiah is considered as a single book, because that is the canonical form in which we have it. (Some introductions to the prophets deal with Isaiah 1—39 separately from chs 40—55 and 56—66; e.g. von Rad; Koch (see chapter 1).) The different original settings of parts of the book are also dealt with. But the main level of interpretation is of the book in its final form. I have followed Childs' lead in this respect, therefore.

However, that is not the main focus of this section of the discussion of each book. A further level of canonical meaning is how the book related to its Old and New Testament contexts, and that is where our interest lies here. This too has a number of levels, however. First, each book has immediate neighbours in the canon, and sometimes it seems as if the order of the books has been deliberately arranged in order to bring these out. For example, in Joel 3:16 [4:16] we read:

> The LORD roars from Zion
>> And utters his voice from Jerusalem.

And this same phrase then appears again in Amos 1:2. In English Bibles this is only a few verses later, and the effect is to produce a catchword link between the two books. The force of the saying in each case is different, as in Joel it heralds sayings about the safety of Judah, while in Amos it leads into judgement. It may be that Joel has been placed first in order to soften the effect of Amos in the reading of the Book of the Twelve as a whole. (The order of the Book of the Twelve in English Bibles follows the Hebrew Bible. In LXX, Amos and Joel are separated by several books, so this point is weaker. However, in one canonical tradition at least, it seems that someone has had an overview of the books that has influenced how they now appear.)

Second, the individual books have a context in the prophetic corpus as a whole. Another well-known saying has an echo of a different sort. In Isa. 2:4 we read:

> They shall beat their swords into
> ploughshares
> And their spears into pruning-hooks.

But in Joel 3:10 [4:10]:

> Beat your ploughshares into swords,
> And your pruning hooks into spears.

The distance between Isaiah and Joel in the canonical order is not close, but even so the echo is unmistakable (see also Book of the Twelve). The effect is to encourage reflection on how Yahweh's final peace relates to his final war and victory.

Third, the prophetic books have a context in the Old Testament as a whole. The relationships we have noticed between them and the Pentateuch and Psalms and other sections of the canon set up echoes, which can be fruitfully explored. For example, Jeremiah's New Covenant must be understood against the background of the covenantal traditions of the Pentateuch.

Finally, the prophets can be heard in the context of the New Testament (the New Covenant serves as an example of this also). In regard to all these levels it is possible to try to hear echoes from the particular book across the larger canonical context. How the book contributes to the theology of the whole Bible is never easy to state in any conclusive way. It is not a simple matter of lining one up against another and seeing where it might have something different. The point is rather to let the books have a kind of conversation with each other. The meaning of the particular book, therefore, is not finally decided in isolation, but only as a part of a whole. This seems to me to be the most fruitful application of canonical criticism. (This sense also has approval from Barton, for example, who is otherwise critical of canonical criticism; in Barton and Reimer eds 1996, especially pp. 70–71. See also Clements 1996, pp. 211–12.)

Think about
CANON AND BIBLICAL THEOLOGY

Do you see similarities and differences between canonical criticism, as defined here, and what might be called 'biblical theology'? Both these terms can be differently defined, so one has to be careful about what exactly is meant. But the comparison says something about the spirit of canonical criticism. It is at heart theological, and it requires the reader or interpreter, in the end, to make theological connections. This is not an exact science. However, it is perhaps the beginning of theology.

I have tried to say something about canon and biblical theology in 'Biblical Theology: Canon and Plain Sense' (McConville 2001).

FURTHER READING

This bibliography contains works referred to in the Introduction, and also serves as a general bibliography for the whole book. Items marked * are considered suitable as first ports of call, while others are more complex, or relate to specific issues.

INTRODUCTIONS TO THE OLD TESTAMENT

B. S. Childs *Introduction to the Old Testament as Scripture*. London: SCM, 1979.

*R. B. Dillard and T. Longman III *An Introduction to the Old Testament*. Grand Rapids: Zondervan/Leicester: Apollos, 1995.

S. R. Driver *Introduction to the Literature of the Old Testament*. Edinburgh: T. & T. Clark, 1892.

G. Fohrer *Introduction to the Old Testament*. London: SPCK, 1970.

*W. LaSor, D. A. Hubbard, F. W. Bush *Old Testament Survey: the Message, Form, and Background of the Old Testament*. Grand Rapids: Eerdmans, 1996, second edition.

*J. A. Soggin *Introduction to the Old Testament*. London: SCM, 1980, revised edition.

INTERPRETING THE OLD TESTAMENT

J. Barton *Reading the Old Testament*. London: DLT, 1996, second edition.

ONE-VOLUME BIBLE COMMENTARIES

D. A. Carson, R. T. France, J. A. Motyer and G. J. Wenham eds *The New Bible Commentary Twenty-First Century Edition*. Leicester: IVP, 1994.

J. Barton and J. Muddiman eds *The Oxford Bible Commentary*. Oxford: OUP, 2001.

BOOKS ON THE PROPHETS

J. Blenkinsopp *A History of Prophecy in Israel*. London: SPCK, 1984.

R. E. Clements *Old Testament Prophecy: From Oracles to Canon*. Louisville: Westminster John Knox, 1996.

*T. Collins *The Mantle of Elijah; the Redaction Criticism of the Prophetical Books*. Sheffield; JSOT Press, 1993.

P. R. Davies ed. *The Prophets: A Sheffield Reader*. The Biblical Seminar; Sheffield Academic Press, 1996.

R. P. Gordon *The Place Is Too Small For Us: The Israelite Prophets in Recent Scholarship*. SBTS 5; Winona Lake: Eisenbrauns, 1995.

K. Koch *The Prophets 1, 2*. London: SCM, 1982–83.

J. Lindblom *Prophecy in Ancient Israel*. Oxford: Basil Blackwell, 1962.

G. von Rad *Old Testament Theology II*. London: SCM, 1965.

*J. F. A. Sawyer *Prophecy and the Biblical Prophets*. Oxford: OUP, 1993.

OTHER BOOKS AND ARTICLES

A. G. Auld 'Prophets Through the Looking Glass: Between Writings and Moses' in P. R. Davies ed. *The Prophets: A Sheffield Reader*. The Biblical Seminar 42; Sheffield: Sheffield Academic Press, 1996, pp. 22–42.

J. L. Austin *How to Do Things With Words*. Oxford: Clarendon, 1962.

H. M. Barstad 'No Prophets? Recent Developments in Biblical Prophetic Research and Ancient Near Eastern Prophecy' in P. R. Davies ed. *The Prophets: A Sheffield Reader*. The Biblical Seminar 42; Sheffield: Sheffield Academic Press, 1996, pp. 106–26.

John Barton 'The Canonical Meaning of the Book of the Twelve' in J. Barton and D. Reimer eds *After the Exile: Essays in Honour of Rex Mason*. Macon, Ga; Mercer University Press, 1996, pp. 59–73.

W. H. Bellinger *Psalmody and Prophecy*. Sheffield: JSOT Press, 1984.

R. P. Carroll, 'Poets Not Prophets: A Response to "Prophets Through the Looking Glass"' in P. R. Davies ed. *The Prophets: A Sheffield Reader*. The Biblical Seminar 42; Sheffield: Sheffield Academic Press, 1996, pp. 43–49.

R. E. Clements 'Patterns in the Prophetic Canon' in G. W. Coats and B. O. Long eds *Canon and Authority: Essays in Old Testament Religion and Theology*. Philadelphia: Fortress, 1977, pp. 42–55.

R. E. Clements 'Prophecy as Literature: a Reappraisal' in D. G. Miller ed. *The Hermeneutical Quest: Essays in Honor of J. L. Mays for His Sixty-Fifth Birthday*. Allison Park, Pa.: Pickwick Publications, 1986, pp. 56–76; reproduced in R. E. Clements *Old Testament Prophecy: From Oracles to Canon*. Louisville: Westminster John Knox, 1996, pp. 203–16 (cited here).

R. Coggins 'Interbiblical Quotations in Joel' in J. Barton and D. Reimer eds *After the Exile: Essays in Honour of Rex Mason*. Macon, Ga; Mercer University Press, 1996, pp. 75–84.

P. Cotterell and M. Turner *Linguistics and Biblical Interpretation*. London: SPCK, 1989.

J. L. Crenshaw *Old Testament Wisdom: An Introduction*. London: SCM, 1981.

B. Duhm *Das Buch Jeremia*. Tübingen and Leipzig: Mohr, 1901.

B. Duhm *Das Buch Jesaja übersetzt und erklärt*. Göttingen: Vandenhoeck and Ruprecht, fourth edition, 1922; first edition, 1892.

A. R. Johnson *The Cultic Prophet and Israel's Psalmody*. Cardiff: University of Wales Press, 1979.

A. R. Johnson *The Cultic Prophet in Ancient Israel*. Cardiff: University of Wales Press, 1944.

H. Lalleman-de Winkel *Jeremiah in Prophetic Tradition*. Leuven: Peeters, 2000.

A. Malamat 'Prophecy at Mari' in R. P. Gordon, ed. *The Place Is Too Small for Us: The Israelite Prophets in Recent Scholarship*. SBTS 5; Winona Lake: Eisenbrauns, 1995, pp. 50–73.

J. G. McConville 'Biblical Theology: Canon and Plain Sense' *SBET 2* (2001), pp. 134–57.

W. McKane *A Late Harvest: Reflections on the Old Testament*. Edinburgh: T. & T. Clark, 1995.

A. R. Millard 'La prophétie et l'écriture: Israël, Aram, Assyrie' *RHR* 202, 1985, pp. 125–45.

P. D. Miller 'The Theological Significance of Biblical Poetry' in P. D. Miller *Israelite Religion and Biblical Theology*. JSOT Suppl. 267; Sheffield: Sheffield Academic Press, 2000, pp. 233–49.

J. Muilenburg 'Form Criticism and Beyond' *JBL* 88, 1969, pp. 1–18.

E. W. Nicholson *God and His People: Covenant and Theology in the Old Testament*. Oxford: Clarendon, 1986.

T. W. Overholt 'Prophecy in History: the Social Reality of Intermediation' in P. R. Davies *The Prophets: A Sheffield Reader*. The Biblical Seminar 42; Sheffield Academic Press, 1996, pp. 61–84.

D. Patrick and A. Scult *Rhetoric and Biblical Interpretation*. Sheffield: Almond Press, 1990.

D. L. Petersen *The Roles of Israel's Prophets*. JSOT Suppl. 17; Sheffield; JSOT Press, 1981.

H. H. Rowley *Worship in Ancient Israel*. London: SPCK, 1967.

Y. Sherwood 'Of Fruit and Corpses and Wordplay Visions: Picturing Amos 8:1–3' *JSOT* 92, 2001, pp. 5-27.

J. Skinner, *Prophecy and Religion*. Cambridge: CUP, 1922.

J. M. Soskice *Metaphor and Religious Language*. Oxford: OUP, 1995.

G. Steiner *Real Presences*. Chicago: University of Chicago Press, 1989.

L. Stulman *The Prose Sermons of the Book of Jeremiah*. SBL Diss 83; Atlanta: Scholars Press, 1986.

G. M. Tucker *Form Criticism of the Old Testament*. Philadelphia: Fortress Press, 1971.

C. Westermann *Basic Forms of Prophetic Speech*. Cambridge: Lutterworth; Louisville: Westminster/John Knox, 1991.

H. G. M. Williamson 'A Response to Graeme Auld' in P. R. Davies ed. *The Prophets: A Sheffield Reader*. The Biblical Seminar 42; Sheffield Academic Press, 1996, pp. 50–56.

H. G. M. Williamson 'Isaiah and the Wise', in J. Day, R. P. Gordon and H. G. M. Williamson eds *Wisdom in Ancient Israel: Essays in Honour of J. A. Emerton*. Cambridge: CUP, 1995.

R. R. Wilson *Prophecy and Society in Ancient Israel*. Philadelphia: Fortress, 1980.

N. Wolterstorff *Divine Discourse*. Cambridge: CUP, 1995.

ABBREVIATIONS

AB	Anchor Bible
ANET	J. B. Pritchard (ed.), *Ancient Near Eastern Texts*. Princeton University Press, 1969, third edition.
AUSS	*Andrews University Seminary Studies*
BASOR	*Bulletin of the American Schools of Oriental Research*
BBB	Bonner Biblische Beiträge
BETL	Bibliotheca Ephemeridum Theologicarum Lovaniensium
BHT	Beiträge zur historischen Theologie
BST	Bible Speaks Today
BZAW	Beihefte zur Zeitschrift für die alttestamentliche Wissenschaft
CBC	Cambridge Bible Commentary
DSB	Daily Study Bible
ExpTim	*Expository Times*
FOTL	Forms of Old Testament Literature
HSM	Harvard Semitic Monographs
IBD	*Illustrated Bible Dictionary*. Leicester: IVP, 1980.
ICC	International Critical Commentary
JBL	*Journal of Biblical Literature*
JSOT	*Journal for the Study of the Old Testament*
JSOT Suppl.	Journal for the Study of the Old Testament Supplement Series
JSS	*Journal of Semitic Studies*
JTS	*Journal of Theological Studies*
LXX	Septuagint (Greek Old Testament)
MT	Masoretic Text (Hebrew text of the Old Testament)
NCB	New Century Bible
NIBC	New International Biblical Commentary
NICOT	New International Commentary on the Old Testament
NIDOTTE	W. VanGemeren (ed.), *New International Dictionary of Old Testament Theology and Exegesis*. Grand Rapids: Zondervan, 1997.
NIGTC	New International Greek Testament Commentary
NSBT	New Studies in Biblical Theology
OAN	Oracles Against the Nations
OBC	J. Barton and J. Muddimann (eds), *Oxford Bible Commentary*. OUP, 2001.
OS	*Oudtestamentische Studiën*
OTG	Old Testament Guides
OTL	Old Testament Library
POT	De Prediking van het Oude Testament
RevExp	*Review and Expositor*
RHR	*Revue d'histoire et de philosophie religieuses*
SBET	*Scottish Bulletin of Evangelical Theology*
SBL Diss	Society of Biblical Literature Dissertation Series
SBT	Studies in Biblical Theology
SBTS	Sources for Biblical and Theological Study
SOTBT	Studies in Old Testament Biblical Theology
TB	*Tyndale Bulletin*
TOTC	Tyndale Old Testament Commentary
VT	*Vetus Testamentum*
VT Suppl.	Vetus Testamentum Supplements
WBC	Word Biblical Commentary
WMANT	Wissenschaftliche Monographien zum Alten und Neuen Testament
ZAW	*Zeitschrift für die alttestamentliche Wissenschaft*

MAPS

Chapter I

ISAIAH

The Book of Isaiah is perhaps the best known of the prophetic books because of its prophecies of the child called Immanuel (Isa. 7:14), a Suffering Servant (in Isa. 40—55) and a messianic king (Isa. 9:2–7; 11:1–9). These are certainly important in any reading of the book, especially if we want to relate the message of the book to the New Testament. However, as we have seen, prophetic books must be understood first in the world in which they were written. So we will now consider some matters to do with its background, and the way in which it came to be a book.

DATE AND DESTINATION

The Book of Isaiah is attributed in its heading (1:1) to Isaiah son of Amoz, who, we are told, worked in the reigns of Uzziah, Jotham, Ahaz and Hezekiah. To judge by the book's contents, Isaiah's main activity seems to have taken place in the reigns of Ahaz (735–715 BC) and Hezekiah (715–687 BC). However, he may have begun to preach in the last years of King Uzziah (who died in 742 BC. For these dates, which are uncertain, see Dates of Kings and Prophets, also Hayes and Irvine 1987). (This would mean assuming that the famous vision in 6:1–13

was not his first 'call' to be a prophet.) And he continued until at least 701 BC, the year of the Assyrian king Sennacherib's invasion of Judah.

The first narrative about Isaiah records a meeting between him and King Ahaz (7:1–17). The time is 734–733 BC. King and people face a crisis, because of a threat to the region from the growing power of Assyria. The nation, with its power centre in Nineveh, Asshur and Calah on the River Tigris, was in the process of becoming a great power, since the accession of a new king, Tiglath-Pileser III, in 745 BC. When Isaiah meets Ahaz, the immediate problem is to know how to respond to an attack on Judah by an alliance of Israel (the northern kingdom, which had split from Judah after the reign of Solomon in 930 BC) and Syria (also called Aram). The story is told more fully in 2 Kings 16. There we find that Judah was in danger on several sides, losing territory in the south to Edom and threatened in the north by this so-called Syro-Ephraimite alliance (the northern kingdom was sometimes called Ephraim). The uncertainty caused by Assyria's advance was perhaps an opportunity to settle old scores. When Edom recovered Elath (2 Kgs

16:6) they reversed its capture by King Uzziah about forty years earlier (2 Kgs 14:22). It is often said that Israel and Syria may have wanted to secure Judah as part of an alliance against Assyria, but there is no strong evidence for this. Their advance looks more like a war of conquest (Isa. 7:6). It is possible that the pictures of Jerusalem under siege in Isaiah 1 come from this time.

Ahaz' response to the crisis was to turn to the great power itself for help, submitting to Tiglath-Pileser as an obedient vassal, and presenting treasure plundered from Solomon's temple as tribute (2 Kgs 16:7–8). The plan apparently worked (v. 9), although it is likely that Assyria would have gone against Syria in any case! Ahaz' involvement with the empire, however, went beyond simply asking for help, for he deliberately introduced aspects of Assyrian worship in the Jerusalem temple (vv. 10–20). This was the cause of Isaiah's clash with Ahaz, for he maintained that the king and people should not trust an alliance with a foreign power for its survival and prosperity, but rather trust in God (Isa. 7:9b).

The question of making alliances as a means of self-defence continued to be an issue in the reign of Hezekiah, the son of Ahaz. People in Judah knew that rebellion against Assyria could cost them dear, for it was when the northern kingdom, under King Hoshea, turned to Egypt for help against their overlord (2 Kgs 17:1–4), that the Assyrians, under Sargon II, came down heavily and destroyed that kingdom for ever. Even so, later in Sargon's reign, Hezekiah joined other small states (Ashdod, Edom, Moab) in a rebellion against Assyria in 713–711 BC, and these again looked to Egypt for help. Some of Isaiah's sayings, against making alliances with Egypt, were probably given in this situation, for example, Isaiah 18—19, with their mockery of Egyptian pretensions to power and grandeur; note the reference to Ashdod in the immediately following 20:1.

The final important phase of Isaiah's work was in Judah's revolt in the time of Sennacherib (705–701). Here again, Isaiah counselled trust in Yahweh, and prophesied in this case that Sennacherib would be destroyed (Isa. 37:21–38). In addition to the narrative about this event, the sayings of chs 30—31 may belong to this time. (It is possible they could go back to 713–711, but the later occasion is usually preferred; see Sweeney 1996, p. 397.) When Isaiah proclaims that Yahweh will fight for Jerusalem to protect it (31:4–5), the point is that he alone can do this, not the merely human power of other kings (31:8). Isaiah's complaint about the securing of the city's defences without trusting in God (22:8b–11) was probably addressed to Hezekiah in the same situation.

The threat from Assyria was always in the background during Isaiah's ministry. The constant menace of it was the setting in which the prophet called for faithfulness. Yahweh could secure Judah if they trusted him; but equally, if they did not, Assyria could come and overwhelm them. These two possibilities are both presented in the main passages we have noticed concerning both Ahaz and Hezekiah. The negative possibility – of Judah being engulfed by Assyria (Isa. 8:5–8) – became a reality when King Sennacherib devastated the land in 701 BC (2 Kgs 18). Conversely, the possibility of salvation became a reality too, when the same invasion was cut short by the miraculous deliverance of Jerusalem (2 Kgs 19:35–37; Isa. 37:36–38).

A reading of Isaiah makes it clear, however, that the Assyrian period is not the only time in which the book is interested. If anything, Babylon is even more prominent. This means that a major focus of the book is a time well after Isaiah's own life, since Babylon succeeded Assyria as the leading power in the region only in 605 BC, when its forces overcame those of Egypt at the Battle of Carchemish. When Judah fell and went into Babylonian exile in 587 BC, Isaiah had been dead for about a century.

Yet Isaiah 40—55 concerns the people of Judah in the exile (587–539 BC). It tells its hearers that the time of their banishment is almost over, because they have more than paid for the sins that caused it (40:1–2). It promises deliverance, naming Cyrus, the Persian king who would oust the last Babylonian king, as the agent who would bring it about (45:1). And it foresees the release of the exiles from Babylon (48:20–21; 52:11–12; 55:12) and their return to Jerusalem (52:7–10), where Yahweh would again be worshipped, in place of the fallen Babylonian gods (46:1). Finally, it seems that Isaiah 56—66 is concerned with events after the exiles have returned, when worship has again begun to deteriorate (e.g. Isa. 58).

This means that the first hearers of Isaiah's words in his lifetime were not the only intended audience of the message of the book. The point of Isaiah 40—55 is to persuade the people in the exile that they would soon be set free and able to go home. This leads to authorship questions: who wrote this part of the book? And indeed, who was responsible for bringing the book into its finished form? We will come to these questions in a moment. Let us notice for now that the underlying contention in all parts of Isaiah remains the same – it is Yahweh, the true God, who is the only power behind the events of history.

CRITICAL INTERPRETATION OF ISAIAH

IDENTIFYING ISAIAH OF JERUSALEM

We have seen from our look at the historical events behind the prophecy, that the book of Isaiah cannot have been written all at one time. Individual sayings came from different dates, and so must have circulated originally in contexts different from those in which we now find them. What is more, as most writers believe, many of the words recorded apparently came from situations after the prophet's own lifetime. This is because it is assumed that prophets directed their messages to people and issues in their own time. The sayings about trusting Egypt, for example, come out of the prophet's passionate involvement with things that were unfolding before his eyes.

So we have to ask two questions: by what process did separate sayings come to be formed into a single book? And how did this book come to bear the name of Isaiah of Jerusalem?

The traditional view (sometimes called 'pre-critical') was that Isaiah did indeed write the whole book. He wrote down his prophecies as he made them (Isa. 8:16 might be regarded as evidence for this). And he did indeed make predictions about events long in the future (in Isa. 40—66). This view is maintained in the recent commentaries of Motyer and Oswalt. One advantage of it is that it provides an explanation for the unity of theme in the book (see below), and of its attribution to the prophet. Its disadvantage is that it involves a view of the prophet in which he is detached from his immediate situation. In Isaiah, the question is not strictly whether a prophet might speak accurately about the future, but why he should address himself to people two centuries after his own time. This would sit oddly with the passionate engagement we see in the prophecies that belong to Isaiah's own time. And on the other hand, the prophetic passion of Isaiah 40—66 (for example in 48:1–11) would seem to fit better in the mouth of a prophet in Babylon.

In the early nineteenth century readers of Isaiah began to think that it fell into two parts (chs 1—39, from Isaiah of Jerusalem, and chs 40—66, from a prophet in the exile). Since the commentary of B. Duhm (1892), however, chs 56—66 have been marked off from chs 40—55, and attributed to another prophet who worked after the exiles had returned home. (For an account of the history of interpretation, see Hayes and Irvine 1987, pp. 387–400.)

However, the threefold division is not so simple, for much of 1—39 is also thought to be from a later time than the writer. For example, the sayings against Babylon in 13:1—14:23 are usually assigned to the time when Babylon was powerful, that is, close to the time of Isaiah 40—55. Furthermore, many of the hopeful sayings in chs 1—12, such as 2:2–4, have been thought to be later than Isaiah, because they are more like the hopeful sayings in chs 40—55. Chapters 24—27, called the mini-apocalypse, are often given a late date because they have a view of history that resembles other late writings (especially the idea of a final victory of Yahweh over all other powers, and individual resurrection).

It must be admitted that conclusions of this sort involve making judgements as to what a prophet in the eighth century *might* have said. It is one thing to notice signs of a particular historical setting (for example, when a prophecy speaks about the end of the Babylonian exile), but quite another to suppose that an eighth-century prophet *could not* have had a vision of a future in which nations would seek the God of Israel in Jerusalem (2:2–4). A related question is the problem of knowing what a particular saying actually *means*. That is, one might be convinced that Isaiah never gave unconditional promises of salvation, and that might mean ruling out a passage like 29:5–8. However, it may be that 29:5–8 was only intended to be an alternative possibility to the destruction pictured in 29:1–4, and that together the two sayings imply that God will save Jerusalem *if* it returns to him in faithfulness. In that case one could regard 29:5–8 as authentic on the grounds that it is not an unconditional promise after all.

Behind these questions lies the question we discussed in the Introduction: what is the background, or world of thought, of the prophets? On what theological grounds did any prophet presume to speak to his contemporaries at all about how they should behave and what they could expect to happen in the future? How we answer that question will have a big effect on how much of Isaiah 1—39 we will think belongs to Isaiah himself. Since scholars differ on this, it is not surprising that they differ enormously over which sayings may be attributed to Isaiah and which may not. Hayes and Irvine, for example, allow most of Isaiah 1—39 to Isaiah, while O. Kaiser 1983, 1974, denies most of it to him.

THE MESSAGE OF ISAIAH OF JERUSALEM
From what we have just said, it will be clear that there is no certain way of working out

'the' message of Isaiah, once the assumption has been made that he did not say everything written in the book named after him. We will shortly ask whether it is even essential that we should try to do so, since what we have to understand, in the end, is the book that has come down to us as a whole. However, it is important for our profile of prophecy in the eighth century that we notice what is commonly thought about Isaiah's own work.

Isaiah's entire message is based on a single foundation: the belief that Yahweh, God of Israel, is the only one who is 'high and lifted up' (6:1). No other earthly power can challenge him, nor any other god. This explains why the strong condemnation of everything that is proud (2:5–22; note 'high and lifted up' in 2:12) comes so early on in the book. It also explains Isaiah's thinking in three important areas: politics, ethics and the future of Judah and Jerusalem.

In politics, Isaiah consistently argued that in crises the kings should trust in Yahweh, rather than in political measures designed to protect the country (e.g. Isa. 7—8; 18—22; 30—31). Since God alone is 'high and lifted up', he has power over all of history. He had authority not only over the kings of Judah, but also over other nations, and indeed the forces of nature (29:6). That meant that if Judah suffered at the hands of an enemy, it was because Yahweh had decided it should happen. So Assyria could be described as 'the rod of my (Yahweh's) anger' (10:5). The Assyrians themselves would not see things like that, of course, for they have their own plans, as Isaiah well knows (10:7–11). But this is Isaiah's point: leaders may think they can see what needs to be done in a situation, but in reality things are unfolding according to Yahweh's purpose, and so the right attitude is trust in him.

In ethics, God's overriding aim is to establish 'justice and righteousness' (1:26–28; 5:7). We shall see how much a vision for a Jerusalem based on these qualities dominates the whole prophecy. It explains Isaiah's severe criticisms of oppression of the poor and weak (1:17; 5:8–10), the corruption of justice (1:21), drunkenness and self-indulgence (3:16—4:1; 5:11–17). But it is crucial to notice that this vision comes from the nature of God. The key text for the point is 5:16:

> But the LORD of hosts is exalted by justice,
>   and the Holy God shows himself holy by righteousness.

This verse connects God's lordship over everything ('is exalted') with his 'holiness', and his love of justice and righteousness. So God does not just have the power to order events on earth; he desires a certain kind of order, because of what he is like. Justice and righteousness may be summed up as a right ordering of all of society under God. As a characteristic of God, it is the determination to bring such a society about. For this reason, 'righteousness' can even effectively mean 'punishment' (10:22; cf. Williamson 1998, p. 25).

As for what God is like, Isaiah's typical word for it is 'holy'. He frequently calls God 'the Holy One of Israel' (e.g. 5:19, 24; the term appears over twenty times in the book). And in the great vision of God in the temple, the seraphim call him 'holy, holy, holy' (6:3).

This means that God's insistence on Israel not making foreign alliances and his desire for a holy people in Judah are really one and the same thing. His power to save them *is for the purpose of* making them a people that shows justice and righteousness. God's 'order' is both powerful and moral. This is why, when Israel turns away from God, it is not only the moral order that collapses, but also the social and political fabric (the point of Isa. 3:1–12). (See also Barton 1995, pp. 55–57, for this point).

Isaiah's concern for the future of Judah and Jerusalem is, of course, connected to these other concerns. Isaiah believed that what he was saying about trust and obedience was important because it affected how Yahweh would treat the people in the future. His fundamental position is what he says to King Ahaz:

> If you do not stand firm in faith
>   you shall not stand at all (7:9c).

This suggests that Ahaz has a chance of continuing in God's favour as the Davidic king, if only he will act faithfully. Similarly, the saying in 1:18–20 spells out the opposite possibilities that lie before Judah, prosperity or destruction. In the same passage, the commands in 1:16–17 imply that obedience will hold back God's anger at the sins described in 1:10–15:

> Wash yourselves, make yourselves clean;
>   remove the evil of your doings from
>   before my eyes;
> cease to do evil,
>   learn to do good,
> seek justice,
>   rescue the oppressed,
> defend the orphan,
>   plead for the widow.

Some passages appear to hold out the prospect of either salvation or judgement without any conditions (e.g. unconditional blessing in 8:1–4; 29:5–8; 31:4–9; unconditional doom in 29:1–4). However, it is unlikely that Isaiah preached either of these messages 'neat'. The best guide to how he used them is likely to be the fact that opposite oracles are sometimes put together (8:1–4, 5–8; 29:1–5, 5–8). So salvation and judgement again represent opposite possibilities, depending on the people's response.

However, Isaiah may not always have held out hope in this way. In some passages it seems as if the people cannot repent; Isa. 6:9–12 is the leading example of this, in Isaiah's vision about his calling. Here it seems as if he must keep preaching without response from the people, until the punishment finally comes. At times it looks as if it has become too late for the people to repent. Isa. 30:15–17 speaks of repentance, but the prophet looks back on the people's response and says:

> *But you refused* and said, 'No! We will flee
>   upon horses' –
>   therefore you shall flee! (30:15c–16a)

Finally, there are promises of salvation at a time in the future. If God's judgement becomes inevitable because the people will not repent, even so, *after* the punishment, he will again have mercy. This can be seen from the verses immediately following the ones just quoted. Isa. 30:18 pictures Yahweh *waiting* to bless 'those who *wait* for him'. If this verse were taken by itself, it might simply mean that God will bless all who remain faithful ('who wait for him'). In the context, however, it must mean that he 'waits' patiently to bless in the end, even though he is bound to punish sin in the immediate future. This is borne out by vv. 19–26, in which the joy of Zion follows a time of 'weeping' (v. 19), and God 'heals the wounds inflicted by his blow' (v. 26).

At this point we face the question as to which sayings about the future really came from Isaiah. (Barton, identifying five different types of saying about the future, offers a discussion of this; 1995, pp. 64–82.) Isa. 30:18–26 is often regarded as an addition in a much later time than Isaiah (Clements 1980, pp. 249–50). Some commentators regard all such passages as additions (see Clements on 1:27–28, pp. 36–37). However, others accept that some are genuine. Barton, accepting that 10:5–9 and 1:24–27 are from Isaiah, writes:

> There is no reason why he should not have looked beyond the disaster which he was certain would come, and foreseen a bright future for the survivors and their descendants (Barton 1995, p. 79).

A special class of sayings about the remote future concern the promised king (9:2–7; 11:1–5; 16:5–6; 33:17). The idea of the king as one who rules justly, and therefore ensures a just society, is deeply embedded in Israel's hopes and beliefs (2 Sam. 8:15; Ps. 72). So it is not surprising that Isaiah should hold out a hope of a king who would live up to the ideal. It is important to note that these prophecies all occur within chs 1—39. Williamson, who believes the sayings about the king come from Isaiah, argues that there are clear stages within Isaiah on the topic of kingship: while Isaiah hoped for a Davidic king, Deutero-Isaiah (chs 40—55) saw God alone as king, and Trito-Isaiah (chs 56—66) followed him in this (Williamson 1998, pp. 4–8).

In spite of questions about which sayings come from Isaiah himself, we have now seen the main features of that message. It is a 'vision' (1:1) in every sense. It shows Isaiah's insight into the nature of God and reality. And it unfolds a view of what society could and should be like. More than that, it declares that it is God's intention to make his chosen people into such a society, even though they have so far failed. We can now take further the question of how his words came to be the basis of the great book that bears his name.

THE COMPOSITION OF ISAIAH 1—39

In discussing some of the sayings about the future in Isaiah, Williamson says that, even if they are not from Isaiah, 'they are still of great importance in demonstrating that . . . those who developed Isaiah's writing in later times did so with a considerable degree of insight into his own way of thinking' (Williamson 1998, p. 23). With this in mind, let us go on to ask how these different sayings have come to form the unified composition that we now have. The debate in Isaiah is not so clear-cut as with Jeremiah. Whereas the issue in Jeremiah is whether Jeremiah himself might have written much of the book, or whether it is the work of scribes, in Isaiah there are more possibilities. This is no doubt because of the long period between Isaiah's life and matters dealt with in the book. How do we bridge the gap from the man Isaiah who lived in Jerusalem in the last decades of the 700s to texts that address situations two hundred years later?

There is some evidence that parts of the book existed in an earlier form than the one in which we know it. For example, it may be that the 'Woe'-sayings (or 'Ah'-sayings, NRSV) in 5:8–24 and 10:1–4a originally belonged together, since they all follow a similar pattern. In the same way the sayings in 5:25–30 and 9:8–21 share the refrain:

> For all this his anger has not turned away;
> his hand is stretched out still (5:25; 9:12, 17, 21)

IS PROPHECY PREDICTIVE?

It is often said that prophecy is primarily 'forthtelling', not 'foretelling'. That is, prophets had a message for people of their own time, and were not in the business of revealing the future. Perhaps these two possibilities are not at odds with each other. For example, a promise of salvation might have the 'rhetorical' intention of encouraging people who are struggling or depressed.

Why do scholars differ over predictive prophecy, and why do they accept some kinds and not others? One critical commentary, Hayes and Irvine, takes almost all of Isaiah 1—39 as coming from the prophet. They accept that there are different kinds of sayings about the future in Isaiah 1—39 (one of the reasons sometimes given for thinking they could not all come from one person), and explain the differences by supposing that the prophet was addressing ever-changing situations. They call these 'rhetorical situations' (e.g. p. 63), that is, situations in which some particular problem is found, which the prophet then addresses in order to suggest a way of thinking about it or dealing with it. (See Introduction, on rhetorical criticism.) On this view it is possible to explain why a single prophet might say quite different things, even about the future. He need not have an entirely consistent message, because he simply meets different needs as they arise.

But why do Hayes and Irvine come to quite different conclusions about individual sayings compared with other scholars such as Clements and Barton? To answer this we have to think of a bigger picture than the idea of prediction in itself. Scholars always have a concept of what Isaiah's message was. This concept, of course, has to come primarily from the sayings. But which sayings really came from the prophet? Well, that depends on the concept of the prophet! So the prophet is identified by the sayings – but the authentic sayings are identified by the concept of the prophet. There is obviously a danger of a circular argument here. Inevitably, each scholar applies some way of judging what is authentic. And this is where differences occur. Clements and Barton look for consistency in the prophet's sayings. Hayes and Irvine, who give the benefit of the doubt to Isaiah, construct a rather different portrait of him.

There is more to the difference between them than this, however. When scholars think a saying is inauthentic, it is because they believe they know something about the kind of ideas found at different periods in the Old Testament's history. So the process may be considered not entirely circular. Thus Clements says of 30:18–26, with its 'dramatic change in the natural order', and its 'extreme assurance that the light of the sun and the moon will be increased to an extraordinary degree':

and also may have formed a group of sayings. Clements even thinks these original groupings should be restored, and he has done so in his commentary (Clements 1980, pp. 60–70). Other parts of the book have also been identified as originally separate sections. For example, 6:1—8:18 is often called the 'Isaiah memoir', since it is a narrative based on his personal account of events in the Syro-Ephraimite war (Clements 1980, p. 70). The heading to chapter 2 (2:1) looks as if it might have stood at the beginning of a collection at one time, since it is unusual for such a heading to occur in the body of a prophetic book (Williamson 1994, p. 144). These are just hints. But since Isaiah prophesied over a period of many years it is reasonable to suppose his words may have been preserved at first in small collections, and indeed that these may have been rearranged and given new contexts as they became incorporated into the book as we have it.

One idea is that Isaiah had a group of disciples who gathered his sayings (Jones

The overall impression is of promises that contain an eschatology bordering on apocalyptic in which a totally new world order is envisaged. Clearly the section is not from Isaiah, and is only marginally related to Isaiah's prophecies as a late … expression of the hope which would witness the reversal of all the threats which Isaiah had delivered (Clements 1980, pp. 249–50).

Even this could be a circular argument, since the supposition that such ideas are relatively late in the Old Testament depends in part on the belief that Isaiah could not have uttered these sayings. Moreover, the extravagant language about the natural order may be highly rhetorical, and need not be 'apocalyptic' at all. (See Daniel: Apocalyptic, for a definition of that genre.) Hayes and Irvine treat this passage as relating to Isaiah's message about the defeat of the Assyrians (Hayes and Irvine 1987, pp. 342–45; cf. 10:5–19).

In this connection, it should be said that sayings about the future are often accepted as genuine because they are thought to relate to events close to the prophet's time. (The point about 30:5–19 in the last paragraph is a case of this.) This is why two key prophecies for 'messianic' interpretation, namely 7:14 and 9:2–7 [1–6] are often accepted as original to Isaiah. That is, it is held that they were not originally meant as predictions of events in the far future, but related to events in the prophet's time. In its context, the Immanuel prophecy (7:14) refers to the immediate crisis, the threat to Judah from the Syro-Ephraimite alliance. The 'sign' that Isaiah gives to Ahaz is that within a very short time – before a child about to be born has grown very old – that threat will have disappeared (v. 16). The young woman who is to be the child's mother is presumably someone present or at least known to Isaiah, Ahaz and other onlookers. How this prophecy came to refer to the birth of Jesus Christ must be considered a little later, when we turn to the interpretation of the Book of Isaiah. Similarly 9:2–7 [1–6], with its great vision of a Davidic king, may have been a conventional coronation hymn, using extravagant language in homage to the king (cf. Ps. 72 for something similar). Its messianic application would then be a development in the text's interpretation.

Predictive prophecy cannot be ruled out in principle. Equally, it should be recognized that there are different kinds of prediction. We should always ask what the prophet meant to say or do by pointing to future events. Moreover, predictions are sometimes taken up later in quite unexpected ways (see on Hos. 11:1). It is important to understand, not only what prophecies originally meant, but how they came to be understood in new ways.

1955 and Eaton 1959). We saw above that Isa. 8:16 might be evidence for Isaiah having written down his sayings. Equally, it could be evidence for disciples having done so. These could have formed a 'school' that continued even after his lifetime, passing his words on, and adding new ones, for example after the fall of Jerusalem in 587 BC. On this view, even the author of Isaiah 40—55, late in the exile, can be seen as a disciple of Isaiah (Jones 1955, p. 245). (See the account of this theory in Williamson 1994, pp. 6–8.)

More common is a redactional theory (see Introduction). Applied to Isaiah, this means that the book of Isaiah came about as collections of sayings that were gradually formed into a book. This would have been the work of scribes who were not followers of Isaiah in particular, but who may have worked on a whole range of writings, adapting them to new circumstances. They could have been the same people, often called the Deuteronomists, who worked on the Historical Books, Joshua, Judges, Samuel and Kings. Successive redactions would have borne the marks of their time. For example, some think there was a major redaction in the time of King Josiah (640–609 BC), when it is thought that there was great optimism among the people that God was saving them from the oppressive powers around them (see Collins 1993, p. 38). This is largely based on the story of Josiah's religious reform, in which we read that he re-occupied Israelite land formerly captured by Assyria (2 Kgs 22—23). The Josianic redaction would have offered great hope, while still calling the people to faithfulness in response to Josiah's lead. On this view, Isa. 9:2–7, perhaps originally a coronation hymn for King Hezekiah, could have been re-used to celebrate King Josiah as one who would bring about the former glories of King David's reign (Collins 1993, p. 39). The redactional point is also about the climactic *positioning* of this saying in relation to the preceding section (chs 7—8), which had held out opposite possibilities of blessing or disaster.

Further redactions continued into the exilic period. The careful structuring of the book, for example the alternation of judgement and salvation sayings throughout Isaiah 1—12, is the result of redactional shaping. The narrative section, Isaiah 36—39, has been deliberately placed to form a connection between Isaiah's prophecies about Assyria and the prophecies about the Babylonian exile in Isaiah 40—55. The important point about redactions is that they reflect an interpretation of the sayings as a coherent whole. The purpose of a redaction, whether Josianic or exilic, might be to say that, while Isaiah once announced judgement, that time is now over and the time of salvation has come. Alternatively, Isaiah did promise salvation; it did not come about in his day, but is now at hand (Collins 1993, 39).

ISAIAH 1—39 AND 40—66

When we spoke of the redaction of Isaiah 1—39, we found that we had to think also of chs 40—66. This is because some of the linkages that we noticed seemed to make sense when we thought about the book as a whole, or at least chs 1—55. This is clearly true of chs 36—39, whose purpose is to connect the prophecies about the Assyrian time with those relating to Babylon. But it may be true about the way in which the parts of the book are organized, even within chs 1—39.

The first question to notice in this regard is whether Isaiah 40—55 (or 'Deutero-Isaiah') was written as a separate, independent prophecy, or in order to fill out or complete the prophecies of Isaiah. Until relatively recently it was common to suppose that Deutero-Isaiah was indeed a separate work. R. N. Whybray, for example, thought that it was simply added to the older collection of Isaiah's oracles by redactors who saw similarities between the two prophets in their love of Jerusalem and its religious traditions. At the same time, they wanted to claim the authority of the older prophet for the newer sayings, and indeed to add a note of hope to Isaiah's work (Whybray 1983, pp. 4–5; cf. Davies 1989).

However, many scholars think that Isaiah 40—55 never existed independently, but that its author was deliberately looking back to Isaiah. Clements writes: 'from the outset, the material in chs 40—55 was intended to develop and enlarge upon prophetic sayings from Isaiah of Jerusalem' (Clements 1985, p. 101). Williamson goes further, arguing in great detail that Isaiah 1—55 as a whole is the product of Deutero-Isaiah, who built Isaiah's words into his own new composition. Parts of chs 1—9, therefore, come from Deutero-

Isaiah himself. For example, he re-used 2:2–4 from an older form of the book, putting it in its present position, and adding v. 5; and he composed 11:11–16, as a deliberate balance to 5:25–30 (Williamson 1994, p. 154; see also Collins 1993, pp. 42–43).

The reasons for these connections are that some language and themes are shared by the two parts of the book. Examples are Israel's blindness and deafness (6:10; 42:7, 18–19), and its election (Deutero-Isaiah reverses Isaiah's rejection of his people). These are the two main examples given by Clements. An example of a verbal link is 29:16 and 45:9 (Williamson 1994, p. 63; and see his further examples, pp. 63–91).

While Isaiah 40—55 is dominated by the expectation of salvation, chs 56—66 re-introduce notes of accusation and warning that we found in parts of Isaiah 1—39. Chapter 58, for example, calls people to observe a true 'fast', meaning to stop oppressing the weak (vv. 6–9). There are also signs of discord within the community, which have suggested to some that a powerful religious group has begun to oppress a weaker group (63:9), and that as a result this weaker group has come to see itself as the true 'servants' of Yahweh (e.g. 65:9c). While there are clear connections with Isaiah 40—55, for example in chs 60—62, the mood is in general different. Since the commentary of B. Duhm in 1892, many have thought that this part of the book originated after the return to Jerusalem, in a time when some of the old bad habits had reasserted themselves. It may have been written by a prophet who wanted to continue the work of Deutero-Isaiah, applying it to the time in which he lived.

The language of the promises leads some scholars to think that these chapters see the beginning of 'apocalyptic', that is, a vision of the renewal of the whole world order in the future (Hanson 1979, especially pp. 150–61). On this reading, the 'servants' are identified as a visionary group oppressed by a powerful ecclesiastical hierarchy. However, the visions of Isaiah 56—66 do not have to be read in that way (see Carroll 1979 and Emmerson 1992, pp. 85–95).

READING ISAIAH AS A UNITY

Our overview of criticism of Isaiah shows an important development. Early criticism treated the different parts of the book as quite distinct, different messages from different prophets for different times. There are still introductions and commentaries that follow this approach, with separate sections for the treatment of each part of the book (e.g. von Rad; Koch).

However, much modern study thinks that the book has been deliberately shaped as a whole into its present form, even though this was a lengthy process. As a result, it is common now to interpret the book as having unity and coherence in its themes and theology. One strand in this development is redaction criticism (which we have described above). Another landmark of a different sort was B. S. Childs' *Introduction to the Old Testament as Scripture* (1979). Childs' treatment of Isaiah in that book was one of the best examples of his belief that biblical books should be read for their theological meaning in their final 'canonical' form. He thought the Book of Isaiah had been deliberately set free from its various original historical settings in order to express a theology of judgement and salvation that was valid for many times and places (pp. 325–27).

The structure and outline that follow cover the whole book of Isaiah. This is done to make the point that the book should indeed be treated as a book, since we have received it in that form. The section on Theological Themes that follows the outline will also be based on the belief that the theology of Isaiah is only properly understood by a reading of the whole book.

STRUCTURE AND OUTLINE

STRUCTURE

The Book of Isaiah falls into clearly identifiable sections. Chapters 1—12 are characterized by prophecies about Judah and Jerusalem, alternating between judgement and salvation. Chapters 13—23 consist of sayings about nations other than Judah and Israel. Chapters 24—27 continue this theme, but picture God's final establishment of his kingdom among the nations. Chapters 28—35, like 1—2, have words of judgement and salvation, and a vision of a righteous king. Chapters 36—39 are a distinct section because they consist of narratives about Isaiah and Hezekiah. Chapters 40—55 are concerned with the return of the exiles from Babylon. And chapters 56—66 address a new situation after the return. This structure may be set out as follows:

1—12	Jerusalem judged and redeemed
13—27	God's righteousness established among the nations
28—35	A righteous king in Jerusalem
36—39	Jerusalem saved, but the shadow of Babylon looms
40—55	The return to Jerusalem from Babylonian captivity
56—66	New heavens and a new earth.

OUTLINE

The structure above may be broken down further, and gives the following outline of the book.

1—12: Jerusalem judged and redeemed

1:1—5:30 In these chapters, the scene is set for the prophecy of Isaiah in the reigns of Uzziah to Hezekiah. Chapter 1 sets the direction of the whole book, because it contains aspects of both judgement and blessing. For this reason some scholars think it was deliberately composed as an introduction to the whole book. Judah is accused of unnatural unfaithfulness to Yahweh (1:2–3), and a connection is made between this and the suffering of Jerusalem (1:5–9). This may refer to the Syro-Ephraimite invasion (734–733 BC). Empty worship is also condemned (1:10–15). However, Jerusalem will be saved, but only after a purging, which will make it righteous once more (1:21–26). This is like chapters 2—55 as a whole, in which judgement, in the form of exile, is followed by restoration. The picture in 1:27–31 makes a distinction between the righteous and the wicked even within the redeemed Zion. This has an echo in chapters 56—66.

A new heading at 2:1 leads into a vision of a future time in which other nations will make pilgrimage to Jerusalem (2:2–4). This reverses an idea found in other Zion literature, in which Yahweh has to defend Jerusalem against enemies (Ps 2). There are echoes of the salvation of the other nations elsewhere in the book (especially in 40—55, but also in 19:24–25 for example).

Isaiah 2:2–4 is regarded as Isaianic by Wildberger, because it is based on an ancient idea of the pilgrimage of the nations to Jerusalem (Wildberger 1991, pp. 85–86). (An almost identical saying appears in Micah 4:1–4. As Micah was another eighth-century prophet, there is a question as to which prophet may have used it first. (See also on Micah.) (See also Predictive Prophecy.)

In 2:5–22, the focus shifts, and a major theme of the book is introduced, the pride of human beings, and the folly of thinking that they can reckon without God in their planning. This is subject to his judgement (2:12). In 3:1–12 Isaiah portrays a topsy-turvy world in which proper authority has been removed. The least qualified rule, and all is chaos and oppression (3:3, 13–15). The form in 3:13–15 is a 'covenant accusation'. (For more on this see on Mic. 6:1–6.) The 'haughty', fashionable women of Jerusalem are humiliated in the violations of war, and their last desperate plea (4:1) is for a return to any kind of social order.

Think about
DELUSIONS OF GRANDEUR
One of the great themes of the book is Isaiah's call to recognize who is *really* 'high and lifted up' (6:1), rather than just imagining oneself to be. Isaiah uses the image of tall trees to symbolize pride (2:13). What might be the modern symbols of this? See also Theological Themes: Trust in God.

This horrible picture is balanced and answered by another vision of salvation (4:2–6), which reminds us of the exodus from Egypt and the tabernacle in the desert (v. 5, cf. Exod. 40:34–38). This salvation, however, only comes after a judgement, and is known by only the 'survivors' of the people.

Chapter 5 then switches back to the prophet's present critical view of the people. The beautiful and tragic 'song of the vineyard' (5:1–7), like a love song, expresses God's longing for his people to be faithful (see the panel). What he desires is 'justice and righteousness' (v. 7), as in the vision of 1:26–28. Instead, there is the very opposite in Judah, and this accusation is filled out in

5:8–23. The accusation is grounded in God's 'holiness' (5:16), which is also the reason why he seeks justice and righteousness. And we now meet for the first time the name 'the Holy One of Israel' (v. 19), used for Yahweh (see Message of Isaiah of Jerusalem). As well as saying that holiness is the most important thing about him, it also points to the fact the God and Israel belong closely together. This is ironic in view of Isaiah's message here. And so another image of judgement finishes the chapter, and this section of the book (5:24–30).

These opening chapters signal the book's vision of a righteous city of Zion. It does not exist in reality, but only in prophetic vision, and in the determination of God to bring it about in the end.

6:1—9:7 In this section, Isaiah himself is introduced, in what some call the Isaiah 'memoir' (6:1—8:18; see Composition of Isaiah 1—39).

As we saw in the Introduction, the account of Isaiah's vision is a key passage for the whole body of prophetic literature. In picturing Isaiah in the divine presence it is set apart from other stories of prophets' calls (such as Jer. 1). It serves to show that Isaiah's words are truly from God (here we see Isaiah 'standing in the council of God', to use Jeremiah's description in Jer. 23:22). The vision-report gives an account of a prophet's experience of God, which leads him to worship, to understanding, and finally to action.

Isaiah's vision of God (6:1–13) is 'in the year that King Uzziah died' (642 BC). It is vital to the whole message of Isaiah. God is 'high and lifted up (v. 1). These very words were used in 2:12, about everything that was '*falsely* high and lifted up'. Only God is truly

Think about
THE SONG OF THE VINEYARD AS POETRY

Isaiah 5:1–7 is a superb example of Isaiah's poetry, and also of the power of poetry to express deep things about God (see Introduction: Rhetorical Intention). It is a love song, and like the Song of Songs, it is set in a vineyard or a garden (cf. Song 1:5–7). Even Genesis 2 can be read as a love song in a garden.

Think about how Isaiah's song creates its effect.

1. Notice who is speaking, and how the speaker changes in the course of the poem. Consider how this produces a dramatic effect.

2. What effect do you think the prophet/poet aims to achieve by referring to God as 'my beloved' in the opening line? And why does he choose a 'song' to make his point?

3. Think about the other imagery and metaphors. What does the 'vineyard' refer to? And how is the metaphor developed in the poem? Notice how the vineyard metaphor appears in other places in the Bible (e.g. Ps. 80:8–18 [9–19]; John 15:1–17).

4. The poem ends with a sharp and terrible contrast between 'righteousness' (sedaqa) and 'a cry' (se'aqa). This cry is the desperate cry for help of someone in great distress (as in Exod. 22:23 [22]; Job 19:7). It is the opposite of 'righteousness'. And this corruption of what God wants in his people is expressed by two words that sound almost the same. What effect does this create at the end of the poem?

5. Taking all these points into account, think again about the power of poetry as described in the Introduction: its openness to the imagination, and its capacity to express profound things. What is lost when you try to boil down this poem to its 'ideas'?

6. Can you think of any modern poem (whether overtly 'religious' or not) that shows some of the qualities of this one?

so. And it is because people put themselves or others in that place that trouble comes. He is also 'holy' (6:3), meaning that he rejects all evil, so that Isaiah feels unworthy in his presence (v. 5) (see Message of Isaiah of Jerusalem on this). His 'glory' is this holy character made known, as once at Mt Sinai (Exod. 24:16), then in the tabernacle and in the temple (Exod. 40:34; Ps. 29:9). Later in Isaiah it will be revealed to all people (40:5). Finally, he is 'king' (v. 5), in a way that puts all other claims to kingship in the shade (it is not accidental that the account opens with a note about the death of King Uzziah; see Theological Themes: King and Messiah).

The vision explains the crisis that has been unfolded in chs 1—5 (since God has not been honoured by Judah). God speaks into that crisis, and now we see that Isaiah will be his messenger. We have already seen that salvation is promised for Judah, but only after judgement (1:21–26). Isaiah will now have to proclaim this mix of bad news and good (6:10–13). Verse 13c is sometimes regarded as a late addition to the vision account, but it accords well with the shape of chapters 1—5.

We find Isaiah at the heart of the life of Judah. His vision of God on his heavenly throne (6:1–13) is located in the temple (v. 1). And in chapters 7—8 he is in dialogue with the king. The issue in 7:1–11 has been outlined above (Date and Destination). Ahaz is told to trust God in the crisis, not human

Map 1
The Two Kingdoms
Showing the principal places which
figured in the history from the reign of
Saul to the Fall of Jerusalem in 587 BC.

Tyre

PHOENICIA

Mt. Lebanon

Dan

A R A M

THE GREAT SEA
(MEDITERRANEAN SEA)

Mt Carmel

Yarmuk

Megiddo

Shunem

Jezreel

Bethshan

Ramoth-
gilead

Tishbe

Dothan

Cherith

Plain of Sharon

Samaria

Tirzah

Shechem

Mahanaim

I S R A E L

Jordan

A M M O N

Bethel

Rabbah

Gibbethon

Gibeon

Mizpah

Jerusalem

Ashdod

Ekron

Shephelah

PHILISTIA

Gath

J U D A H

Lachish

Hebron

M O A B

Gaza

Dibon

Engedi

Arnon

Dead Sea

Beersheba

Kir-haresheth

15

power, and that his true security depends on this (7:9c; this is also the theme of 2:5–22). The Immanuel sign (7:14) assures him that God will overcome the immediate threat (see above, The Message of Isaiah of Jerusalem). But the sign is double-edged. The prophecies immediately following picture invasion by Assyria (ironically, since that is where Ahaz turned for help), and poverty in the land (7:18–25). And 'Immanuel' ('God with us') turns out to mean that God may be 'with us' for judgement as well as blessing (in 8:8c the name comes at the end of a judgement saying). It speaks of blessing again in 8:10c (there translated as 'God is with us' – but the Hebrew is simply 'Immanuel'). Yet the final pictures of chapter 8 are of judgement, at least for some in Judah (8:11–22).

The alternating images of disaster and salvation correspond to the basic choice offered to King Ahaz. The section is rounded off with one of the great promises of the book, 9:[1] 2–7. Verse1 gives a historical context, which many think refers to the beginning of the dismantling of the northern kingdom by Tiglath-Pileser III in 734–732 BC (Childs 2001, p. 79). The oracle (vv. 2–7 [*Heb*. 1–6]) may have originally been a coronation hymn (see Message of Isaiah of Jerusalem). But it has been linked with its context here (note how it picks up the darkness theme from 8:22) in order to round off the whole section (6:1—9:7) on a note of hope for future salvation. It promises a time of great and lasting blessing for the people under a king who will restore the glories of David, and especially, 'justice and righteousness' (v. 7). The new thing here is that this vision of a future Jerusalem (cf. 1:26–28) is now linked with the promised king. This is why the passage can be called 'messianic'. The term 'messiah'

itself (literally 'anointed one') is not here. But the idea essentially lies in the individual who will bring in the promised new age. The remarkable names applied to him (v. 7b [*Heb*. 6b]) speak of his bearing the mission of God in his own person. These may be regarded as throne-names, given at the king's coronation to express hopes of what he would be like as king. (It is not clear whether the oracle in vv. 2–7 would have been given at the birth or the coronation of the king; see Williamson 1998, pp. 42–43, and n. 22.) Commentators often point out a parallel with Egyptian practice, though the number of names given there was five (Sweeney 1996, p. 182). (See below, King and Messiah, for more on this.)

Children play an important part in these chapters, and their names are significant. Isaiah takes his son Shear-Jashub ('a remnant shall return') to meet Ahaz (7:3). We have met Immanuel ('God with us'). Perhaps Immanuel was Isaiah's son also, like the other children in this section? (Note 8:18.) Maher-shalal-hash-baz (8:1, 3) is another child of Isaiah's ('the prophetess', 8:3, just means the prophet's wife). The name means 'spoil speeds, prey hastes', and its interpretation in 8:1–4 is very like the first interpretation of Immanuel (7:16), spelling salvation. However, like that word, this too is followed by less hopeful sayings (in 8:5–22). The promise of a child in 9:2–7, therefore, who also has special names, brings all these 'child' sayings to a conclusion. When we read of the child that is born (or to be born), we think that the Immanuel prophecy may after all have a significance far beyond the immediate Syro-Ephraimite crisis.

9:8—10:34 This section develops the idea of Assyria as 'the rod of God's anger' (10:5, connecting with 7:17c, 18–20; 8:7). It traces the path of God's judgement against Israel and Judah at Assyria's hands, illustrating its thoroughness with the refrain:

> For all this his anger has not turned away;
>   his hand is stretched out still (9:12, 17, 21; 10:4).

However, the logic of the whole section is that Assyria has served unknowingly as God's agent (10:7). It is also wicked and subject to judgement, and will in turn be judged (10:12, 15–19), and a remnant of Judah saved (10:20–27). The section began with boasts of Israel about trees (9:10; recalling the tree-imagery for pride in 2:12–13). But this is turned against Assyria's pride (10:18–19). 10:33–34 is also against Assyria, and so the promises of salvation in chapters 11—12 are prepared for.

11:1—12:6 The 'shoot from the stump of Jesse' (11:1) is clearly another way of speaking about a king in the line of David (alongside 9:2–7). In 6:13, devastated Judah was likened to a tree that has been destroyed, leaving only a stump. 6:13c promised new life from it. Now a shoot springs out of it, in the form of a Davidic king who will bring a new age of righteousness and justice for Judah. The imagery is of an ideal world, a kind of paradise, with peace even from dangerous animals. And there is a hint that not only Judah but all people will know Yahweh, recalling 2:2–4 (11:6–9). The vision shifts to a return of exiles from many countries (11:12–16), anticipating chs 40—55.

Chapter 12 is a song of praise taking up themes from chs 1—11. God's anger, which had not turned away (9:12, 17, 21; 10:4), has now done so (12:1). The speaker will *trust* in Yahweh, the main virtue required of Judah

and its kings (v. 2). Yahweh will be known among the nations, and Zion will be restored (vv. 3–6).

13—27: God's righteousness established among the nations

Isaiah is like other prophetic books in having a section devoted to pronouncements about the nations in general (see Amos 1:1—2:3; Ezek. 25:1—32:32; Jer. 46:1—51:64). These are sometimes called Oracles Against the Nations (OAN), but the name is not wholly accurate, as the sayings include promises of salvation. Isaiah's OAN are crucially important for his whole message, because they speak about God establishing justice and righteousness in the whole world, not just in Judah. A 'messianic' note is even struck in the middle of an oracle about Moab (16:4b–5).

Chapters 13—23 are often marked off from 24—27, but in fact these two blocks belong together, as the latter four chapters form a climax to the themes in 13—23.

13:1—14:27 The first and longest group of sayings concerns Babylon. This fits with the importance of Babylon in the book as a whole, and the message of the salvation of the remnant of Judah from Babylon after their exile (chs 40—55). The word of salvation for Israel in 14:1–2 shows that God's purpose in overcoming Babylon is the restoration of his people (note the parallel with Assyria in 10:12–19). The tone of the prophecy in 13:1–22 reminds of Isaiah's warnings against pride in 2:6–22, and Yahweh's 'day' of punishment (v. 9, cf. 2:12). But the scope of it is all the world (13:5, 11), and the language speaks of disruption in all creation (13:10). The theme of pride brought low recurs in chapter 14. The centrepiece is the fall from heaven of the

'Day Star, son of Dawn' right down to the Sheol, the underworld (14:12–21). Like Ezek. 28:12–14, this applies an ancient myth to the fall of a king. In this case, it may be a myth about the planet Venus (or *helel* in Canaanite; see Childs 2001, p. 126). The fall of a proud tyrant is in line with Isaiah's theme that only God is truly 'high and lifted up' (6:1).

The last paragraph of the sayings against Babylon (14:24–27) switches suddenly back to Assyria (v. 25). This shows that in God's eyes the fate of Assyria and that of Babylon are one and the same. It may also mean that 'the destruction of Babylon represents the final fulfilment of the anti-Assyrian prophecies' (Blenkinsopp 2000, p. 289).

14:28—23:18 The main section of the OAN consists of sayings against the nations around Judah, and Judah itself. Here too we find not just pronouncements of judgement, but other themes, making connections with other parts of the book of Isaiah. A connecting thread is how some of these nations fared in the time of Assyria's and Babylon's power.

Philistia (14:28–32). The 'rod that struck you' (14:29) refers to Assyria (cf. 10:5), which had repeatedly attacked the Philistines in Isaiah's time. The *broken* rod probably points to the death of Tiglath-Pileser III in 627 BC, the same year as King Ahaz died (v. 28). This reminds us again of the true weakness of the seemingly powerful, even if it brings no comfort to Philistia.

Moab (15:1—16:14). In the middle of the pronouncements of judgement on Moab for its pride (16:6, cf. 2:12 again), an appeal is made to *Judah* (presumably) to accept Moabite refugees (16:1–4a). To care for the stranger (or 'alien') was part of Israel's call to

act justly (cf. Deut. 14:29, for example). And in this connection comes a messianic promise of a Davidic king who seeks justice and righteousness (vv. 4b–5; cf. 9:7; 11:4).

Damascus (Syria) and Israel (northern kingdom) (17:1–14). These were the two enemies that threatened Judah in 734–733 (cf. chapter 7). Israel is sharply accused, because it has *forgotten* Yahweh (cf. 1:2–3). Verses 12–14 are addressed to nations in general, but are linked to vv. 1–11 by the theme of the defeat of the enemies of Judah.

Ethiopia (18:1–7). Again, a proud people is brought low. But in the end they will bring gifts to Zion (v. 7; cf. 2:2–4).

Egypt (19:1—20:6). The sayings against Egypt show how foolish it was for any of the smaller nations to think Egypt could help against Assyria. Not only Ashdod (20:1) but also Judah did this (cf. 30:1–5). (For Ashdod's rebellion, see *ANET*, pp. 286-87). In fact, Egypt will be torn apart internally (19:1–15), and finally overcome by Assyria (20:4–6). Isaiah's walking naked and barefoot (20:2–4) is a symbolic action illustrating what happened to captive people.

The middle part of the sayings about Egypt is remarkable, because it pictures Egypt turning to worship Yahweh (cf. again 2:2–4, and the 'light to the nations' in 42:6; 49:6). Even Assyria is counted in this vision, using language of election more usually applied to Israel and Judah (19:24–25).

Southern peoples (21:1–17). The prophet's vision sweeps over the Negeb (southern Judah, 21:1), Edom (Seir, and probably Dumah, 21:11), and Arabia (21:13). The people's desire for the fall of oppressive Babylon is at the centre (21:8–9).

Jerusalem and Judah (22:1–25). The oracle in vv. 1–14 makes clear that the Valley of Vision is Jerusalem (22:8, 9–11). The Valley itself is probably the Valley of Hinnom, south of the city. Judah's trust in its own strength (vv. 8b–11, cf. 2 Kgs 20:20), and its refusal to repent (vv. 12–14) are criticized. The tone is like that of Isaiah's words to Ahaz in chapter 7. The 'day of the LORD' language (cf. 2:12) reappears here to warn of judgement (vv. 5, 8b, 12). The second oracle (vv. 15–25) uses a saying accusing the official Shebna to reaffirm the promise that David's dynasty would continue. It contains the famous phrase 'Key of David' (v. 22), which was later applied messianically to Christ. The two oracles together represent both judgement and salvation, reflecting this balance in the book.

Tyre (23:1–17). The poem about the destruction of Tyre by Babylon (v. 13) and its later restoration is used to fit the theme that the nations will one day bring tribute to Jerusalem (23:17–18; cf. 60:8–13). There is an echo of King Hiram of Tyre's provisions for Solomon's temple (1 Kgs 5:7–12).

The OAN seem rather haphazard, but they strike familiar Isaianic themes. The oppression of nations by Assyria then Babylon, and then the fall of each of these in turn, weaves through the oracles. So too does the idea that Yahweh, the God of Israel and Judah, stands behind all the events of history, which themselves seem haphazard and contradictory. The judgement on Judah stands alongside the punishment of the other nations. Yet there are notes of promise too.

24:1—27:13 These chapters are often treated as a separate section because they contain some ideas like those found in apocalyptic literature (especially a final victory of God over death, and over hostile powers in heaven as well as on earth; see on Daniel in this volume). For this reason they have been called Isaiah's 'mini-apocalypse'. However, it is better to see them as the conclusion to the OAN in chapters 13—23. In those sayings, the fall of Babylon (and Assyria) was a kind of symbol of the final victory of God in all the earth (e.g. 13:4–5, 11). Descriptions of changes in the sun and moon (24:23) were also in the earlier chapters (13:10). Vivid metaphors were used to describe earthly events. So the present section continues that thread. The central point is that God, in bringing judgement on the nation Babylon, shows that he is God over all heaven and earth. However, it is also clear that his victory in the historical situations known to the people of the time is only a hint of his intention to bring about deeper and more long-lasting peace and righteousness in the world.

At the heart of the section is a contrast between two cities (note the title for this section, 'A Tale of Two Cities', in Seitz 1993, p. 172), one that has fallen (e.g. 24:10; 25:2), and the righteous city, which is a kind of ideal Jerusalem (26:1–2). The first question is what city is described as destroyed: Babylon, Jerusalem, some other? Probably the idea is that all cities that have shown pride and rebellion, including Jerusalem, Babylon and the other nations accused in the OAN, must be brought low so that God's victorious rule can be established (Seitz 1993, pp. 187–92). The inhabitants of the righteous city are 'a righteous nation that keeps faith' (see also 1:26), but this too is not restricted to Jerusalem. The picture of feasting on 'this mountain' has echoes of Mt Zion and pilgrimage, and of the covenantal meal before God at Mt Sinai (Exod. 24:11; Motyer 1999, p. 209). Zion is extended to become the dwelling-place of 'all peoples' (cf. 2:2–4), and the victory of God there will mean nothing less than the overcoming of death (25:6–8). The reference to 'his people' (25:8) should perhaps be taken inclusively (in line with 'Egypt my people' and 'Assyria, the work of my hands' in 19:24).

LIFE AFTER DEATH IN THE OLD TESTAMENT

Did the Old Testament writers believe in life after death? The topic is certainly much less to the fore in the Old Testament than the New. Salvation in the Old is often expressed as salvation of the people of Israel from enemies (e.g. Psalm 74), or of the individual from some terrible situation (Psalm 18). Happiness is long life, health, peace, children. There are even passages that seem to deny life after death (Ps. 6:5 [6]). But there are hints of another side to the story. Psalm 73 suggests that the innocent person who suffers may have his cry for justice finally answered beyond the grave (Ps. 73:24). Psalm 16:10 expresses a trust in God that is not limited by death. All of these passages are open to more than one interpretation, as a glance at the commentaries on them shows. But it is likely that the idea of resurrection in Dan. 12:1–3 did not come out of the blue (cf. Blenkinsopp 2000, p. 359).

Isaiah 25:6–8 is part of the Old Testament picture on this. The image of 'swallowing up death' probably comes from the Canaanite myth in which the god Mot 'swallows up' the fertility god Baal (ANET, pp. 138–41). The same Canaanite god is mentioned in Isa. 28:15. The image of God destroying death is powerful. The passage is used by Paul in 1 Cor. 15:54, along with Hos. 13:14, in his great argument about the resurrection (Thiselton 2000, p. 1299).

The book of Isaiah draws elsewhere on motifs from myths. In another, Baal overcomes the god Yam (literally 'Sea', ANET, pp. 129–31), and this lies behind Isa. 51:9–10. Isaiah 14:12–14 probably draws on a myth about the god helel, but we do not know in what form or forms such a myth existed.

28—35: A righteous king in Jerusalem

28:1—31:9 The section is structured by five 'woe'-sayings (28:1; 29:1, 15; 30:1; 31:1), setting a tone of judgement. The focus shifts back, after the visions of the fate of the nations, to the historical situation of Judah. These chapters are like chapters 7—12 in that sense. The pride and sin of Israel (Ephraim) are condemned (28:1–8). The picture of the 'covenant with death' (28:15, 18 – contrast the victory over death in 25:7!) refers to some form of commitment to the god Mot, the god of the underworld (Sheol). This shows that their false trust is religious as well as political. God's justice and righteousness will be the measure of their falsity (28:17). The false wisdom of the religious (28:9–10) is contrasted with the true wisdom of God in his purposes (vv. 23–29; 29:14).

The folly of trust in Egypt is ridiculed in 30:1–7; 31:1–3. It is part of a deep malaise. The idea of rebellious children, who reject God's word with determination (29:9–10), recalls 1:2–4 and 6:9–10. The typically Isaianic message in 30:15 ('In returning and rest you shall be saved; in quietness and trust shall be your strength'; cf. 7:9b) is reported only to show how it has not been heard. The saying about God's deliverance of Jerusalem (31:4–5) means first of all that it is God alone who can do what Egypt cannot. It is no promise of cheap salvation. As in 8:16, Isaiah is told to write his words down, for a time when they will be heard (30:8), since they are not heard now.

Yet the story of judgement has its other side in salvation here also. In 30:19–33 a picture of the destruction of Assyria (vv. 27–33) is side by side with one in which God (the 'Teacher') is present among the people of Zion (vv. 19–22), and giving prosperity (vv. 23–26).

The structure of these sayings shows again that God intends salvation to come out of his judgement on the nations. This involves looking beyond the immediate horizon. The judgement saying in vv. 27–28 has no clear reference, and need not be confined to Assyria. God sifts 'the nations' (v. 28). And indeed 'Zion' (v. 19) should perhaps be understood in an inclusive way after the visions of chs 24—27: 'the more plainly he (Isaiah) engages with history the more easily he moves into eschatology' (Motyer 1999, p. 227).

32:1—33:24 In these chapters too there is a mixing of salvation and judgement, and especially the idea that the one who once acted as the instrument of judgement will be judged in turn (33:1–2; cf. 31:8–9, and 10:12–19). But the announcement of a righteous king (32:1) gives a new focus. In 33:17–22 the theme of judgement on the instrument of judgement (Assyria) and the theme of the coming righteous king (see below, Theological Themes: King and Messiah on 33:17) are combined in a new picture of a righteous and peaceful Zion. This vision of Zion is tempered by the distinction still between righteous and wicked (33:14; cf. 1:27–28, and see on chs 56—66).

34:1—35:10 In chapter 34, Edom stands for the nations (note v. 2), and the judgement on her for the judgement against all. There is an echo of the sayings against the nations in chs 13—23, and also of the 'day of the LORD' (v. 8; cf. 2:12). It is a 'no-kingdom' (v. 12), in contrast to the messianic kingdom (32:1). The real subject of this vision is the evil 'city' that is opposed to God's city of righteousness (cf. on chs 24—27).

In contrast, chapter 35 is a majestic poem on God's final salvation of his people. The blossoming desert (vv. 1–2, 6b–7) recalls Israel's first march to freedom through a desert (Exodus–Numbers), and also speaks of a restoration of all creation. The healing of blind, deaf and lame symbolizes salvation that goes beyond mere restoration to the land of Israel (vv. 5–6). The 'highway' (v. 8) recalls the way from Assyria to Egypt, where those peoples would worship Yahweh (19:23–25), but now the image is paradisal (v. 9, cf. 11:6–9). The return to Zion (after Babylonian captivity) shades over into a greater salvation (v. 10).

Think about
ISAIAH 35 AS CENTREPIECE

Chapter 35 may be seen as the centrepiece of the whole book of Isaiah. Why do you think this is so? Consider its themes, and its position in the book.

36—39: Jerusalem saved, but the shadow of Babylon looms

As we have seen, Isaiah's own work took place in the Assyrian time. However, we also saw that the book covers the Babylonian captivity of Judah as well as the Assyrian wars. Furthermore, the role of these two nations is the same, God's judgement on his people. Yet they also illustrate pride that deserves judgement in its own turn. In the structure of the book of Isaiah, chs 36—39 are pivotal, because they provide the link between the defeat of Assyria and the captivity in Babylon. Beyond that, in chs 40—55, will be the defeat of Babylon too. The narrative in these chapters is closely parallel to 2 Kgs 18:13—20:21.

36:1—37:36 We return to the time of Isaiah and Hezekiah, and the siege of Jerusalem by

continue to be trusted? The speech-forms serve the purpose of persuading the people that God can be believed. They are used freely by him. Scholars often try to recover original separate sayings underlying the present text, but this is uncertain. Here, chs 40—55 will be treated as a continuous argument. The basic premise is that the time of salvation has now come. (The subdivisions used in the following are not hard and fast. The student should notice how different commentators break down the text.)

40:1—41:29 The key to 40:1–11 is its similarity to the call-vision of chapter 6 (see Seitz 1990; cf. also 1 Kgs 22:19, Motyer 1993, p. 299). In the heavenly council, God tells angelic beings to 'comfort his people' (the verb is plural). The basis of the message of salvation to come is in 40:2 – Jerusalem has been punished enough. When God rescues his people it will be revealing his 'glory' to all the world (v. 5), instead of only in the Jerusalem temple (6:3). All people will know that God has kept his word.

The voices in vv. 3, 6 are angelic voices carrying out the command of vv. 1–2 (cf. the seraphim in 6:2–7), and the prophet replies (v. 6b). His message will confirm that after the punishment (vv. 6b–8) comes salvation. The point of 'the word of the LORD will stand for ever' is that after the 'flower has faded' (meaning the judgement now past; cf. 28:1–4) the Isaianic words of salvation will still be fulfilled. The judgement-salvation structure is taken over from chs 1—39 (e.g. ch. 10).

The return to Jerusalem is a movement home through wilderness (like the exodus), with Yahweh leading powerfully (v. 10). Chapters 40—41 consist largely of arguments (including Disputations in 40:12–17, 18–26) persuading the exiles that Yahweh alone is God and has power over all nations and all history (this in response to Israel's question in 40:27). One important argument is that only Yahweh has the power to reveal events before they happen (41:21–24). This is related to the idea that the message sealed up by Isaiah (8:16; 30:8) is now revealed to the later prophet.

Isaiah 41:2 (cf. v. 25) announces the rise of Cyrus (not mentioned by name till 44:28), the conqueror of Babylon, in a rhetorical form that claims it was Yahweh who did this, not any other god. This leads to reassurance to 'Israel' (v. 8). Note the repeated 'Do not fear' (vv. 10, 14), and the promises of rich blessing (vv. 17–20; cf. ch. 35). Israel is here referred to as 'servant', in the first use of this important term in chapters 40—55.

Think about
HOW CAN THE EXILES BE 'ISRAEL'?

In Isa. 41:8 the prophet addresses 'Israel'. Historically, however, Israel no longer existed, since the largest part of it was destroyed for ever in 722 BC, and the Jewish exiles in Babylon had come from Judah. Why, then, does the prophet use this term (and its parallel, Jacob)? It seems that 'Israel' did not have a fixed reference once and for all, but was a matter for interpretation. For more, see again Introduction: Theological Themes: Patterns in the prophetic books.

42:1—44:23 This next section develops the topic of the 'servant'. (See box on the Servant Songs.)

In 41:8–9 the servant referred to Israel, Yahweh's chosen one, offspring of Abraham.

24

In 42:1–7 the natural sense is that 'my servant' still refers to Israel, who is now seen as the one who will bring justice to the world, 'light to the nations' (v. 6). As 'a covenant to the people' he embodies God's covenantal relationship with all peoples ('people' is probably inclusive, in parallel with 'nations'). This is in contrast to Cyrus, who is depicted as an ordinary conqueror (41:25). 42:1–4 is usually described as the first 'servant song' (with 49:1–6; 50:4–9; 52:13—53:12), as identified by Duhm. This tends to make the reader think of the 'servant' as a particular individual. In fact, that understanding of the servant does not emerge clearly from this passage (cf. Childs 2001, pp. 323–25; Motyer 1993, p. 318). However, the servant here is 'Israel' in a special sense, for this servant will open eyes that are blind (42:7) – yet it is Israel that is blind (see on vv. 18–20)! So we may wonder how 'Israel' will carry out this mission. And we will recall that it is very like the mission of the messianic king in 11:1–5.

The rest of chapter 42 recalls how Yahweh's new salvation of Israel (vv. 10–17) is coming through the people's rebellion and punishment. The servant Israel was 'deaf and blind' (42:16, 18–20, cf. 6:9–10). Chapter 43 then develops the deliverance from Babylon by means of a highly poetic parallel with the first exodus of Israel from Egypt (Exod. 14—15; cf. vv. 2–3, 16). The way back to Judah from Babylon was not literally through water. The point is that this new event – the 'new thing' (v. 19) – is even greater than that ancient marvellous salvation. It is a new 'creation' of Israel (43:15).

A typical prophetic accusation follows (43:22–24) – but only, surprisingly, to lead into further declarations of coming salvation (43:25—44:8). The biting criticism of idol making (44:9–20) is part of the insistence that Yahweh alone is God. The present section ends with another celebration of Yahweh's salvation of Israel, 'my servant' (44:21–23).

44:24—48:22 A major theme of this long section is the fall of Babylon. Yahweh, declaring that he is about to fulfil his word (44:26), refers to Cyrus in remarkable ways, as 'my shepherd' (44:28), and 'my anointed' (45:1). These terms are more usually applied to leaders in Israel. For kings as shepherds, see Jer. 23:1–4. 'Anointed one' is applied to priests (Lev. 4:3, 5, 16) and the king. The word is *mashiah*, 'messiah', and strangely it is used in Isaiah only here, applied to Cyrus. Cyrus therefore is portrayed as an instrument of Yahweh's victory in the most exalted and intimate terms (note 'I call you by name', 45:4; cf. 43:1), and his actions are part of the establishment of righteousness in the world (v. 8).

The sayings against Babylon (45:9–25) are interwoven with assertions about the supremacy of Yahweh, and his plan to save Israel. These assertions are directed against the Babylonian gods. This is the point of 46:1–2, where the idols of Bel (Marduk) and Nebo are depicted going into exile, as part of the humiliation of a defeated enemy. One effect of a victory in war was that the victor's god seemed to be more powerful than the god of the defeated nation (the Assyrian Rabshakeh had made the point very clearly: 36:18–20). Yahweh, having no image, could never be humiliated in that way. Even so, it must have seemed to the exiles that he had been defeated, among the impressive statues and images in the great city of Babylon. So the prophet spells out that the splendid Babylonian gods were powerless after all (cf. 46:5–7).

THE SERVANT SONGS (ISAIAH 42:1–4; 49:1–6; 50:4–9; 52:13—53:12)

The Servant Songs are among the greatest and best known parts of the Old Testament. Because they introduce and share the profound idea of salvation through suffering, they have often been marked out as forming a special class of sayings within Isa. 40-55.

This separation of the Songs goes back to Duhm's commentary in 1892, and it was sometimes held that they had no real connection with the message of the surrounding sayings. Westermann still regarded them as a later addition to chs 40—55 (Westermann 1969, p. 92). So are they separate from chs 40—55, or integrated into the context? Most scholars now regard them as integrated, and the interpretation offered here takes that position. For a review of opinions up to the 1970s, see Kruse, 'The Servant Songs'. T. N. D. Mettinger (*Farewell to the Servant Songs*) is an example of a modern author who rejects the thesis of a group of sayings separate from the context.

More importantly, who was the servant? Some have taken the servant as collective, not individual (e.g. Eaton 1979). Some signs point to a prophet, for example, the call language (49:1), and there are other similarities to Jeremiah (see Whybray 1983, pp. 74–78). Whybray favours a prophetic interpretation, and indeed that the servant was Deutero-Isaiah himself (Whybray 1981, 1978). Hugenberger (in Satterthwaite et al. 1995) has argued that the servant is a second Moses, pointing, for example, to exodus imagery in the Songs. Other signs are royal, especially bringing justice and giving law to the nations (42:4), and an interpretation of the servant as king is favoured by, for example, Eaton (1979) (though note that his interpretation is also collective). Westermann sees these two figures united in the servant (1969, p. 97).

In some modern readings the search for an original identity of the servant has been given up, since the text itself makes no identification, and the emphasis is placed instead on literary or theological readings of the songs (e.g. Clines 1976, for a literary reading of Isa. 53. Childs 2001 offers a 'canonical' reading, where the message of the songs is closely bound up with the developing theology of chs 40—55.)

Christians have long identified the servant with the messiah. The New Testament makes the connection in a number of places, primarily with the fourth song, 52:13—53:12 (e.g. Matt. 8:17; John 12:37–40; Acts 8:26–40; 1 Pet. 2:18–25). The servant is thus identified with Jesus Christ. The connection between the two lies in the willing acceptance of the role of Israel in bringing salvation to the world; the acceptance of suffering in fulfilling that mission; that the suffering is on behalf of others ('many', 53:11), and that it brings them 'righteousness' (53:11, cf. Rom. 3:21–26). This 'vicarious' suffering of the servant (i.e. on behalf of others') brings in an element that goes beyond the royal or prophetic, and likens the work of the servant-Christ to a sacrificial victim (53:7, 10). The effect of the work of the servant-Christ goes beyond Israel, because he is designated 'light to the nations' (42:6; cf. Luke 2:32). (Motyer's exposition of the fourth song brings these connections out very fully; 1993, pp. 422–43.)

The nature of the relationship between the songs and the New Testament's understanding of Christ remains

---

Babylon's humiliation is pictured in ch. 47. Its boasting is taunted mercilessly, in a parody of what Yahweh says about himself (47:8b). Not even its famous sorcerers can cast spells to save them (47:12–13).

Yahweh now stresses to the exiles (Israel) that he is bringing about what he promised long ago (48:1–16, especially vv. 3–8). This is part of his demonstration that he alone is truly God (cf. 41:21–24). The voice in 48:16c anticipates 49:1–6 and 61:1; it is the voice of the 'servant', whose mission is to proclaim the salvation after the judgement. This is an important step in the definition of the servant as an individual with a mission in Israel.

to be considered, that is, a hermeneutical question. In traditional theology, the servant simply was Christ, revealed to the prophet as a future deliverer. Motyer's understanding of the servant is subtle, as he allows the identity to be revealed gradually from song to song, and thinks of the songs as integrated into the context (1993, p. 318). In his exposition of 52:13—53:12, however, he clearly regards the portrayal of the servant as Isaiah's portrayal of Christ. More commonly in recent times, the Christological meaning is found by analogy with the contextual meaning of the songs. This means one can suppose that Deutero-Isaiah may have had an individual of his own time in mind, but that that figure embodied truths about God's dealings with humanity that were later seen to be embodied in Christ in a definitive way.

The shaping of the book of Isaiah itself already shows that the deeper meaning is more important than the identity of the figure, since it conceals that identity. The next hermeneutical question is how the theology of Isa. 40—55 came to form the New Testament writers' view, and indeed Jesus' own. On this we may suppose that the New Testament writers were deeply influenced by their knowledge of the Old Testament, but also that they were ready to see new dimensions of old truths (on this see Childs 2001, pp. 420–23). It should be added that treatments of the songs as referring originally to their own times will not necessarily be governed by Christian interpretation. For example, Whybray denies that the fourth song teaches the servant's vicarious suffering (Whybray 1983, pp. 77–78; 1978).

A final reproach (48:17–19) is a prelude to a ringing command to go out from Babylon in joy, on the way through the desert towards home (vv. 20–21). The literal going out of Babylon is paralleled by a 'going' (v. 17c) that refers to way of life. Mere return to Jerusalem can never be salvation in itself. The final verse (v. 22) also darkly hints at this.

Think about
THE FALL OF BABYLON

In Rev. 14: we read: 'Fallen, fallen is Babylon the Great!' Its fall in the sixth century BC, long before Revelation, was sudden. But in the time of the Jewish exile, Babylon was indeed great. King Nebuchadnezzar had built it up to be as splendid as any city that had been seen before. His kingdom was the superpower of the day. In its famous 'hanging gardens' it had one of the seven ancient 'wonders of the world'. Its palaces and temples were magnificent. See the illustrations at 'Babel' and 'Babylon' in *IBD* I, pp. 155–62. Hardly surprising, then, if the defeated Jewish exiles felt that the Babylonian gods were more powerful than Yahweh. What is more, they may have been impressed by the great images of gods like Bel (Marduk) and Nebo (46:1). Was there a challenge in the splendour of Babylon even to the most sacred belief of Yahwism, that God could not be imaged? The prophet opposes this in 44:9–20.

49:1—50:11 In the so-called second Servant Song (49:1–6) the servant (heralded in 48:16c) speaks in his own voice (contrast 42:1). The servant seems more like an individual in this song than in 42:1–4, and he speaks like a prophet about his call (49:1, cf. Jer. 1:5). He has a mission to Israel (v. 5), yet he himself is called 'Israel' (v. 3). The mission of Israel to the nations is apparently focused on an individual who bears it specially. Perhaps this was the prophet. Verse 4 could refer to the prophet's sense of failure for some reason unknown to us, but it could also be a confession of Israel's past failure in its mission to the world. The individual and collective interpretations of the servant cannot be separated here. The servant as an individual has a mission to bring Israel back to its own mission (vv. 5–6a). But now he is to expand that mission to take in other nations (vv. 1a, 6b). The Servant Song is followed by words of Yahweh to the servant (vv. 7, 8–12), assuring him of success despite his own sufferings. The passage ends in a hymn of praise (v. 13).

In 49:14—50:11 the people ('Zion') express doubts in Yahweh's purpose to save, while the servant accepts his mission (50:4–9; Childs 2001, pp. 390–91). 49:14–26 consists of a debate between Yahweh and Zion, in which Zion expresses doubts (49:14, [21], 24) and Yahweh reassures in strongly persuasive words (vv. 15–20, 22–23, 25–26). God's word in 50:1–3 deplores Israel's lack of faith in response to the message of salvation.

In contrast, the servant takes up the challenge of faith (50:4–9 – the third Servant Song). The servant is now (literally) 'one who is taught' (like those who sealed up Isaiah's teaching in 8:16. See above, Message of Deutero-Isaiah, and Williamson 1994, pp. 106–09). On Israel's behalf he accepts the teaching of Yahweh (cf. 48:17). He has suffered but will be vindicated, and he challenges others to stand with him (v. 8). Another voice continues the challenge (vv. 10–11).

51:1—52:12 In this unit Yahweh addresses Israel in 51:1–8 (where the call to 'listen' is repeated three times); 51:17–23; 52:1–6, while Israel addresses Yahweh in 51:9–11. The appeal in 51:1–8 again follows the servant's challenge in 50:4–9, and goes to those in Israel who are willing to seek righteousness (vv. 1, 7), for it is in this way that the promise to Abraham of many descendants (Gen 15:5) will be fulfilled. The call is defined as the mission given to the servant, to bring salvation and justice to the nations (vv. 4–5). Israel replies with a prayer (petition) familiar from Psalms of lament (v. 9; cf. Ps 44:23 [*Heb.* 24]). In doing so they affirm what Yahweh claims of himself, that he alone is God. This is reinforced by the mythological language for creation, borrowed from Canaan and Mesopotamia (vv. 9–10).

In these chapters we do not hear the doubting voice any more (as in 49:14–26). Even so, the people need to be strongly exhorted to 'listen', and 'awake', in order to take the opportunity of salvation. The section is rounded off with an image of good news brought to Jerusalem, that the exiles are returning (vv. 7–10), and a final command to leave Babylon (vv. 11–12). The promise in v. 12 contrasts this exodus with the exodus from Egypt, which was 'in haste' and 'in flight' (cf. Exod. 12:11).

52:13—53:12 This passage is identified in scholarship as the fourth Servant Song, and in the interpretation of the New Testament and the Church as a profound vision of the atoning death of Jesus Christ. The song takes further the idea of the servant as an individual who suffers because of his mission to proclaim salvation, first seen in 49:7; 50:6. Now his suffering is visible and striking (52:14), and the effect of it makes an impact even on kings (52:15). He has endured some terrible pain and humiliation (53:1–3). His suffering is described by speakers who remember their own reaction to it ('we held him of no account', 53:3). They now see him differently, for they confess that his suffering was for them (53:4–6). He was killed, without complaint and with great injustice, for he was innocent (53:7–9). Moreover, it was God who caused his suffering to bring about his purpose (53:10a). Yet the servant, mysteriously, will see life again. He will be an agent of God's will (v. 10d), and through him many will become 'righteous' (v. 11).

It is clear from this how the song has become a key text in Christian atonement theology. (For comment on the basis of this interpretation, see box on the Servant Songs.)

54:1—55:13 This joyous section crowns the whole argument in chs 40—55. Especially, however, it grows out of the fourth Servant Song, which has just gone before. The 'many' children of the barren woman (54:1) recall the 'many' whom the servant will make righteous (53:11). These 'children' are established in 'righteousness' (54:13–14). In this way, the new life given to Zion is shown to be the result of the servant's sufferings in 52:23—53:12. (These links were noted by W. A. M. Beuken 1979–89; cited by Childs 2001, p. 426.) Most important is that the inhabitants of the new Zion are called 'the servants of the LORD' (54:17). All this suggests that the salvation of Zion, promised since chapter 40, is achieved by means of the suffering ministry of the servant on behalf of others. The 'servant' gives rise to the 'servants'. This term is used several times in chapters 56—66 for the faithful in the returned community. Another link with the servant is in 54:13, where all Zion's children will be those who are 'taught' (54:13), like the servant (50:4).

The images of new birth and new beginning in these chapters link with the preceding chapters (51:18, 20), and also rest on the ancient promises to Abraham and Noah (Gen. 12:1–3; 9:1–17). The 'everlasting covenant' once made with David (55:3, cf. 2 Sam. 23:5) is now extended to the servants of Yahweh in the new Zion. So the eschatological vision, already seen in 2:2–4,

will be accomplished (55:5). The exiles must only grasp the opportunity to leave their captivity (55:6–7). So God's word will surely be fulfilled (55:10–11). And the new exodus will be like a new creation, described in terms that remind of Eden itself (55:12–13).

56—66: New heavens and a new earth
Introduction These chapters continue the salvation theme of chapters 40—55. Yahweh will act to save the people of Jerusalem and Judah (Zion), and overcome their enemies in order to restore them to their land. The salvation will happen before the eyes of the world, and even be assisted by foreigners (60:1–3, 10). The vision of salvation suggests that God's hopes for his people will now finally be realized, his former disappointment (5:7) being overcome because they will truly be faithful (60:21). The extravagant language of 60:17–20 tends to spiritualize the relationship between God and people. Walls (that is, of Jerusalem) are not mere walls here, but 'salvation', and gates are 'praise'. Even the sun and moon, the natural created lights will no longer be needed, because God himself will be the people's light (vv. 19–20).

We saw in chapters 40—55 hints that not all in the new Zion would be faithful to the mission of creating a just and righteous city (48:22). And in fact, in the new situation, some at least are unfaithful (hence the sayings that we have already noticed in ch. 58). The situation here is not far from that which we meet in the books of Ezra and Nehemiah, though it is not possible to fix on a specific time that our chapters address (Childs 2001, p. 444). In Isaiah 56—66 there is a passionate concern that those who have been saved should not only worship rightly, but behave well ethically. Isaiah 56:1 significantly adds this dimension to the idea in 46:13, which it otherwise resembles (Emmerson 1992, p. 101). The call to right fasting (ch. 58) insists that worship cannot consist in outward observance alone. The picture of people going about religious observances without true worship or love of neighbour is very like Isa. 1:10–17. Yet the outward aspects of religion are not denied in themselves, for the sabbath is regarded as important (58:13).

In Isaiah 56—66, the people of Yahweh are those within the new community who are truly faithful, according to standards that are familiar from Isaiah's preaching in the early part of the book. The division within the community is clear in chapter 65. God expresses his anger against some people who have rejected him and worshipped other gods (vv. 1–7). But he will protect and save his 'servants' (v. 7). These 'servants' are then equated with his chosen ones, using the language of election, and calling them the descendants of Jacob (v. 9). The contrast between the 'servants' and the faithless is pursued in vv. 13–16. We saw in 54:17 that these servants were those who would carry on the mission of the Servant.

Part of the conflict seems to be over the covenant and who belongs to it. The group that is accused here claims some sort of 'righteousness' (57:12), but it is to no avail. On the other hand, there are some members of the true covenant community who might not be expected to be in it. These include the 'foreigners' (56:3, 6), and the 'eunuchs' (56:4). The first of these groups is hard to identify. The second group may have felt excluded because of the law in Deut. 23:1 (*Heb.* 23:2). One theological contribution of Isaiah 56—66, therefore, is a warning against pride and false religious security *following* God's salvation, and a call to acceptance of the outsider in the community of faith.

While the servant theme has developed to a theme of 'servants', the Servant figure himself is also present as the speaker in 61:1–3, who speaks in the power of the spirit, like the Servant in 42:1. The thread of hope placed in a special gifted individual continues into this last part of the book, therefore. There are also links with the messianic text 11:6–9 in 65:25. The changing shape of this figure throughout the book of Isaiah is explored by Williamson (1998).

56:1—57:21 The new section opens with an exhortation to do justice and righteousness, and this stands over all that follows. A distinction is made straight away between the faithful and unfaithful, with the sabbath (perhaps unexpectedly) playing a symbolic part in this (56:2). Foreigners and eunuchs are (unexpectedly) counted in to the new people, in line with the eschatological vision (vv. 7b–8; cf. 2:2–4; see Introduction to chs 56—66, above). On the other hand, leaders of Israel are condemned ('sentinels', 'shepherds', 56:10–11). The distinction between righteous and wicked continues in ch. 57. The 'righteous', who should be at the centre of the new city, perish (57:1). Meanwhile, the sins that were the cause of Israel's problems before the exile have returned (v. 5, cf. Jer. 2:20; Hos. 4:13). The idolatry on a 'high mountain' (v. 7) contrasts with 2:2. A false righteousness is 'exposed' (NIV) in 57:12. But yet it is the righteous who know true peace (57:2), and the wicked who are denied it (57:21). And the true dwelling of God is 'with the contrite and humble in spirit' (57:15; cf. 6:1).

58:1—59:21 The accusation in chapters 58—59 majors on the lack of justice and righteousness in Jerusalem, which shows that the new Jerusalem has not been fully established (cf. 1:21–26). The exposition of the 'true fast', and the possibility of enjoying God's blessing (58:6–14), reminds of the analysis in 1:12–20. Chapter 58 is a prophetic accusation. In ch. 59 Israel confesses its sin (vv. 9–15a). Even so, the outcome of the sin is Yahweh's coming in wrath to establish righteousness (vv. 14–19). However, the anger against Judah shades over into his judgement on all nations, which leads to Judah's salvation (vv. 20–21). This becomes a preparation for chapters 60—62. (Motyer marks off this middle section as 59:14—63:6; 1993, p. 489.)

60:1—63:6 This exultant middle section of chapters 56—66 is addressed to Zion as such, that is, not just some within it. It opens with words that draw on some of the great promises in the whole book so far (60:1–2, cf. 9:2 [*Heb.* 9:1]; v. 3, cf. 2:2–4; v. 4b, 9, cf. 43:6). Exiles' children return; oppressors become servants. Jerusalem is restored, but its restoration is put on a higher plane by the use of metaphors (60:17–20). Renewed Zion is not quite encompassed by the ordinary city. Yet the ordinary city remains at the centre of the vision (60:21–22).

A voice that reminds of the Servant speaks again (note the 'spirit', 61:1a, cf. 42:1; 48:16c; cf. also v. 1 and 49:9). In addition, the verb *mashaḥ* ('anoint') appears (v. 1b), which might suggest 'messiah'. *Mashiaḥ* ('messiah'), however, is used only of Cyrus in Isaiah (45:1). Motyer thinks Isaiah 56—66 presents the Messiah as the 'Anointed Conqueror' (1993, p. 461), using the term 'anointed' on the grounds that the figure is given the spirit (pp. 492–93). There is indeed a certain combining of the book's deliverer-figures in this passage. Williamson

finds a reference to one who takes it on himself to proclaim 'all the as yet unrealized tasks entrusted to a variety of figures in Deutero-Isaiah' (1998, p. 187), and thinks this conscious combining of offices a good reason to see the figure as messianic (p. 188). It is not for nothing that these words were taken up by Jesus (Luke 4:18–19) to describe his messianic role.

The proclamation is in terms of release from bondage in the land. The 'year of the LORD's favour' (v. 2) reminds of the jubilee, when people returned to ancestral land lost through debt (Lev. 25:10–17).

A first-person voice speaks again in 62:1, echoing 61:1, and so drawing on the Servant idea. A promise of peace for (earthly) Jerusalem (62:6–9) is enclosed by visions in language that once again pushes the limits well beyond the ordinary (vv. 1–5, 10–12). The section is rounded off with a picture of Yahweh coming in anger to vindicate his people (63:1–6).

63:7—64:12 The victorious tone changes again. Now someone speaks on behalf of the people. The whole passage is similar to psalms of lament, with elements of confession, petition and praise. (The confession makes a link back to 59:9–15a, which came just before the middle section, announcing good news.) The recounting of God's past deeds is like Ps. 106, which also tells of Israel's rebellions, and turns to petition and praise. The petitions here are in 63:15–19; 64:1–2, 8–12. The speaker seems to speak for Israel as a whole ('your servants' in 63:17 is parallel to 'the tribes that are your heritage'). And the request is apparently to restore Zion after it has been defeated by enemies (63:16–19). The vision of the future is immediately balanced by a cry from a present time that still longs for salvation. (See above on Hanson's different view of this text: Isaiah 1—39 and 40—66.)

65:1—66:24 Chapter 65 brings to a head the theme that has been present since 1:28–31, the fate of those who continue to be rebellious even after Zion has been restored. Where God's wrath had previously been against Zion's enemies – 'I will not keep silent' (62:1) – the same language is now used against these enemies within (65:6). Their fate will be as that of their ancestors, and their crimes are the same (65:7). The 'servants' of Yahweh are now emphatically separated from these (65:8–16). The servants will fulfil the ancient promises to Abraham (65:9), but the wicked will be cut off (vv. 11–12).

The wonderful situation depicted in 65:17–25 is a completion of God's own desire for Jerusalem (cf. 1:26; 5:7). The joy of it is his as well as the people's (vv. 18–19). The future foretold is one of the great Old Testament pictures of blessing, with long life, many children, peace and plenty (65:1b–25). Is this a real or ideal picture? The last image (v. 25) is shared with that of the messianic age in 11:6–9. And the passage opens with the promise of 'a new heaven and a new earth' (v. 17).

Indeed God can never be limited to Jerusalem. The terms 'throne', 'footstool' and 'resting-place' are usually applied to the city and temple (Ps. 132:7, 14; 99:1, 5). The temple, rebuilt soon after the exiles returned there, can never be a sufficient dwelling-place for him (66:1–2; cf. 1 Kgs 8:27), and true worship is of the spirit.

The last chapter strikes some of the balances we have seen throughout the book. It returns to a theme that we saw right at the beginning:

the pointlessness of the rituals of worship for their own sake (66:2b–5). Then there is a picture of Zion's miraculous restoration, with judgement on his enemies (vv. 7–17). Verses 18–23 draw together the return from exile and the worship of the nations at Jerusalem. The vision is again eschatological (vv. 22–23). And the final note shows that rebellion against God will continue to the end (v. 24).

THEOLOGICAL THEMES

We began to think about the theological themes of the book of Isaiah when we asked what the message of the prophet Isaiah himself would have looked like (The Message of Isaiah of Jerusalem). There we saw that the idea of God as 'high and lifted up' explained important elements of Isaiah's message (God's lordship in politics, ethics and in history itself). However, we must now look at the book as a whole, to identify its great themes, and to see how Isaiah's message is developed.

THE 'STORY' BEHIND THE BOOK

The book began and ended with the city of Jerusalem (1:21–26; and see 66:20). Many of the important events happen there. The city is besieged (chs 1; 7); Isaiah has his vision in the temple there (ch. 6); Isaiah meets Ahaz and Hezekiah there (7:3; 38:1); it is saved from the Assyrian siege (ch. 37); it falls to Babylon (presupposed in ch. 40); the exiles will soon return to it (chs 40—55); other nations will also worship there (2:2–4; 66:20). Why is Jerusalem so important to Isaiah? One might say that it was simply because that was the centre of his world and he was bound to be interested in it. But there is more to it than that.

The events listed above tell a certain story (Jerusalem is accused, punished, restored, promises are made about its future). However, another 'story' lies in the background, and we need to understand that story in order to understand what motivated Isaiah (and later authors) as he spelt out his 'vision'. This story has to be pieced together from our wider reading of the Old Testament.

To the people of Old Testament times it was no accident that their capital city was Jerusalem. They knew that they were God's chosen people since ancient times, when he saved them from slavery in Egypt, to become his people by the covenant made at Sinai (the story told in Exodus; Exodus 19—24 is a central text). When the Israelites came out of Egypt, they had a destination, the 'promised land' of Canaan, where they would have 'rest from their enemies' (Deut. 12:10). That 'rest' was finally achieved, not by Joshua, but by King David, who first subdued all those who threatened Israel (2 Sam. 7:1), and captured Jerusalem. David's son Solomon then built the temple in Jerusalem (2 Kgs 5—8). City and temple became the symbol of the covenant between God and Israel, and of God's protecting presence. The temple was a kind of earthly image of God's dwelling in heaven. He was 'enthroned' there. When King Hezekiah prayed in the temple for the deliverance of the city from Sennacherib he prayed: O LORD, God of Israel, *enthroned upon the cherubim* (2 Kgs 19:15). He was referring to the cherubim in the 'most holy place' (or 'holy of holies'), whose wings were stretched out over the ark of the covenant (Exod. 25:10–22). (The 'holy of holies' in the temple was like the one in the tabernacle in the desert period.)

God was 'king' in heaven (Isa. 6:5). For Israel, like other nations, this idea was fundamental, and it explains many other things that they believed. Most importantly, they believed that God who was king in heaven had demonstrated his kingship in saving Israel, giving them their land, and dwelling in the Jerusalem temple, or 'Zion'. This is reflected in many parts of the Old Testament. Psalm 78, for example, tells the story of Israel and God, with its climax in his choice of Judah and Mt Zion (Ps. 78:67–72).

God is king in heaven, but he also appoints a king to reign in Jerusalem (as the end of Psalm 78 also showed). Psalm 2 is a key text, where God, as king in heaven, rules the nations through the king of Israel in Jerusalem, whom he calls his anointed ('messiah'), and his 'son' (vv. 2, 7). Following God's promise to King David (2 Sam. 7:8–17), he and his successors had a covenant of their own with the God of Israel, which was understood to be 'everlasting' (2 Sam. 23:5; Ps. 89:3–4 [*Heb.* 4–5]). Kings in the ancient world, however, had a responsibility from their god to maintain justice in society (this is clear from the prologue to the Babylonian King Hammurabi's law code; see *ANET*, p. 164). This is no less true of the King of Israel, as Psalm 72 shows clearly (Ps. 72:1–7).

This Old Testament story explains much in Isaiah. It explains why God might be expected to defend Jerusalem (Isa. 29:5–8), and why King Ahaz can be referred to as the 'House of David' (7:2; that is, the promises and responsibilities related to David applied to him as David's successor). It also clarifies why Jerusalem should be a city of justice and righteousness (1:26–28; 5:7). And it shows why the promise of a king, a son of David, who would reign in justice and righteousness (9:7 [*Heb.* 6]; 11:1–5), could be so important.

Finally, the theological 'story' that lies behind

Isaiah helps us understand the issues that Isaiah thought it worth fighting over. What would happen if in fact Jerusalem did not exemplify God's desire for righteousness and justice? How could God's commitment continue in those circumstances? These are the basic issues that are played out in the book.

ZION, CITY OF GOD

Isaiah is sometimes portrayed as one who believed in God's protection of Jerusalem, because of sayings like 29:5–8. In this he is contrasted with Jeremiah, who never spoke in this way, but showed that Judah's hopes in the old traditions were futile (Jer. 7:1–15). This contrast is misleading, however. We saw earlier (Message of Isaiah of Jerusalem) that Isaiah probably did not make unconditional promises about Jerusalem's safety. In fact, the book of Isaiah presents Jerusalem as a problem from the beginning, and works through to a conclusion that is quite different from a simple belief that God would always protect the city.

The book in its final form is written in the knowledge that the judgement of God fell on Judah. This is the point of view that we should take into account when we read the different parts of it. In a sense it is not possible to be sure how much Isaiah himself knew or believed about this. But in the canonical book of Isaiah, the question of God's plan for Jerusalem is worked out in the light of the fact that Jerusalem – the city from which God overcame and scorned his enemies – was destroyed.

What, then, is the book's vision for Jerusalem? There are, of course, very positive salvation sayings about this, mainly in chapters 40—55, but also elsewhere. The city and temple will be rebuilt (44:26–28), foreign kings will assist (60:10–11), and the nations will come to seek the God of Israel there (2:2–4; 66:20).

However, the vision is not of a simple return to the way things were in the good old days before the Babylonians came. Those days, as Isaiah shows us, were not so good. Instead there is a vision of a city in which God's desired righteousness is really found and remains. In one sense, this city will be the historical Jerusalem after the exiles have returned to it; in another it is a city that is greater than that Jerusalem.

This 'double focus' can be seen in the parts of the book that speak about salvation. In chs 40—55 the historical return of the exiles to Jerusalem and Judah is obviously in view. Passages like 40:9–11; 52:7–12 depict the departure from Babylon and the triumphant return to Jerusalem. However, there are pictures of a future, perfected city that go beyond this situation. The vision of a feast for all nations on Mt. Zion and the destruction of death is an example of this (25:6–9). So is the promise of 'new heavens and a new earth' (65:17–18), in which Jerusalem is created a joy and its people a delight, and wolf and lamb shall feed together (v. 25). So too is the beating of swords into ploughshares, as the nations flock to Jerusalem to learn the law of God, and war is a thing of the past (2:2–4). As we saw on chs 24—27, the righteous city pictured there is a kind of ideal, contrasted with the wicked city. The wicked city too, in this contrast, is also idealized, so that it is neither quite Babylon, nor wicked Jerusalem, but a type of all wickedness. In chs 40—66 there are hints that Jerusalem is becoming transcendent, for example in the highly poetic renamings of the city in 60:17–22; 62:12 ('you shall call your walls salvation and your gates praise', 60:18).

'Zion' in chs 40—66 tends to become the place where God's righteous people dwell, rather then the city of wood and stone (see above on 25:8; 26:2). This also fits with the vision of salvation being extended to all nations (42:6; 49:6; 56:3–8; 60:1–2). In some of these visions the nations are coming to Zion; in others the light of salvation is going out to all the earth.

The genius of the poetry in Isaiah is such that these twin visions – of the actual restored Jerusalem and a future city that fully embodies God's righteousness – cannot be cleanly distinguished from each other. The poetry is such that one can imagine the situation portrayed as real or ideal (65:18–25), so that the vision of the heavenly does not let the earthly off the hook of the command to faithfulness.

KING AND MESSIAH

In The 'Story' Behind the Book (a few pages back) we saw that the idea of God as heavenly king was a very basic metaphor lying behind much of the prophecy. Isaiah himself, responding to his temple-vision, declares: 'my eyes have seen the King, the LORD of hosts' (6:5). God's kingship is associated with his holiness and glory (6:3), and this is why Isaiah feels his sinfulness in God's presence (v. 5). It is because God is king that he imposes an order on the world in ethics, politics and history (explained above, Message of Isaiah of Jerusalem).

The belief in God as king runs through the book. In his disputation with other gods Yahweh is called 'King of Jacob' (41:21), 'King of Israel' (44:6), and 'your King' (43:15). As king, he alone is holy and has power to save. References to God 'reigning' are part of this theme (52:7; 24:23). Other passages portray God as king even though they do not use the term (66:1). These passages point to the future salvation of Israel, whether the immediate deliverance or the eschatological kingdom (24:23).

What is the place of the human king in relation to the kingship of God? According to the Davidic theology (outlined above, The 'Story' Behind the Book) the king of Israel rules in Zion by appointment of the heavenly king. So Isaiah can see God 'the King' in his vision (6:5), and then bring his message to Ahaz, the 'house of David' (7:2–3). The human king in Israel is God's means of establishing justice and righteousness among his holy people.

This belief also lies behind the promises that we call 'messianic'. In 9:2–7 [*Heb*. 9:1–6] and 11:1–5 the expectations of a time of justice, righteousness and peace are based on the hope of a king who will fully match God's requirements of him. The picture is of an enduring kingdom ('endless peace', 'from this time onward and for evermore', v. 7), and this is based on the original promise to David (2 Sam. 7:13). The names given in v. 6b [5b] bring out the king's wisdom (Wonderful Counsellor), the power of God (Mighty God), the king's fatherly relationship with the people (Everlasting Father), and his reign of peace (Prince of Peace).

What do these names say about the person of the promised king? As we saw (Structure and Outline) they are probably throne-names that express hopes for what the king will be like. The things that are said of the king are very like things that can also be said about God. 'Mighty God', for example, is used for God in 10:21. 'Wonderful counsels' (or 'plans') are attributed to God in 25:1 (for the translation see Blenkinsopp 2000,

p. 360; the standard translations do not bring out clearly the connection with 9:6 [5].) 'Eternal Father' could of course be said of God, but eternity can also be attached to the king in the language of royal honour (Ps. 72:5). Prince of Peace can be ascribed directly to the king who brings peace. The four names could have been given to the king without the implication that he was himself divine. Some of them are best seen as 'theophoric', that is, they are names given to a human being but they say something about God. 'Immanuel', 'God (is) with us', is also like this. The first two, or perhaps three, throne-names are best seen this way. (Indeed some think the four phrases should be read as a pair of theophoric names: 'A wonderful counsellor is the mighty God; the father of eternity is a prince of peace'; see Williamson 1998, pp. 42–44.)

The names given to the king, therefore, are intended to say something about God. They do not mean that the king is himself God. The Christian doctrine that the Messiah Jesus was divine must be justified in other ways. The emphasis in Isaiah's messianic visions is firmly on the fact that God himself will bring the hoped-for time of justice and peace. The 'messiah' will be an instrument in achieving God's purposes. The mission of the messianic king is so closely attached to the idea of God as saving king that at times it is not clear whether a text refers to the one or the other. Isaiah 33:17 could be taken either way.

The emphasis on God as king fits with the fact that the messianic visions retreat from view in chapters 40—55. There God alone is king. (Note that most of the passages cited above for the kingship of God come from the second half of the book. Williamson draws attention to this; 1998, pp. 1–10.) The

promises to David are extended to the people as a whole (55:3, where 'you' is plural), and the central human figure is the Servant (see below).

THE SERVANT AND THE NATIONS

While the emphasis in the second half of Isaiah falls on salvation, at the same time the dominant figure is the Servant. We have begun to think about the significance of the Servant in the Servant Songs (see box on pp. 26–27). So we focus now on the place of the idea in the book. We shall find that the 'servant' idea is closely related to the salvation of the nations other than Israel.

King and servant are not in themselves widely different ideas, since the king could be described as God's servant (Ps. 89:3 [4], 20 [21]). The king-as-servant had the task of carrying out God's plans for a people. In Isaiah, King-Messiah and Servant have in common the task of bringing justice, righteousness and peace. So the change from king to Servant in chs 40—55 could be just a shift in emphasis, to bring out the servant role of the king-messiah.

However, we saw that the identity of the servant was complicated. He sometimes seemed to be a royal figure, and sometimes a prophet. And above all, he was in places identified with Israel. A key text is 55:1–5. There the covenant once made with David is now made with the whole people (v. 3). And moreover, the people take on David's role as a witness to the nations (v. 4, cf. 43:9–10; 44:8–9). The servant as an individual appears to call the nation back to exercise this role properly (see Williamson 1998, pp. 113–66, for a full explanation of Israel, the servant and the nations). Israel (the nation) is still 'deaf and blind' (49:18–20; cf. 6:9–10). So it falls to the Servant to hear obediently

(50:4b–5), and to proclaim the light of salvation to the world (49:6). The suffering of the Servant in 52:13—53:12 could be that of an individual endured in the course of his ministry. Or by extension it could be that of an obedient servant people as they witness to God in a hostile world.

The servant theme goes hand in hand with the message of salvation to the nations. This is one of the most important developments in the Book of Isaiah. The salvation of the exiles from Babylon, as we have seen, is not a mere return to the way things were before. God wants a truly righteous people to inhabit his 'city'. And that people will be composed of people from many nations.

TRUST IN GOD

Isaiah's insistence that kings trust God instead of making alliances can seem a naïve and unrealistic demand of rulers. Did not Kings Ahaz and Hezekiah, faced with the threat of their country being overrun, simply do what any responsible ruler would do? Today's political world is hardly thinkable without alliances of nations, for security and other purposes. Even in our ordinary daily lives, most of us take precautions for our security and wellbeing as far as it lies within our power to do so (though some Christian groups refuse to use insurance companies for their protection). In an important way, this is only to exercise human responsibility. The Old Testament's Wisdom literature (especially Proverbs) praises prudence, that is, the practical wisdom that works and provides for foreseeable needs. So trust in God does not always mean we should take no sensible precautions. In words famously attributed to Oliver Cromwell as he counselled his soldiers: 'Put your trust in God, my boys, and keep your powder dry!'

Isaiah is not against prudence as such, but against a false reliance on human power that takes no account of God. The power of Assyria and Babylon, as portrayed in Isaiah, thought itself equal with God, as the Rabshakeh's speech in the siege of Jerusalem shows (Isa. 36). The folly of this has always been exposed in the end. The history of the world could be told as a succession of great empires that have risen only finally to fall exhausted, with their mighty pride in ruins. (The visions of the Book of Daniel depict things exactly like this; Dan. 2; 7. And the Tower of Babel story expresses the same point as a kind of parable; Gen. 11:1–9.) A nation may be powerful but can never be all-powerful. To be human, even though organized politically as a super-power, is to be weak. In the aftermath of the attack on New York's World Trade Center we are painfully aware of this. Isaiah's prophetic perception in the Syro-Ephraimite crisis – that that dangerous-looking threat to Judah was destined to run out of steam – is a warning for all time that human power always pretends to be greater than it is. Ahaz was wrong because he

Think about
POLITICAL PLANNING

Does the message of Isaiah mean that all strategic planning is wrong, whether in politics or in other parts of life? Is all human calculation about events ruled out by definition? Isaiah did not deny Ahaz' or Hezekiah's right and responsibility to rule. In the modern world, there are real and difficult issues about how nations organize and defend themselves. Isaiah says to human authorities that they should recognize that their power and authority are not absolute, and that they could come under God's judgement.

thought human power was overwhelming. His failure to understand how things truly lay also shows up how limited human comprehension and planning are. This is why wisdom in the end must always come back to trust in God.

The other side of trust, as we have seen, is obedience. To trust God for our own safety while at the same time we exploit our own power in the world is a contradiction. Nor is it right to say that we will put our own safety first, and only then think about others. To trust God is to live according to his ways. And that means that we attend to the demands of justice and righteousness in every place where it is within our power. In God's world, we do not have a right to absolute security, or to ever-increasing prosperity without reference to others' poverty. The people of Judah discovered this the hard way. No 'city', whether Jerusalem, Asshur, Babylon, or the powerful modern western alliance, is God's 'Zion'. We wait for that to come. Our attitude in the meantime is that which Isaiah urged on Ahaz and Hezekiah: 'In quietness and trust shall be your strength' (30:16; cf. 7:9). This surely means that trusting God is the best way for human beings, here and now as well as in the future. However, the vision of Zion, the city of righteousness that God is establishing beyond all the conflicts of the present world, also means that the dangers and deprivations of whatever we have to endure in our present situations can never have the final word.

RHETORICAL INTENTION

Whom does the Book of Isaiah seek to persuade, and about what? The answer to this is partly given by the Theological Themes, set out above. These are the content of the message the book tries to get across. But the 'rhetorical' question tries to set the discourse in a context, with a speaker or writer and an 'audience'. What specific need (or 'exigency', to use the rhetorical critics' term) made the prophet speak, or the writer write?

It will be clear from all that has been said so far that there can be no single answer to this question. Isaiah spoke to people who were threatened by first the Syrian-Israelite alliance then Assyria; Deutero-Isaiah spoke to people in Babylon not long before Babylon fell to Persia; perhaps a third prophet spoke afterwards in Palestine again. Between the prophets' speeches and the finished book a process of writing took place, perhaps with other situations in mind than those we have thought about. So the rhetoric of the book operates at a number of levels.

One level is that of the prophetic speeches. One of the great contributions to this topic is that of Yehoshua Gitay. His two books consider the speeches of Isaiah in Isaiah 1—12, and of Deutero-Isaiah in chs 40—48. In his view these sections of the book consist of the spoken addresses of the two prophets in their different times and places (Gitay 1981, p. 26; 1991, pp. 1–4). Gitay does not find it strange that speeches giving promises of salvation should alternate with threats of judgement hope in Isaiah 1—12. This is because he looks for the *effect* of speeches on listeners. The speeches of salvation have the effect of showing 'the prophetic vision of the "true" world; the world as it should be' (Gitay 1991, pp. 4–5). This is not at odds with the threats of judgement, just the other side of the coin. He is critical of much Isaiah scholarship, which has looked for the words of Isaiah in short sayings, and rejected many sayings on the grounds that they are in prose. Isaiah, he believes, spoke in extended speeches, and used different kinds of style for different effects (Gitay 1991, pp. 3, 5–6). This emphasis on the rhetorical function of the speeches is important. In particular, it helps us get away from the old question of how a prophet who spoke words of judgement could also utter words of hope. In Deutero-Isaiah, he is able to interpret the discourse as a series of connected arguments, rather than disconnected units.

Gitay helps us to focus on the rhetorical power of the prophet's speech. The power of prophetic speech as such is a vital aspect of rhetorical effectiveness. Other studies have focused on the poetry and metaphors of the book (e.g. Nielsen 1989). Some feminist writers have stressed the feminine imagery for God in texts such as Isa. 42:14; 46:3–4 (Sawyer 1996, p. 203). The power of the speech in itself is perhaps the most important single reason why the prophetic books are still effective today.

When we think about the power of the speech as such, we tend to think about the speech of the prophet(s) in its original situations, as far as we can discover them. However, this level of interpretation, which we have noticed in Gitay's approach to rhetorical analysis, does not deal adequately with the rhetorical intention of the *book* of Isaiah. He sees, of course, that the speeches came into written form, but pays little attention to the importance of the written text as such, think-ing only that they may have been written to be read aloud (Gitay 1981, p. 233). So his method does not seem to answer the question of how the book came to be in its present form, and what *its* rhetorical purpose might have been. The strong connections between the two parts of Isaiah must influence us when we try to evaluate the effect of the whole.

We have seen in outlining the stages of the book that the two 'horizons' of Assyria and Babylon are merged. Assyria and Babylon are morally one; they served God's purpose in their turn, but each fell in the end because of its pride. Some texts in the Book of Isaiah could apply equally to Assyria or Babylon or even Judah (as we saw in chs 25—26, with their contrast between the evil and the righteous city). So the 'audience' of the book in its final form is not Isaiah's original audience, or Deutero-Isaiah's. Rather, it is an audience that can see the connections made by the author (or authors) who brought the book into its final form. This is more likely to be an audience of readers than hearers (though of course the book may have been read aloud, presumably in 'readings', in liturgical settings).

The rhetorical intention of the book is to persuade that God overrules in all human

Think about
PROPHECIES IN NEW SETTINGS

We saw earlier that the book of Isaiah sets prophecies free from their original settings, in order to be able to speak in new situations (Critical Interpretation: Reading Isaiah as a Unity). One of the key moments in Isaiah is when the prophet says to Ahaz: 'If you do not stand firm in faith you shall not stand at all', Isa. 7:9c. This came in a crisis that faced Judah in Ahaz' time. How do you think an audience in the exilic or post-exilic time might have heard this message for them-selves? How might a modern audience hear it?

In this connection, think also about the very solemn note on which the book of Isaiah ends (66:24). How might a modern reader respond to this?

affairs. The great sweep of history, from Assyria's destruction of the northern kingdom in 722 BC to a time after the exile, allows this point to be made on a broad canvas. Not only Assyria and Babylon but all nations come within God's power both to judge and save. The fusing of Assyria and Babylon is even more effective than this, because it is a way of showing that certain things are always, or typically, true. (This explains why some passages in the book are notoriously hard to place historically, because certain types of historical situation tend to recur, e.g. 1:5–9.)

ISAIAH IN THE CANON

It seems that Isaiah was reckoned to be of first importance at the time when the canon was formed between the end of the exile and the New Testament period. Even its position at the head of the prophetic books suggests this. Isaiah is named first (after Elijah) in the celebration of heroes of the faith in Ecclesiasticus (Sirach) 48:17–25. In the New Testament the book is quoted, together with the Psalms, more than any other part of the Old Testament (Sawyer 1996, p. 21). Jesus read from Isaiah in the synagogue in Nazareth at the beginning of his ministry (Luke 4:17–19; Isa. 61:1–2). When the apostle Philip met the Ethiopian eunuch, it was Isaiah that he was reading (Acts 8:32–33; Isa. 53:7–8). It is likely that Isaiah was widely known and used by Jews of the period as well as the early Christians.

No doubt, an important reason for this was Isaiah's vision of the fall of oppressive empires and of a heavenly city (see on the 'two cities', Outline: 24:1—27:13). It is noticeable that the majority of allusions to Isaiah in the New Testament are from the second half of the book, which, as we have seen, promised the Jews liberation from Babylon (e.g. 2 Cor. 6:2, citing Isa. 49:8, to take one of many examples). In New Testament times, Rome could be thought of as another Babylon, and indeed this connection is made in the Book of Revelation (see Aune 1998, pp. 829–30, on Rev. 14:8).

Furthermore, the heavenly city was not confined to Jews. This hope could appeal to Jews and Christians alike: to Jews because the city was in some way identified with Zion (Jerusalem), and key texts portrayed foreigners coming to worship there, and even to build it up (2:2–4; 60:10–12); and to Christians, because they could see the city as genuinely inclusive of all peoples, and not restricted to Judaism. The importance of the idea of the heavenly city to early Christians may be seen from the number of allusions to Isaiah in the Book of Revelation (Sawyer 1996, pp. 28–29), especially in Revelation 21—22, which portray the new heavens and

Think about
ROME, BABYLON AND THE GOSPEL

Notice how the announcement of the fall of 'Babylon' in Rev. 14:8 immediately follows another angelic announcement, of 'an eternal gospel' (Rev. 14:6). The gospel as the reign of God has been contrasted with the reign of the Roman Caesar. In what ways do you think these two reigns are opposed? What might correspond to Caesar's claims in today's world, and how does the gospel relate to it?

For help, see R. W. Wall, *Revelation*, 1991, pp. 183–85, and in more detail, N. T. Wright, 'Paul's Gospel and Caesar's Empire'.

new earth (Rev. 21:1, cf. Isa. 65:17), with a transformed city of Jerusalem in a central place (Rev. 21:10). Isaiah's vision of the salvation of the nations played a very important role in the early church's understanding of the need to take the gospel to the Gentiles. It may be that Jesus himself came to understand his mission by reflection on the Servant of the Lord, both in respect of the Servant's suffering, and of his worldwide mission.

The mission to the Gentiles seems to be in the forefront of the New Testament writers' minds when they use the Isaiah texts. The Servant's commission to be a 'light to the Gentiles' (42:6; 49:6) occurs in important positions in Luke's writings to show his view of Jesus' ministry (Luke 2:32; Acts 13:47; 26:17–18). And the Servant passage in Matt. 12:18–21 is quoted to explain why Jesus told people not to speak about his miracles (Matt. 12:16–17), that is, his work would remain quiet until he brought justice and victory to the Gentiles (Sawyer 1996, p. 35; cf. Hagner 1993, pp. 337–39).

If the gospel was for the Gentiles, then what did that mean about the Jews? Here Isaiah also had things to say that the New Testament takes up. If some Jews rejected Jesus, perhaps it was because they were 'blind', as Isaiah had said of his fellow-Israelites of old (Isa. 6:9–10; 29:9–10; 42:19). Isaiah 6:9–10 is quoted in Mark 4:12 to explain why some do not understand the parables. John's Gospel uses it also, to explain why so many Jews did not believe in Jesus (John 12:37–43). And the Book of Acts justifies the Gentile mission in this way (Acts 28:25–28; cf. 13:46–47). In a similar way, Isaiah's Song of the Vineyard (Isa. 5:1–7) lies behind Mark 12:1–12; Luke 20:9–19. These parables are based on the criticism of the Israelites in that prophecy, and justify giving the 'vineyard' to 'others'.

The apostle Paul also wrestles with the question of Jews and Gentiles. From Isaiah, he takes up the idea of a 'remnant', that is, those who would be left after the judgement fell (Isa. 10:21–22; 1:9; Rom. 9:27–29, cf. 11:5). The 'remnant' in Isaiah is a rather negative idea ('only a remnant'). But Paul turns to it in order to show that 'Israel' (that is, the Jews) still has a place in God's plan of salvation for the world. (This is explained fully by N. T. Wright 1991.)

Isaiah has been criticized for the harshness of the saying in Isa. 6:9–10. This text was found so difficult to accept that some later translations toned it down, so as to imply that those who were 'blind' were so by choice rather than by a decree of God. The Greek translation of the Old Testament (LXX) gave a lead in this, and is followed in Matthew (13:14–15) and Acts (28:26–27). However, the Book of Isaiah's portrayal of Israel is complex. Its vision of redeemed Zion certainly has a place for Jews. It is the place of Gentiles that is more ambiguous: are they on the same level as the Jews in God's plan, or inferior (Van Winkle 1985)? Paul in Romans takes up the same issue as Isaiah faced, but from a different angle. For him, it is the salvation of the Gentiles that is clear, and the position of the Jews that is in question. However, in his expectation, like Isaiah's, the people of God would consist finally of Jew and Gentile alike. Isaiah had opened up the way to this by showing that the 'city of God' could only be based on righteousness, and this made it impossible to be identified with one people only. For Paul likewise, the key is faith, not belonging to a chosen nation.

Think about
PROPHECY, JEWS AND CHRISTIANS

Christians claim the Old Testament as their Scripture, and that its promises are fulfilled in Jesus Christ. How can they do this without taking a negative view of Jewish people? The point made in the preceding paragraph may be part of an answer to this. See also on Jonah: Theological Themes, God's forgiveness extended to all?

At the heart of the Gentile mission in New Testament thinking is the Messiah Jesus. How far do the New Testament writers frame their view of him from Isaiah? Isaiah's messianic prophecies have played a very important role in Christian thought about Jesus. So it is surprising to find, as Sawyer has pointed out, that some of the texts we might expect to find in the New Testament play little or no part in it. The famous celebration of the birth of a king (Isa. 9:7 [6]) is missing, for example – a particular surprise to those who are familiar with Handel's *Messiah*! Moreover, as we saw, some of the texts that do identify Jesus as the Servant are most concerned with the Gentile mission.

However, the servant is certainly linked with the person of Jesus Christ. The connection is made, as we saw, in Matt. 12:18–21 (Isa. 42:1–4), which tells us that Jesus' ministry 'fulfils' what Isaiah said about the Servant. The same text (or at least 42:1) is probably in mind in Matt 3:17, when the voice from heaven speaks at Jesus' baptism. Philip's explanation of Isa. 53:7–8 to the Ethiopian eunuch shows that Luke understood the suffering of the servant to refer to Christ's atoning death (Acts 8:32–35).

The Immanuel prophecy, though it appears only once in the New Testament (Matt 1:23), is important nonetheless, because it is the basis of the doctrine of the virgin birth. This is the point of Matthew's narrative in 1:18–25. We saw in our interpretation of Isa. 7:14 (Structure and Outline) that it related to a political crisis in Isaiah's time. In addition, there was no indication that the 'young woman' was a virgin (but see Wenham 1972). However, the way to Matthew's interpretation was prepared by LXX, which translated the Hebrew *'almah* ('young woman') by the Greek *parthenos* ('virgin'). The force of this was increased by the fact that LXX was a Jewish translation from two centuries before Christ. The passage appears to have become more important in the post-New Testament period than in the New Testament itself, as is suggested by the second-century work by Justin Martyr, 'The Dialogue with Trypho'. This is a controversy between Justin and Trypho, a Jew, in which Justin argues that the Old Testament proves that Jesus was the Messiah.

FURTHER READING

Items marked * are considered suitable as first ports of call, while others are more complex, or relate to specific issues.

COMMENTARIES

Note: references to Motyer in the present work are to the 1993 commentary. The later volume is a different work, with fresh interpretations, and may be the better starting-point for some. Both take the conservative view of authorship. Clements and Whybray are good starting-points for critical commentaries. Seitz and Childs offer 'canonical' approaches.

W. A. M. Beuken *Jesaja II–III*. POT. Nijkerk: Callenbach, 1979-89.

J. Blenkinsopp *Isaiah 1–39*. AB. New York: Doubleday, 2000.

*B. S. Childs *Isaiah*. OTL. Louisville: Westminster/John Knox, 2001.

*R. E. Clements *Isaiah 1–39*. NCB. London: Marshall, Morgan and Scott, 1980.

B. Duhm *Das Buch Jesaja übersetzt und erklärt*. HK 3/1. Göttingen, 1892; 4th edition 1922.

*J. Goldingay *Isaiah*. NIBC. Peabody, Mass.: Hendrickson; Carlisle: Paternoster, 2001.

J. H. Hayes and S. A. Irvine *Isaiah the Eighth-century Prophet; His Times and His Preaching*. Nashville: Abingdon, 1987.

O. Kaiser *Isaiah 1–12*. OTL. London: SCM, 1983.

O. Kaiser *Isaiah 13–39*. OTL. London: SCM, 1980.

J. A. Motyer *Isaiah*. Leicester: IVP, 1993.

*J. A. Motyer *Isaiah*. TOTC. Leicester: IVP, 1999.

J. Oswalt *Isaiah 1–39*. NICOT. Grand Rapids: Eerdmans, 1986.

J. Oswalt *Isaiah 40–66*. NICOT. Grand Rapids: Eerdmans, 1998.

J. F. A. Sawyer *Isaiah 1–39*. DSB. Edinburgh: St Andrew Press/Philadelphia: Westminster, 1984.

*C. R. Seitz *Isaiah 1–39*. Interpretation. Louisville: John Knox Press, 1993.

M. Sweeney *Isaiah 1–39*. FOTL 16. Grand Rapids: Eerdmans, 1996.

C. Westermann *Isaiah 40–66*. OTL. London: SCM Press, 1969.

*R. N. Whybray *Isaiah 40–66*. NCB. London: Oliphants, 1975; Grand Rapids: Eerdmans, 1981.

H. Wildberger *Isaiah 1–12*. Minneapolis: Fortress, 1991.

H. Wildberger *Isaiah 13–27*. Minneapolis: Fortress, 1997.

OTHER BOOKS AND ARTICLES

D. E. Aune *Revelation 6–16*. WBC. Nashville: Thomas Nelson, 1998.

*J. Barton *Isaiah 1–39*. OTG. Sheffield: Sheffield Academic Press, 1995.

J. Blenkinsopp 'Second Isaiah; Prophet of Universalism', in P. R. Davies ed. *The Prophets: a Sheffield Reader*. The Biblical Seminar 42. Sheffield: Sheffield Academic Press, 1996, pp. 186–206.

J. Blenkinsopp *A History of Prophecy in Israel*. London: SPCK, 1984.

R. P. Carroll 'Twilight of Prophecy or Dawn of Apocalyptic', *JSOT* 14, 1979, pp. 3–35.

B. S. Childs *Introduction to the Old Testament as Scripture*. London: SCM, 1979.

R. E. Clements 'Beyond Tradition-History: Deutero-Isaianic Development of First Isaiah's Themes', *JSOT* 31, 1985, pp. 95–113.

R. E. Clements *Isaiah and the Deliverance of Jerusalem: a Study of the Interpretation of Prophecy in the Old Testament*. JSOT Suppl. 13. Sheffield: JSOT Press, 1980.

D. J. A. Clines *I, He, We, and They: A Literary Approach to Isaiah 53*. JSOT Suppl. 1. Sheffield: JSOT Press, 1976.

T. Collins *The Mantle of Elijah*. Sheffield: JSOT Press, 1993.

G. I. Davies 'The Destiny of the Nations in the Book of Isaiah' in J. Vermeylen ed. *The Book of Isaiah*. BETL 81. Leuven, 1989, pp. 93–120.

J. H. Eaton 'The Origin of the Book of Isaiah', *VT* 9, 1959, pp. 138–57.

J. H. Eaton *Festal Drama in Deutero-Isaiah*. London: SPCK, 1979.

G. I. Emmerson *Isaiah 56–66*. OTG. Sheffield: Sheffield Academic Press, 1992.

Y. Gitay *Isaiah and His Audience: the Structure and Meaning of Isaiah 1–12*. Studia Semitica Neerlandica. Assen/Maastricht: Van Gorcum, 1991.

Y. Gitay *Prophecy and Persuasion: a Study of Isaiah 40–48*. Linguistica Biblica Bonn, 1981.

D. A. Hagner *Matthew 1–13*. WBC. Dallas: Word Books, 1993.

P. D. Hanson *The Dawn of Apocalyptic*. Philadelphia: Fortress Press, 2nd edition 1979.

G. P. Hugenberger 'The "Servant of the Lord" in the Servant Songs of Isaiah', in Satterthwaite et al. eds, *The Lord's Anointed*, pp. 105–40.

D. R. Jones 'The Tradition of the Oracles of Isaiah of Jerusalem', *ZAW* 67, 1955, pp. 226–46.

C. G. Kruse 'The Servant Songs: Interpretive Trends since C. R. North', *StBTh 8*, 1978, p. 1–27.

T. N. D. Mettinger *A Farewell to the Servant Songs: A Critical Examination of an Exegetical Axiom*. Lund: Gleerup, 1983.

K. Nielsen *There is Hope for a Tree*. JSOT Suppl. 65. Sheffield: JSOT Press, 1989.

*P. E. Satterthwaite, R. S. Hess and G. J. Wenham eds *The Lord's Anointed: Interpretation of Old Testament Messianic Texts*. Grand Rapids: Baker Book House, 1995.

J. F. A. Sawyer *The Fifth Gospel: Isaiah in the History of Christianity*. Cambridge: Cambridge University Press, 1996.

D. Schibler, 'Messianism and Messianic Prophecy in Isaiah 1—12 and 28—33' in Satterthwaite et al. eds *The Lord's Anointed*, pp. 87–104.

R. Schultz 'The King in the Book of Isaiah', in Satterthwaite et al. eds *The Lord's Anointed*, pp. 141–65.

C. R. Seitz,'The Divine Council: Temporal Transition and New Prophecy in the Book of Isaiah', *JBL* 109, 1990, pp. 229–47.

A. C. Thiselton *The First Epistle to the Corinthians*. NIGTC. Grand Rapids: Eerdmans; Carlisle: Paternoster, 2000.

D. W. Van Winkle 'The Relationship of the Nations to Yahweh and to Israel in Isaiah xl–lv', *VT* 35, 1985, pp. 446–58.

R. W. Wall *Revelation*. NIBC. Peabody, Mass.: Hendrickson; Carlisle: Paternoster, 1991.

M. Weinfeld 'Justice and Righteousness – *mishpat usedaqa* – the Expression and its Meaning', in H. G. Reventlow and Y. Hoffmann eds *Justice and Righteousness; Biblical Themes and Their Influence*. JSOT Suppl. 137. Sheffield: Sheffield Academic Press, 1992, pp. 228–46.

G. J. Wenham 'Betula: a Girl of Marriageable Age', *VT* 22, 1972, pp. 325–48.

*R. N. Whybray *The Second Isaiah*. OTG. Sheffield: JSOT Press, 1983.

R. N. Whybray *Thanksgiving for a Liberated Prophet: an Interpretation of Isaiah Chapter 53*. JSOT Suppl. 4. Sheffield: JSOT Press, 1978.

H. G. M. Williamson *The Book Called Isaiah: Deutero-Isaiah's Role in Composition and Redaction*. Oxford: Clarendon Press, 1994.

*H. G. M. Williamson *Variations on a Theme: King, Messiah and Servant in the Book of Isaiah*. Carlisle: Paternoster, 1998.

N. T. Wright *Climax of the Covenant: Christ and the Law in Pauline Theology*. Edinburgh: T. & T. Clark, 1991.

N. T. Wright 'Paul's Gospel and Caesar's Empire', in C. Bartholomew, J. Chaplin, R. Song and A. Wolters eds *A Royal Priesthood: The Use of the Bible Ethically and Politically*. Grand Rapids: Zondervan, 2002.

Chapter 2

JEREMIAH

The Book of Jeremiah is one of the longest in the Bible, and a favourite for a number of reasons. It paints the most vivid picture of any Old Testament prophet, in all his weakness as well as strength. And it contains the famous prophecy of a New Covenant (Jer. 31:31–34), so important to the New Testament's understanding of who Jesus is. Jeremiah's sufferings on behalf of the people to whom he ministered illustrate the burden that a call to live and speak for God can place on a person. For this reason his life can be compared with the picture of the Suffering Servant in Isa. 52:13—53:12.

DATE AND DESTINATION

The Book of Jeremiah tells the story of the last generation of the kingdom of Judah, from the time when Jeremiah heard the call to be a prophet as a young man, in 626 BC, to the conquest of the kingdom by the forces of Babylon in 587 BC. The story of that conquest is told twice, in Jeremiah 39 and 52, so it is clearly an important climax of the book's narrative, and almost the last event recorded in it. So the book stands on the verge of the long exile of the Jewish people (587–539 BC). During this time they had to

learn to live without the mainstays of their faith – the temple, the king descended from David, and the land itself.

However, the fall of Judah is not quite the last event recorded in Jeremiah. Rather, we are taken into exile itself. When the Babylonian army carried off many of the people in chains, they left many others behind in the land under their own appointee (the story is told in Jeremiah 40—44). These were probably the poorest, and those who were least likely to trouble the new regime. And we follow these people as they escape from Babylonian overlordship by going to Egypt. They even force Jeremiah and his assistant Baruch to go with them, though Jeremiah told them strongly that it was against God's will (Jer. 43:1–7). One of our last glimpses of the people to whom Jeremiah had preached for much of his life is of their turning to the kind of religion that he had preached against (44:15–19).

Even this is not quite the end of Jeremiah's story, for we are also taken to Babylon, and a small incident that occurred twenty-five years after the destruction of the temple. In 562 BC, the exiled Judean king, Jehoiachin, was released from his Babylonian jail, and given an honourable place in the king's household (Jer. 52:31–34).

The story of Jeremiah comes to us therefore from a double exile, and this has left its stamp on the book. The book in its finished form looks back on the life and ministry of Jeremiah, and reflects on the outcome of his prophetic work. It is one of those Old Testament books, therefore, that tries to understand why the terrible fate of exile has overcome God's people. This is why it was aligned, in some versions of the canon (the one familiar to Christian readers), with Lamentations, a book of laments on the same theme. (Traditionally, indeed, Jeremiah was thought to be the author of that book too. See Lamentations, Date and Destination).

This is the first answer to the question of the book's date and destination. It was written in the exilic time for exiled people, who wondered if God had abandoned them for ever, and whether they might hope to return to their historic land in the future. It might have been known, possibly in different forms (see next section) in both Babylon and Egypt. This is because we read of Jeremiah's words being written in different forms (Jeremiah 36), and that they could be carried by messengers to Babylon (Jeremiah 29). And he could have taken them himself to Egypt.

That is not the whole answer to the question of the date, however, because it is clear that Jeremiah's words were not all spoken at the same time, but rather over a long period. He tells his listeners at one point that he has been preaching to them continuously for twenty-three years (Jer. 25:3; this was in the year 605 BC, so even then he still had some way to go). So we can try to discover the particular occasions on which certain words and oracles were spoken. As we have just noticed (about 25:3), some of the sayings are dated. Another example is 26:1–6, where a sermon preached at the gate of the temple at a great festival can be dated to 609 BC, because we know that that is the year in which King Jehoiakim began to reign (26:1). Even when dates are not actually given, it is sometimes possible to imagine which parts of Jeremiah's ministry a saying was spoken in. Many of the oracles in the first main section of the book, chs 2—6, are thought to belong in the earliest stage of his career, because in general they seem to suppose that the punishment that the prophet is pronouncing on Judah may still be avoided if the people repent (e.g. 4:1–4). A time comes when this is no longer the case (for example ch. 24). We shall think a little more about this as we look at the individual sections of the book.

The issue of dating has a further complication, however. As with Isaiah, many scholars think that the Book of Jeremiah does not derive in its entirety from the man whose name it bears. Rather, it is widely held that it contains reflections that go well beyond his life and the immediate circumstances of the exile, and that parts of it may belong to the post-exilic period and come from people who have returned to the land.

One important factor that has encouraged this way of thinking is the fact that the book exists in two main forms. The Greek version (LXX) is a translation of a Hebrew form of the book that is about one-eighth shorter than the Hebrew version that underlies the text in the English Bible (the Masoretic Text, MT). The elements missing from MT range from short phrases to a long passage such as 33:14–26, and it is a complex matter to document them. (Readers of the Hebrew Bible can use the critical apparatus to follow where the Greek lacks words and phrases that are present in the Hebrew.) The differences between LXX and MT are not only a matter of length but also of organization of the material (see below on Structure).

This means that at a time before the texts reached the settled forms in which we know them there was no single fixed text. It is usually thought (though not always) that the shorter form of the text underlying LXX is more original. And this makes it likely that there was a period when additions could be made to the text, perhaps reflecting the interests of different groups who possessed it. It is possible that different forms were known in Babylon, Palestine and Egypt. However, we cannot trace the separate developments of the two textual traditions with any certainty. Remarkably, fragments of both forms of the text were found at Qumran (in the library of the first-century BC community of the Dead Sea Scrolls; Carroll 1986, p. 51). This may simply mean that the book was circulating in two separate forms. But it may also mean that the contents were not finally settled until well into the post-exilic period.

If the book was a long time in the making one consequence is that the events and issues that appear on the surface of the narrative are really speaking obliquely about quite other events and issues. For example, the oracles in ch. 24 appear to concern the question of whether those who were left in Judah after the first wave of deportation to Babylon (in 597 BC) should seek refuge in Egypt. In some estimates, however, this is really about who are the rightful occupants of the land in a time when exiles are returning and there are disputes about who are the true partners in God's covenant (e.g.

Carroll 1986, pp. 482–84). The question of dating thus overlaps considerably with that of interpretation. For many scholars, the real cradle of the book is not the last days of Judah and the exile, but the early stages of what we now call Judaism. Dating the book, therefore, is not an exact science, but many possibilities are opened up by some critical approaches.

CRITICAL INTERPRETATION OF JEREMIAH

PROPHECY AS POETRY?

The remarks just made about dating lead us to consider now some of the ways in which the book has been understood by scholars. In the late nineteenth century, scholars thought that the genuine prophecy was spoken in poetry (see Introduction). Most modern English Bibles distinguish, by the layout of the text, between poetry and prose in prophetic books. (For example, ch. 2 is mainly poetry, while chs 1 and 3 are mixed.) And indeed there are stylistic differences between parts of the book that give some justification to this. B. Duhm, in his commentary, picked out of the book the words that he thought really belonged to Jeremiah, and this habit of thinking the poetic oracles more 'authentic' has had an influence on scholarship to the present day.

Successors of Duhm took the analysis further. It was noticed that a large part of the prose consisted of narrative about Jeremiah, much of it in chs 32—45, and this seemed to form a special class of material in the book. This left another class, namely sayings of Jeremiah that were not poetic, and these were called 'prose sermons' (e.g. Jer. 7:1—8:3; 11:1–17, 21–23; 13:1–14; 16:1–18; 17:19–26; 18:1–12; 19:1—20:6). It was S. Mowinckel who first made these observations (1946), and he called the categories A (poetic oracles of Jeremiah), B (narrative) and C (prose sermons). This A-B-C analysis is found in many introductory works about the book. The 'A' group contained Jeremiah's prayers known as the 'Confessions' (see at 11:18–23).

'DEUTERONOMISTIC' SERMONS?

An important extension of this approach is the idea that the prose sermons are 'deuteronomistic'. That is, they bear a resemblance in style and content to themes in Deuteronomy, and to parts of the Historical Books (Joshua–Kings), which are also held to be dependent on that book. In order to appreciate the force of the idea that parts of Jeremiah are deuteronomistic it is necessary to remember that Deuteronomy, or an early form of it, is widely thought to have been written near the end of the kingdom of Judah. Not only that, but it led to a whole movement that produced or edited many books of the Old Testament. Their work is recognized by style and content: for example, it is prosaic, it repeats key ideas, it has a developed theology of conditional covenant (see L. Stulman 1998, for a characterization of the sermons).

There are indeed important similarities between Jeremiah and the Historical Books, especially Kings. Both tell the story of the last days of Judah, even if Kings covers a much longer time. Indeed, they even share an account of those days, since Jeremiah 52 is very similar to 2 Kings 25. Both books end, therefore, with the short report of the release of King Jehoiachin from his Babylonian prison. In addition, it is important to remember how much the Book of Jeremiah is a *narrative*, like Kings. The books may be said to share a purpose, therefore, to explain why the exile happened and to help people think about how to live with God in the new age that was opening up. In doing so, they emphasized the role of the prophet as God's spokesperson (2 Kgs 17; Jer. 1), and saw the sin of Judah as a breach of the covenant (2 Kgs 22; Jer. 31:32). There are also striking similarities in the way in which some of the speeches in the two books are structured, as E. W. Nicholson has shown (1970, especially pp. 20–71).

If the prose sermons are really 'deuteronomistic', and did not come from Jeremiah himself, then where and when did they originate? This question is answered in several different ways. One answer is given by Nicholson (1970). In his view the prose sermons were composed in Babylon and addressed to the exiles there (pp. 116–38). The basic reasoning is that the thought of Jeremiah was held in esteem following the fall of Judah, and that the exiles worked out new implications of what he had said in a tradition of preaching relevant to their new circumstances. An example is Jer. 17:19–27, which deals with the sabbath. Nicholson found that this fitted the style of the deuteronomists, and doubted that it came from Jeremiah (who does not mention the sabbath otherwise). The topic was more likely to have been of interest to the exiles in Babylon (pp. 65–66, 124–25). The idea that the sermons come from a tradition of preaching in or after the exile is quite common, though many have placed this activity in Judah rather then Babylon (see H. Lalleman-de Winkel 2000, and her references there to German literature on the subject).

A DEUTERONOMISTIC EDITION?

The deuteronomistic theory does not necessarily depend on the idea of a preaching tradition, whether in Babylon or Judah. Often it is seen in terms more of literary and theological development. The strong tendency in modern criticism is to move away from the old distinction between poetic oracles and prose sermons and narratives, to see the whole book as the product of deuteronomistic editing. On this view the poetic oracles may or may not be Jeremiah's own. They too may be the result of theologizing from a later time. This editing process is not restricted to a single time or place, but is seen instead as a process that grew haphazardly out of the needs and experiences of many post-exilic communities.

The idea of a deuteronomistic edition of Jeremiah was suggested by J. P. Hyatt (1951). It has been adopted recently by W. McKane (1986; 1996), who thought of the book as a 'rolling corpus' (that is, additions were gradually made to the book, interpreting it, as it was handed on). R. P. Carroll has also developed the idea (1986). An example of this in practice is Jeremiah 3, in which the oracle in vv. 1–5 is said to be subjected to a variety of new interpretations in the rest of the chapter. Carroll, for example, thinks the development concerning Israel and Judah rests on a failure of the editor to see that 'Israel' in the passage that leads up to the oracle (ch. 2) means Judah (1986, p. 145). (I will comment on this interpretation below.)

IS JEREMIAH FROM JEREMIAH?

In spite of the dominance of the theory we have been describing, a number of scholars have held that Jeremiah is distinct from the deuteronomistic literature and that it comes from the prophet himself, or is at least closely dependent on his work. An important landmark in this scholarly development was J. Bright's article (1951).

Bright showed that there were differences in vocabulary and style between the 'deuteronomic' literature and Jeremiah's prose (recall that this was an important criterion for the deuteronomistic theory). His *Anchor Bible* commentary carries his theory through in detail, trying to place the speeches and sermons of Jeremiah in his life. If Bright could be criticized for attaching too much importance to vocabulary as a guide to authorship, the same point might well be made in return – if vocabulary cannot demonstrate different authorship can it demonstrate identical authorship?

W. Holladay's *Hermeneia Commentary* is a massive contribution to the argument for Jeremiah's authorship. Holladay too attempted to place the words of Jeremiah in his lifetime. In doing so he revised the usual dating of Jeremiah's life, believing that he began his ministry only in the reign of King Jehoiakim (i.e. not in 626 BC, but in 609). He also developed a special theory of the book's composition, based on the seven-yearly cycle of readings of Deuteronomy at the Feast of Tabernacles (prescribed in Deut. 31:10–11). Holladay recognizes that there may be broad similarities of style, yet works that share it can still be distinct from each other. This is important even if one does not accept Holladay's special theory. (As background to this discussion, some have spoken of a type of speech that is characteristic of seventh-century Judah; Driver 1895, p. xci.)

Perhaps the most important argument in favour of Jeremiah's authorship lies in the shape and theology of the book as a whole, rather than in stylistic features. A problem that has long been observed in Jeremiah seems to arise in connection with a number of theories of authorship, namely why the book gives no evidence that Jeremiah supported the reform of King Josiah. According to the dates of Jeremiah's life given in Jeremiah 1, he began his ministry in 626 BC. The reform of Josiah reached a climax in 621 BC with the discovery of the 'book of the law' in the temple during repairs sponsored by the king (2 Kgs 22:8). However, it had been in train in 628 BC, according to the chronology found in 2 Chronicles 34 (note v. 3; and see E. W. Nicholson 1981, pp. 8–10). So if the book really reflects the ministry of Jeremiah, and he supported a return to the covenant, as Josiah did, why did he not support the reform? Instead he makes no clear mention of it, and only gives slight praise to Josiah in his otherwise devastating critique of the kings of Judah (Jeremiah 22, note vv. 15–16). Equally, if the book is deuteronomistic, why did its authors not depict Jeremiah as an enthusiast for an event that they regard as decisive in their composition of Kings? Kings, on the other hand, is just as cool about Jeremiah. It doesn't mention him, and when Josiah wants a prophet to consult when he repents and decides to renew the covenant he sends his officials to the prophetess Huldah, who is otherwise unknown to us (2 Kgs 22:14–20).

In other ways too Jeremiah differs from Kings. In its hopes for a restoration to the ancient land (Jer. 31:38–40; 32) it goes beyond Kings, which expresses hope only for the compassion of the exiles' captors on them (1 Kgs 8:46–53 – v. 34 of that chapter does not refer to a return from exile). And its vision of a glorious restoration of the Davidic monarchy (Jer. 23:1–8) has no counterpart in Samuel–Kings. Jeremiah's relationship with Deuteronomy itself is undeniable. Its hopes for a return to the land echo those of Deut. 30:1–10, for

example. In this way Jeremiah stands closer to Deuteronomy than the Books of Kings.

These comparisons between Deuteronomy, Kings and Jeremiah show that the relationships among them cannot be fully explained by a single, uniform movement. For these reasons some have looked elsewhere to explain the special features of Jeremiah, namely to the prophetic tradition. That is, Jeremiah has characteristics that can also be found in other prophetic books, especially Hosea.

One form of this view is expressed by R. R. Wilson, who spoke of an 'Ephraimite' tradition (see Introduction). This strand was essentially 'covenantal', that is, it took its cue from the Mosaic covenant, with its emphasis on the 'word' of Yahweh, rather than from the 'presence of Yahweh' traditions that placed more weight on the visual. Typical of the 'southern' traditions were ark, tabernacle and temple. Jeremiah, though he ministered in Jerusalem, hailed from Anathoth, somewhat to the north, and was evidently influenced by the strong covenantal theology of Hosea. His 'temple sermon' (Jer. 7:1–15), with its clear echoes of the Ten Commandments (v. 9) and its severe criticism of false temple worship, typified the northern values. Even the prophetic formula, 'the word that came to Jeremiah from the LORD' (e.g. 7:1; 11:1) is part of this picture (contrast the southern Isaiah's vision of Yahweh in the temple, Isaiah 6).

The north-south distinction can be overdrawn (on Isaiah, we saw that word and vision were not necessarily incompatible). And it is clear that Amos, who went from southern Tekoa to preach in northern Bethel, thought that north and south shared a heritage on which he could base his appeal. Furthermore, Hosea and Amos, in different ways, appear to have influenced Jeremiah (see Holladay 1989, pp. 44–47), as did the other major southern prophets Isaiah and Micah (Holladay, pp. 47–51).

However, the most striking similarities are with Hosea. Hosea's analogy between Israel's unfaithfulness and an unfaithful wife (Hosea 2—3) appears in Jer. 2:2–3, 20–25; 3:1–5. Both prophets draw on the law against a remarriage to a first husband (Deut. 24:1–4) in Hos. 2:7 [9 *Heb*]; Jer. 3:1–5. Both call Israel to 'return' to Yahweh, or 'repent' (the Hebrew verb *shub*; see also Lalleman-de Winkel 2000, pp. 90–115, 132–155 on this topic). Both are critical of kings (Hos. 8:4; Jeremiah 22), and stress the need for the people to return wholeheartedly to Yahweh in covenant faithfulness. Both express the deep compassion of God for his people, so that he recoils from abandoning them absolutely (Hos. 11:8–9, Jer. 31:18–20). Both suffered as a direct result of their call (Hosea in his unhappy marriage; for Jeremiah, see on his 'confessions', at 11:18–23). And both see a time when Yahweh will restore his people even after he has punished them (Hosea 14; Jer. 31:31–34; 32). (See further McConville 1993, pp. 149–71.)

These observations mean that Jeremiah can be placed within a line of prophets from both Israel and Judah, who preserved theological beliefs that go back to the time of the formation of the people. In terms of the question of date and destination, it means that we can think of the prophet as having exercised an actual ministry among the people who lived through the last days of Judah. The words of Jeremiah, however, have been collected and given their present shape by someone (or perhaps more than one) who could look back on Jeremiah's ministry, see

the result of it, and reflect on what it might mean for people who lived after the events themselves. Some concept of a 'redaction' of the book is necessary, even if we attribute the activity of redaction to Jeremiah himself (see McConville 1993, pp. 27–41, on the present form of Jeremiah 3:1—4:4).

STRUCTURE AND OUTLINE

Jeremiah is a large and varied book, and the division of the material in it is not immediately obvious. There are some points to guide the reader, however. First, the distinction between poetic oracle and speeches and narratives helps. Second, there are expressions that regularly introduce new words of the prophet, especially: 'The word that came to Jeremiah from the LORD' (7:1). Third, there are some blocks of distinctive material, such as the call-narrative (Jeremiah 1), the so-called Book of Consolation (Jeremiah 30—33), and the Oracles Against the Nations (Jeremiah 46—51). This last section is confirmed as a separate block, because it appears in a different position in LXX, immediately after Jeremiah 25:13, and thus roughly in the middle of the book. Taken together, these factors give a structure like the one that follows.

STRUCTURE

1:1–19   The call of Jeremiah
2:1—6:30   Poetic pronouncements of judgement and
             calls to repent
7:1—10:25   The people's falseness in worship
11:1—20:18   Falseness in the covenant; Jeremiah and
             God wrestle over the people's sin
21:1—24:10   The failure of Judah's kings and prophets
25:1–38   God's judgement on all the nations by
             Babylon – and Babylon judged in turn
26:1—29:32   Foreshadowings of Babylonian supremacy
30:1—33:26   The 'Book of Consolation'
34:1—36:32   King and people refuse the word of
             Jeremiah

OUTLINE

1:1–19: The call of Jeremiah

The introduction (vv. 1–3) dates Jeremiah's prophecy from 626 BC (the thirteenth year of King Josiah). A young man at the time, he went on to minister through the reigns of four kings, up to and beyond the fall of Jerusalem in 587 BC (see Introduction).

His protest against God's call reminds of Moses' (Exod. 4:1–17) and Gideon's (Judg. 6:15), though they all give different reasons. The objection of his youth is overruled by God's reply that he has intended to call him since before he was born. Jeremiah's life from the beginning is bound up with God's plan for many nations (vv. 4–8). God assures Jeremiah that he has given him authority to declare what God plans to do. The centre of the message is that the kingdom of Babylon, the new power in the region, will come as an enemy against Judah. Jeremiah will be severely persecuted for declaring this, but God will protect him (vv. 9–19).

Think about
GOD'S CALL

Compare the calls of Jeremiah, Moses and Gideon. What do they have in common? Why do you think God called these people? Other passages to consider are: Isaiah's vision of God (Isa. 6:1–3), though it is not usually considered a 'call'-narrative; and the story of God's choice of David (1 Samuel 16).

2:1—6:30: Poetic pronouncements of judgement and calls to repent

The collection of sayings in these chapters have often been regarded as among Jeremiah's earliest words, and have even been equated with his first scroll, which King Jehoiakim destroyed (Jer. 36:23; Holladay 1989, p. 16). They contain vivid images of coming battle and defeat, interspersed with calls to repent. It is not always possible to know where one saying ends and another begins, nor to date any exactly.

2:1–37 Israel's former faithfulness Like Hosea (Hos. 2:14–15), Jeremiah recalls the time in the Sinai desert, after Israel came out of Egypt, when the people were faithful to God (2:2–3). (Contrast the picture of that time in Ezek. 20:13. Jeremiah and Ezekiel use the memory of the period quite differently, according to their own rhetorical purposes.) Their former faithfulness is used as a starting-point for the main message, that they have now become unfaithful.

In vv. 4–13 Jeremiah uses a 'covenant accusation' (see on Mic. 6:1–6). God asks in what way he has failed in his obligations to Israel, since they have abandoned their obligations to him. The assumption of mutual obligations is covenantal (cf. Hos. 4:1–3; Mic. 6:1–4; and Huffmon 1959). Israel is then characterized as a slave (v. 14), rather than the free people delivered from slavery in Egypt; as a harlot, rather than a bride (v. 20); as a wild vine, not a cultivated vine (v. 21; cf. the vine image in Ps. 80:8–13), and as a thief (v. 26).

Jeremiah points to what happened to Israel in the past, in order to appeal to Judah. Judah has come to embody the historic people, since the northern kingdom was taken into Assyrian exile a century before, in

722 BC (Jer. 2:36). Verse 36 also foreshadows the fact that a remnant in Judah will look to Egypt for help in the time of the Babylonian invasions (cf. ch. 24). (See How can the exiles be 'Israel'?, at Isaiah 40—41.)

3:1—4:4 Calls to repent This is a key passage about repentance. Jeremiah 3:1–5 is based on the idea that a woman, once divorced from her husband, may never remarry the same man (Deut 24:1–4). Consequently, Israel, once separated from Yahweh, should by rights never be taken back by him. However, the appeal in the chapter assumes that such a thing could indeed happen. The experience of the exiled northern kingdom of Israel is used rhetorically by Jeremiah, who proclaims repentance towards the north (3:12–14). This is to show that God could take back those he has cast off. The point is directed towards Judah, however. Judah is just as bad as Israel (3:6–11). Jeremiah tries to persuade them to return to God, because he will not always be angry, but is merciful (3:15—4:4). The perspective in this chapter takes in the whole span of the book's events, and sees beyond the judgement to the possibility of a new salvation.

The last passage, Jer. 4:1–4, sees a repentant people fulfilling its role as God's chosen means of blessing all nations (v. 2, cf. Gen. 12:3). It asks for 'truth, justice and uprightness', the essential qualities of faithfulness to God. And it introduces the metaphor of circumcision of the heart for true faithfulness (v. 4, cf. Deut 10:16; 30:6).

4:5—6:30 Visions of judgement Jeremiah turns back from a long-term view of God's mercy to the imminent danger. This section contains vivid, horrific images of approaching war. In 4:5–8 there is a rallying-cry to people throughout the land to take refuge from the

> **Think about**
> **'CIRCUMCISION OF THE HEART'**
>
> What is the real point of this metaphor? Circumcision was the mark of belonging to the people of God (Gen. 17:9–14). Do you think the re-framing of it in Deuteronomy and Jeremiah means to do away with the practice of circumcision? The question is a bit like the question whether prophets (and psalmists) meant to do away with sacrifice (cf. Ps. 50:14, and the translation in NRSV and the alternative in the margin).

enemy in the fortified cities, and in Jerusalem (i.e. Zion, vv. 5–6). The enemy, savage as a lion, will come 'from the north'. This piece of information does not yet identify it as Babylon, since the north is a direction from which many enemies might come (due west is the sea, and due east a vast desert). Jeremiah 4:13–18 pictures the terror coming to the land in a north-south progression from Dan (far north) through Ephraim to Jerusalem. Jeremiah 4:19–22 gives a first insight into the pain of the prophet himself at the coming disaster. The vivid language of v. 19 probably indicates psychological and emotional distress rather than physical.

Jeremiah 4:23–28, in an echo of Genesis 1, shows the whole creation lying waste because Judah is devastated. The failure of God's covenant with Judah (standing now for the whole covenant people Israel) means a kind of undoing of the creation itself. A further picture of war (4:29–31) gives a female personification to Jerusalem, first portraying it as a harlot, then showing the suffering of its women (similarly to Lamentations; Lam. 1:1–2, 8–9, 15).

Chapter 5 continues to depict Judah's evil. Justice and truth are again the measure of faithfulness (5:1). And, if even one person practised these, the city of Jerusalem might be saved (cf. Gen 18:22–33). In a way Jeremiah himself will fulfil this role. The evil runs through the whole people (vv. 4–5, 7–9, 20–29). The remnant idea is introduced in vv. 10a, 18, that is, the destruction will not be complete. So also is the idea of the special responsibility of some for the evil of all (e.g. v. 26). Most importantly, the prophets and priests, charged with leadership, lead others astray – yet the people are willing to follow (vv. 30–31).

In 6:1–8 Jerusalem is again personified as a woman (v. 2, as in 4:30–31), now complacently delighting in her beauty. But an idyllic picture of shepherds grazing around her turns quickly to a picture of war (vv. 3–6). Jerusalem should be a city of righteousness, but nourishes wickedness. The prophet expresses horror because the city that was intended to show God's righteous character has turned into a byword for evil. Verse 8 is based on the relationship between God and Jerusalem, now under unbearable strain.

God's punishment is thorough; even after the first 'gleaning' he will return to mop up what is left (v. 9). The picture of God's wrath (vv. 11–12) reminds of the curses of the covenant (Deut. 28:30). Reasons are given for this: the people have lusted after their own gain, and the leaders have misdiagnosed deep-seated ills as of no consequence (vv. 13–14).

The cure is to return to the 'ancient paths' (v. 16), that is, to keep the covenant made long ago under Moses. Instead they persist in false worship (v. 20), another major theme of the prophets (Isa. 1:10–17; Amos 5:21–25). So the enemy will come. And

Jeremiah himself is an 'assayer', one who refines metal (v. 27). This just gives an element of hope, that the refining may leave something pure behind (cf. Isa. 1:21–26).

Digging deeper:
A COMPARISON

We have made several comparisons between Jeremiah 6 and Isaiah 1. Draw these similarities together to say what the two passages have in common, and how, if at all, they differ.

7:1—10:25: The people's falseness in worship
This section of the book has the general theme of the people's falseness in worship. It mixes oracles in poetic style with more connected, sermonic speeches.

7:1–15 False temple worship This is the so-called temple-sermon, and this is a fuller account of the same episode told in 26:1–6. The date is early in the reign of Jehoiakim (609–608 BC). People are pouring to the temple to worship at some great event, perhaps the Feast of Tabernacles. Jeremiah stands in the gate to show that mere feast-keeping is no substitute for real worship. He

Digging deeper:
THE TEMPLE AND SECURITY

According to Jeremiah, the people falsely believe the temple cannot be destroyed, and that they themselves are permanently secure. Why do you think they might have thought this? Texts to consider are: 2 Samuel 7; Ps. 89:1–37 [2–38]; 2 Kings 19. How does Jeremiah show they are wrong?

recalls a number of the commandments (v. 9) as well as covenant obligations expressed more generally (vv. 5–7). The logic is that Jerusalem is no more immune from God's judgement than Shiloh was before it (v. 12). Shiloh had first qualified as the place 'where I first made a dwelling for my name' (the terms of Deut. 12:5; see 1 Samuel 1—3), but this had not stopped its destruction by the Philistines.

7:16—8:3 Idol worship The scene changes to various kinds of idolatrous worship outside the temple. The 'queen of heaven' (v. 18) could be the Canaanite goddess Anat, or the Babylonian Ishtar/Astarte. Topheth, in the Hinnom Valley south of the city, was the scene of child-sacrifice, in imitation of Canaanite and Phoenician practice. God's words 'which I did not command' (v. 31) may refer to the people's wrongly using Exod. 13:2 as a pretext. (Note also Deut 12:31.) The worship of sun, moon and stars (8:1–3) was widespread in the ancient Near East, and resisted in the Old Testament (Gen. 1:14–19 shows them as merely created things).

The people's idolatry is so bad that Jeremiah is told he must not even pray for the people, one of the prophet's roles (7:16, cf. Moses, Exod. 32:11–14).

8:4–21 False leadership Far from repenting (turning to God), Judah is a people that perpetually turns away (vv. 4, 6). The leaders are rebuked again, perverting their God-given responsibilities: to teach Torah (law, v. 8), to show wisdom (v. 9) and to announce judgement when it is due (v. 11). Jeremiah's own grief pours out in vv. 18–21.

8:22—9:16 [15] Falseness pervades Judah. Jeremiah, 'the weeping prophet', weeps

because of the people's sin, and also because of the judgement it brings. His grief reflects God's own grief over his people (note the phrase, 'declares the LORD', in vv. 3 [2] and 6 [5], showing that these feelings are really his). The passage is a terrible accusation of a society shot through with falseness (vv. 2–9 [1-8]). Verses 12–16 [11–15] explain the coming judgement in terms of Judah's neglect of God's law (cf. Deut. 9:6).

9:17–26 Visions of the end The suffering of the women of Jerusalem is taken up again, as typifying the agonies of the people (cf. the female images in 4:30–31; 6:24–26).

10:1–25 Yahweh unique Jeremiah proclaims that Yahweh is the one true God. His exposure of the falseness of other gods is full of irony, like the prophecy in Isa. 44:9–20. In both places the prophet knows that the defeat of the people may make them think other gods are stronger. In a wonderful hymn Jeremiah celebrates Yahweh as creator (vv. 12–14). He once again expresses his personal anguish at the coming destruction (cf. 4:19–22), which is mixed with a wish for God's judgement (vv. 24–25).

11:1—20:18: Falseness in the covenant; Jeremiah and God wrestle over the people's sin
11:1–17 Covenant broken These verses are based closely on the language and ideas of the covenant. The 'terms', or literally, 'words' of the covenant (vv. 2, 8) refer to the curses in, for example, Deut. 28:15–68. This passage (apart from the somewhat poetic vv. 15–16) is a good example of the logical style of the 'sermons'.

11:18–23 Plots against Jeremiah Jeremiah's preaching leads to threats on his life, from the people of his own village (cf. Luke 4:24). His prayer for God's punishment on them

(v. 20) is the first of the so-called 'confessions', in which he turns his anguish into protest. God's promise of protection recalls the assurance given at his call (Jer. 1:18–19).

Digging deeper:
JEREMIAH'S 'CONFESSIONS'

Jeremiah is well known as the 'weeping prophet'. But a number of his poems have been singled out as expressing his grief particularly deeply. They are: 11:18–23; 12:1–6; 15:10–14, 15–21; 17:14–18; 18:18–23; 20:7–12, 14–18). These are known, rather misleadingly, as his 'confessions'. In them, the prophet protests to God about the pain and grief he is suffering, and about how he has treated him, and even prays for the punishment of his enemies. The 'confessions' are often compared to Psalms of Lament. For parallels, see W. Baumgartner 1998, pp. 41–62, 79–101.

Are the 'confessions' private prayers, cultic prophecy, or public proclamation? For a review of interpretation, and the contribution of the 'confessions' to Jeremiah's theology, see McConville 1993, pp. 61–78.

12:1–17 Abandonment and restoration
Jeremiah's note of protest continues in another 'confession' (vv. 1–4), which this time brings a rebuke (vv. 5–6). If Jeremiah has been abandoned by his 'house' (v. 6 – NIV has 'family'), God now plans to abandon his 'house', namely Judah (v. 7). Judah is also his 'inheritance' (cf. Deut. 4:20), and his 'vineyard' (v. 10, cf. 5:10; Isa. 5:1–7). The 'shepherds' (v. 10) are Judah's rulers (cf. 23:1). Verses 14–17 give a glimpse of the salvation after the judgement (like 3:15–17 – note the good shepherds there).

13:1—14:22 Judgement and penitence
Jeremiah's acted parable of the loincloth (13:1–11; cf. Isaiah 20; Ezekiel 4—5) speaks of the corruption of Israel and Judah. Israel, once close to Yahweh by virtue of the covenant, is now fit only to be cast off. Perath (NIV) is the Euphrates, and the parable therefore relates to the exile in Babylon. (On symbolic actions see at Ezek. 4:1—7:27. Compare Jer. 16:1–9). The following parable (13:12–14) uses drunkenness to convey the helpless confusion that would come with the judgement.

The poetic oracles (13:15–27) imagine the misery of land and prophet (e.g. v. 17). The metaphors of vv. 22–27 picture some of the real cruelties and violations of war.

A famine affecting Judah (14:1–6) leads to words of repentance (vv. 7–9), but these are rejected by God (v. 10), presumably because insincere. No prayer or speech of prophets can help Judah at this stage, and false prophets will be punished (vv. 11–16). The chapter closes with another impassioned prayer for mercy by the people (vv. 7–22). The next verses (in ch. 15) suggest that this too is not a true repentance.

15:1—16:21 Jeremiah suffers for the people
Even if Moses and Samuel, the great intercessors (Exodus 32; 1 Samuel 12), prayed for Judah they would not be heard (15:1–2). Manasseh (v. 4) was king before Jeremiah's time (687–642 BC). His sins are singled out also in 2 Kgs 21:23–26 as the main cause of the punishment.

After another judgement saying (vv. 5–9), Jeremiah again expresses his great anguish (vv. 10–14, 15–21 are his third and fourth 'confessions'). Verses 11–12 are a reassurance (like 1:18). Verses 13–14 are an oracle against Judah reminding Jeremiah of the purpose of his calling. Even so, his grief verges on accusation of God (vv. 15–18). And this draws another assurance, tinged with rebuke (vv. 19–21).

Jeremiah is forbidden to participate in the usual routines of life, including even marriage, as a sign that all these will cease (16:1–9). The sins of the present generation are the immediate cause of their fate (vv. 10–13, despite 15:4). In the midst of the judgement sayings, a vision of a salvation afterwards is unexpectedly inserted (v. 14), echoed at the end by penitent words of other nations who recognize Yahweh as God (vv. 19–20).

17:1–18 The blessing and the curse The people's sin written on the heart (v. 1) makes a contrast with the New Covenant, which will also be written on the heart (31:33). God's anger 'for ever' (v. 4) will be overwhelmed by the grace of that covenant. The covenant is also reflected in the formulae of curse and blessing in vv. 5–6, 7–8, the latter very like Ps. 1:3. With these words the possibility of blessing is raised again, and applied to those in Judah who remain faithful. Jeremiah himself is one of these, and in another 'confession' (vv. 14–18) he pleads for God's judgement on his own enemies.

17:19–26 The Sabbath It is quite unusual for Jeremiah to make so much depend on one particular commandment. However, the Sabbath was a concern also of Amos before him (Amos 8:5). This saying might have had special importance in the exile, when other symbols of the worship of Yahweh had disappeared.

18:1—19:15 Visits to the potter Pot-making, a common activity in ancient times, provides

two illustrations in this section. First Jeremiah shows how the fate of every nation is in God's hands (18:1–11). Failure to keep his covenant is therefore dangerous (18:13–17). The 'stubbornness' of Judah (v. 12) is borne out with the story of plots made against Jeremiah (18:18, like 11:18–23), and another 'confession' (18:19–23) in which he prays for God's punishment on them.

The second potter incident (ch. 19) involves an acted parable in which a pot is broken and cannot be remade, signifying that judgement on Judah is inevitable.

20:1–18 Compelled to speak Jeremiah's physical suffering reaches a new height with his mistreatment by the priest Pashhur (20:1–6). So too does his cry of protest at a vocation that makes him a victim of his message (vv. 7–12). Like Job, he even wishes he had never been born (vv. 14–18, cf. Job 3). The two protests (the last of his 'confessions') are separated by a shout of praise (v. 13), allowing a word of salvation to come even into this dark moment.

The anguished cry brings this long section of the book to a close, with Jeremiah's question about the purpose of his life ringing in our ears. There will be an answer to this by the end of the book.

21:1—24:10: The failure of Judah's kings and prophets
This section covers the reigns of all the kings of Judah in Jeremiah's time, but focuses on the last of them, Zedekiah. The point is to show how they all failed, and that the only hope for Judah is to undergo the punishment of God by means of Babylon.

21:1—22:12 Zedekiah seeks reassurance
Jeremiah, though mistreated by an official in

Chapter 27 shows that not only Judah but also other nations are to be punished by God through Babylon. We remember that Jeremiah is a 'prophet to the nations' (1:5). This is now in the time of Zedekiah, between the first and second invasions of 597 and 587 BC (27:1).

Some prophets challenge Jeremiah's message, and say that the punishment will not last long (27:16). The temple treasures removed in 597 will soon be brought back. Jeremiah opposes this strongly, especially in his showdown with the prophet Hananiah (ch. 28). When Jeremiah declares that Hananiah will die (28:16), and he does, it shows that Jeremiah's message was the right one (see Deut. 18:20–22 on one test of a true and false prophet). (See also Theological Themes.)

In chapter 29 Jeremiah sends a letter to the first set of exiles, who were taken to Babylon in 597 BC, telling them not to expect a quick return, but to make new lives in Babylon. This would be the beginning of the new future that God promised for a time after the punishment (24:4–7). The key phrase 'I will bring you back from captivity' (v. 14 NIV, otherwise, 'I will restore your fortunes') occurs first here. The seventy-year period is reaffirmed (v. 10). It is clear that the question of whether the exile would be long was hotly disputed in both Judah and Babylon (vv. 20–32).

30:1—33:26: The 'Book of Consolation'
This is the 'Book of Consolation', the heart of the book, where Jeremiah finally unfolds the great promises of salvation that await those who endure the exile. The phrase 'I will bring you back from captivity' occurs six times in these chapters (30:3, 18; 31:23; 32:44; 33:7, 11; cf. 29:14). Chapter 30 makes salvation sayings follow judgement sayings

(e.g. vv. 4–7, then vv. 8–9), to show that this is the order of events in God's plan. Some judgement sayings here exactly recall sayings earlier in the prophecy, but are now set side by side with salvation (e.g. 30:12, 15 are like 6:14; 8:21). The time set aside for punishment is now presented as near its end.

Chapter 31 is full of visions of glad resettlement in the promised land. The ones saved are the 'remnant of Israel' (31:7). The one who scattered Israel is now their redeemer (31:10–11). While God has punished his people he has also yearned to save them (vv. 18–20). The punishment is put in the past (vv. 29–31). In this way the New Covenant is introduced (31:31–34). It looks forward to the day when the people of Israel and Judah shall again live in their land, now needing no law to compel their obedience to God, but obeying him because their hearts are changed. God himself will help them be faithful (31:33, cf. 32:39–41). Because of this the New Covenant will be better than the Mosaic covenant, which they could not keep. (See Theological Themes.)

The story of Jeremiah buying a field (ch. 32) continues the theme of chapters 30—31, because it illustrates the great turning in Judah's fortunes – even though Jeremiah buys the field at the time when Jerusalem is just about to be taken by the Babylonian army (32:2)! Normal life *would* resume in Judah, in God's time (contrast ch. 16). When Jeremiah says, 'Is anything too hard for the LORD?' (32:27), the point is that God can save and change even those who had been so hard-hearted as to rebel constantly against him in the past. In chapter 33 the pictures of salvation include a promise of a new messianic king, together with a new temple and priesthood (33:14–26).

34:1—36:32: King and people refuse the word of Jeremiah

The Book of Consolation has given a glimpse of the future. But the focus now switches back to the midst of the crisis. Again, the prophecy follows a thematic development, not a chronological one. The first episode in this section concerns Zedekiah (597–587 BC, ch. 34), then the next two chapters take us back to Jehoiakim (609–597). The theme is how the kings resisted God's word by Jeremiah, and how that led to the exile. The incidents tell much about the kings' and people's stubbornness. Zedekiah's decision to release slaves was in keeping with God's law (Deut. 15:12–18), but the leaders and people had not the resolve to carry it through (34:8–11). In their unfaithfulness they compare badly with the sect known as the Rechabites (ch. 35), who were able to stick to their peculiar vows of an ascetic, nomadic lifestyle. And Jehoiakim's burning of the scroll containing the words Jeremiah had spoken up to that time (36:23) is a wonderful symbol of the kings' refusal to hear God's message. The word of God could not be destroyed, however. Jeremiah simply wrote the words on a new scroll, with more besides. Kings would be powerless in the end to stop God's purpose. (See Introduction: The prophets: Did they write?)

37:1—39:18: Up to the fall of Judah

We are now in the last days of Judah before the axe falls in 587 BC. As the Babylonian empire besieges Jerusalem, Jeremiah is put in prison. His constant message that Judah should submit has been taken as treason, and he is even suspected of deserting to the enemy (37:11–15). Even so the indecisive Zedekiah, who is probably dominated by powerful officials, seeks Jeremiah out. However, Jeremiah can give no relief from his usual message (37:16–21, also vv. 3–10).

His enemies want to put him to death, and he is rescued only by a powerful friend (38:1–13). Zedekiah meets him secretly. The message does not change but Jeremiah appears to have the king's protection (38:14–28).

The city falls. The Babylonians take official control of Jerusalem by setting up court there (39:3). Zedekiah's sons are killed to prevent any thought of the royal line of Judah continuing (39:6), and he himself is disabled (v. 7). Many people are taken into exile in Babylon, but some of the least important politically are left (vv. 9–10). Jeremiah now has the protection of the Babylonians, who apparently respected him as a prophet (40:2–3). They may have known the Judean view that he was a sympathizer. The prophecy of doom against the city has now been fulfilled. Jeremiah's supporter Ebed-melech will have to endure the collapse of the city, but his life is assured because of his faithfulness (39:15–18).

40:1—45:5: The fate of those who were left

These chapters tell the story of those who were left in the land, which is not told anywhere else in the Old Testament. Jeremiah remains with this group, and joins Gedaliah, the newly appointed governor (40:4–6). There are immediate signs that God is beginning to bless the land again (40:11–12). However, the group immediately faces danger from an ambitious chieftain, Ishmael, son of Nethaniah, whose name shows he is an Israelite. He is supported by the old enemy the Ammonites, who no doubt see the weakness of the land and its wealth (40:13–16).

When Gedaliah is murdered, the new leader, Johanan son of Kareah, wants to take refuge from Babylonian rule in Egypt

(41:17–18). The people ask Jeremiah for a word from God (42:2–3). Jeremiah's message is now to stay in the land (42:7–22). This is in line with his former message, because he still says that the people should accept Babylonian rule, and not go to Egypt (cf. 24:8–10). The new leaders, however, reject this, and go to Egypt, taking Jeremiah and Baruch with them, and those who had returned to Judah to enjoy its blessings (43:1–7, cf. 40:11–12). The situation has hardly changed, therefore. Like Zedekiah, the people want to hear the prophet's word, but they do not like it when it comes.

In Egypt, Jeremiah declares that Babylon will come and defeat Egypt (43:8–13). This shows again that God's message affects all nations (cf. chs 25; 27). It also shows that he will carry out his judgement against those who have sought refuge in Egypt by bringing Babylon against that nation too. There is no avoiding God's word. The people quickly return to old idolatrous ways, confirming that they themselves merit God's judgement (44:11–19).

Like Ebed-melech (39:15–18), Baruch will have to experience the devastation of war, but his life is assured (ch. 45).

46:1—51:64: Oracles Against the Nations

This is the major collection of Oracles Against the Nations (OAN) in the book. It has a similar message to chapter 25. This long section is positioned differently in the Greek LXX, after 25:13. Its importance is shown by the fact that one ancient text (LXX) places it in the middle of the book, while the other (the Hebrew, or MT) places it in this climactic end-position.

The OAN show again that Jeremiah's message is for all the nations, not just Judah.

The nations mentioned include many of Israel and Judah's neighbours and historic enemies. Egypt's prime position follows naturally from the story in chs 43—44 (note 46:13, and the phrase 'Pharaoh and those who trust in him', v. 25, which includes the Judeans who have gone there). The punishment of the nations will have as its outcome the salvation of Judah (46:27–28).

There follow sayings against the Philistines (ch. 47), Moab (ch. 48), Ammon (49:1–6), Edom (49:7–22), Damascus (Syria, 49:23–27), Kedar (49:28–33 – these were desert-dwellers from the east, like the Midianites in the time of the judges, Judges 6—8), Elam, a nation far to the east (49:34–39). In some cases, there are remarkable assurances that God has future plans for these nations too (48:47; 49:6; 49:39).

The main part of the OAN is reserved for Babylon, in two long chapters (50—51). This comes last because it occupies such a key role in the book. It is Babylon that brings God's judgement, but this does not mean it has acted for the right motives (see also Isaiah on Assyria, Isa. 10:5–12). Instead it has acted only cruelly and in its own interests. So it too will be punished, and this is emphasized to show that everything that has happened to Judah was part of God's greater purpose to judge the peoples of the earth. The judgement on Babylon is at the same time the salvation of Judah. This means that the OAN are like the Book of Consolation (chs 30—33), because they show that salvation comes after punishment. This is why God is described here as Judah's 'redeemer' (50:34).

As Jeremiah wrote down his words concerning Judah, so he does for Babylon, sinking them in the River Euphrates, to await the day when they would be fulfilled (51.59–64).

52:1–34: Further account of fall of Jerusalem, the temple destroyed

This tailpiece partly repeats the events of ch. 39, but is more like the ending of Kings (2 Kgs 25). It adds to ch. 39 the story of the plunder and destruction of the temple (52:17–23), and also the note about the release of King Jehoiachin, who was exiled in 597 BC (vv. 31–34). Some writers see in this a hint of the future restoration of the rule of a Davidic king again in Israel.

THEOLOGICAL THEMES

SIN AS FALSENESS

Jeremiah portrays Judah as everything that it should not be. The people were in a relationship with Yahweh, their God, based on the covenant made centuries before at Mt. Sinai (Exodus 19—24). They were to worship Yahweh alone (Exod. 20:2–3), and keep his laws. Instead, they have become worshippers of Baal (or 'the baals', 2:8, 23). This topic, set at the beginning of the prophecy in ch. 2, is the key to the whole accusation of Jeremiah. Instead of 'loving' Yahweh, they have made 'lovers' of other gods (v. 33). In the covenant, Israel would be faithful and Yahweh would bless them (2:7, cf. Deut. 7:12–13). Now they have trusted gods that have no power, and therefore they will find no help (2:5, 28).

This basic falseness is found from the top of Judah's society down. The leaders have abandoned their true responsibilities. Priests did not serve Yahweh, or teach his law, and prophets prophesied by Baal (2:8), giving the false message that all was well when the foundations were rotten (6:14; 23:9–40; 28).

Rulers generally (literally 'shepherds', 2:8; 23:1) have failed to lead. The kings had special responsibilities because of the covenant Yahweh made with David (2 Sam. 7). They were to rule according to the law given by Moses, and in justice (2 Sam. 8:15; Jer. 22:16), but they became oppressors and looked only for their own advantage (22:13).

The falseness of Judah is most fully portrayed in 9:2–9, a terrible accusation, which assembles a whole range of words for lies and deception. Judah's sin becomes its own punishment, because honest, trusting relationships have become impossible. This horror of a society based on the lie is the very opposite of what one based on covenant should be.

In this situation, the people falsely believe they are secure. This is why the sin of the leaders is so tragic. Jeremiah's attack on the false worship in the temple (7:1–15) goes to the heart of the problem. Though they are at heart worshippers of Baal, they still flock to the feasts of Yahweh at his temple. The temple is the symbol of the promise once given to David, and it seems to guarantee safety from every kind of evil. Safety is a covenant blessing (Deut. 12:10; 28:7). But there can be no covenant blessings where there is no truth in worship, and the commandments are openly flouted (7:9–11). The same point is made in 11:1–5, which implies that some covenant celebration is in process, but says that the people can only expect the covenant curses, not its blessings.

The blessings of the covenant are in fact systematically denied. The dreadful images of drought in ch. 14 are a kind of falseness, for land should be fruitful. But land is a part of the covenantal order. Desperate people recognize that rain is not given by the skies themselves, nor by powerless gods, but by Yahweh (14:22, cf. v. 7, and Deut. 28:23–24). The expected bounty of the promised land is withdrawn.

Even the rights of Judah as Yahweh's chosen people are now suspended. The dramatic reversal of the idea of the Holy War drives this home. Where once Yahweh had overcome enemy armies in order to bless his chosen people with land, now he turns enemy armies against them (21:1–10). This is like saying that Judah is no longer Yahweh's people. The logic of this is pursued in chapter 27. If Judah is not Yahweh's people then it can have no further right to the land it received as his people. Yahweh now declares that he has given the lands of all the nations to Nebuchadnezzar (27:6). This obviously includes Judah. Indeed, in this passage, Judah is no different from the other nations.

In the end all the marks of Judah as Yahweh's people are taken away. The Davidic king has to flee as the representatives of the King of Babylon enter Jerusalem and set up his court there (39:3). The temple is destroyed (52:17–23). And the people are driven from their land. The logic of falseness has been fully worked out. Falseness in covenant spells loss of the marks and blessings of covenant. There is nothing vindictive in Yahweh's punishment of his people. In failing to be the covenant people in truth, they have failed to display his justice and righteousness before the eyes of the nations, which was their calling (Deut. 4:6–8), and therefore their position is untenable.

JUDGEMENT AND SALVATION

There is a movement in the book from judgement to salvation. This movement does not lie on the surface of the book in an obvious way, but can be seen when we look carefully at the book as a whole. It seems that Jeremiah began by preaching that Judah should repent. This is clear in texts like 4:1–4. Even sayings that just accuse the people, like many in chapters 2—6, were probably originally meant to turn them to repentance. So it is quite likely that in his early years Jeremiah did not think of the exile as inevitable. If Judah kept the covenant it could continue to be the people of Yahweh in the promised land. However, at some time, which we cannot pinpoint, he realized that the people would not change, and that Yahweh was going to punish them. We see this in the two stories of the potter in chapters 18 and 19. The first of these stories leaves the door open for the people to turn, but the second portrays the destruction of the nation as fixed and final, a broken pot that cannot be mended.

This means that the way of salvation has changed. Judah can still be the people of Yahweh but only after going through the exile. Salvation will come, but only after judgement has come first. This pattern can be seen in a number of places. In the midst of Jeremiah 16, for example, which mainly confirms that all life in the land is going to stop, there is a glimpse of the end of exile (16:14–15). The same thing may be seen in 3:15–18. Jeremiah probably did not say these words of hope after exile at the same time that he said the words of judgement. More likely his sayings have been arranged in a certain order, either by himself late in his life or by someone else. These arrangements of his sayings have been done by someone who saw the path of development that his ministry had in the end.

A key text spelling out the role that the judgement has in God's plan is chapter 24.

In that place there is no longer any question of avoiding the invasion by Babylon, but only of which group will enjoy Yahweh's favour after it is all over. It is in fact those who actually go through the punishment who will be saved. The structure of the book in its present form (in Hebrew) is at pains to spell it out that this is one of its key concepts. Between Jeremiah 24 and the Book of Consolation (chapters 30—33) it is made very clear that salvation will not come quickly. Jeremiah will finally preach salvation, but he is certainly not to be confused with those who say salvation will come immediately, like Hananiah (ch. 28).

THE NEW COVENANT

Now the New Covenant comes into play. How will the situation after the exile be any different from the situation before it? How can anyone guarantee that afterwards the people will be faithful, when they had shown for generations that they could not be? Jeremiah knew that the people were very unlikely to change (see 5:21, 23 see also Deut. 9:4–6 for the same problem). This is one of the hardest questions that the writers of the Old Testament had to face. The New Covenant provides an answer.

The important elements in the New Covenant (31:31–34) are the following. First, it is made with 'the house of Israel and the house of Judah' (v. 31). This is an ideal, because 'Israel', that is, the northern kingdom, no longer existed in Jeremiah's time. The New Covenant looks forward to a restoration of the people in a form that has passed away. The same idea is found in 3:12–13, where the prophet preaches towards the north, in a symbolic act that speaks of a salvation that could hardly be imagined as a possible event. Even so, the New Covenant is another covenant with the same historic people who made a covenant with Yahweh in the time of Moses.

Second, it is 'new', however, not just in the sense of 'renewed', as any covenant might be renewed (Joshua renewed the covenant in Joshua 24; Josiah did it in 2 Kgs 23:1–3). It is new because it is not like the old (v. 32). It is going to be different because the people broke the old one. A new covenant is needed *because* another of the same would just be broken again.

Third, in the New Covenant the 'law' (torah) will be written on the people's hearts (v. 33). This is in contrast to the stone tablets on which the commandments of the first covenant were written (Exod. 32:15). The 'torah' itself is the same. But this is a bold image of a people whose wills have been changed. They will not be simply compelled by a law they did not choose, but they will desire to keep it. And this change in the people is to be brought about by God himself. In this way the covenant will again be in force ('I will be their God, and they will be my people').

Fourth, the New Covenant people will be a community that knows God intimately, and that shares the knowledge of him together (v. 34). There will be no need for one to teach another to follow Yahweh (rather than some other god), because all will be in a close relationship with him.

Fifth, because they will now be a faithful community, Yahweh will put the former sins behind (v. 34b).

This vision of a transformed people is what makes the turning from judgement to salvation possible in Jeremiah. If there were no such hope the covenant would simply

65

have to come to an end. When the terms of an Ancient Near Eastern treaty were not kept, then the penalties for breaking it were imposed, and that was the end of the matter. The Mosaic covenant was in some ways like such a treaty (see the volume on The Pentateuch in this series). The Books of Kings, which like Jeremiah tell the story of the fall of Judah because it broke the covenant, hold out very little hope for life afterwards (just a prayer that the Babylonians would have mercy on their captives, 2 Kgs 8:46–51). Deuteronomy 30:1–10, however, is like Jeremiah's New Covenant in some ways. It too knows that Israel was unable to keep the covenant. To use its metaphor, Israel could not 'circumcise its heart' (10:16 – the same metaphor is used in Jeremiah 4:4). Therefore, after the curses of the covenant have come upon the people (Deut. 30:1), God himself will 'circumcise their hearts' (Deut. 30:6). The thought is like Jeremiah's, because God acts to change the situation *because* the people are unable to do it for themselves.

This line of thought can be called 'Deuteronomic', or sometimes 'deutero-nomistic'. That is, it is within the kind of thinking set off by Deuteronomy that this question about covenant-keeping and failure arises. We have noticed that Jeremiah is often thought to be very close to Deuteronomy in its language and ideas. Here too, then, is a similarity between them. Their idea of an act of God that solves the problem of human sin is carried into the New Testament, when the New Covenant is made real by the perfect obedience of Christ, which is then extended to those who are 'in Christ' by the work of the Holy Spirit.

It is because of the New Covenant that the changes pictured in the Book of Jeremiah can be brought about. A key phrase is in

Jer. 32:17: 'Nothing is too hard for you' (also v. 27: 'Is anything too hard for me?'). In the context this means that he can even bring salvation out of desolation, and obedience

Digging deeper:
ISRAEL'S RETURN TO ITS LAND

This is a controversial issue in some modern biblical interpretation. Do the Old Testament prophecies of a return to the land find their fulfilment in the modern return of Jewish people to the land of Israel? The remarkable story of this return, with the revival of the Hebrew language as a unifying force, the strange course of political events that helped bring it about, the winning of wars against the odds, and the occupation of something like the borders laid down in the Bible, have led some to think so.

In evaluating the question, these points might be considered:

1. Recall what has already been said about the meaning of 'Israel' (Introduction: Theological Themes, and Isaiah: How can the exiles be 'Israel'?). Where is 'Israel' truly to be found, according to the prophets? Does the adoption of the name 'Israel' for a modern state guarantee that it is the 'Israel' of which the prophets spoke? How might modern Israel (like any other nation) meet the prophets' standards?

2. What attitude do you think Christians should have to all the peoples of the Holy Land?

For a balanced and well-documented treatment of these issues see Chapman 1983 and for a thought-provoking analysis of the paradoxes of the 'Holy Land' see Cragg 1992. See also the reflections below, in Jeremiah in the Canon.

out of stubborn rebellion (32:39–40). For the same reason the people who once lost their land because of their falseness might have their land again, with all its abundance instead of drought, with joy instead of mourning, and with the round of feasting, and the priests playing their true part (31:7–14). They can have the city of Jerusalem again, the symbol of the Davidic covenant (31:38–40), and David himself (30:9), and even the full temple institutions and a promise of permanence (if 33:14–26 is original – it is missing in LXX). For this reason Judah can be redeemed while Babylon faces its turn to be overthrown (50:34).

THE INDIVIDUAL

The Book of Jeremiah is sometimes regarded as the beginning of individual religion in the Old Testament. J. Skinner (1922) made the classic case for this. The two main arguments used are the New Covenant prophecy, because of its idea of a torah written on the heart, and the prayer life of Jeremiah himself. 'Individualism' is not quite the right understanding of Jeremiah, however. As we have seen, the New Covenant prophecy is about a renewal of the whole people of Israel and Judah. It is not necessarily more individualistic than the Mosaic covenant. The key concept is 'inwardness' rather then individualism. So while people are brought to faithful obedience in the New Covenant they are still part of a community that belongs together in relationship with God. That remains the point of the 'covenant' idea, expressed in the words 'I will be their God and they will be my people' (31:33b).

The life of Jeremiah does play an important role in the message of the book. Parts of the book have been called 'biographical', because they tell us so much, not just about things that happened to him, but about his inner life. This is more true of Jeremiah than of any other prophet. And some think this shows an interest in the religious life of the individual as such.

There is some truth in this. Jeremiah's prayers reveal a deep love of both the people of Judah and of God. He is caught between that love and his sense of justice (compare 8:22—9:1 with 9:2). He is also tormented by his calling itself, which has made him the enemy of everyone (15:10). There is a tremendous honesty in these prayers, as one individual struggles openly with God. (See p. 56, Jeremiah's 'confessions', at 11:18–23.) In a sense, of course, this is no different from many of the Psalms, which also display people's anguish, as well as their joy and thankfulness. Indeed, Jeremiah's prayers are often very similar to the language and ideas of the Psalms (e.g. 11:19, cf. Ps. 44:11 [12]). Perhaps they strike us more forcefully as the prayers of an individual because we get to know the person involved.

The life of Jeremiah is mainly important, however, because it shows the power of an individual in the life of the community. It is not *just* an illustration of personal piety. Instead, Jeremiah is one person who keeps alive the community's ancient traditions and obligations. He is an example to Judah of who and what they are meant to be. For him, to be a prophet is not just to speak words that he is given as if by some divine dictation, but to challenge the people by his own life. The message was unpopular because they knew it to be true, and this is why they tried to kill him. They would scarcely have resisted a dreaming mystic with such hatred.

This is the real 'individualism' in Jeremiah, not a personal private piety that owes nobody anything and keeps itself to itself, but the willingness of an individual to stand against a whole society's corruption, and take the burden of living the truth on his or her own shoulders.

There is even more to it than this, for in Jeremiah God reveals his own passion for his covenant people. This is clear because in some places we do not immediately know who is speaking, Jeremiah or God. The best example of this is 8:22—9:3 [2]. Here we think at first that Jeremiah himself is grieving over the people, and wants to go away from them and weep over their sin and fate. And that is true; the idea of getting away to a place to stay in the desert (9:2 [1]) could only refer to Jeremiah. But at the end of 9:3 [2] we realize that this whole passage has been expressing the feelings of God. This is not a contradiction. It shows that in the faithfulness and suffering of Jeremiah God reveals something of his own heart. Jeremiah is a bit like Isaiah's 'Suffering Servant' in this sense. We can even say that there is a foretaste of the 'incarnation' in Jeremiah (that is, where God becomes human, as he would do in Jesus).

THE MESSIAH

Though it is not a major theme in the Book of Jeremiah, the hope of a future Davidic king who will reign in justice and righteousness is held out. The key text is 23:5–6, where this king is called a 'righteous branch', where 'branch' means one descended from an ancestor as a shoot grows from a tree (the same phrase is found in Zech. 3:8; 6:12–13; and Isa. 11:1 is also similar). This prophecy says, therefore, that the old promise to David – that his line would rule for ever – will be fulfilled in the end. The righteous king who will fulfil the promise is contrasted with the kings of

Judah since Jehoiakim (in ch. 22), who have failed to live up to the obligations imposed on them (cf. 1 Kgs 2:2–4). A kingdom of righteousness is just what Jeremiah has shown to be lacking in Judah, which was shot through with falsehood (Jer. 9:2–9). The hope for a righteous king, therefore (the term 'Messiah' is not actually used in Jeremiah) is a hope for a society in which truth overcomes falsehood.

The passages that express this hope belong to those parts of the book that look beyond the exile to a time of restoration, and thus with the idea of the New Covenant. As well as in 23:5–6 the promise of a king is found in 30:9 and 33:14–26, that is, within the Book of Consolation (chs 30—33), which has the New Covenant promise at its heart (31:31–34). Just as the New Covenant would not be fulfilled by a return of the Judean exiles to the land in itself, so this promise of a righteous king would not happen just by turning the clock back and giving the descendants of David another chance. The promise belongs to the vision of a wholly renewed people, as in the New Covenant. In the perspective of the New Testament, this would only happen when Jesus came as Son of David, to establish a kingdom based on justice and righteousness that would go beyond the limits of ancient Judah and extend to all peoples and all times.

RHETORICAL INTENTION

The Book of Jeremiah has many hearers. When we ask what it *means* we have to go back a step and ask what audience we have in mind. Do we mean those who first heard Jeremiah preach? Even these will have varied in their fears and expectations over the long period of his ministry. Or do we mean those communities that gathered the prophet's words and used them again and again in their worship? These too varied, since groups of Jews began to live in different parts of the empire from the time of the exile on. And the different forms of the book (LXX and MT) show that the process of gathering the words of Jeremiah, and perhaps expansions of his words, was not uniform.

The very existence of the book, therefore, testifies to the different ways in which the prophet's words were heard. His words come to us, indeed, very indirectly. Often the layers look like this: the narrator says Jeremiah says the LORD says, say to x: ". . ." (The point is illustrated by the several levels of speech-marks that some translations use in order to clarify who is speaking – see RSV at the end of 29:28, for example.)

This means that his words have been mediated to us by a process of reflection on them, and also that they may still be heard on different levels. As an example we may take the theme of repentance. In his preaching, it seems that Jeremiah called the people of Judah to repent (as we saw above, Theological Themes: Judgement and salvation). The force of this call comes across strongly in a passage like 4:1–4, and it can still be a dominant note in a reading of Jeremiah today. However, as readers of the book, we know that the people did not repent. This is clear in Jeremiah 2—3, which contain reflections on their failure to do so (3:6–10), and which already consider the consequences of the fact (3:1–5). The book of Jeremiah has been put together for, maybe by, people who knew they had not listened to Jeremiah and had suffered the consequences. The same people also hoped that God would still have mercy on them

and give them a new start (3:14–18). These people, then, are quite different from those who had persecuted Jeremiah and thought him a traitor. If they had not been convinced that Jeremiah was right after all, his words would hardly have been preserved.

How did these people understand Jeremiah's words when they were read to them, perhaps in a synagogue in Babylon or Egypt – or back in Judah? While Jeremiah's first hearers refused to believe they needed to repent, and looked to their king and temple as signs of God's favour, these people could not put their hope in those institutions. They knew that temple and kings were not, after all, guarantees of security. In a sense too it was now too late for them to hear the call to repent, since repentance could no longer forestall the disaster that had befallen them.

Everything, therefore, is now heard in a new key. They could not repent in such a way as to avoid the exile, yet they knew that Yahweh demanded their complete loyalty, and that he would hold them to it. The message of repentance could always be heard in a fresh way, whenever people were tempted to place their hope elsewhere than in Yahweh alone. They knew that loyalty to Yahweh did not depend on maintaining the national institutions of politics and worship, but that they could show it by being a faithful, obedient community, even in exile. They knew that obedience to Yahweh had to be a matter of the heart.

While people were still actually in exile, they might have pondered long on their past failings. The Book of Lamentations is one evidence of the grief and penitence of people who knew their sins and the consequences of them. For them, there was the hope that in due course there could be salvation. The hard lesson was that the consequences of sin could not lightly be passed over. This was involved in admitting that Jeremiah had been right, whereas Hananiah (ch. 28) and other prophets who had played down the seriousness of both the sin and the punishment had been wrong. Exilic hearers of Jeremiah's words knew that God was both judge and saviour, and they had to reckon with what that meant, even as they held out hope that one day salvation would come. The core of the book that addresses such people is chs 24—29, with its reflections on the way to salvation through exile (ch. 24), its period of seventy years as a time in which justice might be seen to be done (25:12; 29:10), and its letter to the exiles, counselling acceptance of their lot in Babylon, with the reassurance that God had not abandoned them, even though life had not turned out as they had hoped (29:4–28). The same people might also have come to know, through Jeremiah's experience, how God was with them in their suffering.

After the restoration the key changes once again. Salvation has come after all. The challenge for Jeremiah's hearers in this new situation is not to go back to the old complacency, but to build a society that is worthy to be God's covenant partner, and to receive the benefits of land and blessing. In this setting the New Covenant comes not only as promise but as challenge. Can they be people who have God's laws written on their hearts (30:3)? A true hearing of this note in the book involves admitting that obedience is not natural, but that people need the help of God (30:3; 32:39–40). This is the rhetorical effect of the idea that God himself will enable them to obey. Seen in this way it is not a hard problem to puzzle over (does God overrule human free will?), but

instead it drives hearers to a humble acceptance of their weakness. The figure of Jeremiah himself might have given them an example of a broken and devoted life, vindicated finally when events proved that he had been God's servant all along. Their acceptance of their weakness might finally have been put in the perspective of a new understanding that Yahweh their God was Lord of all the nations, and that he would bring his judgement and salvation in due course not just to people of Judah but to the whole world (chs 46—51).

Think about
FREE WILL

Look again at Jer. 32:39–40. Does this seem to say that God, having found that people were disobedient, changed his mind about allowing them to make free choices? How would this tie up with the challenges to repentance and obedience in the book? Does it help to think about a text like this in terms of the rhetorical effect it was meant to have, rather than see it as a theological conundrum?

JEREMIAH IN THE CANON

The book of Jeremiah was influential from its earliest days of existence. The books of Chronicles and Daniel both refer to the 'seventy years' of exile, in different ways, as we have seen (2 Chron. 36:21; Dan. 9:2). In Daniel, the idea of restoration from exile is already being stretched to mean a final victory over all evil.

Jeremiah's place in the Canon may be considered more broadly, however. Along with Hosea, Jeremiah plays an important part in the biblical idea of God's personal involvement with people in history. Both these prophets, in their suffering, display something of the suffering of God (see Theological Themes: The individual, last paragraph). God's suffering arises both because of people's sin, and because of their anguish. In this sense Hosea and Jeremiah are forerunners of Jesus, who also grieved over both the sin of Jerusalem and its consequences (Matt. 23:37–39; Luke 13:34–35), and who participated in the joys and sorrows of human existence (John 2:1–11; 11:32–35). Jesus displays the Incarnation uniquely. Yet, Jeremiah and Hosea show beforehand that God's way of dealing with the world was 'incarnational'. The point is made not only in the suffering of the prophets themselves, but in direct sayings of God which express a longing love that strives with the impulse to judge sin (Jer. 31:20, cf. Hos. 11:8–9).

The connection between judgement and salvation also throws light on God's personal involvement with his world. For the place where judgement and salvation are finally shown is in the life and death of Jesus. The anguish of God seen in his longing over Israel is expressed in both judgement of sin and salvation from it. And this paradox has its climax in the cross of Christ. Like Jeremiah, Jesus came to a people that was in a kind of exile, though in its own land (under Roman rule) and showed them that the way to the kingdom of God was not easy, but meant 'taking up the cross' (Matt. 10:38). To do so would mean entry in the end to the kingdom of God. But that would not be immediate, for generations of followers of Jesus. The Book of Jeremiah shows that the principle of judgement followed by salvation applies to all history and every dimension of life. While we await

the kingdom of God, we are in a sense between judgement and salvation, and – like the exiles – we hear the call of God to bring justice and righteousness into our lives, not only individually, but also in the church and in the wider world.

A comparison of Jeremiah and the New Testament also shows how major themes can be understood in fresh ways. This can be illustrated by the topics of temple, land and king. When people in the exile heard Jeremiah's prophecies of a restoration to the promised land, of a renewed temple and priesthood, and of a Davidic king, they might well have expected that he meant these things in the sense in which they had known them before. After all, the New Covenant promise (31:31–34) continues by describing a rebuilt Jerusalem in terms that would have sounded familiar to them (31:38–40). And the Book of Consolation (Jeremiah 30—33) is full of pictures of returning joyfully to the land. The force of these pictures is still felt by many today who think that the modern return of Jews to the Holy Land is a fulfilment of them.

For Christian readers, however, these topics in Jeremiah are read within the larger biblical narrative, which stretches from the creation to the final establishment of the kingdom of God, and in which the coming of Jesus Christ plays the central part. In that perspective, a renewed land is only a partial glimpse of a renewed earth. It is real enough, in the sense that the visions of a happy and righteous people in a fertile land (such as Jer. 30:10–14) show the sort of desire that God has for his human creatures. And they call all people to work towards building societies like these. But the full realization of the land promises is bound up with the full realization of the kingdom, and the New Covenant community, which is and will be brought about by the life, death and resurrection of Christ.

In the same way the themes of temple and kingship are brought to fullness in Christ. If temple means the presence of God among his people then this is accomplished by Jesus, who makes the divine presence possible in a quite new way (this is why the curtain of the temple is torn as Jesus dies, Mark 15:38). And kingship means no less than the kingship of the Son of David who was also Son of God, who is king of all nations, and who brings in an everlasting kingdom. For these reasons it is misguided to look for 'fulfilments' of Old Testament promises in specific events of our own times. Such fulfilments, if taken literally and pressed to logical conclusions, mean making divisions among human beings again, after such divisions have been broken down by the reconciling work of Christ (Gal. 3:28).

FURTHER READING

Items marked with * are considered suitable as first ports of call, while others are more complex, or relate to specific issues.

COMMENTARIES

In addition to the commentaries marked *, Carroll is important for its scholarship, and for its thesis that the book was compiled over a long period. The Word Commentaries give useful help on the text.

J. Bright *Jeremiah*. AB. New York: Doubleday, 1965.

R. P. Carroll *Jeremiah*. OTL. London: SCM, 1986.

P. C. Craigie, P. H. Kelley and J. F. Drinkard *Jeremiah 1–25*. WBC. Dallas: Word Books, 1991.

*R. K. Harrison *Jeremiah and Lamentations*. TOTC. London: Tyndale Press, 1973.

W. L. Holladay *Jeremiah 1, 2*. Hermeneia. Philadelphia: Fortress, 1986; Minneapolis: Fortress, 1989.

*D. R. Jones *Jeremiah*. NCB. Grand Rapids: Eerdmans; London: Marshall Pickering, 1992.

G. L. Keown, P. J. Scalise and T. G. Smothers *Jeremiah 26–52*. WBC. Dallas: Word Books, 1995.

J. R. Lundbom *Jeremiah 1–20*. AB. New York: Doubleday, 1999.

W. McKane *Jeremiah 1–25*. ICC. Edinburgh: T. & T. Clark, 1986.

W. McKane *Jeremiah 26–52*. ICC. Edinburgh: T. & T. Clark, 1996.

*H. McKeating *Jeremiah*. Epworth Commentaries. Peterborough: Epworth Press, 1999.

*J. A. Thompson *Jeremiah*. NICOT. Grand Rapids: Eerdmans, 1980.

OTHER BOOKS AND ARTICLES

The following include items mentioned in the discussion. General studies are those by Nicholson and Stulman. Note: the essays of Bright and Hyatt are also in the collection of Perdue and Kovacs.

W. Baumgartner *Jeremiah's Poems of Lament*. Sheffield: Almond Press, 1988.

J. Bright 'The Date of the Prose Sermons of Jeremiah', *JBL* 70, 1951, pp. 15–35.

C. Chapman *Whose Promised Land?* Tring: Lion, 1983.

K. Cragg *The Arab Christian: a History in the Middle East*. Louisville: Westminster/John Knox, 1991; London: Mowbray, 1992.

S. R. Driver *Deuteronomy*. ICC. Edinburgh: T. & T. Clark, 1895.

J. P. Hyatt 'The Deuteronomic Edition of Jeremiah', *Vanderbilt Studies in the Humanities*, 1951, pp. 71–95.

S. M. Kang *Divine War in the Old Testament*. BZAW 177. Berlin: de Gruyter, 1989.

H. Lalleman-de Winkel *Jeremiah in Prophetic Tradition*. Leuven: Peeters, 2000.

T. Longman and D. G. Reid *God is a Warrior*. SOTBT. Grand Rapids: Zondervan, 1995.

J. G. McConville *Judgement and Promise: an Interpretation of the Book of Jeremiah*. Leicester: IVP; Winona Lake: Apollos, 1993.

E. W. Nicholson *Preaching to the Exiles: A Study of the Prose Tradition in the Book of Jeremiah*. Oxford: Basil Blackwell, 1970.

S. Mowinckel *Prophecy and Tradition*. Oslo: Jacob Dybwad, 1946.

E. W. Nicholson *Deuteronomy and Tradition*. Oxford: Basil Blackwell, 1981.

L. G. Perdue and B. W. Kovacs *A Prophet to the Nations: Essays in Jeremiah Studies*. Winona Lake: Eisenbrauns, 1984.

G. von Rad *Holy War in Ancient Israel*. Grand Rapids: Eerdmans, 1991; original: Göttingen: Vandenhoeck and Ruprecht, 1958.

J. Skinner *Prophecy and Religion*. Cambridge: CUP, 1922.

L. Stulman *Order Amid Chaos: Jeremiah as Symbolic Tapestry*. The Biblical Seminar 57; Sheffield: Sheffield Academic Press, 1998.

L. Stulman *The Prose Sermons of the Book of Jeremiah*. SBL Diss 83. Atlanta: Scholars Press, 1986.

M. Weinfeld *Deuteronomy and the Deuteronomic School*. OUP, 1983.

Chapter 3

LAMENTATIONS

DATE AND DESTINATION

Lamentations is not a prophetic book, but finds itself in the prophetic section of the Christian canon. This is because the book is traditionally associated with Jeremiah. The Septuagint (LXX, the Greek translation of the Old Testament) not only attributed it to the prophet, but placed it after his book in its canonical order. (In the Hebrew canon, in contrast, it comes in the third division, known as the Writings, between Ecclesiastes and Esther.)

Lamentations is a book of laments about the fall of Jerusalem and the horrors experienced by the people of Judah in their defeat by the Babylonians. There are hints of this loss of land, king and temple in the text (1:3, 10; 2:2, 7). It is not hard to see why the book could have been thought to come from Jeremiah. He too spoke about the exile, and his life and work continued after the fall of Jerusalem. Jeremiah uttered laments, as we have seen (e.g. Jer. 11:18–20; 15:15–18). And some of the expressions in Lamentations are similar to expressions of Jeremiah (e.g. Lam. 3:48–51, cf. Jer. 14:17).

We cannot be sure if there was a historical connection between Jeremiah and Lamentations. But it is natural to suppose that the laments come out of the experience of the exiles. The fifth lament (ch. 5) could come from a later point in the exile than the first four, as it seems to reflect a situation that has gone on for some time.

CRITICAL INTERPRETATION OF LAMENTATIONS

Lamentations falls into five separate poems, corresponding to the chapter divisions. Each is a 'lament', like a number of the Psalms (e.g. Psalms 44; 74; 79; 80; 89, which also express the pain of Judah because of the exile; cf. Westermann 1965, pp. 173–76). Lament Psalms typically pour out complaints and protests to God about some circumstance of the author or the community. They also usually have a note of hope or confidence, suggesting a sense that the prayer of lamentation has been heard and answered (e.g. Psalm 13, where vv. 5–6 turn from grief to confidence). Lamentations strikes a note of joyful hope in the middle of the book (3:22–39). Since Lamentations has only one such main high point (there is a brief one in 4:22), it is in one sense a single lamentation, the five separate poems adding up to a unified work.

The most striking formal feature of the book is the acrostic form of the poems (see Freedman 1986). That is a poetic arrangement in which each line begins with the next letter of the alphabet. Acrostic Psalms can sometimes be easily spotted because they have twenty-two verses, that is, one verse for each letter of the Hebrew alphabet (e.g. Psalms 25; 34). There are variations of this pattern. Psalm 119 has twenty-two stanzas, in which each line within a stanza begins with the same letter. Lamentations has three twenty-two-line poems (chs 1; 2; 4). Lamentations 3 is a variation of this, because it has three lines for every letter of the alphabet, resulting in its sixty-six verses. Lamentations 5 does not fit the pattern.

On these formal grounds, then, we find once again that ch. 3 has an important central place in the whole composition, and that ch. 5 stands somewhat apart from the rest. It remains to be seen if we can explain why the work has been structured in this way.

STRUCTURE AND OUTLINE

The structure of the book is straightforward, as it falls into the five poems that we have already identified.

STRUCTURE
1:1–22 Jerusalem mourns
2:1–22 The LORD's anger and the people's grief
3:1–66 The poet's suffering and the LORD's compassions
4:1–22 Siege
5:1–22 A people subdued

OUTLINE
1:1–22: Jerusalem mourns
1:1–7 Jerusalem was once the chosen city of God, the place where he set his Davidic king, and where he dwelt in the temple (Ps. 2:6; 2 Samuel 6—7). Now it has fallen from grace, and lost its marks of his favour. Pilgrimages have ceased (v. 4, cf. Ps. 84:5). The people have been dragged off into exile (v. 4). The enemies that God had once defeated now lord it over them (v. 5, 7). In this misery, Jerusalem is personified as a woman ('widow'; 'princess', v. 1; 'daughter of Zion', v. 6). The 'lovers' metaphor is part of this (v. 2, cf. Jer. 3:1), for Jerusalem is not innocent (cf. v. 5). The personification helps portray not only the sin but also the extreme suffering of the people.

1:8–22 The personification continues in these grim pictures of the violence and humiliation inflicted on the defeated people (1:8, 10–11), and the sense that the humiliation is public (v. 12). Again, sin is acknowledged (vv. 8a, 9a). But even so, Jerusalem appeals to Yahweh, and repeats the pathetic cry that there is 'none to help' or 'comfort' (vv. 9, 16, 17, cf. vv. 7, 21).

The closing appeal to God (vv. 18–22) admits sin, but, in keeping with the lament form, also seeks his punishment on his enemies.

2:1–22: The Lord's anger and the people's grief
2:1–10 The theme here is God's anger against his people. This is a shocking reversal of expectations, for in the past God had shown his anger against Israel's enemies. This reversal of the Holy War idea was also a feature of Jeremiah's prophecy, as we have seen (Jeremiah 21). This poem records the dismantling of the whole nation of Judah and its institutions: temple, sacrifices and pilgrimage-feasts, prophets, law (torah), king (vv. 5–9). (Note also

'footstool', v. 1, a reference to Jerusalem, and possibly the ark of the covenant; cf. Pss 132:7; 99:5.)

2:11–22 The poet's grief now comes to expression. He weeps, as Jeremiah did (v. 11, cf. Jer. 9:1 [8:23]), because the people's grief is also his own. He wants to meet their felt need of a 'comforter' (v. 13, cf. 1:9). His grief has anger in it, because the leaders had failed the people (v. 14). He bewails the mockery of his people by other nations (vv. 16–17). But all this is in fact because the covenant curses are falling on the people for their unfaithfulness (v. 17, cf. Deut. 28:15–68).

The final verses (vv. 20–22) plead in great anguish that the punishment is simply excessive. Yes, the people had sinned, but should they suffer this much?

3:1–66: The poet's suffering and the Lord's compassions

3:1–21 The poet now laments his own suffering. His complaint reminds us of other sufferers: Job (Job 3:11–19; 19:21); Jeremiah (Jer. 20:7). God has deliberately marked him out for torment (cf. especially Psalm 88), and refused to hear his prayer (v. 7), a typical Psalms theme (Ps. 10:1; 13:1 [2]). He has lost all peace (v. 17). But at his lowest point he remembers God's goodness (v. 21).

3:22–39 This mid-point of the present poem and of the book is a hymn to God's compassions. The first key terms (v. 22) are *ḥesed*, 'steadfast love', and *raḥamim*, 'compassion', both celebrated also by the prophets (see Hosea: Theological Themes). God's 'faithfulness' is also essential to his character, for it is that which makes Israel able to trust that he will keep covenant. The poet comes to a confident faith because the

Lord himself is his 'portion' (v. 24; i.e. his blessing or prosperity). In this he is like the psalmist in Ps. 73:26. Present affliction is not the whole story. The faithful should wait for the Lord (vv. 25–26).

This thought is developed in vv. 31–39. God does not willingly afflict human beings. If he punishes sin, he will also have compassion. The order of judgement and compassion here is like what we find in the prophetic books also.

3:40–66 The poet now speaks of 'us' in vv. 40–47, and calls to repentance, the right response to sin according to the prophets (vv. 40–42). This turns again to complaint (vv. 43–47), in contrast to the insight that the faithful must wait for God (vv. 25–26). And v. 48 comes back to the poet's own weeping over the suffering of the people.

The last section (vv. 49–66) again focuses on the poet's own distress, caused now by his personal enemies who have thrown him into a pit (cf. Jer. 38:6), and plot against his life (cf. Jer. 11:19; 18:18). Because of its place in the book, it seems that the poet's suffering stands symbolically for the people's. In his expressions of hope for his own deliverance (vv. 55–60, 64–66), there is hope for the people's.

4:1–22: Siege

4:1–10 This passage depends on a contrast between past and present. A once precious people has become common and worthless (4:2), their beauty ruined (vv. 7–8). At the same time they have been dehumanized, showing less natural affection than animals (v. 3), and even devouring their own young (v. 10). Such were the horrors of the siege, a worse affliction than sudden death or mere famine (vv. 6, 9). Prophets too had depicted the appalling fall from refinement into humiliating poverty (Isa. 3:18—4:1; Amos 4:1–3).

4:11–22 The theme is again the LORD's wrath (v. 11). This has come in spite of the belief (of Judah and also of other nations) that it could not do so (v. 12). The cause is attributed to the faults of the leaders, especially prophets and priests (v. 13, cf. Jer. 6:13–15). The people had misguidedly placed their trust in them, as also in foreign alliances (v. 17) and their own king (v. 20). All had failed to save.

Judah's enemies, typified (here as elsewhere, by Edom, cf. Isaiah 34; Mal. 1:2–6) may rejoice for a little while. But the last note is one of hope, for their turn will come to be destroyed (vv. 21–22).

5:1–22: A people subdued

These poignant pictures of terrible hardship are the opposite of what life in covenant with God should be. The land was an 'inheritance' from Yahweh (v. 2, cf. Deut. 4:21), but is now, ironically, controlled by foreigners. The people who should have been free, and who were called to ensure the good of the disadvantaged (Deut. 14:28–29), are now no better than slaves, permanently disadvantaged themselves (vv. 3–10). The complaint in v. 7 is common (cf. Ps. 79:8), possibly reflecting Exod. 20:5, and coming out of great distress. Past generations had indeed sinned (cf. 2 Kings 17), but the exile generation was wrong to think their punishment was due to those generations alone. This complaint was squarely answered by Jeremiah (Jer. 31:29–30) and Ezekiel (Ezekiel 18; see Joyce 1989).

The pictures of wretchedness in vv. 11–16 reveal a regime of ruthless, cruel oppression, in which all values are inverted. It is the corruption of all that society should be. The prophets said that such a transformation would come as a result of the people's sin (cf. Isa. 3:1–12, and note vv. 9b, 11). Sin is acknowledged here (v. 16b). There is a confession of faith in God as king (v. 19), and a prayer for restoration (v. 21, cf. Jer. 31:18). But the poem, and the whole collection, ends on a bewildered note, without a sign of the reassurance found in 3:22–39. (See Gordis 1974.)

THEOLOGICAL THEMES

COVENANT CURSE AND CONFESSION OF SIN

The underlying assumption in Lamentations is that God is king (5:19), the one who ordains everything, whether good or evil (3:37–39). Closely linked to the idea of God as king in the Old Testament, is the covenant. For it is kings who make covenants, and Yahweh is the 'great king' (cf. Mal. 1:14), who made a covenant with Israel. In all the bitter lamentation, our poet knows that the suffering of Judah is a result of its sin (1:18; 5:16b). And this is because God has brought about the curses of the covenant (2:17, cf. Deut. 28:15–68). All the afflictions known in Lamentations find an echo in that catalogue of curses. In his lamentation, the poet freely admits that Israel has sinned. In this he is in line with the prophets, though not with other laments about the exile (Psalms 44; 74; 79; 80; note especially Ps. 44:17–19, which claims the people is innocent).

The other temptation felt by the sufferer is to blame it all on others. Lamentations flirts with this solution (5:7), but the confessions of sin show the poet knows it is not the whole truth. The most telling confession of sin is probably that one at the end of the central hymn of confidence and praise (3:39). Here the poet agrees entirely with the prophetic view, that punishment is due to sin, and if one must wait for God to turn again in mercy, this is because the time of punishment must come first.

LAMENTATION AND BITTER SUFFERING

While sin is acknowledged, the lamentation has all the other expected elements (complaint against God, lament over personal and communal suffering, complaint about the enemy's oppression and taunts; Westermann 1965, pp.176–81). The admission of sin does not make it any easier to bear the pain. Indeed the poet's protest is as deep and grievous as any psalmist's, and he feels the overwhelming afflictions are excessive and unjustifiable. His appeal to God in 2:20, and implicitly in 5:11–14, calls on God to recognize that there are limits to what is just and tolerable, even in due punishment.

This puts Lamentations among the greatest and boldest protest literature of the Old Testament. It penetrates to the depths of bitter experience, and expresses a sense that humanity should not be subjected to unnatural cruelties, to the point of being utterly crushed (3:17; 5:15). (Joyce (1993) has read Lamentations in relation to the grief process, with reference to E. Kübler-Ross 1970.)

'THE STEADFAST LOVE OF THE LORD'

The final questions of the book express the deepest fear of the lamenter: Have you utterly rejected us? Are you exceedingly angry with us? (5:22). What if God really is absent, and has abandoned us for ever? The final position of these questions gives them a terrible solemnity. Yet the answer to them is already contained in what has gone before: 'For the LORD will not cast off for ever!' (3:31).

The greatest lamentation in the Old Testament also contains one of the greatest confessions of God's love. The ideas are familiar from the prophets, especially Hosea. As the prophets work through Israel's experience of God, from judgement to a renewed relationship with him, the concepts of his steadfast love, compassion and faithfulness are crucially important. So it is for the author of Lamentations. The idiom is different, however. The lament form allows the confession of faith to come from within the experience of suffering. The suffering itself is in no way diminished by this, for it is unequalled in its intensity, and it tends to reassert itself, even when the confession has been made. But just for these reasons the confession of faith, which is also intense, is particularly effective.

The hardest part of the confession was perhaps God's *faithfulness* (3:23). Was it possible to think that God had been faithful to his promises when he had done these things to his people? This was certainly an acute problem for the author of Psalm 89, whose questioning about the exile (vv. 38–51 [39–52]) is carefully designed to call in question God's faithfulness (vv. 1–37 [2–38]).

WAITING FOR GOD

The counterpart of the confession of faith is the spiritual attitude of waiting (3:25–26). We find this theme elsewhere in the prophets (e.g. Habakkuk, and see panel at Mic. 7:8–20). It finds expression also in Psalm 73, another lament in which the psalmist is tempted to think that God has been untrue to his promises. He too finds that there is blessing in patient contentment, and in simply being near God (Ps. 73:23–26). Job too, the best-known Old Testament sufferer, finally bows before God, before he has any prospect of relief from his sufferings (Job 42:1–6). In these moments when the author of Lamentations finds peace, he is close to the Old Testament's superb literature of quiet trust (Psalms 23; 131). Even there, such trust often thinly veils the dangers that threaten life (Ps. 23:4–5).

A COMFORTER

The people in exile had a need to be 'comforted', in the sense of Isa. 40:1. In Isa. 40—55, 'comfort' is a regular expression to describe God's deliverance from exile. In Lamentations the people is still in distress, and seeks someone to 'comfort' (1:9, 16–17). The absence of anyone to do so is a great desolation.

Lamentations is closest to the prophets when it portrays the poet as a sufferer, in terms that remind us of Jeremiah. The poet's suffering is caused, in part at least, by the suffering of the people. This is clear when he longs to be able to meet their need for a comforter (2:13). In 3:40–66 he even seems to bear the sin of the people, again like Jeremiah, and also recalling the Suffering Servant of Isa. 52:13—53:12.

RHETORICAL INTENTION

The power of Lamentations as an act of communication lies in its great intensity, wrapped up in a highly disciplined form, the acrostic (see Critical Interpretation). The form of the poems lies on the surface for all to see, so that we cannot miss the act of composition. It is effective because the intense feeling seems to contrast so sharply with the discipline needed to write the poetry.

Such discipline is no doubt needed for all poetry writing, but the artificiality of the acrostic is a particularly striking case of it.

The use of this form has a number of effects. It was a spiritual discipline for the author (or authors). The acrostic form in general shows the devotion of the poet. As a formal A-Z, it symbolically expresses wholeness. This might mean that it covers the whole subject, or that it expresses the whole devotion of the writer.

In Lamentations there is a further dimension, because of the subject matter. Here the disciplined form may be the only way in which the extreme emotion of the topic may be articulated. Webb calls it 'ordered grief' (Webb 2000, pp. 60–61). The writing of the poem(s) in itself is a triumph of the faith that is expressed at the high point of the book (3:22–39). If the close of the book leaves a doubt about the poet's trust, this is met by the sheer finished presence of the composition.

However, even this must be qualified, because in the final poem (ch. 5) the acrostic form breaks down. The twenty-two-verse length remains, so that the acrostic is shadowed here. (Some have tried to restore an actual acrostic, but this has not met with acceptance.) The form finally also allows the doubt to have its say.

The form should be considered in terms of its effect on an audience as well as on the author. Its power lies in its capacity to express the deep anguish of people. As with all the biblical laments, it allows people to express feelings that they might not even dare to formulate in words. The poet's creativity permits readers to interpret their world in the way in which he leads them. He leads to faith and confession. But there is no compulsion in this, because of the untidiness at the end. The closest Old Testament poem to Lamentations in this respect is Psalm 88, which barely touches base with faith, and finishes on the bleakest of notes. Its power is to reach into the depths of the most disturbed soul, and give the merest contact-point with God. Lamentations can work in a similar way. It may be laid alongside the most traumatic events a broken world can produce, and used to express the most inexpressible grief (see Linafelt 1998). Yet it will not force faith. It is prepared to wait for faith, just as it recommends the sufferer to wait for God.

LAMENTATIONS IN THE CANON

Lamentations, as we have seen, is not the only protest literature in the Old Testament. Its canonical significance lies in its response to the prophetic books in which it is embedded, at least since LXX aligned it with Jeremiah. Among the prophetic books, it hardly expresses a distinctive theology, since it accepts the prophets' analysis of Israel's and Judah's sin and its consequences. However, it allows a different voice to be heard. It is a voice that rarely comes to expression within the prophetic books. The prophets themselves lament, of course. But their lamentation comes from their special insight, from the prophetic role. They are, by definition, outsiders to most people's view of things. When they allow other voices than their own to be heard in their books, those voices are either suspect (e.g. Jer. 3:21–25), or resistant (Mal. 1:2, 6). The voice in Lamentations is not restricted to the poet's own, but stands in a way for all who are addressed in the prophetic books. They were warned of judgement. Now it has

come, and here they speak out of their agony. There is no doubting the authenticity of this voice, for it shouts at us as we read.

The 'lament' form is absent in the New Testament (though indirect allusions to Lamentations may be found, Webb 2000, pp. 79–81). A possible reason for this is that in the New Testament the horizon for possible faith changes, and the cry for 'comfort' is met by Jesus Christ, whose experience of dereliction then resurrection parallels that of the ancient people of faith. If we move from identifying here with the sufferers of Judah to identifying with Jesus' words on the cross: 'My God, my God, why have you forsaken me?', it may be possible to move on with the gospel story to the triumph of the resurrection.

FURTHER READING

Items marked with * are considered suitable as first ports of call, while others are more complex, or relate to specific issues.

COMMENTARIES
D. R. Hillers *Lamentations*. AB. New York: Doubleday, 1972.

*I. W. Provan *Lamentations*. NCB. London: Marshall Pickering, 1991.

OTHER BOOKS AND ARTICLES
D. N. Freedman 'Acrostic Poems in the Hebrew Bible: Alphabetic and Otherwise' *CBQ* 48, 1986, pp. 408–31.

R. Gordis 'The Conclusion of the Book of Lamentations (5:22)' *JBL* 93, 1974, pp. 289–93.

*N. Gottwald *Studies in the Book of Lamentations*. SBT 14. London: SCM, 1962 second edition.

P. Joyce *Divine Initiative and Human Response in Ezekiel*. JSOT Suppl. 51. Sheffield: JSOT Press, 1989.

P. Joyce 'Lamentations and the Grief Process: a Psychological Reading' in *Biblical Interpretation* 1, 1993, pp. 304–20.

E. Kübler-Ross *On Death and Dying*. London: Tavistock, 1970.

T. Linafelt *Surviving Lamentations: Catastrophe, Lament and Protest in the Afterlife of a Biblical Book*. Chicago/London: University of Chicago Press, 2000.

T. Linafelt 'The Impossibility of Mourning: Lamentations After the Holocaust' in T.

Linafelt and T. K. Beal eds *God in the Fray: a Tribute to Walter Brueggemann*. Minneapolis: Fortress Press, 1998, pp. 279–89 .

R. B. Salters *Jonah and Lamentations*. OTG. Sheffield: Sheffield Academic Press, 1994.

B. G. Webb *Five Festal Garments: Christian reflections on the Song of Songs, Ruth, Lamentations, Ecclesiastes and Esther*. NSBT. Leicester: Apollos, 2000.

C. Westermann *Praise and Lament in the Psalms*. Edinburgh: T. & T. Clark, 1965.

Chapter 4

EZEKIEL

DATE AND DESTINATION

PLACE

Ezekiel's is the only prophetic book whose sayings and action happen entirely in Babylon. We have seen, of course, that the prophetic author of Isaiah 40—55 probably lived and worked in Babylon. But his work has been absorbed into a larger book, set mainly in Judah. Daniel, to which we have still to come, is also set in Babylon, but is a different kind of work, as we shall see. So Ezekiel gives us one of the Old Testament's most important glimpses of the exile. In his work, and in the people to whom he spoke, we have an idea of the turmoil caused in people's minds by the terrible loss of temple, city and land. We also see the beginnings of Jewish life without these things.

TIME

Ezekiel's prophecies fall at the early end of the exilic period, unlike those of Deutero-Isaiah, who (apparently) worked close to the end of it. Ezekiel stands closer to Jeremiah. While Jeremiah never went to Babylon (he was taken in the end to Egypt), the young Ezekiel may well have known him, or known of him, in Judah, before he was taken off in Nebuchadnezzar's first wave of exiles in 597

BC. This could explain why some of the things Ezekiel says are quite like sayings and ideas of Jeremiah (e.g. Ezek. 11:19–20, cf. Jer. 31:33; 32:39–40).

CHRONOLOGY IN EZEKIEL

The dates in Ezekiel are part of the difficult question of the dating of the exile. There has been disagreement over whether the fall of Jerusalem occurred in 587 BC or 586 BC (in Ezekiel commentaries, for example, Wevers places it in 586 BC, while Allen prefers 587). It is agreed that Ezekiel followed the Babylonian calendar, in which the new year began in the spring, and not the traditional Israelite calendar, which began in the autumn. This is sometimes thought to solve the problem – but even so, the difference of opinion about the year persists (contrast Wevers 1982, p. 179, and Wiseman 1993, p. 313).

The date of 587 BC gives a difficulty with Ezekiel, because the announcement of the fall of the city in 33:21 seems to come too long after the event (seventeen months). See the different solutions of this in Allen (1990, p. 152; Wevers 1982, p. 179). In the chronology I have adopted, Jerusalem fell in 587 BC (see The dates of kings and prophets).

(For a chronological table of Ezekiel's dated sayings and visions, see Greenberg 1983, p. 10; or Wevers 1982, p. 2).

We first hear Ezekiel's voice in 593 BC, that is, the fifth year of the exile of King Jehoiachin in 597 BC (1:2).

The disaster that had fallen on the city, therefore, was still very fresh. That is, in itself, the great problem that the prophet and others are facing at the time. These are disoriented people, wondering what God has done to them, and what they should expect him to do next. The big issue has changed dramatically since Jeremiah tried to wake people up to the danger that the land might be invaded and they themselves made captive. For the people already in Babylon, these things have now happened.

Yet the events that Jeremiah warned of have not yet fully run their course. For the temple in Jerusalem still stands, and people left behind still worship there. Ezekiel, like Jeremiah, had to preach that the temple would fall. This was so that the exiles, in their early years of separation from the land, might accept that what had happened to them was indeed a work of God's judgement, and that it had only just begun. In the politics of the time, there was some hope that Egypt might regain control of Palestine, and end Babylonian power. This was to prove an illusion. Jeremiah had said that the exile would last seventy years (Jer. 25:11–12), in order to oppose false prophets who tried to play down the seriousness of the situation. And Ezekiel, at the beginning of his prophecy, is having to ram home the same message.

TO WHOM IS HE SPEAKING?

Though he is a prophet to the exiles, Ezekiel reserves his fiercest criticism for Jerusalem itself. In chs 8—11 Ezekiel sees in visions the idolatry being practised in the temple there. The portrayal of the temple, and the actions and people named, make it look as if Ezekiel must have been physically present. Commentators at one time thought that Ezekiel must have exercised at least some of his ministry in Judah, either before he was taken into exile, or by making one or more journeys to Judah from exile (McKeating documents this; 1993, pp. 36–37; cf. Zimmerli 1979, pp. 234–35; Fohrer 1979, pp. 406–08). Another view is that what he is said to have seen in visions was no more than he could have known from the time before he was taken into exile, or found out from later information (Fohrer 1979, p. 407).

But prophets did have visions (cf. e.g. Amos 7:1–8), and they also spoke oracles about cities and nations that were far away, often as if directly addressing them (e.g. Isa. 14:4b–21; Jer. 49:4–5; cf. Greenberg 1983, pp. 15–17). So it is likelier that Ezekiel spoke, as the narrative tells us (8:3), because of visions he was given. As a priest (1:3), he would have had a close knowledge of the temple, so the visions were of very familiar places, and the leading people named were probably people he would have remembered from when he lived in Jerusalem only a few years before.

While the words the prophet speaks in these chapters seem to be directed to the people of Jerusalem, their real audience is the exiles. This is very clear in 11:14–15. There we get an insight into the way people were thinking in Judah and Babylon. Some at least of those who were left in Judah were saying that the exiles had lost their stake in the land that God had promised to Israel in ancient times (v. 15b). They reasoned that as they had not been taken into exile they must be the ones God favoured. (They may have drawn on the official 'Zion-theology' that we outlined in the chapter on Isaiah.) We hear in these verses an echo of a division between the two groups. This is another point at which Ezekiel takes up a teaching of Jeremiah. He had taught that God's plans for a future for his people lay, not with those who had stayed behind in the land, or gone to Egypt, but with the Babylonian exiles (Jeremiah 24). Ezekiel continues this argument. The exiles are the true Israel (v. 15a); and in due course God will bring them back to the land to purify it (11:16–25).

Ezekiel continued to preach in Babylon for twenty-two years. The last dated prophecy is in the twenty-seventh year (29:17), that is, 571 BC. This means that we have words that he spoke well after the temple had fallen. It follows that his message must have changed during that time, since after 587 BC he would no longer have to insist that the temple would fall. This is the usual explanation given for the movement within the book from sayings of judgement to sayings that promise salvation. When the exiles had come to accept the idea that they really were suffering God's punishment, then Ezekiel could begin to emphasize the promise that they would be rescued from their captors and restored to their homeland, even though it would be the next generation that would have that privilege.

The vision of the renewed temple is dated in the twenty-fifth year of the exile, namely 573 BC. This twenty-fifth year could be symbolic (half-way to a jubilee). Furthermore, the date of the latest vision is not necessarily the date of the book (even if we assume Ezekiel is the author of it; see next). It is possible, therefore, that the real audience of Ezekiel's prophecies is late in the exile (see Renz 1999, p. 10). B. S. Childs thinks it is impossible to specify an audience (1979, pp. 357–58).

CRITICAL INTERPRETATION OF EZEKIEL

The unity of thought in Ezekiel has meant that it was common to suppose that Ezekiel himself had written all or most of the book, long after the authorship of the Books of Isaiah and Jeremiah had been questioned (McKeating 1993, pp. 30–31). S. R. Driver, in his classical critical introduction to the Old Testament, could say:

> No critical question arises in connexion with the authorship of the book, the whole from beginning to end bearing unmistakably the stamp of a single mind (1892, p. 261).

Literary criticism, however, found grounds to separate sources. The different settings in Judah and Babylon were one reason for division (but see previous section). Some saw the real Ezekiel as a poet only (as we saw was the case with Jeremiah); and some regarded him as a prophet of doom only. There were doubts about how Ezekiel could be both a prophet and priest. (For a further account, see McKeating 1993, pp. 32–41.)

However, modern criticism of the book has been more influenced by the features that suggest unity. Much current scholarship favours a redaction-critical approach, that is, where a core of the book derives from Ezekiel and this has been gradually expanded into the book that we have today. The chief influence in this direction was the huge commentary of Zimmerli (originally 1969, English 1979; 1983). Zimmerli observed that elements in the book were not simply the written reports of the prophet's speeches, but narrative additions (e.g. 3:15; 11:25; Zimmerli 1979, p. 68). He went on to suppose that the speeches themselves underwent a development. Ezekiel 17 gives an example of his method. The poetic allegory in 17:2–10 has been supplemented by an interpretation in prose 'which must have had in mind the events of 587 BC' (Zimmerli 1979, p. 69).

This process of expansion is attributed to an Ezekiel 'school'. This is because the expansions show so much consistency with Ezekiel's own thought (Zimmerli 1979, pp. 70–71). (This is different from the widely held idea that all the prophetic books have been edited by a single group, the Deuteronomists.) In fact, Zimmerli thinks it is hard to distinguish between the work of the prophet and that of the school and that Ezekiel himself could have been responsible for much of the editing of his own work (1979, p. 71). Other authors have come to similar conclusions (Fohrer 1979; McKeating 1993, p. 45; Greenberg 1997, p. 396; Childs 1979, p. 360–61).

One difficulty of distinguishing between Ezekiel and a hypothetical 'school' lies in the 'scholarly' nature of Ezekiel's own thought (for example in the development of the well-known prophetic marriage metaphor in ch. 16; or the theological discussion arising out of Jeremiah's proverb in ch. 18; see comment below on these passages). The term 'scholarly' is quite suitable for Ezekiel, because he draws consciously on a whole range of theological currents in Israel's traditions. (Zimmerli documents this; 1979, pp. 41–52; more briefly, McKeating reviews the influence of other prophets on Ezekiel; 1993, pp. 92–98.)

The intellectual scope of Ezekiel counsels caution in deciding with certainty what is his and what is not. Greenberg in particular advocates a strongly 'holistic' view of the book (1997, pp. 18–27), and urges alertness to the uniqueness of this book over a range of factors (p. 21).

Digging deeper:
WAS THERE AN EZEKIEL 'SCHOOL'?

We saw that some scholars think an Ezekiel 'school' was responsible for the shaping of the book of Ezekiel. But there have been other ways of thinking about this. Consider some of the arguments used. Note R. E. Clements' criticism of the idea of a 'school', and his own alternative: a final shaping of the book *late* in the exilic period, by someone steeped in the same traditions as Ezekiel (Clements 1982). Wevers has a similar redaction-critical view (1982, pp. 22–30).

Follow up Greenberg's criticism of such views (noted in the previous paragraph). Then see Davis's criticisms of both Zimmerli and Greenberg; 1989, pp. 11–24, as part of her proposal that 'Ezekiel's prophecy was actually conceived in writing' (p. 27).

Consider Ezekiel 16 as an example. Note the criteria used in assessing primary and secondary parts of the chapter (e.g. in Wevers 1982, p. 94).

McKeating (1993, pp. 42–61) gives a helpful overview of critical approaches since Zimmerli.. What do you make of his judgement on Greenberg's holistic and Childs' canonical approaches (pp. 60–61)?

STRUCTURE AND OUTLINE
STRUCTURE
The book of Ezekiel may be divided into three main sections: chs 1—24; chs 25—32; chs 33—48. The first concentrates on the

condemnation of Jerusalem for its unfaithfulness; the second consists of sayings against foreign nations; and the last is dominated by visions of restoration and salvation. The basic structure, therefore, is similar to those of Isaiah and Jeremiah. A message of judgement against Yahweh's own people, Judah, is followed by a larger perspective, in which Yahweh is seen as judge of all the nations. And finally there is the prospect of a better future.

Think about
GOD'S PRESENCE IN EZEKIEL'S STRUCTURE

Notice how this structure can be further illustrated by the important theme of God's presence (see Theological Themes). Compare three visions relating to this theme (1:1—3:15; 8:1—11:25; 40:1—48:35). Note especially the echo of 11:23 in 43:1–2. What do you think Ezekiel is saying about the presence of God by this double journey of God's 'glory' to Babylon and back?

See Outline on chs 8—11.

Another element in the narrative structure is the connections between things that Ezekiel himself reports. For example: 'the word of the LORD came to me' (3:16); 'the hand of the LORD was upon me' (3:22), and numerous references to experiences of 'the spirit' (3:12, 24). Ezekiel's message is bound up with his own life. In the ninth year of the exile (590 BC), Ezekiel's wife dies, and he himself is struck dumb (24:1, 15–17, 25–27). He remains dumb until the city falls (33:21–22). These events in Ezekiel's life parallel the events in the narrative. At this

stage we notice this simply as another example of how carefully the book is structured, with ch. 24 anticipating the report of the fall of the city in ch. 33.

So there is more to the structure of Ezekiel than a simple chapter-division. The architectural quality of the Book of Ezekiel is one of its outstanding features. It may have something to do with the orderly mind of a priest, although that is really just a guess.

With the qualifications just made, the structure of the book may be set out as follows:

1—7	the prophet and the coming fate of Jerusalem
8—11	a vision of Jerusalem's sin
12—15	Ezekiel, elders, prophets
16—24	allegories and parables
25—32	oracles against nations
33—39	Jerusalem falls; oracles of salvation!
40—48	vision of a renewed city, temple and land

OUTLINE
1—7: The prophet and the coming fate of Jerusalem
1:1—3:27 Ezekiel is introduced to us as a priest (1:3). The thirtieth year could refer to his age (1:1), maybe the year in which he would have entered priestly service (cf. Num. 4:3; 1 Chr. 23:3; Allen 1994, p. 20). The River Chebar (1:3) is an unknown place, perhaps remote, where the exiles were settled.

The action begins with a remarkable vision (1:4–28). The vision of the strange creatures and their wheeled chariot leads up to the vision of God enthroned in heaven (1:26–28). Elements in the vision are partly familiar. The creatures with touching wings (v. 11) remind us of the golden cherubim in the inner sanctuary of tabernacle and temple (Exod. 25:18–20; 1 Kgs 6:23–28). The wheeled chariot echoes the chariot that carried the ark in ceremonial procession (2 Sam. 6:3). The creatures are like the 'seraphim' that surround God's throne in Isaiah's vision, with wings stretched out and others covering their body (v. 11; Isa. 6:2). The creatures have mainly human features (v. 4b, 10a), but mixed with other beasts (vv. 6–10), symbolizing all creation.

God's presence is denoted by fire (v. 13, cf. Isa. 6:6; Exod. 19:18). The movement of the chariot expresses his freedom to go and be wherever he wishes. The vision of God himself is surrounded in mystery. The observer's eye is drawn up above the creatures and chariot, above a 'dome' (the same word as used for the 'dome', or 'firmament' of the sky in Genesis 1:7), to unimaginable height. Even the language ('the appearance of the likeness of . . .') puts God at due distance. Yet the divine figure is also human-like (v. 26), in an inverted echo of humanity as being 'in the image and likeness of God' (Gen. 1:26).

The vision cannot be fully imagined, being a powerful impression of the unimaginable God. If it is 'out of focus' (Clements 1996, pp. 12–13) this is in keeping with its subject.

Chapters 2—3 tell of the prophet's call, addressed to him as 'son of man', as regularly in the book. The meaning of this is simply 'human being' (hence 'mortal', NRSV); it is not a messianic term here (contrast Dan. 7:13). We are also told that 'the spirit' (or 'a spirit', NRSV) came into him. The spirit will play an important part in his prophetic experience. In 3:12–14 it physically lifts him up, and later it will transport him to Jerusalem in visions (8:3). He is to carry words of judgement to a rebellious people. This familiar kind of mission (cf. Isa. 6:9–10; Jer. 1:17–19) applies to the exiles in particular (3:9–11). The message given him is to become part of him, as symbolized by the eating of the scroll (2:8—3:3; cf. Jer. 15:16). The 'sweetness' is odd and unexpected, but means that the truth and goodness of what God seeks and intends exceeds the pain of the present judgement. Ezekiel is bound over to be faithful to his calling as a watchman, and will be held responsible for the fate of his people if he is not (3:16–21). He is personally overwhelmed by the vision of the glory that he has seen (3:23), and will be able to speak only with God's permission (3:25–26).

4:1—7:27 In 4:1—5:4 Ezekiel performs four symbolic actions, vividly picturing the coming siege and destruction of Jerusalem. Prophets before him had performed such actions (e.g. Isaiah 20; Jer. 13:1–11; 18–19). Ezekiel's acts involve his own person in a way that seems shocking (especially 4:4–8). This too is not new (Hosea had married a prostitute, Hos. 1:2; Jeremiah was forbidden to marry, Jer. 16:2). Ezekiel combines symbolic act and personal suffering more than any other, and the visual side of his message is more pronounced. There is a priestly aspect to his suffering in the phrase 'bear the punishment' (4:5–6; cf. Exod. 28:38; Lev. 16:22), which hints that Ezekiel's suffering had an atoning effect for Israel. (On the lengths of time in 4:5–6, see Greenberg 1983, pp. 105–6.)

The reasons for the punishment are breach of God's covenant, with its 'statutes and ordinances' (5:6), a phrase common in Deuteronomy, the Old Testament's greatest document on the covenantal law (see e.g. Deut. 4:1–8). The central offence is idolatry (5:11), which breaks the first and second commandments (Exod. 20:3–6). Some of the

Think about
PROPHETIC SYMBOLIC ACTIONS

Try to visualize Ezekiel's performance of the siege of Jerusalem. What is signified a) by Ezekiel lying down; b) by his bared arm (cf. Deut. 4:34; Jer. 21:5)? Does he represent the suffering of Jerusalem, or the anger of God – or both?

Why do you think symbolic actions were thought effective? What does it tell us about how to understand the 'word of God'?

For help in answering this question see W. D. Stacey 1990, pp. 260–82 (reprinted in Gordon 1995, pp. 112–32). Stacey reviews some possible understandings of symbolic actions, and especially shows the inadequacy of the idea that they are just 'visual aids'. J. Lindblom 1962, pp. 165–73, also gives a general explanation of symbolic actions, though he deals at length there with Hosea's marriage. (The following passage in Lindblom, on 'The Revelatory State of Mind', pp. 173–82, is also relevant to Ezekiel.) Further short treatments are in Sawyer 1993, pp. 11–13; Petersen 1981, pp. 30–34.

language is familiar from Hosea and Deuteronomy (Ezek. 6:13, cf. Hos. 4:13; Deut. 12:2; Ezek. 5:11, cf. Deut. 12:31; 29:17 [Heb 16]). The punishments come in the triad well known from Jeremiah: sword, famine and plague (5:12a, 17; 6:12), with exile added (5:12b; cf. Jer. 15:2).

Ezekiel promises that a small remnant would survive (5:1–4; 6:8–10; cf. Isa. 6:13c; 10:20–21; Jer. 6:9). This should encourage the exiles, in the midst of the terrible judgement sayings. Chapter 7 has further conventional messages of judgement. Verses 26–27 are notable because they show that the accusation and judgement affect all levels of society. In this chapter we meet the phrase: 'And they shall know that I am the LORD' (7:27), which becomes a refrain in the book. The judgement is intended to lead to better knowledge of God. The cry 'End!' (7:2; cf. Amos 8:2) seems unconditional, but is qualified by the promises of survivors both before and after (cf. 9:4).

8—11: A vision of Jerusalem's sin
These chapters are carefully constructed to portray the situation in Jerusalem from the perspective of Babylon. They tell the story of Ezekiel's vision-journey to Jerusalem and back to Babylon (8:3; 11:24–25). He is taken by a figure that looks human, but is evidently a heavenly being (8:2). This is the first Old Testament occurrence of the idea of a superhuman guide, which is developed by apocalyptic books (cf. Dan. 10:5–6). It is the 'spirit' that actually transports Ezekiel, however (cf. 3:12–14).

Ezekiel's journey is matched by a journey of God. His 'glory', the symbol of his presence, progresses gradually from the inner sanctuary (9:3) to the threshold of the house, where the cherubim-chariot awaits (10:18), then to the east gate of the temple (10:19), to the mountain east of Jerusalem (the Mount of Olives; 11:23). This second vision of the creatures (10:1, 9–21 – now called cherubim, 10:1) has the purpose of showing this progress of God towards Babylon. The picture is completed by 10:15, which shows that these were the creatures Ezekiel had seen in Babylon.

The images in ch. 8 depict various forms of worship that offend Yahweh's command that he alone should be worshipped, and that images should not be made, not only of him, but of any living creature for the purpose of worship (Exod. 20:3–5). The people and their leaders clearly brought in aspects of the worship of other gods than Yahweh. The cults of Tammuz (8:14, a dying and rising god) and the sun (8:16) were widespread in the ancient Near East.

In ch. 9, the six executioners and the man clothed in linen with the writing-case probably represent Babylonian soldiers and an official (Clements 1996, pp. 40–41). The official marks out some to be spared (v. 3). These military and political figures are put in a special light, however, recast as agents of Yahweh's anger. The depiction is in line with the concept of God using foreign powers for his purposes of judgement and salvation (like Assyria, Babylon and finally Cyrus in Isaiah). The theological perspective in 9:4 overwrites the political one: the official will have had his own reasons for sparing people, but Ezekiel puts another light on it. That is, God spares those who lament the false worship from the heart. The man's book also has echoes of the 'book of life' passages (Exod. 32:32; Ps. 69:28 [*Heb* 29]). There may also be echoes of the Passover (Exod. 12:29–32).

The LORD's departure from the temple in ch. 10 is followed by another reassurance that he will spare a remnant, namely those who have gone into exile (11:13, 14–17). They will be renewed spiritually, so that they will be God's obedient people truly, from the heart (11:19–20), an echo of Jeremiah's New Covenant idea (Jer. 31:31–34). With the destruction of the physical temple, God himself is a 'sanctuary' to the exiles for a time (11:16). This further spiritualization has the irony that the true 'sanctuary' is not in Jerusalem but on foreign, enemy soil.

12—15: Treachery in Babylon

The focus in these chapters switches back to Babylon. It becomes clear that the exiles themselves are rebellious too, just like the people back in Jerusalem (12:2). When the 'elders of Israel' in Babylon come to Ezekiel to consult him (14:1–3), they probably want him to give oracles that promise that salvation will come quickly (just as King Zedekiah was asking Jeremiah to do as the Babylonian armies besieged Jerusalem in the last days before its destruction; Jer. 21:1–2). But the LORD says they have idolatry in their hearts (14:3, 4, 7), so they are still a long way from the 'heart of flesh' that God wants to give his renewed people (11:19).

The main aim of these chapters is to reinforce the point that Jerusalem will soon fall. When Ezekiel acts out a going into exile (12:3–7) he means that there will be more exiles yet from Judah. King Zedekiah will be among them (vv. 10, 12). He is here called a 'prince', not a full king, because in political reality he was a mere puppet of Babylon. (The king is called *naśi'* also in 21:25 [30]; 34:24; 37:25, and several times in chs 45—48.) The reference in 12:12 is to his attempted escape and blinding (2 Kgs 24:4–7).

Ezekiel's message is opposed here to all who think the judgement will not come, whether by popular wisdom (12:21–28), or by false prophets, 'who prophesy out of their own imagination' (literally 'hearts'; 13:17, possibly 13:2, see NRSV; see also Jer. 23:16), or by divination (13:17–23).

On the contrary, the end is certain to come, because God has decreed it. Chapter14:9 contains one of the strongest statements of this in the book (cf. 20:25–26, and see Theological Themes: Sovereignty of God).

Noah, Daniel and Job are named as well-known righteous people (all non-Israelite; Daniel is probably not the Daniel of the Old Testament book, but a figure of antiquity, known in the Canaanite Ugaritic texts; see *ANET*, 'The Tale of Aqhat', pp. 149–55. See also Ezek. 28:3). Noah's righteousness was so great that because of him the LORD did not destroy the world entirely. But he will destroy Judah. The language of destruction is like that of Leviticus 26, where it is in the form of covenantal curses (the land is desolate, because of the *faithlessness*, or treachery, of the people; Ezek. 14:13; 15:8, cf. Lev. 26:32–35, 40).

Think about
INTERCESSION

One of the prophets' roles was prayer for the people (Gen. 20:7; Exod. 32:11–14). Ezek. 14:13–20 is sometimes compared with Jer. 15:1–2 (see Jeremiah: Outline). What are the similarities and differences between these two passages?

God has two aims in taking the people into exile. First, he will demonstrate his own justice. This is the point of the repeated 'they will know that I am the LORD' (12:15, 16, 20; cf. 14:23). It applies even to 12:16, where survivors are sent to exile simply as witnesses to God's judgement on their sin. Second, punishment is not the whole story, for he intends to create a cleansed and renewed people (14:21–23; cf. again Lev. 26:40–45)

16—24: Allegories and parables
16:1–63 The idea of Israel as an unfaithful bride (ch. 16) is taken over from Hosea (Hosea 1—3) and Jeremiah (Jer. 2:2—3:14).

The point of the metaphor is that Israel, once 'married' to God in covenant, became unfaithful by taking other 'lovers', that is, by worshipping the gods of other nations. In a grotesque development of this, Ezekiel takes the image of Israel as a woman to an extreme, depicting graphically the physicality of birth, maturity (vv. 4–7) and marriage consummation (vv. 8–9). Various elements in the tradition are taken further in this vivid depiction: for example, God's gifts prostituted to other gods (16:16–21; Hos. 2:8 [10]); the 'lovers' named (vv. 26–28); the faithless sister Israel (Jer. 3:6–7) becomes a family of mother and sisters (vv. 45–46)!

The twists to the familiar theme are designed to shock: where Jeremiah had promised that God would 'restore the fortunes' of Israel (29:14), Ezekiel applies this to others (16:53; but note Jer. 48:47). The extreme language is designed to shock people out of their complacency. After it, the restoration and forgiveness are remarkable, but even in them there will be shame (v. 63), now in penitence (contrast v. 52).

Think about
JERUSALEM AS FEMALE

Julie Galambush (1992) argues that Ezekiel's female personification of Jerusalem in chs 16 and 23 associates women with infidelity and pollution. Do you think this imagery does betray a patriarchal view of women as inferior? Or is it 'just' a metaphor?

See Isaiah: Outline on Isa. 5:1–7, and the panel there on the Song of the Vineyard, for pointers on the prophets' use of metaphor.

17:1–24 The background of ch. 17 is very like that of 12:1–16, Zedekiah's rebellion against Babylon, and his punishment. Again, traditional images are used in the poetic allegory' (vv. 3–10; cf. Ps. 80:8–19 [9–20]; Isa. 2:12–13).

Digging deeper:
TWO POLITICAL ALLEGORIES

1. Consider how the political issues behind Ezekiel 17 are represented in the allegory. Who are the 'eagle', the 'top of the cedar', and the 'seed' (vv. 3–5)?

2. What attitude to kingship in Israel do you find in ch. 17? Levenson (1976, pp. 77–84) thinks Ezekiel's allegory is based on Jotham's fable in Judges, which is critical of kingship, but differently developed. How does Ezekiel's view differ from Jotham's? Is Ezek. 17:22–24 messianic?

3. Is the point of view the same in the allegory in ch. 19? Use a commentary to identify the characters. What is the significance of vv. 11, 14 in relation to Gen. 49:10?

18:1–32 Chapters 18 and 20 form an unusual contrast and counterpoint. Each is crucial to the thought of the book in its own way. The argument in ch. 18 is that each person is responsible for his/her own life before God. In context, the 'individualism' probably refers to the responsibility of each generation. This is in answer to the fatalistic belief that the fate of a generation is beyond its control (the proverb in v. 2 expresses this, taken over from Jer. 31:29–30). To the exiles, this would mean that they had been punished for the sins of previous generations. Chapter 18 opposes this with Ezekiel's usual

rigour. The aim of the argument is twofold: to show that God is just (vv. 25–29); and to encourage the exiles that they do have a future with God if they repent (vv. 30–32; cf. 11:19–20).

Digging deeper:
DIVINE INITIATIVE AND HUMAN RESPONSE

Consider further the interpretation of Ezekiel 18 as addressing the exilic *generation*. Read Paul Joyce 1989, pp. 33–60. How does the message of ch. 18 fit with other parts of the book, e.g. 14:13–20, and 11:19–20?

20:1–44 The bleak picture in ch. 20 is Ezekiel's response to an enquiry by a deputation of the exiles' elders (vv. 1–3). We do not know what they asked; perhaps, as some have thought, they were considering building a temple to Yahweh in Babylon. Whatever their plan, Ezekiel dismissed it scathingly as idolatrous (vv. 30–32).

Ezekiel's version of Israel's past history with God is his way of answering the elders. It is a terrible litany of the people's unfaithfulness. Here again, everything is put in extreme terms. Ezekiel has no memory of a golden age in Israel's relationship with God (contrast Hos. 2:14–15 [16–17]; Jer. 2:2–3). God many times held back from punishing them only 'for the sake of his name' (vv. 8–9, 13–14). While ch. 18 stressed the responsibility of each person, or each generation, for their own life before God, ch. 20 portrays the people down the ages as having a solidarity in sin against God. The present generation, because of its intentions, is shown to be part of this picture.

But God's power will prevail. Verses 25–26 contain another strong statement that everything that happens to Israel is under his control (cf. 14:9; and see Theological Themes: Sovereignty). The promised future salvation also reflects this (vv. 33–44). But it comes with strong warnings to be faithful. Chapter 20 is in the end like ch. 18: both aim to persuade the exiles not to be like their ancestors, and to turn to God in truth.

Think about
EZEKIEL 20 AS 'RHETORIC'

Ezekiel 20 poses problems for the reader. We saw that it differs from Hosea and Jeremiah in its depiction of Israel's history. The statement in v. 25 seems perverse. Does it help to think of this chapter in terms of its rhetorical effect? Notice especially how the chapter nears its climax with a well-known refrain: 'You shall know that I am the LORD' (v. 44), which usually occurs in judgement contexts.

20:45—24:27 The sayings in this section lead inexorably to the climax in 24:25–27, which points to the news that the city has fallen. Note the 'news' in 21:7, with its echo in 24:26. The tone of these chapters is all judgement, with no more pointers to salvation. When Ezekiel 'moans' (21:6–7) he is anticipating the terrible news of the fall of Jerusalem, and the effect it will have on the exiles in Babylon. The first major part of Ezekiel's message is coming to a head.

The sayings in these chapters are mixed. The attack on Jerusalem is vividly imagined (ch. 21). (There is a hint that Babylon will be punished in its turn in 21:30–32. And 21:28 anticipates 25:1–7. Ezekiel 21:27 [32] has

been taken messianically, because of a supposed echo of Gen. 49:10. However, the sense requires a threat rather than a promise; Wevers 1982, p. 127.) Accusations are piled up in ch. 22, mixing ritual and moral offences, rather like Leviticus 19 (there are also echoes of Leviticus 18 and 20 in the sexual sins within families; 22:10–11). There is an emphasis on ritual 'uncleanness' and 'profanation', reflecting Ezekiel's priestly perspective (22:15–16; 24:12–13). Chapter 23 returns to the prostitution metaphor as in ch. 16. The metaphor shades over into pictures of the violence and rape that accompanies defeat by foreign armies.

Ezekiel's own life has been used to exemplify his message. Now it does so in a terrible way. His wife, 'the delight of your eyes' (God's words to Ezekiel, 24:15) dies, in a picture of the destruction of the temple, also 'the delight of your eyes' (Ezekiel's words to the people, 24:21). Ezekiel is now dumb until the day when the news comes (in 33:21). There is no more to be said.

25—32: Oracles Against the Nations
The three major prophets have extensive sections of OAN (see Isa. 13—27; Jer. 46—51, which have oracles against all the nations mentioned here; cf. also Amos 1—2). The general reasons for them are to show that all nations are in God's power, and responsible for acting justly in obedience to his law.

Ezekiel's choice of nations is partly traditional, but reflects current events. Of the smaller nations, Moab and Ammon had taken advantage of Judah in the final siege (2 Kgs 24:2; and cf. Jer. 41:11–18, noting v. 15). But two nations dominate the series, Tyre (Phoenicia) and Egypt. The sea power of Tyre was besieged by Babylon for thirteen years beginning soon after Jerusalem fell

(586–573 BC), and suffered greatly but held out (29:17–20). The reason for opposing Tyre may have been Ezekiel's perception that Babylon was God's instrument of judgement in the region at the time. Egypt, as we saw in both Isaiah (19—20; 30:1–4; 31:1–3) and Jeremiah (21—24; 40—44), was a focus of resistance to Babylon.

Babylon itself is a striking omission from this catalogue, in contrast to Isaiah's and Jeremiah's extensive criticisms (Isa. 13:1—14:27; Jeremiah 50—51). Ezekiel has perhaps taken his cue from Jeremiah's concept that salvation for the Jews lay through submitting to Babylon, and in resisting the temptation to trust in Egypt (Jeremiah 24). Unlike the two other great prophets, he does not go on to say that Babylon would meet its own punishment at God's hands in due course (though there is a hint of this in 21:30–32).

A high point in these oracles is the splendid portrayal of the pride of Tyre and its king. Like Isaiah in his oracle against Babylon (Isa. 14:12–20), Ezekiel (in 28:11–19) uses a myth about a fallen angel from 'Eden' (v. 13), or the 'mountain of God' (v. 14), to depict this king's overweening pride.

Think about
THE OAN AS RHETORIC

What effect do the OAN have, coming at this point in the prophecy? Do they delay the forward movement of the book in a dramatic way? Notice what will be the main event in the chapter immediately following. How is the fall of Jerusalem put in the context of God's wider action and plans?

In the midst of these prophecies we find an affirmation that Judah will be saved (28:25–26; 29:21). The latter text – 'I will cause a horn to sprout up for the house of Israel' – echoes Ps. 132:17, a messianic promise ('sprout' is akin to the noun 'branch' that is also used messianically in Jer. 23:5; Zech. 6:12).

33—39: Jerusalem falls; oracles of salvation!
33:1—37:28 Curiously, the news of the fall of the city unlocks a series of prophecies of salvation. Chapter 33, having re-emphasized Ezekiel's special responsibility (33:2–9, cf. 3:16–21), carefully spells out that words of judgement need not be final (33:10–20): God in his justice will save the penitent. The news comes (vv. 21–22), and Ezekiel can speak again. The critical saying that follows (33:23–33) once more justifies the punishment in order to lead into the new promises.

Chapter 34 is an extended meditation on Jer. 23:1–6. God himself will 'shepherd' his people in place of the wicked 'shepherds' (ruling classes; 34:1–10, 15). The messianic Davidic king (Jer. 23:5–6) is now cast as God's appointed 'shepherd' too, under God (34:23–24). The 'sheep' will not only have shepherds, but a good and fruitful land (13–14; 25–31). The lavish pictures of plenty echo other prophetic visions (cf. Isaiah 35; Hos. 2:18 [20]), and some Psalms (Psalm 72). The point of these visions is that the ancient promises of a bountiful land (e.g. Deut. 8:7–10) will at last be fulfilled again.

The salvation of Israel is a vindication before those who tormented and despised them. Edom (35:1—36:7; note 35:15; 36:7, 13–15) serves to typify Israel's enemies (note 36:5), as it does in Isaiah 34. Moreover, God himself will no longer be despised by other nations. His reason for saving Israel can even be seen as his action for his own reputation (36:22–23).

The restoration of Israel is expressed in several theological ways. It is a story of ritual defilement (36:16–21) and cleansing (36:23–25). That is, Israel's sin is seen in 'holiness' terms, as we might expect from Ezekiel the priest. Sin defiled people and thus the land, which 'vomited them out' (Lev. 18:24–30). The exile came as a result of the profanation of the land (36:20), and restoration is a purification (vv. 23–25). But the renewed salvation is also a new creation (like the 'garden of Eden', 36:35), and like the New Covenant (36:26–28; cf. 11:19–20; Jer. 31:31–34). The story of salvation is told as a contrast to the former judgement, to emphasize the grace of God

See the panel on Israel's return to its land, in Jeremiah: Theological Themes.

The famous vision of the valley of dry bones (37:1–14) is another image of God's completely new act of salvation. The valley could be a real battlefield. The graphic picture of bones being reassembled is typical of Ezekiel's stark imagery. The coming of the 'breath', or 'spirit', into the bodies recalls the first human creation (Gen. 2:7). God can save and renew Israel, even though it was hopelessly sinful. This is not a doctrine of personal resurrection in the later sense, yet the assumption behind it is the same; God who created can recreate.

The vision is integrated into the thought of chs 34—36. In 37:15–28 it is interpreted to mean that a unified Israel will once more live in its own land, under a Davidic king. Interestingly, David is actually called 'king' here (37:24), though the term 'prince' is preferred elsewhere (e.g. 34:23–24; ch. 45), and even in the present verses, as if to qualify it, the term 'king' is quickly followed by 'prince' (v. 25). In their land, under their king-prince, they will also have once more God's temple in their midst (37:28). These verses anticipate the themes of chs 40—48.

38:1—39:29 The promises of salvation will continue with the vision of the temple in chs 40—48. But once again the action is held back by an interlude concerning foreign nations (as chs 25—32 held back the news of Jerusalem's fall in 33:21). These chapters are different from chs 25—32. They concern a period after the people have resettled in the land, and picture an invasion by an overwhelmingly mighty army (38:4–6). The narrative tells how that army would be defeated by God, and that by delivering them from this attack, he will once again show that he is God, and will always be faithful to his people (39:25–29). (Note how Gog's burial, 39:11–14, has an ironic echo of 37:1–14.)

Magog is mentioned in Gen. 10:2, in a broadly 'European' grouping of primeval nations (see Wenham 1987, pp. 216–17). While Gog has been seen as a reference to Alexander the Great, among others (see Clements 1996, p. 170), he cannot be identified, nor can an occasion that the prophet may have had in mind. Some scholars think the vision must be dated to a time after Ezekiel, when there was a real threat to the post-exilic community (Clements 1996, p. 170). Others treat at least a core of it as from Ezekiel, so that it does concern a still-future situation (see Allen 1990, pp. 202–04, and his account there of theories of redaction of the chapters).

The chapters include themes from other prophecies in new ways. The enemy is raised up by God for God's purpose, but has his own evil plans (38:10–16), just like Assyria in Isaiah's day (Isa. 10:5–11). Isaiah provides a number of other motifs, such as the re-inhabiting of waste places (38:12, cf. Isa. 49:19), and the turning of weapons into implements for peaceful purposes (39:9–10; Isa. 2:2–4). In this way, Ezekiel builds on past instances of God's actions in both judgement and salvation. In doing so, he says that, in a final great showdown between good and evil, God will give victory and salvation to his faithful people. The vision is taken up in the Book of Revelation to make a similar point in anticipation of the final victory of Christ over the forces of evil (Rev. 20:7–10). That is the true horizon of

Digging deeper:
ON THE REINTERPRETATION OF PROPHECIES

Ezekiel 38—39 draws on previous prophecies, and also feeds into later writings. We have noticed some of these links already. Follow up further allusions to other prophecies in Ezek. 39:8 (cf. Isa. 2:12); 39:17–20 (cf. Isa. 25:6–12); 38:15 (cf. Jer. 6:1); (39:25; cf. Jer. 29:14); 38:8, 16 (cf. Isa. 2:2).

What do these links tell us about how traditional ideas and beliefs were re-used and developed by the prophets? For example, in 39:17–20 (cf. Isa. 25:6–12), in what particular ways has the image of the feast on the 'mountains of Israel' been developed? (On 'mountains of Israel', cf. Isa. 14:25.) How should we read Ezek. 39:18, in view of Lev. 17:10–16?

Also consider Dan. 11:40–45. This could be influenced in turn by Ezekiel 38—39, as Rev. 20:7–10 would be even later.

this vision; it should not be considered a veiled account of specific events in the modern world.

40—48: Vision of a renewed city, temple and land
The book comes to its close with a vision of the future Israel, with a renewed temple at its centre. The temple itself is described (40:1—43:9); regulations for the community's life are then given (43:10—46:24), and finally the vision expands to the whole land.

40:1—42:20 The description of the temple takes place in another vision of Ezekiel, as in chs 8—11 (40:2). It is dated in the twenty-fifth year of the exile (40:1), a number suggesting the exiles are halfway to a 'jubilee', that is, a release and restoration (cf. Lev. 25:9–10; Allen 1990, p. 229). The 'very high mountain' (40:2) is a reference to Mt Zion, yet with mythological overtones (see Theological Themes).

The proportions of the temple are revealed in great detail, as were those of the tabernacle to Moses (Exod. 25:1—31:17). In receiving such instructions, Ezekiel is like a new Moses. The care for such details comes from a concern to deal properly with holy things. The pattern is not quite like either the tabernacle or the temple of Solomon; for example, the rooms for the priests north and south of the temple courtyard (42:1–20) are new. It has been questioned whether Ezekiel's vision was meant to be practical, or was ideal only. Ezekiel might not have distinguished in this way.

43:1—46:24 With the renewed temple in place it is time for the glory of God to return to his dwelling-place, which he had left because of its corruptions (43:1–5; cf. 9:4; 11:1, 23). This completes an important narrative arc. God has been a 'sanctuary' to his people 'for a little while' in exile (11:16); the vision points to the end of that time, and God dwelling in Jerusalem once more. The spirit is part of this pattern too: as it had taken Ezekiel on his first vision-journey to Jerusalem, it now does so again (43:5).

The vision continues with instructions for altar, sacrifice, priesthood, the 'prince' and the annual festivals. Therefore, Ezekiel's programme provides for all the elements of Israel's religious life that the Pentateuchal law-codes did. The priesthood has a hierarchy, as in Numbers 3—4. Here the Zadokites have the priestly role because they are regarded as faithful (44:15), and the Levites' lesser role is attributed to an unspecified sin (44:10–14; see the 'Digging deeper' box). The priests and Levites are to occupy an area around the temple in the middle of the land (45:1–6). The 'prince' (*nasi*') also has holdings alongside the priestly land (45:7–8; for a diagram of how this looks, see Levenson 1976, p. 120). There are rules for atonement (cf. the Day of Atonement, Leviticus 16), Feasts of Passover and Unleavened Bread, and the sabbath.

In Ezekiel's Israel, priests and prince govern the religious life. Ezekiel himself is the only prophetic figure, like Moses in Deuteronomy (Deut. 18:15–20). There is no high priest. And the king has become a 'prince' (Hebrew *nasi*'), which makes him like a tribal chief from Mosaic times (cf. Numbers 2, throughout). This seems to warn against a too-powerful monarchy, and to insist that the political chief is subject to the Sinai covenant and law of Moses. (See Levenson 1976, pp. 57–69; 111–25.) Similarly, K. R. Stevenson argues that the spatial geography of Ezekiel aims 'to restructure society from pre-exilic monarchy to a post-exilic temple

society without a human king' (1996, p. 160). And S. S. Tuell sees Ezekiel 40—48 as a 'polity', 'like Deuteronomy and the Book of the Covenant' (1992, p. 275).

ROLES OF PRIESTS AND LEVITES

The respective roles of priests and Levites in Ezekiel 44 are striking, because Zadok is in the place of Aaron, and the priest-Levite division is made for quite different reasons than those given in Numbers 3—4. This has suggested to scholars that some controversy about the legitimacy in the priesthood lies behind Ezekiel 44. And in the critical reconstruction of Israel's history that prevailed for a century after Wellhausen, Ezekiel has been seen as the first to demote the Levites, and thus as a staging-post on the way to the structure of the priesthood found in Numbers 3—4 ('P'). In addition it has seemed to scholars that a contemporary controversy has intruded into Ezekiel's vision.

Allen reviews the discussion (1990, pp. 249–56). Levenson thinks the regulations are in line with Ezekiel's basic vision, and that the underlying concern is the equality of all Zadokite priests; there is no high priest here (contrast Lev. 21:10–14; Levenson 1976, pp. 129–44). A recent full-length discussion is found in Duguid 1994. See also Duke, 'Punishment or Restoration', for the view that Ezekiel 44 does not demote the Levites, but honours them.

47:1—48:35 The river that flows from the threshold of the temple to fill the land is an extravagant image based on a motif in the Zion-theology of a river in Jerusalem (Pss 36:8 [9]; 46:4 [5]). This does not correspond to real geography, but is a mythological motif in which rivers are at the source of all life (cf. Gen. 2:10–14). The dwelling of the gods is a 'cosmic mountain', which is also the source of the primeval rivers (Clifford 1972, pp. 131–60). In 38:12, Zion is called the

polemic against Babylonian gods is not a prominent theme in Ezekiel as it is in Isaiah (there are hints of Babylonian religious influence in 13:17–23; and Ezekiel's response to the elders in ch. 20 implies they are coming under similar influence). And the visions of God's enthronement are not a simple spiritualization of God's presence. In all the portrayals of God's presence in the book, Ezekiel uses imagery and language from the world of priest and temple. So when Ezekiel sees that God can still be 'present' even though the temple is in ruins, this is not an abstract theory of the divine presence. Rather, the presence is specifically with the exiles, who will be the core of the renewed Israel. In this way the presence theme is tied in with Ezekiel's narrative of salvation.

Moreover, the visions of the cherubim-throne do not mean that Ezekiel cares nothing for the temple. This is clear when God says that he himself will be a 'sanctuary' for the exiles during their time in Babylon (11:16), and from the final vision (chs 40—48), in which he sees the future of Israel in connection with a renewed temple. He establishes a continuity of God's presence throughout the crisis of the exile until the restoration to the land. (See also Salvation below, on the nature of the programme of restoration.)

SIN, JUDGEMENT, PURIFICATION

We saw above (Sovereignty of God) that Ezekiel stresses the sovereignty of God in judgement and salvation. Ezekiel aims to make a clean break with the past. Israel had for generations rebelled against God, and was now being judged for its sin. When Ezekiel insists that Jerusalem will fall, he is not just making a tactical point (to stop wishful thinking about a quick end to the exile), but he is showing that the 'old Israel'

(represented by the terrible corruption in the temple, chs 8—11) has come to a complete end (the term 'old Israel' is used by Renz 1999 e.g. pp. 142, 160, 182).

We have seen, in relation to the 'presence' theme, that Ezekiel typically uses language and images drawn from Israel's 'religious' world. He does so too in the realm of sin and judgement. Israel's sin is portrayed as defilement or profanation of the holy. These concepts belong in the world of temple, priests, sacrifices and holy events. People might be unable to come into the 'holy' sphere of worship because of some 'uncleanness'. This could be caused by a range of conditions or circumstances, such as injury or conditions related to sex and childbirth (Leviticus 12—15). Uncleanness must not come into contact with the 'holy'. Those who were ritually unclean could be made 'clean' again, by various purification rituals.

Digging deeper:
'HOLINESS'

Holiness is a potentially misleading term for Christian readers of the Old Testament. For explanations of the theology of holiness in Israel's religion, see Wenham 1979, pp. 18–25, or (in more detail) Jenson 1992, pp. 40–55.

For Ezekiel the priest, Israel's sins have made them 'unclean' (22:15a). This does not mean they are guilty only of 'religious' sins in the strict sense. Their sins were both religious (e.g. ch. 8) and moral (they did not keep the 'statutes and ordinances', that is, the covenant laws, 20:11–13; cf. 34:3–4). Ezekiel often speaks of Israel's sin in general as 'rebellion' (e.g. 2:5–8), meaning that they have rejected God, who had known them personally in a covenant relationship. In this he is similar to Isaiah (Isa. 1:2–4).

However, Ezekiel uses language about idolatry to portray Israel's unfaithfulness ('abominations', 'detestable things', 20:4, 8; cf. Deut. 7:25–26; Hos. 9:10; 2 Kgs 23:13, 24). They defiled the land of Israel by their sins (36:16); and they defiled the name of God among other nations because the nations thought the destruction of Jerusalem and Judah meant that he was weak (36:20–22). God's action in judgement, therefore, is a purification, or ritual cleansing (22:15b; 36:25). This removal of ritual uncleanness can be a 'purging', referring to judgement by itself (22:17–22; contrast Isaiah's use of the smelting image, where the result is a renewed people; Isa. 1:21–26). But it can also be a cleansing restoration (36:25, where it is part of the giving of a new heart, vv. 26–27). Finally, in saving Israel, God 'sanctifies' his name, that is, he makes it holy again (36:23).

SALVATION: A RADICALLY NEW BEGINNING; ZION AND EDEN

As we have seen, Ezekiel aimed to show that there had to be a completely new start. God himself would ensure this by giving the renewed people a 'heart of flesh', so that they would be able to keep his commandments, and so they could once again occupy the holy land (11:19–20; 36:26–28). The theology of this is very like that of Jeremiah's 'New Covenant' (see on Jer. 31:31–34 in this volume). In Ezekiel, however (more than in Jeremiah), there was to be a break with the past, as is clear especially in chs 14; 18; 20. Previous generations did not determine the exiles' fate (ch. 18); moreover, the exiles must become utterly different from those generations (ch. 20).

But what kind of hope did Ezekiel hold out for the renewed community? The answer to this lies mainly in chs 33—48. As Renz has shown, this is dominated by the idea of God as 'king' (Renz 1999, pp. 47, 102). Chapter 34 is the main statement: God himself will be the people's 'shepherd' (34:15), and under him David will be their 'prince' (34:25. See above on chs 37; 45). The idea of a human king under God is not new in the Old Testament (Ps. 2:6). However, in Ezekiel's programme, the kingship of God is emphasized by the lower position taken by the human king. Ezekiel is thus somewhat like other parts of the Old Testament, which speak of God's kingship apart from a human king (e.g. Psalms 93—99). Most akin is perhaps Deuteronomy, which, like Ezekiel, carefully subordinates the human king to the law, and permits him a very limited role (Deut. 17:14–20).

If Ezekiel 40—48 is taken as a realistic programme, then it gives an important place not only to the plan of the temple (chs 40—42) but also to the arrangements for the specifically religious life of the people (chs 43—46), and the priests (ch. 44). Yet this does not mean that Ezekiel only foresees a 'religious' community (as the post-exilic Jews are often portrayed). The prince's special territory close to the temple (45:7–8) shows that the concept is still political. The king is recognizably Davidic (the king's house was beside the temple of Solomon; 1 Kgs 7:8). This is explicit in Ezek. 34:23–24; 37:24–25. To call him a 'prince', however, using the old tribal title, may intend to bring him more obviously under the authority of the Sinai (Mosaic) covenant (Levenson 1976, p. 69. See also Joyce 1998). (See above on ch. 44.) The reunion of the two houses of Israel in 37:15–23 is another way of reaffirming the unifying role of the Davidic king in Israel's history.

But how far is Ezekiel's programme meant to be practical and realistic? There are elements in his hope for the future that stand close to 'apocalyptic', with its separation between the present age that is passing away and a new age to come (for more on 'apocalyptic', see Daniel, panel on Apocalyptic). History gives way to a 'transcendent' order, that is, one that lies beyond history. The portrayal of the final battle between good and evil in chs 38—39 leans in that direction.

The vision of the new temple also has features that point beyond immediate political conditions. Solomon's temple was built on Mt Zion. The new temple is situated on 'a very high mountain' (40:2). In a way, this is just Zion. Yet we have seen that it draws on mythological language (see Outline on ch. 47). Ezekiel uses the language not only of Zion but of Eden. 'God's holy mountain' in Ezekiel can be either Mt Zion (as in 20:40) or Eden (28:14; note the parallel with Eden in v. 13; Levenson 1976, p. 25, and see his discussion on pp. 25–34). In dwelling on Zion, the God of Israel is king of all creation. This points to the hope of a much greater salvation than the return to Judah and a priestly theocracy (Levenson, p. 33).

POLITICAL/FORMAL AND SPIRITUAL RELIGION: EZEKIEL AS PROPHET AND PRIEST

We have already noticed the paradox that Ezekiel stresses both God's sovereignty and people's responsibility for their own standing before God. A second paradox, which we have also just seen, is the need to establish an actual society with day-to-day arrangements for running it, and at the same time to herald a whole new age. Related to both of these is another tension, between the practical and political aspects of religion and the dimension of real personal faith. This tension is sometimes seen to put Ezekiel at odds with Jeremiah, for example. Jeremiah criticized the worship in the Jerusalem temple, and declared that people should not take its permanence for granted (Jer. 7:3–7, 12–15). Obedience to God's laws was more important (Jer. 7:6, 9). His New Covenant promise seemed to abolish the need for mediators between God and his people (Jer. 31:33–34). A lead in this direction had already been given by Hosea, where God says: 'For I desire steadfast love and not sacrifice, the knowledge of God rather than burnt offerings' (Hos. 6:6; cf. Mic. 6:6–8; Amos 5:21–24). With this prophetic trend in mind, Ezekiel gives an unexpectedly prominent place to legal and ritual instructions in his vision of the new society. McKeating, for example, thinks the contrast with Jeremiah and other prophets is very clear. While they had seen little hope for the future in cultic arrangements, Ezekiel has made them central: 'the stone that Jeremiah and the rest rejected, is in Ezekiel made the head of the corner' (1993, p. 91).

This way of seeing things needs some qualification. Jeremiah does have texts that envisage a renewed place for kings, priests, city and temple (Jer. 30:9; 31:14; 31:38–40; 33:14–26). The last of these texts, which strongly asserts a permanent role for king and priests, is closest to Ezekiel. It is, admittedly, a suspect text as a guide to Jeremiah's thought, as it is missing in LXX, and widely thought to be out of keeping with that prophet's message. Perhaps it is best seen as an answer to a question that is inevitably posed by Jeremiah's teaching: how shall the restored community organize itself in practice? It is Ezekiel who gives the fullest answer to this question.

The important theological question, however, is whether Ezekiel's practical and political programme is compatible with the religion of the 'heart' that is also so important to him, as it is to Jeremiah (Ezek. 11:19–20; 36:26). This is an important question in today's world, because it is often said that religion is a private matter for the individual and has no place in public policy-making. The idea of a religion of the heart can easily be taken as support for this view. However, as we saw on Jeremiah 31:31–34, this is a mistake. When Old Testament texts demand obedience from the heart, they are not talking about 'individualism' in a modern sense, but saying that the people of God together should adhere truly to God's commands (this is also true of Deut. 6:5, the famous 'Shema').

In this connection it is important that Ezekiel is both prophet and priest. As we saw, scholars used to think these roles could hardly be reconciled (Introduction: Theological Themes). The prophet was seen as one who warned against the dangers of formal, ritual religion (Amos 5:21–24; Isa. 1:10–17; Hos. 6:6). The prophetic side of Ezekiel's ministry is very clear. The phrases 'the hand of the LORD was upon me' (3:22), and 'the word of the LORD came to me' (6:1) stress his prophetic role as one who receives and transmits God's word. The 'spirit of God' plays a key part in his experience, for example in his visions of Jerusalem (8:3; 43:5), and in giving God's word to the prophet (11:5; see Carley 1975, pp. 23–37). The symbolic actions (chs 4—5) are typically prophetic. In this way Ezekiel's experience has a strong 'charismatic' side. He has direct revelations and experiences from God that do not depend on his role as priest. And his message of repentance and the need for a 'heart of flesh' (11:19–20) stresses the inner reality of religion in true prophetic style.

Yet Ezekiel is introduced very deliberately as both prophet and priest: 'the *word* of the LORD came to the *priest* Ezekiel . . . *and the hand of the LORD was upon him there* (1:3). To call for true repentance and obedience from a 'heart of flesh' does not contradict the obligation on a people to organize itself under God's laws. We can go farther. Ezekiel lets us see that the formally organized side of religion can and ought to be part of a full response to God. This is part of a broader picture for, in the Old Testament, formal religious life is not separate from political organization. The 'prince' still has a role alongside the priest, as we have seen.

Ezekiel makes an important contribution to the Old Testament's theology of politics and the spiritual. It is common to be told today that there is no place for God in the public, political sphere. In general, Muslims have understood this fundamental point more clearly than modern Christians. The issue in today's dialogue with Muslims about the relation of God and the state should not be *whether* politics is essentially theological, but *how*. In that connection, we have to observe the transcendent dimension of Ezekiel's vision of the future. The sovereignty of God in Israel's life means that ultimately he will establish his kingdom beyond the limits of any immediate earthly arrangements.

RHETORICAL INTENTION

Who were the 'audience' of the Book of Ezekiel? Whom does the book try to persuade and about what? There are really two audiences. The first is the hearers of Ezekiel himself, the exiles in Babylon. These are the ones we actually meet in the narrative of the book. They were represented by the elders, who came to Ezekiel to ask for guidance on certain things (e.g. 20:1–3). They are presented in the book as thoroughly rebellious against God (2:2–7), and Ezekiel is told beforehand that they will not listen to him (3:7). His role as a 'watchman' is to deliver God's words faithfully, even though they are unlikely to be heard (3:11, 16–21). To these people, Ezekiel's message, as we have seen, was that they should agree and accept that Jerusalem should be judged, that the exile was deserved and would be long, and that they themselves should turn from the sins of former generations.

Indications in the text are that Ezekiel's ministry to this audience was unsuccessful. They treated his words and actions as a performance to be enjoyed rather than as a solemn message to be heeded (33:30–33). As Renz argues, this last passage is decisive for Ezekiel's 'rhetorical situation'. He must carry on with his ministry, even though it is not heard (Renz 1999, 32). Ezekiel's enforced silences (3:25–26) were a symbolic action signifying this rejection of the message (Renz 1999).

A message that would not be heard may seem pointless. But this brings us to the second audience. This audience is not seen in the book, but is those for whom the book was written. It is important to realize that the whole Book of Ezekiel is a record of words he was told to say at certain times. The dating system shows that the book looks back on the words and actions recorded in it. For example, Ezekiel records that his vision of the new temple came 'in the twenty-fifth year of our exile' (40:1). This means, of course, that its point of view is from a time well after the fall of Jerusalem (33:21). The fall of Jerusalem was the key event for Ezekiel in regard to his 'first'

audience. But for the readers of the book it is well in the past. How far in the past we cannot know for sure, but it is likely to be before the fall of Babylon and the first stage in the return of exiles to Judah, since there is no indication of these things in the book.

What, then, is Ezekiel saying to this second audience? To them he is saying that they should think about all that has happened to them in a certain way. The exile was the work of God, as was the destruction of the temple. To this audience the message was no doubt urgent and sought a response. It was by no means hopeless. To them the possibility of being freed from the effects of their ancestors' actions was real (ch. 18). God was planning a new future for them, not in Babylon, but in the land, with a renewed temple, priesthood and political structure. This may have been a highly debatable issue among the later exiles. A whole generation had been born in Babylon, and for them the idea of a return to Judah may have seemed strange and improbable. Whereas the first generation needed to know that Jerusalem would fall, this one had to understand that Jerusalem was 'the navel of the earth' (38:12), that is, the place in which he ruled all time and space. They had a duty to be thoroughly renewed spiritually, and become fit to be God's covenant people again in his holy land.

The difference between the two audiences can sometimes be hard to define. For example, when Ezekiel quotes the people who have stayed in Jerusalem and their arrogant belief that they were God's favoured ones rather then the exiles (11:14–15), this fits within his message to the first audience in Babylon, for they may have been tempted to think that was true.

However, it takes on a new significance for a later generation who are being urged to prepare to return, for they too might have greatly feared that the Jerusalemites might not welcome them. This point can be applied to many sayings of Ezekiel. We need to be aware of the potential of the prophets' sayings as heard by quite different audiences at different times.

EZEKIEL IN THE CANON

We have already observed Ezekiel's relationship to other prophets. In his criticisms of both idolatrous practices and social sins he is in line with the main streams of prophetic thought (Theological Themes: Political/formal and spiritual religion). We saw that he was distinct from other prophets in the extent of his thinking about how the renewed people should live, in practice, in the land, and in his harmonization of prophetic and priestly emphases in religion. Yet that was a matter of style and degree, rather than a contradiction.

We have also noticed Ezekiel's 'scholarly' reflection on other Old Testament writings (Critical Interpretation). In his interest in 'holiness' he draws on the Priestly parts of the Pentateuch, especially Leviticus 17—26 (the Holiness Code). He seems also to be influenced by Deuteronomy in his vision for a return to the land in renewed obedience to the 'statutes and laws' promulgated by Moses, and in rooting out idolatry (Ezek. 11:16–21, cf. Deut. 4:25–31; 26:16; 30:1–10). Ezekiel 20:32 is like Deut. 12:30, in warning against the temptations to be like the surrounding nations. Ezekiel's 'heart of flesh' as a condition of true obedience also echoes Deut. 6:5; 10:12). (See further Carley 1975, pp. 59–60.)

This drawing on Israel's theological traditions is not just a matter of style, but very important to Ezekiel's message. It is a kind of rebuilding of the foundations of the faith of Israel, from the Mosaic law and the occupation of the land by Joshua, to the post-exilic conditions. Like Deuteronomy, Ezekiel not only insists on true obedience, but brings the rulers and officials in Israel strongly under the authority of the Mosaic law (cf. Deut. 16:18—18:22). Like Exodus–Leviticus–Numbers it provides for the fabric and maintenance of the worship life of Israel. Like Joshua, it allots land to the tribes.

Ezekiel's first special contribution to Old Testament theology, therefore, is in absorbing the prophetic theology of thorough moral and spiritual regeneration, and bringing it into a vision for the ongoing political and religious life of the people of God.

A second contribution is in his portrayal of the final conflict between God and evil in Ezekiel 38—39, the war of Gog of Magog against God's people. This establishes, as we saw, that the final victory of God will not come immediately, but after an unspecified time. The arrangements for daily life in the land, while they are utterly serious and important, are temporary. The life of faith is lived between deliverance from slavery (in this case Babylon) and final deliverance. Ezekiel holds together these two aspects of reality: the present life of obedience (itself both spiritual and institutional) and the vision of a greater salvation beyond the present time. A similar capacity for both the 'now' and 'not yet' will be found in Daniel (for quite different circumstances). But it is this broad horizon of Ezekiel that caused his prophecy to be so readily taken up in the Book of Revelation, where the believers in Christ are sustained by a vision of heaven.

FURTHER READING

COMMENTARIES

Note: In addition to the commentaries marked *, NICOT and Word are very useful for detailed discussions.

L. C. Allen *Ezekiel 1–19*. WBC. Dallas: Word Books, 1994.

L. C. Allen *Ezekiel 20–48*. WBC. Dallas: Word Books, 1990.

D. I. Block *Ezekiel 1–24*. NICOT. Grand Rapids: Eerdmans, 1997.

D. I. Block *Ezekiel 25–48*. NICOT. Grand Rapids: Eerdmans, 1998.

*R. E. Clements *Ezekiel*. Louisville: Westminster/John Knox, 1996.

*P. C. Craigie *Ezekiel*. DSB. Edinburgh: St. Andrew Press/Philadelphia: Westminster, 1983.

M. Greenberg *Ezekiel 1–20*. AB. New York: Doubleday, 1983.

M. Greenberg *Ezekiel 21–37*. AB. New York: Doubleday, 1997.

R. M. Hals *Ezekiel*. FOTL. Grand Rapids: Eerdmans, 1989.

*J. B. Taylor *Ezekiel*. TOTC. London: Tyndale, 1971.

J. W. Wevers *Ezekiel*. NCB. London: Marshall, Morgan and Scott, repr. 1982.

W. Zimmerli *Ezekiel 1*. Hermeneia. Philadelphia: Fortress, 1979.

W. Zimmerli *Ezekiel 2*. Hermeneia. Philadelphia: Fortress, 1983.

OTHER BOOKS AND ARTICLES

D. I. Block 'Gog and the Pouring Out of the Spirit: Reflections on Ezekiel xxxix 21–9', *VT* 37. 1987, pp. 257–70.

K. W. Carley *Ezekiel Among the Prophets*. SBT. London: SCM, 1975.

B. S. Childs *Introduction to the Old Testament as Scripture*. London: SCM, 1979.

R. E. Clements 'The Ezekiel Tradition: Prophecy in a Time of Crisis' in R. Coggins,

A. Phillips and M. Knibb eds *Israel's Prophetic Tradition*. Cambridge: CUP, 1982, pp. 119–36.

R. J. Clifford *The Cosmic Mountain in Canaan and the Old Testament*. HSM 4. Cambridge, Mass.: Harvard University Press, 1972.

E. Davis *Swallowing the Scroll: Textuality and the Dynamics of Discourse in Ezekiel's Prophecy*. JSOT Suppl. 78. Sheffield Academic Press, 1989.

S. R. Driver *Introduction to the Literature of the Old Testament*. Edinburgh: T. & T. Clark, 1892, third edition.

I. Duguid *Ezekiel and the Leaders of Israel*. VT Suppl. 51. Leiden: Brill, 1994.

R. Duke 'Punishment or Restoration: Another Look at the Levites of Ezekiel 44:6–16' *JSOT* 40. 1988, pp. 61–81.

G. Fohrer *Introduction to the Old Testament*. London: SCM, 1979, pp. 403–15.

J. Galambush *Jerusalem in the Book of Ezekiel*. SBL Diss. Atlanta: Scholars Press, 1992.

R. P. Gordon, ed. *The Place is Too Small for Us: The Israelite Prophets in Recent Scholarship*. SBTS 5. Winona Lake: Eisenbrauns, 1995.

P. P. Jenson *Graded Holiness*. JSOT Suppl. 106. Sheffield: JSOT Press, 1992.

*P. Joyce *Divine Initiative and Human Response in Ezekiel*. JSOT Suppl. 51. Sheffield: JSOT Press, 1989.

P. Joyce 'King and Messiah in Ezekiel' in John Day ed. *King and Messiah in Israel and the Ancient Near East*. JSOT Suppl. 270. Sheffield: Sheffield Academic Press, 1998, pp. 323–37.

J. D. Levenson *Theology of the Program of Restoration in Ezekiel 40–48*. Missoula: Scholars Press, 1976.

J. Lindblom *Prophecy in Ancient Israel*. Oxford: Basil Blackwell, 1962.

*H. McKeating *Ezekiel*. OTG. Sheffield: Sheffield Academic Press, 1993.

B. C. Ollenburger *Zion, The City of the Great King: A Theological Symbol of the Jerusalem Cult*. JSOT Suppl. 41. Sheffield: JSOT Press, 1987).

D. L. Petersen *The Roles of Israel's Prophets*. JSOT Suppl. 17. Sheffield: JSOT Press, 1981.

T. Renz *The Rhetorical Function of the Book of Ezekiel*. Leiden: Brill, 1999.

J. F. A. Sawyer *Prophecy and the Biblical Prophets*. Oxford: OUP, 1993.

W. D. Stacey *Prophetic Drama in the Old Testament*. London: Epworth, 1990.

K. R. Stevenson *The Vision of Transformation: the Territorial Rhetoric of Ezekiel 40–48*. SBL Diss 154. Atlanta: Scholars Press, 1996.

S. S. Tuell *The Law of the Temple in Ezekiel 40–48*. HSM 49. Atlanta: Scholars Press, 1992.

G. J. Wenham *Leviticus*. NICOT. Grand Rapids: Eerdmans, 1979.

G. J. Wenham *Genesis 1–15*. WBC. Waco: Word Books, 1987.

D. J. Wiseman *1 and 2 Kings*. TOTC. Leicester: IVP, 1993.

Chapter 5

DANIEL

DATE AND DESTINATION

The events recorded in the Book of Daniel span the Babylonian exile. The third year of Jehoiakim (1:1), in its plain sense, is 606 BC. This poses an immediate problem, as Nebuchadnezzar did not ascend the throne of Babylon till 605 BC, nor did Babylon control the region until his defeat of Egypt at the Battle of Carchemish in that year. (Note Jer. 25:1, which puts the accession of Nebuchadnezzar in the *fourth* year of Jehoiakim.) Baldwin proposes a solution to the problem by arguing that in the Babylonian system of post-dating, the third year of Jehoiakim would be 605 (Baldwin 1978, pp. 77–78). If the idea of an attack on Jerusalem in the reign of Jehoiakim is to be feasible, then 605 BC must be preferred. The Books of Kings do not report an exile in this year, but 2 Kgs 24:1–2 tells that Nebuchadnezzar came against Jehoiakim, and 2 Chron. 36:6 adds that he 'bound him in fetters to take him to Babylon'. The latest date given in the book is the third year of King Cyrus of Persia (10:1), that is, about 536 BC, soon after the Babylonian empire had fallen to that king. The chronology of Daniel, therefore, allows the time of the exile proper to correspond fairly closely to Jeremiah's predicted seventy years (Jer. 25:11–12).

The focus of much of the book, however, is a later time – the persecution of Jews under the Greek Seleucid empire in the second century BC, and specifically by one Seleucid king, Antiochus IV Epiphanes (175–164 BC). The visions that compose the second half of the book (chs 7—12) unite in pointing to his reign, and especially to the years 169–67 BC. In 169 BC, Antiochus plundered the temple of its treasures in order to raise revenue. And in 167, he went further, ordering the temple of Yahweh the God of Israel to be ritually defiled (according to the Jews' own beliefs about defilement), and its worship to be replaced by pagan worship. To complete the insult, he erected a statue to the god Zeus Olympios in the temple. This is what is called 'the abomination that makes desolate' (9:27; 11:31). Though the Book of Daniel does not refer to Antiochus IV by name, its visions point clearly to these events.

The Book of Daniel consciously brings these two periods into connection. Both Nebuchadnezzar's dream in ch. 2 and Daniel's vision in ch. 7 map out the history of the period from the Babylonian to the Greek empires. They see four successive empires. The natural interpretation of these four is that they correspond to Babylon, Media, Persia and Greece. This succession is echoed in the narrative and dating system of the book. On the death of Belshazzar, the last king of Babylon (actually co-regent with his father Nabonidus), he is succeeded by Darius *the Mede* (5:30–31), who is succeeded in turn by Cyrus *the Persian* (6:28; cf. 9:1; 10:1). Chapter 10 also refers to the succession of Persia by Greece (10:20). The most detailed recounting of the history of the four empires comes in ch. 11. However, here and in the other visions, it is clear that the interest of the author falls heavily on the reign of Antiochus IV Epiphanes. This is the great crisis that the book addresses. (The dates and identifications just given are not agreed by all. The question of composition is taken up in the next section.)

It is important, therefore, to have an idea of the two different periods portrayed in the book, in order to understand it. The following table gives key dates.

KEY DATES FOR THE BOOK OF DANIEL (all BC)
(after Hartman and Di Lella 1978, p. 30)

605–562	Reign of Nebuchadn(r)ezzar
605	Daniel and others exiled to Babylon
562–560	Reign of Amel-marduk (Evil-Merodach)
560–556	Reign of Neriglissar
556–539	Reign of Nabonidus
549–539	Belshazzar co-regent
539	Babylon captured by Cyrus the Persian
539–530	Reign of Cyrus after capture of Babylon
530–522	Reign of Cambyses
522–486	Reign of Darius I Hystaspes
336–323	Reign of Alexander the Great of Macedonia

Ptolemaic Empire (Egypt)		*Seleucid Empire (Syria)*	
323–285	Ptolemy I Lagi	312–280	Seleucus I
		280–261	Antiochus I
285–246	Ptolemy II Philadelphus	261–246	Antiochus II
246–221	Ptolemy III Euergetes	246–226	Seleucus II
		226–223	Seleucus III
221–203	Ptolemy IV Philopater	223–187	Antiochus III the Great
203–181	Ptolemy V Epiphanes	187–175	Seleucus IV
181–146	Ptolemy VI Philometor	175–164	Antiochus IV Epiphanes

169	Antiochus IV plunders the temple
167	Antiochus erects statue of Zeus in temple; beginning of Maccabean revolt
164	Death of Antiochus and rededication of the temple

Note: The Ptolemies and Seleucids fought at length for control of Palestine. It was only Antiochus III who finally brought Palestine under Seleucid control in 198 BC (see Davies 1985, p. 32).

This table, compared with a reading of Daniel, tells us some important things about the book's relation to history. Daniel makes no mention of the Babylonian kings between Nebuchadnezzar and Belshazzar. Belshazzar, moreover, was not the son of Nebuchadnezzar (5:2), but of Nabonidus. The list of kings does not show a 'Darius the Mede' (5:31 [6:1]) between Belshazzar and Cyrus. These are some of the factors that have led scholars to question the traditional dating of the book in the time of the exile itself.

CRITICAL INTERPRETATION OF DANIEL

The date of the composition of Daniel is contested between critical and conservative scholars. The traditional view has been that the book comes from the time of its central character, that is, from the Babylonian exile. The visions (chs 7—12) are narrated by him, and the detailed accounts of events in the second century are presented as revelations of the future. Since God can inspire prophets to see the future, and indeed, since this is one of the things the Book of Daniel insists on, there seems to be a warrant for taking the book at its face value.

The critical view, however, has been taken for two main reasons. First, the book is said to contain historical errors which would be improbable in a writing of the exilic period, for example in supposing there was an exile in 605 BC, and in its confusion over the succession of kings (see the note at the end of Key dates for the Book of Daniel). Second, the detailed account of key events from the Persian period to Antiochus IV in ch. 11 follows the known course of history up to v. 39, but vv. 40–45 tell of a further Egyptian campaign which is unknown to history. And the rededication of the temple in 164 BC is a surprising omission. It follows from this reading of ch. 11 that it must have been written between the desecration of the temple (167) and its rededication (164).

Conservative scholars have tried to meet these points. Joyce Baldwin has argued that the stories show knowledge of the Babylonian court and its history, and therefore are likely to come from the time in question. She also cites the discovery of the 'Prayer of Nabonidus', on which Daniel 4 appears to be based, as supporting evidence (Baldwin 1978, p. 36; see the 'Prayer of Nabonidus' panel). D. J. Wiseman has offered an explanation of Darius the Mede, along with other historical problems (1965, pp. 9–18), as have Dillard and Longman

---

'THE PRAYER OF NABONIDUS'

Nabonidus (556–539 BC) is one of the kings of the exilic time not mentioned in Daniel. A number of ancient documents relate to him. According to the 'Nabonidus Chronicle' (ANET, pp. 305–07), this king spent much of his time away from Babylon in the desert city of Tema in Arabia. The 'Verse Account of Nabonidus' (ANET, pp. 312–15), written by opponents, deliberately gives the impression that he was out of his mind. Finally the 'Prayer of Nabonidus', discovered at Qumran, tells in his own words how, while at Tema, he was 'smitten with a bad inflammation' by decree of 'the Most High God', but when he confessed his sins, a Jewish soothsayer from among the exiles in Babylon showed him that this was so that he should honour the Most High God rather then worship idols. The 'Prayer' is given in full in Hartman and Di Lella 1978, pp. 178–79.

The connections with Daniel 4 are clear. Observe both the similarities and the differences. What do you think is the relationship between the two texts?

(1995, *Introduction*, pp. 332–337). Possibilities for Darius the Mede include that he was Cyrus (Wiseman), and that he was a vassal of Cyrus, Gubaru, who ruled in practice in the first year of the new kingdom (an old theory revived in recent times by Shea 1982). Joyce Baldwin has found Babylonian parallels to the prophetic visions of Daniel, and thinks this makes it possible that the visions as well as the stories have a sixth-century Babylonian background (Baldwin 1979). K. A. Kitchen has argued that the Aramaic of Daniel is classical Imperial Aramaic and that the dating of the book cannot be settled on the grounds of its language (in Wiseman et al. 1965, pp. 31–79).

GENRE

Daniel consists of distinct types of literature, which can be broadly classified as stories (chs 1—6) and visions (chs 7—12). The stories are most like the Book of Esther, among Old Testament books, and in some respects like the Joseph narrative in Genesis 37—50. These all share the theme of the life of Israelites/Jews outside the land of Israel and under foreign rule. The figure of Daniel is most like Joseph, since both interpret dreams and rise to power in the foreign court. The issues at stake are more like those of Esther, where Jewish people live in danger of oppression because of their Jewish identity. These stories reflect on life in 'diaspora' (that is, Jews living away from the land of Israel; the word is based on the idea of 'scattering') (Humphreys 1973; cf. Redford 1970, pp. 94–97; and Wills 1990, pp. 55–70). Humphreys distinguishes between two types of court-tale in Daniel: 'tales of court conflict' (Daniel 3 and 6) and 'tales of court contest' (Daniel 2; 4; 5). These specifically Jewish stories belong in turn to a broader tradition of stories of wise courtiers that go back to ancient Egypt (Sinuhe)

(*ANET*, pp. 18–22), and that include Ahiqar, the closest non-Jewish story to the biblical examples (*ANET*, pp. 427–30; J. M. Lindenberger, in Charlesworth, ed. 1985, pp. 479–507).

> **Think about**
> **DANIEL AND ESTHER.**
>
> In the Outline below, you will notice a number of comparisons with Esther, especially on Daniel 3—6. Think about the ways in which these two books are similar. Do they regard foreign rulers as potentially friendly, and try to show how life under them as a faithful Jew is possible? Think also about Humphreys' distinction between 'tales of court conflict' and 'tales of court contest'. Is this a valid distinction? Does it tell us anything about the first question (i.e. are rulers potentially friendly)?

In the visions of Daniel, a well-known prophetic feature is developed in a new way. Amos and Jeremiah had visions, which God interpreted to the prophet (Amos 7—8; Jeremiah 1; 24). The visions of Daniel, according to a recent study, come at the end of a development of the prophetic vision, Zechariah being a mid-point (Niditch 1983). Daniel's visions are longer than the early visions, have complex imagery and stress the reactions of the person who sees the vision.

The vision-form says much about the meaning of Daniel. It is suitable to the book's theological emphasis that God is in control of all history and can disclose the course of it to anyone he chooses. The symbolism too is not random, or based on a mere code. Rather, the symbols help to convey the meaning (Goldingay 1989, pp. 147–48). It is not an accident that a cruel, ruthless empire or king should be symbolized by an animal's horn, for example, which symbolized strength. Mixed creatures, as in 7:2–8, were familiar to ancient people, from temple-statues for example (as can be seen in Mesopotamian exhibits in major museums). They are not portraying real creatures, but are combinations for symbolic effect (a lion's strength, an eagle's speed, for example, in 7:4). The symbols used in the visions may have made more – or other – impressions on the first readers of Daniel that do not come across to us with such clarity or force, because of their world of ideas and associations.

It is because of its visions that Daniel is often said to belong to the category of 'apocalyptic'. (See the panel on Apocalyptic.)

UNITY

The difference between the stories and the visions has led a number of scholars to suggest that the book was not originally a unity. Some think that the stories really do show evidence of a Babylonian exilic origin (Davies 1985, pp. 50–55), whereas the visions belong to the second century BC in Palestine. Others insist on the unity of the book, and so conclude either that it is entirely from the second century (Rowley 1965), or entirely from the sixth (Baldwin 1978, pp. 35–46).

In any case, the differences between the stories and visions should not be overstressed. Both address situations of foreign rule and (potential) persecution; both have revelations from the heavenly realm; both have angelic visitations (3:24–25); both have dreams; two of the visions (chs 7 and 8) are dated by the reign of Belshazzar. Wisdom is a shared theme

(the wise Daniel is opposed to the wise men of Babylon, the 'Chaldeans', in chs 1—6; and in chs 7—12 the faithful Jews who are assured of final victory over tyranny are sometimes called 'the wise'). Together the two types of literature convey a whole range of possibilities entailed in life under foreign rule, and assert the rule of God both in ongoing history and in final victory over all tyrannical power.

Think about
DANIEL'S STORIES AS HISTORY?

Conservative scholars have regarded the stories of Daniel as history and the visions as genuine prediction. They have done so because they have thought it important to defend the book's exilic date. Why do they do this, and what theological issues do you think are at stake?

How does the factor of literary genre relate to this issue? Are there reasons to think that the stories may not be correctly classified as history, and/or that the visions may not be genuine predictions? On the visions, see 'Digging deeper' at ch. 11. On the stories see Lucas 2002 (Introduction: Types of literature and interpretation), who thinks that, since the literature that is most like the stories of Daniel is 'story' rather than history, it may not be necessary to think that Daniel's stories intend to tell history.

STRUCTURE AND OUTLINE

STRUCTURE
At first glance the structure of Daniel looks simple. It appears to fall into two main sections, chs 1—6 consisting of stories about the exiles under Babylonian rule, while chs 7—12 contain visions of events yet to

APOCALYPTIC

The term apocalyptic applies to a type of literature known as apocalypses, of which the two biblical examples are Daniel and Revelation. In popular usage, the words apocalypse and apocalyptic tend to refer to a great final conflict, perhaps the end of the world (as in the film title *Apocalypse Now*). This picks up from biblical and Jewish apocalyptic one aspect of *some* of the literature in question, namely eschatology (the study of the *end* – a subject of perennial fascination in popular books on religion).

Daniel and Revelation do have eschatological themes and, in the scholarly literature too, eschatology has sometimes seemed to be essential to apocalyptic (Rowland documents this, 1982, p. 25). But, as Rowland argues, this is not the essential thing about apocalyptic, but rather the disclosure of divine mysteries (Rowland 1982, pp. 23–48, see for example pp. 25–26). (The word apocalypse – Greek *apokalupsis* – means 'disclosure', 'unveiling'.)

Major non-biblical apocalypses are found in 1 and 2 Enoch, 4 Ezra, the Book of Jubilees, 2 Baruch and the Testament of Abraham, among others. See Collins 1984 pp. 6–24, for analysis. The texts may be found in Charlesworth 1983 and Charlesworth 1985.

These apocalyptic disclosures can be about the end-times, but are not always. 1 Enoch, for example, has more to do with understanding the nature of heaven and earth. In Rowland's view, there is not even 'a distinctive apocalyptic approach to future hope' (1982, p. 71).

Biblical apocalyptic has been thought to have its origins in the Wisdom literature (von Rad 1972, pp. 263–83) and in prophecy (Russell 1964, pp. 88–100; Hanson 1979. Note that these are contrasting views – von Rad played down the links between apocalyptic and prophecy, e.g. 1972 pp. 269–74, 282, n. 32). We have already noticed the 'Wisdom'

connection with Daniel in Daniel's conflict with the 'wise' of Babylon, and the emphasis on the 'wise' Jews in the visions. And we have also seen that prophecy has similarities with Daniel's visions (Critical Interpretation: Genre). It is probably misguided to try to draw neat distinctions between the apocalyptic of Daniel and these other major Old Testament categories. Hanson attempted to show that apocalyptic eschatology arose when a visionary group withdrew from the mainstream religious life of post-exilic Judah and abandoned hope of change within history (1979, p. 219). But the radical break between this age and the next, found in some apocalypses, is not present in all. Apocalypses often look for vindication within history (Rowland 1982, pp. 37–38). (For a critique of von Rad's belief that apocalyptic derived from Wisdom, and of Hanson's thesis, see Bauckham 1978. Bauckham argues that apocalyptic is essentially interpretation of prophecy, p. 18; cf. D. S. Russell 1964, pp. 178–202.)

The 'apocalypse' form may be called a genre, yet apocalypses contain a number of forms within them (Collins 1984, p. 3. Collins sets out the range of what he calls 'Basic Apocalyptic Genres' on pp. 6–19). Certain ideas tend to recur within apocalypses, but not in a rigid way. Not all are reactions to persecution, for example (Collins 1984, p. 22). Apocalypses are compatible with other strands in Jewish thought, including the Torah piety that became dominant in first-century Judaism (Rowland 1988).

Daniel may be called 'apocalyptic' in the sense that disclosures of heavenly secrets by angelic mediators play an important part in it. These are not all 'eschatological', however. The disclosures in the stories relate to events within history, sometimes imminent ones (e.g. 5:30). And both stories and visions tell also about the nature of reality, for example, in the human face and mind of good political rule, and in the close relationship between faithful humanity and the heavenly realm (e.g. in 8:15–17).

happen. However, a different division is also possible. A clue lies in the two languages used. The book opens in Hebrew (1:1—2:4a). Then, just before the story of King Nebuchadnezzar's first dream, it switches into Aramaic, and continues in that language to 7:28. The last five chapters (8—12) revert to Hebrew. Chapters 2—7, which are mainly in Aramaic, form a unified section. It opens and closes with dream-visions about the succession of four world empires which are overcome in the end by the kingdom of God (chs 2; 7). The chapters in between also correspond to each other concentrically: chs 3 and 6 are stories about persecution of faithful Jews, while chs 4 and 5 focus on the attitude of two Babylonian kings to the God of Israel (for more on this structure, see Casey 1979, pp. 7–9). Viewed in this way, ch. 1 is an introduction to the whole book, setting out the basic issue of the challenge and possible costs of faithfulness under foreign rule. Chapters 8—12 then consist of visions which elaborate more fully the persecution of the Jews and their deliverance in the end from their enemies. They take their cue from the vision in ch. 7. Despite the variety of form, therefore (the two languages, story and vision), the book has a unity because of its coherence of theme.

STRUCTURE

OUTLINE

1:1–21: Daniel and friends gain acceptance in Babylon, but stay faithful

The opening verse sets the Book of Daniel in the Babylonian exile. When the author places the beginning of the exile in 605 BC (see Baldwin 1978, p. 77; and above, Date and Destination, on the historical problem), he may have in mind Jeremiah's prophecy that it would last seventy years (Jer. 25:11–12; cf. 2 Chr. 36:22–23). The period to Cyrus's edict in 539 BC is then close to seventy years. As in Kings (2 Kgs 24:13), the exile is symbolized by the removal of temple treasures to Babylon (this will come back into the story in ch. 5). (The seventy-year exile will be reinterpreted, however, in Daniel 9.)

The story tells of the attempt to absorb the best of the young Judean exiles into the Babylonian court, its culture and its ways. The fact that they are from royal and noble families means to Nebuchadnezzar that he takes the best of subject peoples to increase his own glory. To the reader it suggests that they bear responsibility for Israel in a special way. They would have the privileges that went with royal service (1:5). But their Judean background would be erased by giving them new, Babylonian names (v. 7). This introduces a strong theme in the stories, the pressure on the Jews to give full loyalty to their new overlords.

An important emphasis is knowledge and wisdom. Just as in the Old Testament Wisdom literature, this is both a natural gift and something learnt (v. 4). For the exiles, the learning was to be Babylonian, of course. This sets up another theme of the stories, namely, where true wisdom and knowledge are to be found.

Finally, Daniel and his friends make it a matter of principle not to touch the food and drink provided by the king, so as not to be 'defiled' by it. Jewish concern to obey the food laws (Leviticus 11; Deuteronomy 14) seems to have led them to abstain generally from the food of the peoples they lived among (cf. Tobit 1:11). This small mark of loyalty to the God of Israel points to the real issue: the followers of God and his law are set against the might of the greatest empire in the world. On the faithfulness of Daniel and his friends rests the future of God's people, after the disaster of the exile.

2:1–49: King Nebuchadnezzar's dream and its meaning are revealed to Daniel; the end of the Babylonian empire is foretold

Daniel is now cast in a role like that of Joseph, who famously interpreted dreams of another king, the Egyptian Pharaoh (Genesis 41). Like Joseph, Daniel is also rewarded with great power in a foreign kingdom (Dan. 2:48).

As the dream is about power, the dream-interpretation is a test of power. The mighty

learning of Babylon is lined up on one side in the introduction of the 'magicians, enchanters, sorcerers and Chaldeans' (v. 2 – in Daniel, 'Chaldeans' sometimes describes the Babylonian people as such (5:30), but here, as perhaps in 1:4, it designates a class of 'magi', masters of all kinds of knowledge, including magical arts). So too is the power of the Babylonian king. His absurd demand for an interpretation of a dream he cannot remember, his unshakeable decree, the exaggerated punishments threatened (vv. 2–5), all show his pretension to absolute power.

God's revelation of the dream and its meaning to Daniel (2:19) is one of the key events in the book. It is God alone who gives wisdom and knowledge, not the magic arts of Babylon, and Daniel praises God for this (2:20–23). The divine revelation of 'mystery', that is, knowledge not accessible by ordinary means, is the essential element in 'apocalyptic'.

The dream is of a statue composed of four types of material (vv. 31–35). Taken by itself, it could mean that the apparent power and glory of Babylon was fatally undermined and would soon collapse (Baldwin 1978, p. 92). The interpretation, however, assigns the four levels of materials to successive kingdoms, beginning with Babylon (vv. 37–39). In modern scholarship, the three kingdoms after Babylon (as we have noted) are identified as Media, Persia and Greece. The traditional view, still advocated by some scholars, sees the four as Babylon, Medo-Persia, Greece and Rome. (For further discussion, see above, Date and Destination.) In the interpretation, the progressive deterioration in quality of the materials (noted in v. 39) does not seem to be the essential thing about the picture, nor even the chronology, strictly speaking. The kingdoms fall together to 'the kingdom that shall never be destroyed' (v. 44). The message for Nebuchadnezzar would be to show that all human power is derived from God (vv. 37–38), and that the king's pride in his power and great culture is misplaced. And he does indeed worship God (v. 47). The real point may be to encourage the Jewish hearers that their domination by a foreign power would soon be at an end.

3:1–30: Shadrach, Meshach and Abednego face martyrdom rather than renounce their God, but are saved

For the first time, Jewish faithfulness to God leads directly to the threat of martyrdom. Nebuchadnezzar's dream of a flawed gold statue (ch. 2) has not chastened him (in spite of 2:47); on the contrary he now erects a gold statue to assert his own power and glory (3:1). The repeated lists of officials (vv. 2–3) – like the pompous lists of musical instruments (vv. 5–7) – parade the power pretensions of the empire with comic irony.

Ambitious people seek their own advantage at the expense of others under a megalomaniac king (vv. 8–12 – like Haman, the enemy of the Jews in Esther). Nebuchadnezzar's enraged challenge to the three Jews (vv. 14–15) shows how convinced he is of his own power. The pride of empire directly challenges God.

Their answer is one of the high points of the book: they believe God's power can deliver them from the tyrant; but they are willing to die for their loyalty to him if he chooses not to deliver them (vv. 16–18). This faith has faced the possibility of paying the ultimate price.

The miraculous rescue proves that God is indeed more powerful than the most ruthless human kingdom. The fourth figure seen in the flames looks like both a man and a god (v. 25). This is a mirror-image of the angelic-human figures who will feature in chs 8—12 in the visions there of the salvation of faithful Israel. Nebuchadnezzar draws a pen-portrait of the ideal martyr-saint (v. 28b). The reversal of the decree (v. 29, in words like 2:5) again reminds of Esther (Esther 8). The three Jews are rewarded (v. 30).

4:1–37 [3:31—4:34]: Nebuchadnezzar praises God after Daniel interprets his second dream

The theme of the story is familiar: the pride of Nebuchadnezzar in the glories of his kingdom (v. 30), and a dream interpreted by Daniel after the 'Chaldeans' had failed (vv. 7, 18). A new feature is that the story is told by Nebuchadnezzar himself (except for vv. 28–33), looking back on the events told in the chapter, and from the standpoint of worship of God (vv. 2–3, 37). He seems to have a close relationship with Daniel (v. 19).

The tree in the dream is like the paradisal tree of life (vv. 10–12; see Goldingay 1989, pp. 87–88 for the widespread mythological background of this idea. Another echo of it is found in Gen. 1:9). Applied to Nebuchadnezzar, it is not wholly negative, even though tall trees are elsewhere applied to kings as symbols of pride (especially Ezekiel 31; also Ezekiel 17, and cf. Isa. 2:12–13). The chapter presupposes that human power is given by God (vv. 17b). Indeed that is what the king is meant to learn by his experience (v. 25), and he is finally restored to his rule, greater than ever (v. 36), but now knowing that real authority comes from God.

The temporary madness of the king, and his expulsion to the 'animals of the field' (v. 15) echoes the contrast between the human and the beastly in ch. 7. The restoration of Nebuchadnezzar from beastly to his true human self shows the possibility of right human rule under God, whose 'works are truth, and whose ways are justice' (v. 37).

Scholars sometimes see Nabonidus' self-imposed exile from Babylon in the Arabian desert, attested by several Babylonian sources, as the true source for this story (see Critical Interpretation, and Hartman and Di Lella 1978, pp. 177–80).

5:1–31 [5:1—6:1]: King Belshazzar defies God, and dies, after Daniel interprets a sign

As in ch. 4, there is a connection with King Nabonidus, for Belshazzar (or Bel-shar-usur) was his son, whom he left in charge of the kingdom during his long absence in the Arabian desert at Tema (Lacocque 1979, p. 75). Belshazzar was in effective control of Babylon when it fell to Cyrus in 539 BC (Hartman and Di Lella 1978, pp. 185–86; Baldwin 1978, pp. 21–23). The setting of the story is just before the fall of Babylon to the Persians. Its opening (v. 1) reminds of King Ahasuerus' banquet in Esther (Esth. 1:1–4). Other ancient sources say that when the Medes and Persians took Babylon, the king was holding an orgy (Hartman and Di Lella 1978, p.187).

Belshazzar represents the opposite possibility of kingship from that which we saw in Nebuchadnezzar in ch. 4. While Nebuchadnezzar worshipped God and respected Daniel, Belshazzar uses the temple treasures in his idolatrous orgy (vv. 2–4), and does not know who Daniel is (vv. 11–12). Belshazzar has no dream, but sees writing on a wall (v. 5). In the interpretation, Daniel expressly contrasts Belshazzar in his pride with the humble Nebuchadnezzar (vv. 18–23). Commentators often see an analogy

between Belshazzar and Antiochus IV, because they both desecrated the temple treasures. The judgement on Belshazzar is swift and dramatic (vv. 24–28, 30).

The brief note in v. 31 [6:1] records the fall of the Babylonian empire, and the coming of the Medo-Persian. On Darius the Mede, see Date and Destination.

6:1–28 [6:2–29]: Daniel faces martyrdom rather than renounce God, but is saved

The story of Daniel's persecution corresponds to that of the three friends in ch. 3. The initiative in this case, however, is taken by jealous officials, not by the king (vv. 3–5 [4–6]; contrast 3:1–7), a first sign that Daniel's promotion caused discontent. The king himself is sympathetic to Daniel, but is easily duped by the intriguers.

The irrevocable edict, 'the law of the Medes and Persians' (v. 8 [9]), plays an important role, for this is what makes the king helpless to save Daniel (vv. 14–15 [15–16]). A similar idea is found in Esther (Esth. 8:8). The law of Daniel's God (v. 5 [6]) is contrasted with an arbitrary law that condemns the innocent (v. 22 [23]), and frustrates the best intention of a well-disposed king to do what is right. His helplessness contrasts with the power of God to deliver Daniel, and the king himself recognizes this (v. 16 [17]). Daniel's deliverance is matched by the condemnation of his enemies (v. 24 [25], cf. Esth. 8:9–14).

7:1–28: God shows Daniel in a dream a succession of kingdoms, followed by the kingdom of God and his 'holy ones'

Chapter 7 begins the series of visions that now dominate the rest of the book. While the stories took us past the end of the Babylonian period into the Medo-Persian (ch. 6), the clock now turns back to the first year of King Belshazzar (about 550 BC). Daniel, who has previously interpreted the dreams and visions of others, now becomes the visionary, and he in turn needs others (heavenly beings) to interpret.

The chapter consists of a dream of Daniel (vv. 1–14), followed by an interpretation by an angelic figure (vv. 16, 17–28). In the dream Daniel sees 'four great beasts coming up out of the sea' (v. 3). We know from ch. 2 – though the image is now different – that these will represent a succession of four empires. The symbolism conveys certain features of the kingdoms, such as strength (the lion) and speed to fall on prey (the eagle, v. 4; and see above, Critical Interpretation: Genre). The 'human mind' given to the first beast makes a link with the restoration of Nebuchadnezzar in ch. 4 (cf. 4:16, 33). It also anticipates the rule of 'one like a son of man' (vv. 13–14). True and good rule is symbolized by humanity, and the vision of the first beast shows that empires are capable of ruling well. The fourth 'beast' has a number of 'horns' (vv. 7–8), that is, successive kings within that empire. The last of these, 'a little horn', is singled out as particularly arrogant (v. 8).

The vision of the beasts is followed by a judgement-scene (vv. 9–14). In this scene, the 'Ancient One' (or 'Ancient of Days') is a way of speaking of God, who is God in long ages past and future (Ps. 41:13 [14]; 93:2). The image of a wheeled throne is like the vision of God in Ezekiel 1. Fire symbolizes God's presence (Exod. 24:17; Deut. 4:11). Images of God enthroned and surrounded by heavenly beings are usually set in heaven (as in Job 1; 1 Kgs 22; Ps. 82:1), but this scene seems to be on earth, where the visions of the beasts are set. In the judgement, the last 'horn' of the fourth beast is destroyed (v. 11). Now 'one like a son of man' (or 'human being') is presented to God the judge, and he is given everlasting kingship over all the nations (vv. 13–14). The humanness of this figure contrasts with the beastliness of the first four kingdoms. Similarly, the 'sea' out of which the beasts come is a symbol of Chaos, in the mythological language that the Old Testament sometimes borrows (cf. Pss 46:2 [3]; 93:3–4; Isa. 17:12; Gen. 1:2). This sea-chaos symbolizes opposition to God's created order (vv. 2–3). The human figure, in contrast, comes 'with the clouds of heaven' (v. 13). Clouds also symbolize the presence of God and the heavenly realm elsewhere (Exod. 13:21, and other 'pillar of cloud' passages in Exodus and Numbers; Ezek. 1:4, 28; Isa. 19:1). Like Adam, this human figure receives authority under God (cf. Gen. 1:26, 28, and Goldingay 1989, p. 168).

The interpretation of the dream is given briefly in vv. 17–18, and more fully in vv. 19–28. In the first interpretation, the four kingdoms are finally replaced by the everlasting kingdom given to 'the saints (or 'holy ones') of the Most High'. In the longer interpretation, the focus is on the fourth beast, and especially on the 'little horn', which persecuted the 'holy ones' severely (v. 21). The defeat of this king, and the giving of the kingdom to the 'holy ones', is told twice (vv. 21–22; 23–28). In the interpretations, the term 'one like a son of man' is not used. It is applied to 'the holy ones of the Most High'.

The 'one like a son of man' and the 'holy ones of the Most High' are interpreted differently by commentators as human or angelic figures (see the panel on the Son of Man). In my view the imagery is primarily human, that is, the 'one like a son of man' and the holy ones' represent faithful Israel.

SON OF MAN

Who is the 'one like a son of man' in Daniel 7? This question is obviously important for Christian readers of Daniel, because Jesus is called the 'Son of Man' in the Gospels, and because the passage in Daniel has traditionally been interpreted messianically. Let us look at some relevant facts in Daniel.

First, the term itself, 'one like a son of man', will not identify the figure in Dan. 7:13. The Aramaic expression translated 'son of man', *bar 'enash*, occurs only here in the Old Testament (perhaps because there is very little Aramaic in the Old Testament). But the Hebrew equivalent, *ben 'adam*, is typically used simply of human beings (as regularly of the prophet Ezekiel, Ezek. 2:1; of Daniel, Dan. 8:17; and of humans generally, Ps. 8:4 [5]).

However, the figure is not just a 'son of man', but '*one like* a son of man'. And this sort of description can apply to heavenly beings. Angelic figures are described in human-like terms in Ezek. 8:2–3 ('a figure that looked like a man', *'ish*); Daniel 8:15 ('having the appearance of a man', *geber*). This last text introduces Gabriel, whose name actually means 'man of God'. When he is introduced in this way, he is instructed by a 'human voice', referring either to another angel, or to God himself. God is described in human-like terms in Ezek. 1:26 ('the appearance of the likeness of a man', *'adam*). In Dan. 10:5 the similarity of an angel to a human is expressed very directly: 'I saw a man' ('*ish*), clearly an angel. And in 9:21 Gabriel is simply 'the man (*ha'ish*) Gabriel, whom I had seen before in a vision' (i.e. in 8:15–26). Several different terms are used to describe human-like figures in these texts, and the phrase 'son of man' does not appear in them. However, it is clear that heavenly figures can have human characteristics both in Daniel and in other places.

Indeed, some emphasis is laid on the similarity between human beings and the heavenly beings. Gabriel addresses Daniel as 'son of man' (*ben 'adam*,

8:17). This is the closest expression to the Aramaic phrase in 7:13. But in the context the point is to suggest a likeness between the angelic Gabriel and the human Daniel (see Lacocque 1979, p. 208).

Having looked at these texts it is clear that the 'one like a son of man' in 7:13 could still be either human or angelic! A further factor now comes in. Who are 'the holy ones of the Most High' (*qaddishe 'elyonin*)? This is related because, as we saw in the Outline on ch. 7, the 'one like a son of man' seems to stand for 'the holy ones of the Most High' (7:18, 21–22, 25, 27). And these too may be either human or divine. The human interpretation is suggested by the phrase in 7:27: 'the *people* of the holy ones of the Most High' (where 'people' and 'holy ones' most naturally refer to the same group; cf. 8:24. Some have taken it otherwise, as 'the people belonging to the [heavenly] holy ones'; but see Goldingay 1989, pp. 182–83, and Casey 1979, pp. 40–41). On this human interpretation, the whole chapter may be understood quite naturally as a vision of the triumph of the faithful people of Israel. That is, when the oppressive kingdoms have perished, God will give kingly authority in his world to the faithful people of Israel. This message would not be far from that of Isaiah 40—55.

The *angelic* interpretation of the 'holy ones' has support in Daniel, however, from 8:13–14, where Daniel overhears a heavenly conversation (here the Hebrew *qadosh* corresponds to the Aramaic *qaddish*). And a series of texts in ch. 4 refers to 'watchers' and 'holy ones' (4:13 [10], 17 [14], 23 [20]). These too appear to be angelic messengers. If the 'one like a son of man' and the 'holy ones of the Most High' are angelic or heavenly figures, the meaning of ch. 7 is that the final conflict between good and evil is fought out in heaven. This has support from 10:20–21, where angelic figures appear to represent nations (the angelic speaker, together with the archangel Michael, contends against 'the prince of Persia', 'the prince of Greece'; cf. Lacocque 1979, p. 128). The defeat of powerful kings on earth, therefore, is paralleled by a war in heaven. This idea appears to find support in several of the Qumran writings (e.g. 1QM [War Scroll] 12:8–9; and see Lacocque, p. 131).

There are now two main possibilities for interpreting 'one like a son of man'. Either he is a human figure who stands for the people of Israel, and thus the 'holy ones of the Most High' in Daniel 7 are human; or both the 'one like a son of man' and the 'holy ones of the Most High' are angelic. Both these views have support in the scholarly literature (see Hartman and Di Lella 1978, pp. 218–20, and Casey 1979, pp. 25–46, for the human interpretation; and Collins 1984, p. 82, and Lacocque 1979, pp. 122–34 for the angelic). Lacocque thinks the 'one like a son of man' is identified with the archangel Michael, 'implicitly in chapter 7, explicitly in several passages of chapters 8—12' (p. 133). There are mediating views. For example, Davies thinks the author of 12:1 probably equates 'one like a son of man' with Michael, though the author of ch. 7 does not (Davies 1985, pp. 105–06).

However, the picture is more subtle than either of these opposed views. The temptation is to insist on one extreme at the cost of forcing the text. (For example, the angelic view does not deal easily with 7:21–22, and its defenders sometimes regard these verses as an addition to the basic text, e.g. Noth 1984, p. 228; cf. Lacocque 1979, p. 126.) The attribution of human features to human beings and to angels alike should not be seen as a confusing problem, but as part of the point the author wishes to make. Lacocque's interpretation, which I have classed as 'angelic', recognizes this. The 'one like a son of man' stands for faithful Israel, 'the personification of the righteous people, the perfect image of the righteous individual' (Lacocque 1979, p. 146). But he also points to a fellowship between Israel and the community of 'holy ones' in heaven (pp. 132–34).

Is the 'one like a son of man', then, messianic? For an answer to this, see below, Theological Themes.

However, the conflict that is played out on earth is closely mirrored by a conflict in heaven.

8:1–27: Daniel has a vision of a tyrant arising from the empire of Greece and finally being destroyed by God

The vision in this chapter is dated two years after the vision of the 'one like a son of man' (8:1, cf. 7:1). Daniel's vision is interpreted by the angel Gabriel (v. 16). (On Gabriel and the 'holy ones', vv. 13–14, and Daniel himself as 'son of man', v. 17, see the panel, Son of Man.) Daniel's behaviour when faced by the angelic being is similar to Ezekiel's (Ezek. 1:28; 2:2; Lacocque 1979, p. 168).

The explanation of the vision (vv. 2–14) is given in vv. 20–25. The focus of the visions on the Greek empire is now explicit. The 'great horn' of the male goat is Alexander the Great (vv. 9, 21). His empire divided among four generals on his death (v. 8, though the fourfold division may be intended symbolically here, corresponding to the 'four winds of heaven'; Hartman and Di Lella 1978, p. 235). The 'little horn' (v. 9) is again Antiochus Epiphanes IV (as in 7:8, though the imagery is now different).

The message to Daniel is that the vision is for the 'time of the end', that is, the time of Antiochus Epiphanes, when he desecrated the temple (v. 11) in 168 BC (cf. 9:27; 11:31; 12:11). The history of the kingdoms is revealed in order to show the people suffering persecution at that time ('the people of the holy ones', v. 24) that their sufferings would soon cease.

9:1–27: After Daniel's prayer of penitence on behalf of Israel, Gabriel reassures him again that tyranny will be overcome

In this key chapter, Daniel interprets Israel's

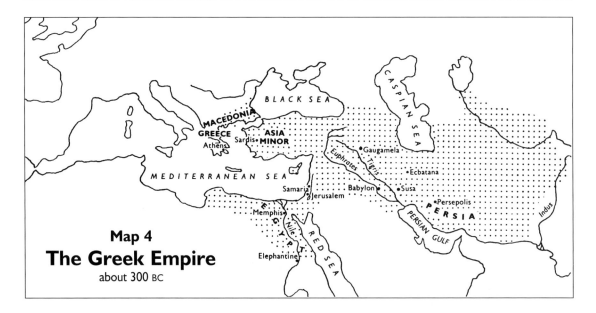

Map 4
The Greek Empire
about 300 BC

BLACK SEA

CASPIAN SEA

MACEDONIA
GREECE
Athens
Sardis ASIA MINOR

MEDITERRANEAN SEA

Euphrates
Tigris

Gaugamela

Ecbatana

Samaria
Jerusalem
Babylon
Susa

Memphis

Persepolis

PERSIA

NILE

RED SEA

PERSIAN GULF

Indus

Elephantine

covenantal and prophetic traditions, and applies them to the crisis of the Jews under Antiochus IV. The key prophetic text is Jeremiah's prophecy that the exile would last seventy years (v. 2, cf. Jer. 25:11–12; 29:10). The exile in the strictest sense (until exiles returned from Babylon) could be measured as about seventy years (see on the Jeremiah texts just mentioned). In Daniel's concept this corresponds to the time from the beginning of the exile in 605 BC (see on 1:1) to the 'first year of Darius the Mede (about 539 BC), or perhaps the 'third year of Cyrus (10:1), that is, about 536 BC. However, the time referred to in Daniel 9 is well after that period (it is fixed once again by the reference to the desecration of the temple in 9:27, by Antiochus Epiphanes IV in 168 BC). The dating of the vision in 539 gives rise to the interpretation of the seventy years that will be offered in this chapter.

The seventy-year exile is re-interpreted by Gabriel (vv. 24–27). Perhaps taking a cue from Lev. 26:18, 27 (which warn of God's sevenfold punishment for breaking the covenant), the seventy years become seventy 'sevens', or 'weeks', of years. (Gabriel's speech has been called an 'exegetical midrash' on Jeremiah's seventy years; Collins 1984, pp. 9–10; Goldingay 1989, pp. 231–32.) The arithmetic cannot be pressed for accuracy (490 years from 597 or 587 would take us too late), but the thought is that Israel has been continuously in 'exile' since the time of Nebuchadnezzar. This fits with the idea of four successive oppressive empires in chs 2 and 7. Only after this long period, and the final intense persecution of Antiochus, will salvation for faithful Israel come at last.

Daniel's prayer (vv. 4–19) is, in its literary type, a communal confession (cf. Ezra 9:6–15; cf. Goldingay 1989, p. 233). It draws on a range of prophecies about the exile, all intended to support the point that the time of exile is finally coming to an end in the time about which he speaks. It especially takes up language of Ezekiel about the restoration of Israel. See, for example, Ezek. 20:40–44, compare Dan. 9:15–19, and note especially the accent on God's grace, not the merit of the people. Daniel, in his prayer, seems to be consciously fulfilling the requirements of the prophecy.

Digging deeper:
PROPHETIC ALLUSIONS

There are many prophetic allusions in Daniel's prayer. For example, with Dan. 9:7 compare Isa. 33:13; Jer. 16:8; Ezek. 18:24 ('treachery'). Dan. 9:26b echoes Isa. 10:22–23. (See also Lacocque 1979, p. 182–87.) Why does Daniel deliberately build this range of prophecies into his prayer? A key phrase may be 'to seal vision and prophet' (v. 24). Note how Lacocque understands this (1979, p. 193), i.e. bringing prophecy to an end once and for all. Porteous offers an alternative to this (1979, p. 140). The idea of completion applies also to *sin*. What 'sin' is referred to in 9:24? (cf. 8:23).

Some think the prayer is out of keeping with the pattern of revelation in chs 8—12 (Hartman and Di Lella 1978, pp. 245–46). How may it fit the thought of the chapter? Does it qualify Daniel as the 'favoured man' (v. 23), who is fit to be given a revelation (Lacocque 1979, p. 178)? Is it a representative prayer by a righteous individual on behalf of Israel, qualifying the faithful to be redeemed (Goldingay 1989, p. 233)? If so how does this relate to Ezekiel's point in Ezek. 14:12–20?

The anointing of a most holy place (v. 24) may refer to the rededication of the temple in 164 BC (cf. 1 Macc. 4:36–59). The 'anointed ones' (*mashiah*, 'messiah') in vv. 25, 26 are probably high priests. But identifications and interpretation are disputed.

Digging deeper:
A 'MESSIANIC TEXT'?

In what sense is Dan. 9:24–26 'messianic' (only here in OT is *mashiah* used in 'absolute' way to refer to 'the messiah'; Selman 1995, pp. 283–84)? Find out the different ways in which commentators have interpreted this text over the generations. Ask what is referred to by the phrase translated in NRSV as 'most holy place' (v. 25). Who are the 'anointed prince' and the 'anointed one' in vv. 25–26? Does the prophecy relate in any way to the coming of Christ? (Traditional Christian interpretation has taken the 7+62+7 non-historically, i.e. [variously] of Christ and the Church; Meadowcroft 2001, pp. 431–32.) A variety of answers to these questions can be found in the commentaries of Porteous (1979, pp. 139–44), Baldwin (1978, pp. 167–78), Lacocque (especially on the 'holy of holies', 1979, pp. 193–94). The New Testament sees the announcement of the kingdom of God inaugurated by Jesus, Mark 13:14 = Matt. 25:15; 2 Thess. 2:4; Josephus: AD 70 (Lacocque 1979, p. 191).

Gabriel's interpretation of the 'seventy years' in vv. 24–27 apparently refers to the initial period after the return from Babylon (the first seven weeks), the long period from then to the Antiochene period (62 weeks), and the time of that crisis itself. 'The abomination that makes desolate' (9:27; cf. 11:31) is the statue erected by Antiochus IV to the god Zeus Olympios in the temple.

10:1—12:13: An angel shows Daniel what will happen to his people in the end time. A preview of history up to Antiochus IV leads into a promise of the final triumph of the righteous

The last in the series of visions that began in 7:1 is dated in the reign of Cyrus (10:1). This is the latest date given for a vision, and signals that the drama moves towards its final scene. The angelic figures in this chapter are not identified by name, and the one in vv. 5–9 need not be the same as the one (or ones) in vv. 10, 16, 18 (see further Goldingay 1989, pp. 290–92). The first figure is particularly impressive in appearance (cf. the vision of God in Ezek. 1:27), and Daniel reacts as if it is a vision of God (vv. 7–9; cf. Judg. 13:20). The point of ch. 10 is to explain why the deliverance of Israel has taken so long to come. The 'princes' of Persia and Greece apparently refer to angelic beings who correspond to those nations in heaven (vv. 13, 20–21). Correspondingly, Michael is the special angelic protector of Israel (12:1). He is distinct from the speaker (or speakers) in 10:13, 21.

Daniel 11 is the most detailed telling of the events leading up to Antiochus IV's desecration of the temple in 168 BC, the event that has been at the centre of each of the visions since ch. 7. Collins classes it as a 'regnal prophecy', one of the types of *ex eventu* prophecy that he identifies, noting Babylonian parallels, and the Jewish Sibylline Oracles 5:1–51 (Collins 1984, p. 12). Antiochus IV comes in at v. 21, his assassination of the high priest Onias III is referred to in v. 22 ('the prince of the covenant', cf. the 'anointed prince/chief' of 9:25), and the desecration of the temple – which he commanded in his absence – is recorded in v. 31 (cf. 9:27). The 'little help' for the faithful (v. 34) could refer to the Maccabean revolt, but this is not certain. Verse 35 refers to the time of suffering the faithful had to endure, in terms that once again recall Hab. 2:2–3 (cf. 8:17b, 26b; 10:14b). Verses 30–35 point to a division between the faithful in Israel, and 'those who forsake the holy covenant' (those who collaborated with the Greek overlords).

The particular arrogance of Antiochus, to the point of his self-deification, is stressed (v. 36). His campaign against the worship of Israel's God (cf. 1 Macc. 1:41–49), may have been intended to increase his own prestige. (On his coins he had the word *theos*, 'god', inscribed, and portrayed Zeus Olympios with his own features; Hartman and Di Lella 1978, p. 301.) This corresponds to other allusions to him in visions (7:8, 25; 8:11). Antiochus IV's arrogance makes an ironic play with the idea of divine figures in human form (chs 7—10), for here is a human figure who wants divine honour.

Digging deeper:
DANIEL 11 AND HISTORY

The historical issues in ch. 11 can only be appreciated by a close reading of the chapter with guidance as to the events referred to, as in a detailed commentary. (Hartman and Di Lella is very full; pp. 286–305. Porteous and Lacocque are more succinct.) A primary source is 1 Maccabees 1—4, which should also be read in conjunction with this text.

The issue about the nature of prophecy in Daniel is sharpest at this point. Joyce Baldwin challenges the usual scholarly assumption that Dan. 11:1–39 is prophecy after the event (*ex eventu*), on the grounds that this is contrary to a natural reading, and therefore calls in question the theology of the book, which sets great store by God's power to reveal mysteries, including the future (Baldwin 1978, pp. 182–85). Goldingay responds point by point (1989, p. 283). The discussion is about genre. Can the integrity of this kind of prophecy after the event be preserved if it is a known type of literature that its intended readers would have understood? Consider Baldwin's concerns and whether Goldingay meets them.

Daniel 11 stays close to known historical events up to v. 39. Verses 40–45 depart from the known history, and tell of a last flourish of this king, ending at last in his downfall. This turn from known history to the unknown and somewhat general is the clue that leads most scholars to date this chapter after 167 BC and before 164, when the temple was rededicated. The omission of the victories of Judas Maccabaeus may suggest 166 BC.

In ch. 12 the expectation of deliverance from exile is combined with the hope of the resurrection. The faithful will have to endure a terrible persecution (12:1; cf. Jer. 30:7), but in the end the faithful people will be delivered (for the 'book', see Exod. 32:32; Ps. 69:28 [29]). The faithful who died during the persecution will rise to 'everlasting life' along with those who remain (v. 2). The separation between those who would rise to life and those who would suffer everlasting contempt corresponds to the division among the Jews in 11:30–35. The resurrection is in the first place applied to the people of Israel, in continuity with Ezek. 37:1–14.

The idea of resurrection is not new here in the Old Testament (see Lacocque 1979, pp. 236–38; Baldwin 1978, pp. 204–05). New is its use in an eschatological context, that is, where it is linked to the final establishment of the kingdom of God, and a general judgement of the righteous and the wicked. This no doubt lies behind the understanding of the idea in the New Testament (e.g. Matt. 25:46; John 5:28–29, cf. 11:24).

The book ends with the promise that the final victory of God for his people will come at a specified time from the desecration of the temple. Daniel will be rewarded at that time for his faithfulness (12:11–13).

THEOLOGICAL THEMES

THE KINGDOM OF GOD

The metaphor of God's kingship runs through the whole biblical story. For example, the covenantal texts of the Old Testament (especially Deuteronomy) put God in the role of the 'great king' who imposes treaties on his vassals. Isaiah and Ezekiel both had visions of God seated on his heavenly throne (Isaiah 6; Ezekiel 1). Daniel's vision of the 'Ancient of Days' and the presentation to him of 'one like a son of man' (7:9–14) is in the same line of descent. All these visions are based on a common Ancient Near Eastern idea of God's heavenly court, in which he is surrounded by other heavenly beings. The similarities of Daniel's portrayal of God to mythological imagery have often been noted (Emerton 1958, cf. Davies 1985, pp. 73–75). The 'great sea', for example (7:2–3), is like the primeval Chaos, and the beasts that come out of it have echoes of the monster that opposed God in the beginning, a myth reflected elsewhere in the Old Testament, where the monster is called Leviathan or Rahab (Job 26:12; Ps. 74:13–14).

But the idea of the kingship of God gains new dimensions in Daniel. Isaiah had already known that God's rule extended to raising up and putting down successive kingdoms (in the sequence Assyria-Babylon). Ezekiel saw a conflict between God and nations beyond the immediate time, in his vision of Gog (Ezek. 38—39). Daniel now presents God's rule in history in the schema of a succession of four kingdoms, followed by the establishment of a kingdom of a different kind. There are several elements in this view.

First, there is the kingship of God, that is, he is the one who rules. The author of Daniel can hardly have thought that these four were the only ones that counted in history. The choice of kingdoms depends on the setting of the book, spanning the Babylonian to the Seleucid periods. The schema is a way of saying that God is behind, and over, all the powers and developments in the human world.

Second, God grants power to kings: not only kings of Israel and Judah, in the line of David, but kings generally. This is clear about Nebuchadnezzar (2:37; 4:25 – 'the Most High has sovereignty over the kingdom of mortals, and gives it to whom he will'). Daniel 4:36–37 shows, moreover, that in his right mind, Nebuchadnezzar could rule well. Isaiah had seen that Cyrus could be chosen for God's purposes (Isa. 45:1), and indeed Jeremiah had seen it of Nebuchadnezzar (Jer. 27:1–7). But Daniel makes it a general principle. The universality of God in his delegation of authority to human beings is accentuated in Daniel by the choice of names for God. Titles like 'God of gods . . . lord of kings', 2:47; 'the Most High', chs 4; 7, cf. 3:26; 'God of Heaven' ch. 2, are typical in Daniel, though traditional Israelite names are used in 2:23 ('God of my fathers'), and in ch. 9 (Yahweh, 9:8, 10 etc.).

Third, Daniel knows not only of the king*ship* of God, but of his king*dom*, in a development that would be important for the New Testament. After the succession of human kingdoms have come to an end in turn, God will set up 'a kingdom that shall never be destroyed' (2:44). This is the forward look that can properly be called eschatological. It is the basis of the hope that current oppressive regimes would fall at last. And it is accompanied by the teaching about resurrection and everlasting life (12:1–3).

It is sometimes said that the schematic view of history, especially in the visions, is deterministic (e.g. Davies 1985, p. 87). Davies sees a sharp distinction between a distant God (in the visions) who has simply prescribed all in advance and a God who is involved in everyday life in the stories. This underestimates the force of the marriage of story and vision in Daniel, and overpresses the four-kingdom schema. It is the 'wise' to whom the message comes in the visions, and the resurrection is offered to these (12:2–3). In the visions too, there is a call to faithfulness.

DIVINE AND HUMAN RULE

Human beings are given astonishing dignity in Daniel. The shape of godly rule is human. The first beast was 'made to stand on two feet like a human being and a human mind was given to it' (7:4, in a reference to the restoration of Nebuchadnezzar after his madness, 4:36–37). The angelic figures who speak to Daniel have human form, and some stress is laid on their correspondence to Daniel in this form (8:15–17). And over all the communication between the worlds of heaven and earth in chs 7—12 is the figure of the 'one like a son of man', who is at home in both worlds at once (see Son of Man).

In this view of the world, human beings take on again their responsibility to rule given at the creation, where the whole created order was made subordinate to them (Gen. 1:26–28). Kings may or may not conform to the 'Adam' pattern. Nebuchadnezzar may do so for a while. But opposite that model of right rule stands Belshazzar (a type of Antiochus IV in the minds of the readers), who symbolizes the worst possibilities of human rule, the pride that wants the rank of god, and self-serving tyranny. The high status of humanity can be corrupted into the worst kind of offence against God. The sin of the Garden of Eden is repeated in the pride of kings.

Think about
THE PRIDE OF KINGS

Look again at Ezekiel 28, and compare how the sin of pride in kings is portrayed there with its portrayal in Daniel.

MESSIAH

The question of whether Daniel has a messianic theology must be seen in the light of the previous section. As we saw (Son of Man), the 'one like a son of man' stands for the faithful Jewish people, for the righteous individual, and points to a fellowship between the 'holy ones' on earth and in heaven. The term 'messiah' itself (in 9:24–26) is not used in a 'messianic' sense. The future hope in Daniel is for the kingdom of God, the resurrection of the faithful to a kingdom presided over by Michael and other angels. The 'one like a son of man' does not yet refer to a messianic figure in Daniel in the sense of a specially appointed individual who comes from heaven in the end to establish a kingdom on earth (see Rowland 1982, pp. 46–47). The Similitudes of Enoch (in 1 Enoch) move closer to this idea of the 'son of man' than Daniel does.

This being so, it is clear that the concept of the Son of Man in the Gospels does not simply lift the idea from Daniel as it is found there, but is a reinterpretation in the light of the coming of Jesus. The coming of the Son of Man in clouds with great power and glory (Mark 13:26) is in line with the New Testament's expectation of the coming of the messiah from heaven (Acts 3:19–21; 1 Thess. 4:15–17; see Rowland 1982, pp. 45–47). The justification of this reinterpretation of the

Son of Man by Jesus and the Gospels is that in Daniel the 'one like a son of man' is part of a comprehensive picture of humanity restored to its proper place in God's world, bearing the responsibility of government under him. Jesus, as Son of Man, does this, where other human beings could not.

GOD'S FAITHFULNESS, HUMAN FAITHFULNESS

The Book of Daniel affirms the faithfulness of God and requires the faithfulness of his people. God's faithfulness is at stake in the situation of exile, as we saw in the first three major prophetic books. The immediate issue has moved on in Daniel, however. Although the book begins with the bringing of Daniel and his friends to Babylon, the exilic background is simply assumed from then on. The faithfulness of God is not made dependent on a return to the homeland, rather it is played out in the exile itself. The issue is now whether God will and can protect his people from the all too visible power of kings who do not recognize the God of Israel, and who may at any time try to assert their power against his claims. In the stories, God's faithfulness is demonstrated in his deliverance of the friends from death in the furnace and Daniel from the lions (chs 3; 6).

These stories serve as a foundation for the promises of God's faithfulness in the end, which are the theme of the visions. The affirmation of his faithfulness calls for faithfulness on the part of the people who suffer under tyranny. Daniel and the three friends are models of piety in these situations. The reader knows the happy outcome of the story of the friends and the fiery furnace but, as they were tied up to be thrown into it, they did not. Their confession of faith that God can deliver them is followed by 'But if *not . . .* we will not serve your gods.' (3:18–19). This is one of the revealing moments in the book. The perspective of the visions (and the book as a whole) is from the midst of persecution, with no obvious end in sight. The affirmations of God's kingship are made in the grip of tyranny. God raises up kings and puts them down, but he has not yet destroyed Antiochus IV, who in fact made many martyrs (Dan. 11:33; 1 Macc. 1:57–63; 2:29–38). In Shadrach, Meshach and Abednego we hear the authentic voice of people whose faith could cost them their lives. This is the vocation of the faithful according to the Book of Daniel.

It is in this context that the major themes of wisdom and knowledge function in the book. The faithful Jews are called 'the wise', again in the footsteps of the wise Daniel. Why *should* pious Jews endure persecution when it might cost them their lives? The answer is that they have been shown the secrets of heaven. Antiochus may still rage, but they have it on the highest authority that he will fall, like all others before him. 'One of the most important contributions of the Book of Daniel is its novel insistence on the linking of faith to understanding' (Lacocque 1979, p. 191). And this understanding is given for the purpose of endurance.

Think about
WISDOM AND UNDERSTANDING

Notice how wisdom and understanding are in parallel with 'purification, cleansing and refinement', and opposed to *wickedness*, in Dan. 12:10. How far is this a typical Old Testament connection? See Prov. 16:6–7, and follow up the parallels between wisdom and righteousness in that book. Does Daniel have the same view of wisdom?

RHETORICAL INTENTION

The rhetorical intention of the Book of Daniel has already been implied in the preceding paragraphs (especially God's faithfulness, human faithfulness). The rhetorical 'exigency' (that is, the crisis that produces the need for the book to be written) is clear. Jewish people are coming under strong pressure to compromise or abandon their faith. The issue is in principle the same for the Babylonian exiles and for the later generation in Palestine. Under Antiochus IV many did give way (1 Macc. 1:43b, 52–53). Antiochus even found willing Jewish collaborators in Jerusalem who were prepared to help him destroy traditional Judaism for the sake of their own advancement (2 Macc. 4:8–19). In this context, the aim of the Book of Daniel is to persuade people who are suffering persecution that it is worth holding fast to their faith and enduring persecution, because God will finally vindicate them, even after death.

The structure and content of the book serve this message. We have seen how the stories support the appeal in the visions. Just as important is the revelation that the conflict on earth is paralleled by conflict in heaven. It is no accident that the human and angelic figures in the visions are in close relationship (see panel on Son of Man), or that scholars have found it hard to decide whether 'one like a son of man' is human or angelic. The persuasive point in this is that the human conflict that people are enduring is *actually* a heavenly conflict. There is a dimension to it that is hidden from natural view. The agents of the tyrant belong to a host that is bound to be defeated because their defeat has already been decreed by heaven itself.

This raises the question how exactly the Book of Daniel wishes its readers to respond. Or to put it differently, which Jewish group of the period stands closest to its message? Was it the violent resistance of the priest Mattathias, who killed a Jew who offered a pagan sacrifice in the Jewish town of Modein, together with the Seleucid official who had come to enforce it, and to turn the population away from their faith (1 Macc. 2:1, 15–26)? He and his sons then began an 'armed struggle', and for a time under Mattathias's son Judas (nicknamed Maccabaeus, hence the name Maccabees for the movement) had astonishing military successes against the imperial armies.

Digging deeper:
DANIEL AND 1 MACCABEES

Read Mattathias's speech to the Seleucid officials in 1 Macc. 2:19–22. Now compare it with the words of Shadrach, Meshach and Abednego in Dan. 3:16–18. What are the similarities and differences? Could the differences be a clue to different persuasive purposes of the books of Daniel and 1 Maccabees?

Commentators usually suppose that the author of Daniel did not approve of the Maccabean revolt, or at best gave it only the faintest of praise in a veiled allusion in Dan. 11:34 ('a little help'). The powerlessness of the faithful Jews in Daniel and their readiness to meet martyrdom is consistent with a more passive style of resistance. The emphasis in the final verses of Daniel is on perseverance and the prospect of a long period of suffering (Dan. 12:11–12). Daniel's 'wise' have been identified with the 'Hasideans' (or hasidim') (1 Macc. 2:42; 2 Macc. 14:6), the group who sought refuge in the wilderness in 1 Macc. 2:29–38 and were killed on the sabbath, and scribes in the line of Ben Sira (see Sirach 38:34—39:11).

Digging deeper:
'THE WISE'

Consider these possible identifications of 'the wise', together with the texts cited, and ask whether any of them is likely. Then see Davies 1985, pp. 121–25 for an evaluation, and a further suggestion. It is not finally possible to identify the 'wise' of Daniel with a particular group.

Finally under this heading, it is important to ask whether Daniel really supports a 'deterministic' view of history, as is often said. This is in reference to the schematic presentation of history in which the four successive kingdoms are replaced finally by the 'kingdom that shall never be destroyed' (2:44). This 'deterministic' concept of history is one of the factors that is thought to set Daniel apart from a prophetic view. (See the panel on Apocalyptic, and the references there to von Rad and Bauckham.)

Think about
A 'DETERMINISTIC' VIEW OF HISTORY?

Do you think this interpretation of Daniel is consistent with its persuasive force as we have tried to describe it? For Daniel's audience much remains uncertain, and they are urged strongly to behave in a certain way. Is this any more 'deterministic' than the message of Isaiah or Ezekiel? Could the schematic presentation of history simply be a device (a convention borrowed from other ancient literature) to reinforce the point that God is ultimately in control?

DANIEL IN THE CANON

In the Christian form of the Old Testament canon Daniel stands among the prophetic books, while in the Jewish canon it is in the Writings section. This difference in the canonical tradition is perhaps not surprising, since the book is unique in the Old Testament in important ways.

Think about
DANIEL AMONG THE PROPHETS?

Consider in what ways the book is like and unlike the prophetic books so far studied. What reasons do you think might have led to its inclusion in the Writings section of the Jewish canon? Notice that we have at various points found similarities between Daniel and other books in that section, such as Esther and Proverbs.

The inclusion of Daniel with the prophets leads us to think of it as somehow related to the emphases of those books, even though Daniel is nowhere called a 'prophet'. A connection is established in Daniel's prayer of penitence. This prayer, as we saw, reinterprets Jeremiah's prediction of a seventy-year exile (9:2), confesses the people's failure to hear the prophets (9:6, 10) and shows that prophetic prediction will be fulfilled in the end (9:24).

The express link with Jeremiah means it is no surprise that Daniel should come soon after that book in the canonical order. It comes immediately after Ezekiel, however, and this may reflect similarities that we have noticed between that book and Daniel, especially the heavenly visions and the explanation of them by heavenly beings. A further link with Ezekiel may lie in Ezekiel's requirement of repentance before the

restoration. Daniel's prayer of repentance in ch. 9 meets the requirement on behalf of the people, and thus declares that the conditions for the end of the exile exist (the main concern of ch. 9). Daniel thus takes on the role of as the intercessor, that is, the one who can make an effective prayer on behalf of the community. This is paradoxical in terms of the relationship with Jeremiah and Ezekiel. Note Ezekiel 14.

Think about
DANIEL AS INTERCESSOR

Why is Daniel's role as intercessor paradoxical in the light of Jeremiah and Ezekiel? Consider this in the light of Jer. 7:16; 11; 14; 15:1; Ezek. 14:12–20.

The inclusion of Daniel among the prophets, and as an interpreter of prophecy, highlights the function of the prophets in general as those who have told in advance of future deliverance. This is consistent with another feature of the Christian canon, which, unlike the Jewish form, closes with the prophetic books, and thus creates an expectation of a fulfilment still to come.

This last point relates to one of the features of the book that is observed in all critical discussion of it, namely that its account of the events in the reign of Antiochus IV Epiphanes departs from their known course at Dan. 11:40. It is interesting to reflect that, in the days following the death of Antiochus IV and the rededication of the temple in 164 BC, those who could follow the narrative of ch. 11 closely enough to identify the events recorded in it (as was presumably the intention of the writer) must have known what modern scholars have observed. Yet the book continued to be regarded as Scripture.

Indeed it was a popular book. A number of Daniel fragments were found at Qumran, and these seem to show the influence of more than one textural tradition (Hartman and Di Lella 1978, pp. 72–73). We know too that the figure of Daniel continued to give rise to further stories about him. (Susanna and Bel and the Dragon, included in the Greek form of the book, are examples of this.)

The departure from known facts about Antiochus IV at 11:40 has the curious effect of diverting attention from the particular circumstances of his persecution. This is paradoxical, of course, because as we have seen, the visions all converged on him, and these verses still purport to do so. Yet Baldwin, noting that '(a)lready before the end of the third century the shadow of Rome was falling over the eastern Mediterranean', continues: 'It is therefore naïve to suggest that the writer thought the end of all things was imminent in the time of Antiochus Epiphanes' (Baldwin 1978, p. 184). Whether or not this was true for the writer, it must quickly have become clear for the readers. The Jewish writer Josephus (in the first century AD) made a comparison between the sufferings of the Jews under Antiochus IV and under Rome: 'In the very same manner Daniel also wrote concerning the Roman government, and that our country should be made desolate by them' (*Jewish Antiquities* x.276; also cited by Baldwin 1978, p. 175). In the same way, for the earliest Christian readers, the assurances initially made in connection with the Antiochene persecution could readily be extended into the establishment of the kingdom of God through Christ. The reception of Daniel in the New Testament witnesses to this development. Mark 13:26–27 shows how the 'son of man' language and imagery was adapted to refer to Christ. And the same chapter anticipates a 'desolating sacrilege' still to be set up 'where it ought not to be' (that is, in the temple, referring to the Roman destruction of the temple in AD 70, and the rededication of the site to Roman worship; Mark 13:14). And the Book of Revelation re-uses motifs from the visions to depict the conflicts that must be endured in the time of the church before the final victory of Christ.

For a detailed treatment of Daniel's influence on the New Testament, see Adela Yarbro Collins, in J. J. Collins 1993, pp. 90–123.

Think about
DANIEL AND REVELATION

Read Revelation 13 and 20 looking for motifs from Daniel. How have they been reinterpreted (the beast, the image of the beast, the sea, the resurrection, the one who sat on the throne, the books opened, the dead judged)?

FURTHER READING

* Items marked with * are considered suitable as first ports of call, while others are more complex, or relate to specific issues.

COMMENTARIES

Baldwin is still an excellent short commentary, favouring the earlier date of Daniel. Porteous is a good general commentary favouring the later date. Lucas is up to date and very useful. Lacocque is stimulating for its theological interpretation. Collins is masterly on interpreting apocalyptic.

*J. G. Baldwin *Daniel*. TOTC. Leicester: IVP, 1978).

*J. J. Collins *Daniel With an Introduction to Apocalyptic Literature*. FOTL 20. Grand Rapids: Eerdmans, 1984.

J. J. Collins *Daniel*. Hermeneia. Minneapolis: Fortress, 1993.

J. E. Goldingay *Daniel*. WBC. Dallas: Word Books, 1989.

L. F. Hartman and A. A. Di Lella *Daniel*. AB. New York: Doubleday, 1978.

A. Lacocque *The Book of Daniel*. London: SPCK, 1979.

*E. Lucas *Daniel*. Leicester: Apollos, 2002.

*N. Porteous *Daniel*. OTL. London: SCM, second edition 1979.

*D. S. Russell *Daniel*. DSB. Edinburgh: St. Andrew Press/Philadelphia: Westminster Press, 1981.

OTHER BOOKS AND ARTICLES

J. G. Baldwin 'Some Literary Affinities of the Book of Daniel' *TB* 30. 1979, pp. 77–99.

R. Bauckham 'The Rise of Apocalyptic' *Themelios* 3. 1978, pp. 10–23.

M. Casey *Son of Man: the Interpretation and Influence of Daniel 7*. London: SPCK, 1979.

J. H. Charlesworth *The Old Testament Pseudepigrapha 1 and 2*. New York: Doubleday, 1983, 1985.

*P. R. Davies *Daniel*. OT Guides. Sheffield: JSOT Press, 1985.

R. B. Dillard and T. Longman III *An Introduction to the Old Testament*. Grand Rapids: Zondervan; Leicester: Apollos, 1995.

J. A. Emerton 'The Origin of the Son of Man Imagery' *JTS* 9. 1958, pp. 225–42.

J. E. Goldingay 'The Book of Daniel: Three Issues' *Themelios* 2. 1976–77, pp. 45–49.

P. D. Hanson, *The Dawn of Apocalyptic*. Philadelphia: Fortress, 1979.

W. L. Humphreys 'A Lifestyle for Diaspora: a Study of the Tales of Esther and Daniel' *JBL* 92. 1973, pp. 211–23.

Tim Meadowcroft 'Exploring the Dismal Swamp: The Identity of the Anointed One in Daniel 9:24–27' *JBL* 120. 2001, pp. 429–49.

S. Niditch *The Symbolic Vision in Biblical Tradition*. HSM 30. Chico: Scholars Press, 1983.

M. Noth 'The Holy ones of the Most High' in M. Noth *The Laws in the Pentateuch and Other Essays*. London: SCM, 1984, pp. 215–28.

G. von Rad *Wisdom in Israel*. London: SCM, 1972.

D. B. Redford *A Study of the Biblical Story of Joseph*. SVT, 20. Leiden: Brill, 1970.

C. Rowland *The Open Heaven: a Study of Apocalyptic in Judaism and Early Christianity*. London: SPCK, 1982.

C. Rowland 'Apocalyptic Literature' in D. A. Carson and H. G. M. Williamson eds *It Is Written: Scripture Citing Scripture; Essays in Honour of Barnabas Lindars, SSF*. Cambridge: CUP, 1988.

H. H. Rowley 'The Unity of the Book of Daniel' in *The Servant of the Lord*. (rev. ed.) Oxford: Blackwell, 1965, pp. 249–80 (previously London: Lutterworth, pp. 237–68).

*D. S. Russell *The Method and Message of Apocalyptic*. London: SCM, 1964.

M. Selman 'Messianic Mysteries' in P. E. Satterthwaite et al. *The Lord's Anointed*. Carlisle: Paternoster; Grand Rapids: Baker, 1995, pp. 281–302.

W. H. Shea 'An Unrecognized Vassal King of Babylon in the Early Achaemenid Period' *AUSS* 9. 1971, pp. 51–57, 99–128; *AUSS* 10. 1972, pp. 88–117, 147–78.

W. H. Shea 'Darius the Mede' *AUSS* 20. 1982, pp. 229–47.

G. J. Wenham 'Daniel: The Basic Issues' *Themelios* 2. 1976–77, pp. 49–52.

L. M. Wills *The Jew in the Court of the Foreign King: Ancient Jewish Court Legends*. Minneapolis: Fortress Press, 1990.

D. J. Wiseman, T. C. Mitchell, R. Joyce, W. J. Martin and K. A. Kitchen *Notes on Some Problems in the Book of Daniel*. London: Tyndale Press, 1965.

THE BOOK OF THE TWELVE

The twelve prophetic books from Hosea to Malachi are sometimes regarded as a single work, and called the Book of the Twelve. There are some grounds for this in ancient literature. Ben Sira, in his praise of the prophets, refers to the Twelve Prophets, in a sequence following Isaiah, Jeremiah and Ezekiel (Sirach 49:10). Some early counts of the books of the Old Testament give totals of twenty-two or twenty-four, instead of the thirty-nine that are listed in modern English Bibles (see Josephus etc). One reason for the difference is that the Twelve were counted as one book.

There are certain features of the Twelve which, on the surface, support this view. For example, the shortest books in the collection, such as Obadiah and Nahum, are scarcely 'books' in the same sense as the bigger ones. These two are quite like the Oracles Against the Nations sections of the larger books, and make sense as parts rather than as wholes. Nahum's denunciation of Nineveh (Assyria) would be narrow and one-sided in itself, but makes sense as a reassurance to Judah (1:15) when we also know that Assyria was, in its time, an agent of God's judgement (Hos. 10:6). So when Nahum is put in the light of Hosea we see a connection similar to the one we saw in Isaiah (Isa. 10:5–11, 12–19).

There are other kinds of inner linkages between the books of the Twelve. For example, we are bound to ask how it is that one book (Jonah) can have a story about Nineveh's repentance and salvation, while another (Nahum) has only words of judgement for it. Similarly, Obadiah's words against Edom continue a series of texts in which Edom stands representatively for nations that will come under God's judgement (Joel 3:19; Amos 1:11–12; 9:12; cf. Collins 1993, p. 70). There are 'catchword' links too. Joel 3:16a ('The LORD roars from Zion, and utters his

> **Think about**
> **READING JOEL BEFORE AMOS**
>
> Collins makes the connection between Joel 3:16 and Amos 1:2. In his view the effect of Joel being placed before Amos was 'that the dire threats against Israel which dominate Amos are softened when read in the light of the more optimistic ending of Joel' (Collins 1993, p. 68). Do you think this is a good way of expressing the effect of reading Joel before Amos?

Digging deeper:
THE BOOK OF THE TWELVE AS ONE BOOK?

Read Collins 1993, pp. 59–84, and work through the connections he makes there between the books in the Twelve. Then consider the theory that the Twelve should be treated as a single work. Here are some questions to ask:

1. Do the thematic and contextual links he identifies demonstrate that the Twelve should be read as a single book?
2. Note the variations in the order between MT and LXX (LXX: Hosea–Amos–Micah–Joel; LXX=MT from Nahum to Malachi). Does this give evidence of canonical thinking about the order of the books? Or does it show, on the contrary, that the order of the books was fluid in the tradition, and thus militate against the idea that the Twelve are a 'book'?

3. Do you think the links between the books of the Twelve might be overemphasized at the expense of links between these books and the major prophetic books (Isaiah, Jeremiah, Ezekiel, Daniel)? For example, Isa 2:2–4 anticipates Mic. 4:1–4; Jeremiah cites Micah 3:12 in Jer. 26:18; the centrality of Jerusalem in vision of the future (Zephaniah) reminds of Ezek. 40---48).
4. Do you think there is as clear a structure in the Twelve as there is in the major books (for example, how are Oracles Against the Nations distributed)? And what do you make of the self-containedness and individuality of a number of the books (e.g. Jonah, Zechariah)?

Notice finally the different kinds of arguments used by Collins (1993), and House (1990).

---

voice from Jerusalem') is repeated only a few verses later in Amos 1:2 (since Amos follows Joel in MT). The context is different in each case (salvation in Joel, judgement in Amos), but such contrasts are perhaps deliberate.

FURTHER READING

R. J. Coggins *Haggai, Zechariah, Malachi*. OTG. Sheffield: JSOT Press, 1987.

R. J. Coggins 'The Minor Prophets; One Book or Twelve?' in S. Porter et al. eds *Crossing the Boundaries: Essays in Biblical Interpretation in Honour of Michael D. Goulder.* Leiden: Brill, 1994, pp. 57–68.

T. Collins *The Mantle of Elijah*. Sheffield: Continuum, 1993.

P. R. House *The Unity of the Twelve*. Sheffield: Almond Press, 1990.

Chapter 6

HOSEA

DATE AND DESTINATION

The Book of Hosea stands at the head of the Book of the Twelve, or the Minor Prophets, as they are otherwise known (Hosea–Malachi). Though it is first in sequence in the Twelve, it is not the earliest in time, since Amos' prophecy is dated a decade or so before the time when Hosea probably began to prophesy in about 750 BC. The order of the books of the Twelve, therefore, is not quite chronological, although generally the books associated with the eighth century precede books from the exilic and pre-exilic periods. However, theological factors have probably contributed to the ordering of the books as we have them in MT and English Bibles (see The Book of the Twelve).

The setting of the book is in the northern kingdom, up to the end of the reign of King Hoshea (732–722 BC) and the fall of that kingdom. The events alluded to cover the period up to that event from about the middle of the century. Jeroboam II (786–746 BC) was still on the throne of the northern kingdom, towards the end of a long and prosperous reign (see The dates of kings and prophets).

In the eyes of the author of Kings, Jeroboam II had been a wicked king, yet he had also been successful (2 Kgs 14:23–25). This seemed odd to the author of Kings, so he added a comment to explain why Jeroboam II had not been cut short in his wickedness (2 Kgs 14:26–27). The background of a number of Hosea's sayings assumes a prosperous situation (2:8 [10]; 10:1).

Hosea also lived through the turbulent time that followed Jeroboam's reign, in which kings succeeded each other rapidly, often by intrigue and murder (2 Kings 15). The dynasty of Jehu came to an end with the short reign of Jeroboam's son in 746–745 BC (2 Kgs 15:8–12). This is recalled in Hos. 1:4, which refers to events recorded in 2 Kings 9—10. Here Hosea proclaims punishment on 'the house of Jehu for the blood of Jezreel' (1:4), a reference to events recorded in 2 Kings 9—10, when Jehu son of Jehoshaphat son of Nimshi wiped out the entire family of King Ahab in a bloodbath (see on Hosea 1 for more on this). The last king of Israel, Hoshea, also came to the throne by conspiracy and murder (2 Kgs 15:30). Hosea's comments in Hos. 7:7; 8:4 probably reflect this.

These last decades of Israel are overshadowed by the rise of Assyria and its threat to Palestine (Hos. 9:3; 10:6). Tiglath-Pileser III (also known as Pul) came to the Assyrian throne in 745 BC and began to exact tribute in Israel and take exiles (2 Kgs 15:19–20, 29). Some passages in Hosea suggest that the Israelite kings were uncertain whether to appease Assyria or look to Egypt for help (5:13; 7:11; 12:1 [2]).

We have seen how this rise of Assyria affected Israel and Judah in our study of Isaiah. Some of Hosea's prophecies may come from the time of the war against Judah by an alliance of Israel and Syria (the Syro-Ephraimite war, 734–733 BC) (e.g. 5:8–11, Wolff 1974, p. xxi). It is interesting to see this crisis from a northern point of view, in contrast to the Judean King Ahaz' view in Isaiah 7. A climax came under Hoshea, who rebelled against his vassal status and looked to Egypt for help (2 Kgs 17:4 – reflected in Hos. 7:11; 12:1 [2]). The Assyrian king finally lost patience and ended the northern kingdom for good by exiling king and people (2 Kgs 17:5–6). Hosea gives a northern perspective on the threat from Assyria, just as Isaiah gave a southern (Judean) one. Hos. 13:15–16 [13:15—14:1] refers to this in a poetic way.

Hosea's setting in the northern kingdom makes him unusual among the prophets. Most of the prophetic books focus in one way or another on Jerusalem, but Hosea never mentions it, or any other city in Judah. The cities he names most are Samaria (the northern capital), Bethel and Gilgal (two important worship centres; see 1 Kgs 12:25–33; Josh. 4:19–24). His horizon is Israel as a whole, or Israel and Judah together (4:15; 5:12–14). The only mention of King David is in 3:5. While this is

sometimes seen as a late text from Judah, it could just as well show a desire in the northern kingdom for a reunion of historic Israel under the Davidic monarch (Andersen and Freedman 1980, p. 307).

DEUTERONOMY AND HOSEA

A glance at Deuteronomy and Hosea reveals similarities between the two books. Look at how Deut. 12:2–4 depicts Canaanite religion, then follow up echoes of this in Hosea (e.g. Hos. 4:13). An account of these similarities is given in Weinfeld 1972, pp. 366–70.

Deuteronomy is sometimes said to have originated in northern Israel, because of features such as its covenantal theology, its apparent low view of kingship (kings are permitted under strict conditions in Deut. 17:14–20), its strong teaching on Yahweh as giver of the land (Deut. 8:7–10) and its opposition to Canaanite religion (these are all features of Hosea too). (For the view that there was a distinctively 'northern' ('Ephraimite') prophetic tradition, including Hosea and linked with Deuteronomy, see R. R. Wilson 1980.)

The similarities between Hosea and Deuteronomy raise the question of which came first. This is strictly an issue in Deuteronomy studies (see G. J. Wenham, *The Pentateuch*, in the present series). Modern Deuteronomy studies are divided over whether Deuteronomy is Judean and Josianic (the classic Wellhausenian view) or northern and Israelite. Andersen and Freedman, in their commentary on Hosea, have taken the view that Deuteronomy (or at least a deuteronomic tradition) came first. An alternative view is that of E. W. Nicholson (1986), who finds a proto-deuteronomic theology in Hosea. This is a slight modification of an influential work in German by L. Perlitt (1969), which was taken up by, for example, R. E. Clements (1975). An important article by John Day (1986) reaffirms the origin of covenantal theology relatively early in Israel's history.

RELIGION IN HOSEA'S TIME

Hosea's criticism of Israel focuses strongly on its false religious practices. His opposition to Canaanite religion has echoes of Deuteronomy, which is also rigorous in its Yahwism. Hosea, however, has more specific targets (not least the god Baal, whom Deuteronomy does not name), and gives a more colourful picture. He picks out sanctuaries for special attack, notably Bethel (which he calls, disparagingly, Bet-Aven, 'house of iniquity') and Gilgal (see 4:15; 9:15; 10:5, 8, 15), and refers to calf-idols (8:5–6; 10:5–6), sacred pillars (3:4; 10:1), self-mutilation in worship (7:14) and temple-prostitution (4:13–14). A world of sacrifice and religious feasts is vividly displayed.

In the opening chapters (1—3) the metaphors of prostitution and adultery are used to depict Israel's worship of Baal (2:8 [10]). The same metaphors appear in chs 4—14 also, always implying that Israel has abandoned Yahweh for the Canaanite god (4:10, 15–19; 5:4; 9:1). 'Baal' is Baal-Hadad, the Canaanite storm-god, known from Canaanite as well as biblical sources. (For the Baal myths found at Ugarit in Phoenicia in 1929, see *ANET*, pp. 129–41; Gibson 1978.) As the storm-god, Baal was associated with fertility, which may explain why Israel was drawn to him in its settled agricultural life in the eighth century. There seems also to be a connection between the sexual metaphors of Hosea and the sexual fertility rites that were an aspect of worship in the Baal cult (4:13–14). (See Wolff 1974, pp. 13–15 for a specific view of this.) The connection between Baal-worship and fertility is clear from 9:1, and also suggested by what Hosea sees as the due penalty for this apostasy, namely barrenness (4:10; 9:14).

The picture is not a simple one, however, because Israelites continued to worship Yahweh as well as Baal. This is clear from passages such as 5:6 ('With their flocks and herds they shall go to seek the LORD'), perhaps 6:1–3 (where Hosea probably quotes words spoken by other Israelites), and 8:2. It may be that the worship of Yahweh and Baal had become confused. It seems from 2:16 [18] that the name Baal was actually applied to Yahweh. The bull- or calf-idol set up at Bethel by Jeroboam I, to which Hosea refers several times (8:5; 10:5), shows that the Canaanite concept of a god (especially El) in the form of a bull had influenced Israel's way of thinking of Yahweh. It is not clear whether Israelites thought of this image as an image of the god, or as a pedestal on which the invisible god was enthroned (Davies 1992, pp. 44–45).

However, Hosea's use of the plural 'lovers' (2:7 [9]) implies that Israel worshipped more than one god, and to these may be added a goddess or two (see note on 4:18–19). There is archaeological evidence that the goddess Asherah was worshipped alongside Yahweh. At Kuntillet 'Ajrud the following blessing-text was found:

> I bless you by Yahweh of Samaria and by his Asherah

where 'his Asherah' probably refers to the wooden pole set up at sanctuaries in honour or the goddess of that name (Deut. 16:21; 1 Kgs 16:33). For more on archaeology and Hosea, see King 1988, pp. 88–107.

CRITICAL INTERPRETATION OF HOSEA

A first reading shows immediately that there are different kinds of material in Hosea.

Like Isaiah, Hosea spoke words of judgement (predominant in chs 4—5, for

Think about
KINDS OF WRITING IN HOSEA

Consider the following passages and notice differences in their form: 1:1–11; 2:16–23 [18–25]; 3:1–5; 4:1–3; 6:1–3; 11:1–4. Ask who speaks. What is the purpose of the saying? In what sort of context might it originally have been spoken?

This approach to the texts of Hosea is 'form-critical' (see Introduction). Davies briefly lists a number of types that occur in Hosea (1992, p. 99). But note his warning about the limitations of form criticism in Hosea:

'. . . a form-critical approach to Hosea will have to content itself with identifying recurring features of his oracles, without necessarily being able to give to whole passages descriptions which group them conveniently into a small number of categories' (1992, p. 98).

2. In the Syro-Ephraimite war (734–733 BC) Hosea saw that Yahweh might use corrective punishment (5:11, 15). Calls to repent (6:1–3; 14:1–3) might come at this stage.
3. With these calls unheeded, he goes back to messages of doom (7:10; 9:17). Only when the nation was about to fall did Hosea see that Yahweh's love could never be overcome (11:8–11; 14:4–8).
4. The calls to repent (6:1–3; 14:1–3) could come after the fall of Israel in 722 BC (Davies 1992, pp. 31–32).

He then finds a corresponding development in chs 1—3. For example, 2:2–3 [4–5] allows for repentance, while 2:4–13 [6–15] supposes that judgement is sure (Davies 1992, pp. 32–33).

This analysis allows for much more of the book of Hosea to be attributed to the prophet than older source-critical approaches did (such as W. R. Harper 1905; see Davies' account of these; 1992, pp. 94–96).

Davies' reconstruction is a reasonable hypothesis, but the book of Hosea as it stands is organized quite differently. This means that someone (Hosea himself and/or others) has taken sayings that were originally self-standing, having their own contexts, and put them into their present order, presumably with a theological purpose.

The sayings have in fact been grouped into blocks that share certain themes. Chapters 1—3 bring together quite different types of material under the theme of the unfaithful wife. Chapter 4 makes a new beginning, introducing a large section of Hosea's oracles (chs 4—14). This block may be subdivided

example) and salvation. The salvation sayings are of different kinds, covering both the immediate and the distant future. For example, some calls to repent imply that that this is all that is needed for Israel to enjoy Yahweh's blessing (5:4; 7:10; 12:6). Other sayings anticipate a period of time before the salvation (e.g. 3:5; 11:10–11; 14:4–7). (For this topic in general see Isaiah: Is prophecy predictive?) One approach to the different kinds of saying in Hosea is to suppose that his message developed in response to changing circumstances. A possible development (within chs 4—14) is suggested by Davies, as follows:

1. Hosea's earliest preaching called people to repent and practice justice (12:6).

into chs 4—11; 12—14 (Wolff 1974, pp. xxix-xxxii). Within each of these blocks, Wolff observes a movement from accusation to threat and finally to deliverance (Wolff, p. xxxi). The middle section (chs 4—11) may be further subdivided (as below, Structure and Outline; and see Davies 1992, p. 103; Andersen and Freedman 1980, pp. xii-xiii).

The thematic grouping of sayings shows that Hosea's sayings were put carefully into their written form by someone who was able to draw out connections between them, and show the theological relations between them. The process from individual speeches to written book (the book's 'tradition history') may have begun in Hosea's lifetime (Wolff 1974, p. xxxi; Davies 1992, p. 101). The organization of the parts into a theological whole (its 'redaction history') may also owe something to Hosea.

It is generally held, however, that the book had a Judean redaction after the fall of the northern kingdom (when it must have been 'rescued' by people who brought it south), and that this accounts for some of the references to Judah (e.g. 1:7, which could be a veiled reference to the miraculous deliverance of Jerusalem in 701 BC, cf. Isaiah 36—37); 3:5, Wolff 1974, p. xxxi; but others defend this verse; Emmerson 1984, pp. 101–05; 6:11a). Some further texts have similarities with Amos, which may suggest that they too have a southern setting, e.g. Hos. 4:15, cf. Amos 5:4–6; 8:14; Hos. 8:14; cf. Amos 1:4 (Davies 1992, p. 105). Finally, the heading of the whole prophecy (1:1) shows that it has been collected finally in Judah, because it is dated by mentioning four kings of Judah, while only Jeroboam II is named among the several northern kings who reigned in the same period.

STRUCTURE AND OUTLINE

STRUCTURE

The main structural divisions, as noted above, are chs 1—3; 4—11; 12—14. This may be given in more detail as follows:

1—3	Hosea's marriage and Israel's unfaithfulness
4:1—7:16	Sins of people, priests and leaders
8:1—11:11	False worship
11:12 [12:1]—14:9	Past and future

OUTLINE

1:1—3:5: Hosea's marriage and Israel's unfaithfulness

Hosea the prophet is introduced with a command from God to undertake a symbolic action (1:2–3). This action is costly and self-involving (as would later be the case for Jeremiah and Ezekiel also; Jer. 16:2; Ezek. 24:15–18). His union with Gomer is to become a symbol of Israel's unfaithfulness to God. The force of the command is 'Go, take a prostitute and have a prostitute's children'. (But see note on Hosea's 'marriage', as this

Think about
'THE HOUSE OF JEHU' – DIFFERENT VIEWS IN HOSEA AND KINGS?

Jehu slaughtered the house of Ahab at the word of the LORD (2 Kgs 9:7–10), and he is commended for his actions in 2 Kgs 10:30. Yet Hosea condemns him. (The 'house of Jehu' refers here to Jeroboam II and his son.) How can these things be reconciled? Notice how 2 Kgs 15:12 interprets the promise to Jehu in 2 Kgs 10:30 (concerning the 'fourth generation'). Does Kings itself give a pointer to Hosea's interpretation? Is there anything in the Kings account of Jehu that might justify Hosea's judgement?

reading is disputed.) Gomer's children by Hosea carry symbolic names (1:4–9; as would Isaiah's, Isaiah 7—8). The children's names stand for God's undoing of his promises to Israel. 'Jezreel' (literally, 'God sows') first reminds of Jehu's violence against the house of Ahab in this place (2 Kings 9; see the panel on this).

On Lo-ruhamah ('not pitied', 'not shown compassion') see Exod. 33:19; Deut. 30:3; 1 Kgs 8:50. On Lo-ammi ('not my people'), see Lev. 26:12; Jer. 31:33. The names symbolize God's rolling back of covenantal promises, and judgement about to fall. Yet, still at the head of the book, these name-connotations are reversed, and the promise of salvation beyond judgement is renewed (1:10–11 [2:1–2]).

The metaphor of the 'woman of harlotry' is now applied to Israel, cast as a mother turned prostitute (2:1–13 [3–15]). Her 'lovers' are other gods, especially Baal. The issue turns on the gifts of land and plenty (2:8–9 [10–11]). These are the signs of Yahweh's favour (cf. Deut. 7:13–14), but the credit has gone to Baal. Yet here too the covenantal promise is renewed (2:14–23 [16–25]). This important text spells out the key qualities of Yahweh (especially 'faithfulness'; vv. 19–20 [21–22]), which are the basis of his demand that Israel should in turn be faithful to him. (See Theological Themes for more on this text.)

Hosea 3:1–5 mirrors ch. 1, with another symbolic action, Hosea's redemption of an 'adulteress'. The woman may or may not be Gomer (see panel on Hosea's marriage), but the author does not say, because he is interested in the symbolism, not in writing a biography of Hosea (Mays 1969, pp. 55–56). Hosea now shows faithfulness and compassion to one who has been unfaithful.

The symbolism appears to mean that Israel would be prevented from worshipping other gods for a time, until they eventually returned to Yahweh of their own will.

4:1—7:16: Sins of people, priests and leaders

4:1—5:7 Faithfulness is once again the dominant theme in this section. It opens with a 'lawsuit' (*rîb*) against Israel (4:1–3). By this legal metaphor (cf. Isa. 3:13–15; Jer. 2:4–13; Mic. 6:1–5) they are accused of not having kept the covenant, by neglecting both its particular commands (4:2; cf. Exod. 20:7, 13–16; Jer. 7:9) and its basic principles (4:1b). 'Faithfulness' (*emet*) and 'loyalty' (*hesed*) (NRSV), or 'truth' and 'steadfast love' are key qualities in Israel's relationship with God (see Theological Themes). The terms are often combined to speak of God's faithfulness (Exod. 34:6; Ps. 89:14 [15]) (Wolff 1974, p. 67).

'Knowledge of God' (4:1; cf. 6:6) implies knowledge of his law, which was the special responsibility of the priests (4:6). The general accusation of Israel now focuses on the priests (4:4—5:7). They are accused of failing in their duty of teaching the law of God (*torah*, cf. 8:1, 12; Deut. 33:10), and even of leading in the worship of other gods (4:7, 12–13). The image of prostitution now comes close to the literal meaning of the term, for Baal-worship involves actual prostitution in that god's temples (4:14, 17–18). Some find a reference here to a ritual undergone by young Israelite women before marriage (Wolff 1974, pp. 86–87). There is a possible reference to worship of a goddess in 4:18–19 (Davies 1992, p. 40). Finally the king is drawn into the accusation of the priests (5:1), and the problem of prostitution is shown to be internalized in Israel (5:4).

5:8—6:6 A major theme in these chapters is Israel's relations with other nations. Hosea's

Digging deeper:
HOSEA'S 'MARRIAGE'

Hosea's relationship with a woman or women in chs 1 and 3 is a puzzle for several reasons. First, if Hosea has married Gomer, why does God say to him in 3:1: 'Go (again), love a woman . . . .'? This seems an unnatural way to refer to Gomer. Second, we are not told in ch. 1 that Gomer was unfaithful to Hosea after he married her. So 3:1 is strangely abrupt for that reason too if the woman here is Gomer.

The real problem felt by readers is a moral one: could God have commanded Hosea to have sexual relations with a prostitute? This seems to be implied if the woman in ch. 3 is not Gomer. NIV's translation in 3:1 is an example of this concern: 'Go, show your love to your wife again'. This is not justified by the Hebrew. (The word *'ishshah* can mean either 'woman' or 'wife'. When it stands alone, as here, it must mean 'a woman'. There is no word for 'your'. The word 'again' goes with either 'the LORD said', or with the command 'Go'.) Stuart meets the problem in a different way, by seeing in ch. 3 a reference to a second marriage (1987, p. 64).

The exegetical difficulties are not limited to ch. 3. The problem of defending Hosea's own morals applies to ch. 1 also. Does he marry a known prostitute? (For ways in which commentators have tried to avoid this implication see Wolff 1974, pp.13–14; Andersen and Freedman 1980, p. 162; Davies 1992, pp. 80–85.) Does he *marry* Gomer at all? Davies points out that the word 'take' followed by *'ishshah* might only mean procure for sex (Lev. 20:14, 17, 21; Davies 1992, p. 90).

The dominant view of chs 1 and 3 is that Hosea marries Gomer and that she is also the woman in ch. 3. (See Wolff 1974, pp. 59–60; Mays 1969, pp. 54–56, and his note on p. 23; Andersen and Freedman 1980, pp. 293–94.)

How do these different interpretations affect the theological reading of the text? For example, if the woman in ch. 3 is Gomer, then a comparison with the law of Deut. 24:1–4 is fruitful (Wolff 1974, p. 63; see also Jer. 3:1–5). Consider also Davies' novel idea that Hosea, in uniting with Gomer, symbolizes not Yahweh (as is usually supposed) but Baal; that is, he acts out the union of Israel with its 'lovers' (2:7 [9]), namely false gods (Davies 1992, pp. 87–92). (If this is correct, the image is different in 2:2–3 [4–5]; 2:19–20 [21–22].)

---

alarm-call (5:8–11) probably comes in the Syro-Ephraimite crisis (5:10 possibly indicating a counter-attack by Judah; Wolff 1974, p. 113). (Beth-aven, v. 8, is a contemptuous name for Bethel, home of Jeroboam I's calf-idol; 1 Kings 12.) Israel sought Assyrian help (5:13; cf. 2 Kgs 17:3), but to no avail. In their distress they repent (6:1–3), but this seems to be rejected by God, who sees deeper and demands *hesed* and the 'knowledge of God' (6:6, cf. 4:1; for repentance rejected, see also Jer. 3:22b–25, followed by 4:1–4).

6:7—7:7 The passage begins with 'transgression of the covenant'. The exact incident is unknown. ('Adam' is a location on the River Jordan, cf. Josh. 3:16.) The covenant is Israel's covenant with Yahweh, dating from Sinai (Exodus 19—24). The string of locations named shows forcefully that guilt runs through all Israel. ('House of

'ON THE THIRD DAY' (HOSEA 6:2)

The penitential song that Hosea quotes in 6:1–3 contains the idea of a raising up 'on the third day'. In the context this means that people in distress will be revived after a short time. However, the idea of resurrection after three days was known in the ancient world in connection with the Sumerian god Tammuz and the Egyptian Osiris (see Wolff's note, 1974, pp. 117–18). It was natural for the text to be applied to the resurrection of Christ, as some early Christian writers did, although not in the New Testament.

Israel' in 6:10 may originally have read 'Bethel'; Wolff 1974, p. 106.) The focus is on corruption within, implicating priests (6:9), king and officials (7:3–7). The theme of prostitution and adultery continues, both symbolically (6:10) and in reality (7:4). The problem is not only religious, however, but a lack of justice (7:1–2, cf. 4:2).

7:8–16 This passage returns to the theme of false political trust, whether in Egypt or Assyria. The 'turning to Yahweh' falsely claimed in 6:1, does not materialize (7:10, cf. v. 14). The note of personal rejection of Yahweh is strong (vv. 13–15). There is an echo of the Baal-worship in the time of Elijah in v. 14 (cf. 1 Kgs 18:28).

8:1—11:11: False worship
8:1–14 Israel is under threat because of its rebellion (the 'vulture' is Assyria, v. 1). Its rebellion against Yahweh is summed up here as breaking law and covenant (8:1). The combination of law (*torah*) and covenant (*berit*) echoes the Mosaic covenant, especially the language of Deuteronomy (note Deut. 4:13). 'Torah' here denotes the whole revealed will of God, as in Deut. 17:18–19 (cf. Wolff 1974, p. 138). A history of

rebellion is then told, with kings not appointed by Yahweh, and the worship of idols. (Idolatry is here typified by the 'calf of Samaria', 8:5–6. As there is no evidence of a calf- or bull-idol at Samaria, this is probably a way of speaking of the calf at Bethel; cf. 10:5, and Mays 1969, p. 118.) Kings and calf-idol are associated, perhaps recalling the apostasy of Jeroboam I (1 Kings 12).

Israel has lost its special (elect) status (8:8; cf. Amos 9:7). So they shall go back to Egypt, where they were first chosen for deliverance, to be God's chosen people (8:13c, cf. Exod. 19:4–6). The whole range of Israel's devotion is rejected by God (8:11–14), with some irony (v. 11). With 8:14a compare Isa. 44:2; 51:13; and with v. 14b compare Amos 1:4, 7 etc.

9:1–17 The command 'Do not rejoice' (9:10) shows that Israel has lost its right to celebrate being God's people ('rejoicing' is a key mark of the people in true worship of Yahweh in Deuteronomy; e.g. Deut. 16:13–15). As in that text, rejoicing is especially in the context of the annual feasts; the Feast of Tabernacles is also in view here in Hosea (9:5; cf. Lev. 23:39; Jdg. 12:19). Their 'prostitution' again disqualifies them (as in chs 1—3).

Hosea's message made him unpopular, like Jeremiah (9:5–7), and like that prophet he also protests, in an intercession that turns to a prayer for judgement (9:14; cf. Jer. 11:14, 18–20; cf. McConville 1993b, pp. 64–65).

Hosea thinks back on Israel's history as one of rebellion (9:17). For Gibeah (v. 9), see Judges 19—21; for Baal-Peor see Num. 25:1–5. Gilgal (v. 15) refers to the very beginning when they entered the land (Josh. 4:19). For 9:10 compare Deut. 32:10.

10:1–15 The 'vine' image again recalls

Israel's history (cf. Ps. 80:8–16 [9–17]). The accusation of unfaithfulness and the message of judgement focuses on kings (king and calf are again linked, vv. 3–6, cf. 8:4–5). The priests of Bethel (Beth-aven) are 'idolatrous priests' (*kemarim*, not the usual *kohanim*, cf. 2 Kgs 23:5). A call to righteousness (*sedaqah*, only here in Hosea) and steadfast love (*hesed*, cf. 6:6), with a promise (10:12) is enveloped in an announcement of judgement (vv. 11–15).

11:1–11 The new metaphor of Israel as Yahweh's 'son' in vv. 1–7 has origins in the story of election and exodus (Exod. 4:22–23; so also in the language). The metaphor is expanded to convey the terrible tension of God's love rejected by his rebellious 'son' (v. 1). The constant rebellion will lead to judgement, a return to Egypt, from where they had first been taken (v. 5, cf. v. 1).

This leads to a passage at the heart of the book's theology, in a great 'illogical' leap (vv. 8–11). Judgement is still the due reward of rebellion. (The images of judgement, Admah and Zeboiim, are neighbouring cities of Sodom and Gomorrah (Gen. 10:19; 14:2, 8) and involved in the total destruction recorded in Gen. 19:24–25; cf. Deut. 29:23 [22].) However, with the sonship idea still in mind, God speaks of his love for Israel in strong emotional language, using human-like metaphors ('my heart recoils', 'my compassion grows warm and tender'; cf. 2:19 [21]; also Jer. 31:20 for a close parallel). God's love is such that he cannot finally give up his 'son' (contrast the law in Deut. 21:18–21, and Davies 1992, p. 30). Though God uses human images of himself, he is also *not* like humans, precisely in his power to decide not to vent his anger (v. 9).

Therefore exile will not be the end of the story, but there will be restoration (11:10–11).

11:12 [12:1]—14:9: Past and future

11:12 [12:1]—13:16 The final section of the book (chs 12—14) begins with a 'covenant-accusation' (12:2–6 [3–7]; cf. Mic. 6:1–4), as the large middle section did (4:1–3). Here it is linked with another historical retrospect ('Judah' in v. 2 may originally have read 'Israel'; cf. v. 12 [13]). The reference is to the life of Jacob (=Israel), specifically to Gen. 25:22–26; 32:22–32; 28:10–22. The passage recalls Jacob's repentance as well as his deceits, and so leads into a call to repentance (12:6 [7]).

Memories of Israel's origins continue to be used to show her unfaithfulness and how judgement is due. (With 12:8 [9] cf. Deut. 8:17; 12:9 [10], cf. Exod. 20:2). The 'trader' in 12:7 [8] (NRSV; 'merchant', NIV) is literally a 'Canaanite', by a development in the meaning of that word. But the echo helps to depict Israel as 'Canaanized', that is, false to the covenant, as prohibited by Deut. 7:1–5. The history is also seen as unfolding under the eye of the prophets (12:10 [11]), including Moses (12:13 [14]; cf. Deut. 18:15–18).

Hosea turns again to the theme of idolatry, with another reference (probably) to the calf-idol at Bethel (13:2; cf. Exod. 34:17). The picture of a people fed by God, then, once satisfied, turning away from him in pride (13:4–6) recalls Deut. 32:10–18 (cf. again 12:8 [9], and Deut 8:11–20). The accusation picks up again Hosea's criticism of kings (13:10–11), and the 'son' motif, but now the compassion of 11:8 is hidden (13:14). The passage ends in a stark threat of unavoidable judgement (13:15–16 [13:15—14:1]).

14:1–9 [2–10] This climax affirms again that God's salvation will have the last word. The word *shub* is frequent here, in the call to 'return' (or 'repent', 14:1–2 [2–3]), and in the important v. 4 [5], literally 'I will heal their 'turning (away)'. This text is very like Jer. 3:22 (and a similar play on *shub* in Jer. 3:12–14; see on that passage, and also Jer. 31:18. For further comparison of Hosea and Jeremiah on this topic, see McConville 1993b, p. 157–62). The theology is like Jeremiah's New Covenant theology, where the problem of Israel's unfaithfulness is solved by a new initiative of God himself (Jer. 31:31–34; 32:39–40).

The book closes with new images of plenty (14:4–7 [5–8], contrast 4:3), and a call to 'wisdom' (14:9 [10]).

THEOLOGICAL THEMES

'NO OTHER GODS'

The First Commandment (Exod. 20:3) stands over the book of Hosea, with its prohibition of the worship of gods other than Yahweh. This may be seen not only from the general opposition to the worship of Canaanite gods, but from allusions to Exod. 20:2 (12:8–9), and to Deuteronomy 32, which is another extended meditation on the same theme (Deut. 32:12, 15–21). This insistence on worshipping Yahweh alone is rooted in the memories of Israel's election by Yahweh, and its exodus from Egypt.

Indeed, much of Hosea can be understood in this connection. This is the context of the idea of Israel as 'son' of Yahweh (Hos. 11:1, cf. Exod. 4:22–23), and of God as Israel's 'Maker' (Hos. 8:14). There is a further echo here of Deuteronomy 32, now vv. 4–6, and also of Isa. 51:13. Creation and election are close in all these texts (note the parallel between 'father' and 'creator' in Deut. 32:6). Finally, Hosea's fondness for historical retrospects is based in a sense of Israel's unique relationship with Yahweh. The historical scope goes back before the time of Moses and exodus to the patriarchs of Genesis (Hos. 12:3–4). And Hosea does not just use history for illustration purposes, but presents it as a unified development. For example, in 12:10–14 he combines Jacob, the exodus, Moses and the sins of Ephraim, that is, Israel after settlement in the land. In this respect Hosea is like certain Psalms, which review Israel's history (e.g. Psalms 78; 105; 106).

It is Hosea's belief in one God, Yahweh, that sets his religion apart from that of Canaan (see Date and Destination: Religion in Hosea's time). It may also explain why human kingship plays so small a role in his thinking (though see 3:5). Kings as Hosea knew them were closely implicated in idolatrous worship (chs 8; 10). As in Deuteronomy, it is Israel itself that is Yahweh's 'son', not the king (Hos. 11:1; cf. Deut. 14:1; 32:5–6; contrast Ps. 2:7). It is in such ways that Hosea is so like Deuteronomy, which has the key 'text' for worshipping God alone in Deut. 6:4 (alongside the First Commandment, Exod. 20:3; Deut. 5:7).

FAITHFULNESS AND STEADFAST LOVE

The idea of God's faithfulness is rooted in the history of election, to which we have

Think about
IDOLATRY

In religion, idolatry is the most serious evil, because it makes 'god' what is not God. Martin Luther said: 'The confidence and faith of the heart alone make both God and an idol' (Large Catechism, 1529: 'The First Commandment'). This is a perceptive comment, pointing out that a religious temperament in itself cannot distinguish between good and bad belief about God. He might have been thinking about Hosea 2! Belief in God needs to know who God is.

What might idolatry mean in a secular society, or even for modern religious people?

1. Is there a clue in the idea of 'consumerism'? (The clue is given in Col. 3:5, cf. Eph. 5:5.) Modern consumerism is more than mere greed, but a way of looking at the world. Did Hosea depict Israel's Baal-worship as 'consumerist' (trying to secure the goods of life without receiving them as God's gift)? For more on consumerism as a world-view, see Bartholomew, ed. 2000. The essays there show how consumerism has affected all aspects of life, including the life of the church.

2. What dangers are there in false views about the nature of God? Think of how people often claim that God made them do certain things. Or how both sides in wars claim that God is on their side.

already referred. It is the point of the dominant metaphor of the book, that of marriage. The marriage-vow which God makes in Hos. 2:19–20 [21–22] attributes faithfulness directly to him, in the terms

hesed and 'emunah ('steadfast love', 'faithfulness', respectively, NRSV). Hesed is the quality by which a covenant is sustained. In Hosea, it is given content, not only by 'faithfulness', but also by the other terms used in this text: sedeq (righteousness), mishpat (justice), rahamim (mercy, compassion) and the idea of 'knowing' Yahweh.

These qualities in Yahweh are mirrored in what he desires in his covenant people, which we see in the opening accusation: 'There is no faithfulness ('emet, close in meaning to 'emunah), or loyalty (hesed = 'steadfast love' in 2:19 [21]), and no knowledge of God in the land' (4:1; cf. 6:4, 6 (hesed); 10:12 (hesed with sedaqah, 'righteousness'); 12:6 [7] (hesed with mishpat, 'justice'). (On these terms see the relevant articles in NIDOTTE. Note that their meanings must be understood according to their various contexts, and also in typical combinations. Such combinations are not mere additions of separate concepts, but the combinations themselves are suggestive of rich and complex meanings.)

Hesed ('steadfast love', 'loyalty') emerges as the key, overarching concept in the book's theology. It is first of all reciprocal, that is, as it is true of Yahweh towards Israel it is to be true of Israel towards Yahweh. Second, it is given content by the other significant terms with which it appears in combination. For Israel to show hesed to Yahweh will mean that it will seek 'justice and righteousness', that is, it will seek to establish right and just relations among Israelites, and take all necessary measures to bring this about. ('Justice and righteousness' is an important combination in Amos – see Amos: Theological Themes.) The currency of these right relationships is God's Commandments, in the context of the historic covenant from Mosaic times, alluded to in 4:2 (cf. Jer. 7:9).

Covenant and *torah*

The main point about this combination has been made in the previous paragraph. The close parallel between covenant (*berit*) and law (*torah*) (Hos. 8:1) is typical of Deuteronomy. This is deduced from the emphasis laid on both ideas throughout that book, as well as from key passages such as Deuteronomy 4—5 (and note Deut. 4:13). It should not be understood in a legalistic sense, as if the association of covenant and law were a reduction of covenant *to* law. For an example of this view, note Mayes on Deut. 4:13: '(*b^{e}rit* [covenant] often refers specifically to the decalogue itself rather than to the relationship between Yahweh and Israel of which the decalogue forms a part' (Mayes 1979, p. 152). For Hosea, covenant clearly does mean the relationship itself, as we see from the emphasis on genuine loyalty, and especially from a text like Hos. 6:6 ('I desire steadfast love and not sacrifice').

'Steadfast love, not sacrifice' (Hos. 6:6)

Meaning can be conveyed by strong oppositions as well as by combinations of terms. It used to be thought that the prophets aimed at the abolition of formal religion, and of sacrificial worship in particular. Texts like Hos. 6:6 suggested such an interpretation (as also Isa. 1:10–17; Amos 5:21–25; Mic. 6:6–8, as well as texts in the Psalms: Ps. 40:6–8 [7–9]; 50:7–15). Modern Old Testament scholarship tends not to see texts like Hos. 6:6 as outright rejections of sacrificial worship, but rather as a strong affirmation of the need for genuine love as indispensable in religion. (For a similar affirmation by strong contrast, compare 'Jacob I loved but Esau I hated'; Mal. 1:2–3.) The prophetic aim is for Israel's devotion to God to be genuine, and to permeate all of life. (In this sense it is like Deuteronomy's call for obedience in Deut. 6:4–5.)

However, Hosea is scathing about any 'magical' understanding of religion, in which rituals themselves were thought to produce certain effects. This was because it was thought that there was a natural connection between ritual performances and the created order. Instead of praying to Yahweh from the heart, Israelites 'gash themselves for grain and wine' (7:14), like the desperate priests of Baal who opposed Elijah (1 Kgs 18:28). The prophets' rejection of this kind of thinking has been called the 'disenchantment of the world' (Nicholson 1986, pp. 201, 207–08).

Think about
THE 'DISENCHANTMENT' OF THE WORLD

In this context, 'disenchantment' means realizing that the world cannot be manipulated by ritual or magical acts. The realization of this in Israel is sometimes attributed to the prophets. However, the Old Testament's covenant theology in general is opposed to Ancient Near Eastern (ANE) religion on this point. Decisive in human affairs is not the success of religious performances, but the obedient response to God in a relationship with him.

Are there ways in which a view of the world as 'enchanted' can still be found today?

For an analysis of the Old Testament's answer to the ANE's religious world-view, see Nicholson 1986, pp. 201–17.

JUDGEMENT AND LOVE: GOD'S DILEMMA

A final implication of Hosea's belief in one God is that judgement and love are held together in tension (Emmerson 1984, p. 16). This is one of the great paradoxes of the Old

Testament. It is true of the flood-story of Genesis 6—9, where one God brings the flood in judgement on humanity and saves humanity from the same flood by sparing Noah and his family. This is in contrast to the flood-stories of the Ancient Near East where these different acts are attributed to different gods (the god Enki, who favours Atrahasis (the 'Noah' figure), and protects him from the flood that is brought about by the god Ellil; see Dalley 1991, pp. 1–39, especially pp. 29–30).

The paradox comes to a head in Hosea 11:8–11, where God is portrayed in a kind of inner turmoil, compelled by his nature both to judge sin and to save his beloved people. It comes across as an illogicality in theology, as in the triple use of 'therefore' in Hos. 2:6 [8], 9 [11], 14 [16], where the last of these unexpectedly follows a declaration of judgement with an intention to save (Emmerson 1984, pp. 21–25). The effect is exactly like Jer. 30:5–7 (where there is no 'yet' in v. 7c in Hebrew; 30:16), in Jeremiah's build-up to his New Covenant theology (see McConville 1993b, pp. 94–95).

Finally, the person of the one God is revealed in human-like terms. The dilemma of judgement or salvation in 11:8–11 is not presented as an intellectual problem, but as a person in an agony of decision. In this aspect, Hosea is close to Jeremiah, where the suffering of God is mirrored in that of the prophet (see on Jeremiah: Theological Themes: The individual). In Hosea too, the suffering of the prophet parallels God's suffering. He comes close to the note of protest found in Jeremiah's 'Confessions' in the prayer of 9:14. The portrayal of God is in a broad sense incarnational, that is, he is portrayed as identified and involved with people. By his own nature he demands judgement, yet he will not judge, because he is holy. The resolution of this, in biblical terms, is the cross of Jesus Christ, where (in Barth's terms) the Judge is judged.

Think about
HOLINESS AND LOVE

God will not judge – because he is holy (Hos. 11:9). This is a quite unexpected connection! What might we have expected here instead? What does this say about our understanding of God's holiness?

RHETORICAL INTENTION

As with other books, the question of rhetorical intention involves asking about the 'audience' of Hosea. Here again, there will have been several audiences, beginning with those who heard Hosea preach. The audience of the book in its final form (certainly after the fall of the northern kingdom, and perhaps in or after the Babylonian exile of the people of Judah) will have heard an explanation of why God has continued to be with his people even after a history of sin and judgement. They will have understood the tension in the book between judgement and salvation when they think of their own history of punishment followed by survival. (These aspects of Hosea's persuasive power are again similar to the rhetorical effect of Jeremiah, where they are developed more fully; see Jeremiah: Rhetorical Intention.) This capacity of the prophetic books to bring alive the preaching of the prophets with great immediacy, while allowing their message to illuminate the new situations of those of a later time, is a powerful force in enabling a people to survive under great pressure.

In thinking about Hosea's rhetorical intention we should notice the tremendous power of the means of persuasion he uses. There are several elements in this. First, the structure of the book serves a rhetorical purpose. The introduction of its themes in chs 1—3 sets a context for the hearing of the oracles that follow. Already in these opening chapters the trajectory of judgement to salvation is mapped out. The device of the naming of children announces first judgement, then salvation, both within ch. 1 (vv. 6–9, 10–11), and between chs 1 and 2 (cf. 2:21–23 [23–25]). The imagery of marriage and prostitution is carried through to a conclusion in a return of Israel to Yahweh (in 3:5). The concept that the words of Hosea relate to a relatively long period is introduced (3:3–4), suggesting to readers that they look for the relevance of the words to their own day.

This introduction to the prophecy allows a balance to be kept in the mind of the hearer between judgement and salvation. Judgement is an ever-present possibility. Yet the tendency of the prophet's thought is towards salvation. The words of judgement, therefore, do not lead to despair but to a call to obey. This is clear in those passages in 4—14 where the voice suddenly turns to Judah (e.g. 4:15a), and we see the purpose for which the words of judgement have been preserved and passed on.

While the structure of the book points us to renewed hearings of the prophet at some distance from his own time, the language and imagery of the book shows us why his words were powerful when he spoke and why they were worth recording. Personal images are at the heart of his appeal. To cast God as husband and father is not just to symbolize a covenantal relationship, but also

to bring to bear the inherent power of such metaphors. The betrayal of a loving husband or father is poignant and moving. The same kind of response is produced in Hosea as in, for example, the story of the Prodigal Son (Luke 15:11–32). Indeed a specific parallel has been pointed out between Hos. 2:7b [9b] and Luke 15:17–18 (where Israel and the prodigal recognize that they were better off with their first husband/father, and resolve to return; Nolland 1993, p. 784). The agony of God in his love-judgement dilemma (Hos. 11:8–11) makes the same kind of appeal to the reader as the unrestrained demonstration of fatherly love at the moment of reconciliation in the parable (Luke 15:20–24).

This last point brings us to metaphor itself. Metaphors are not random images, but

---

Think about
METAPHORS AND SIMILES

Consider Hos. 5:8–15 and the number of metaphors and similes used in that short space (vv. 10, 12, 13, 14). Bear in mind that some metaphors are related to the reality they portray only in some very specific way, while others are much closer to that reality. In what way do you think God is like 'maggots' to Ephraim (v. 12)? Is this image as close to the reality (of God) as the metaphor of a lion (v. 14)? This exercise could be extended throughout Hosea.

We have thought about poetry and metaphor at other points in this volume; see Introduction: Rhetorical intention; Isaiah: the song of the vineyard as poetry, and Joel: Rhetorical intention. G. Morris, 1996, has given a detailed analysis of poetry in Hosea (some knowledge of Hebrew is needed to benefit fully from this).

reveal something essential about the reality to which they point. We have just observed this about the husband and father metaphors. The same is true of the metaphor of prostitution. As Wolff especially has shown, there is a connection between this image and the sexual aspects of Baal-worship. Hosea fixes on cult-prostitution as a religious rite and turns the idea of prostitution into a powerful condemnation of idolatry, the abandonment of Yahweh and the breach of the First Commandment.

Hosea's language is rich in metaphor, as a glance at certain passages shows.

Other poetic devices are used in Hosea, often with ironic effect. An example is Hos. 8:11–14, with its play on 'multiplication'. Ephraim *multiplies* altars to expiate sin – in vain, of course – but they ignore Yahweh's *multitude* of laws. They have also *multiplied* fortress cities (v. 14), but this too is in vain, since they cannot defend against an attack by Yahweh himself. Many of the wordplays are hidden by translation out of Hebrew. They are, however, of the essence of Hosea's persuasive power.

HOSEA IN THE CANON

Canonical interpretation of Hosea refers at one level to the shape of the book in its final form. Childs' treatment of it focused on this, showing how an original message delivered to the northern kingdom was developed in a number of stages to become, in the end, a mature reflection on the relation of judgement and salvation, valid for many situations (Childs 1979, pp. 373–84). What the original message might have been is a matter of debate (see on Critical Interpretation; Childs acknowledges this 1979, p. 381). But the

books of Davies and Emmerson trace this kind of development in Hosea in helpful ways. The adaptation of Hosea's message to the southern kingdom is an obvious stage in this process. A prophecy that began in calls to avoid the judgement due for rebellion against God becomes a retrospect on salvation out of judgement, together with warning to learn from the past.

Canonical interpretation in recent times looks more to the place of the book in a wider context. We have considered the idea of the Book of the Twelve as a coherent entity separately (see Book of the Twelve). It is no doubt significant that the Book of the Twelve should open with a work whose theology can be understood as a development of the First Commandment. The collection of the twelve prophets thus becomes a reflection on what is involved in worshipping the God of Israel and him alone.

In the New Testament, Hosea is remembered above all as the prophet of 'steadfast love', or 'mercy', especially because Jesus quoted Hos. 6:6: 'I desire mercy and not sacrifice' (Matt. 9:13; 12:7). In both these Gospel passages, Jesus uses the prophet's words against exclusive and legalistic interpretations of the law (in these cases, dietary laws and the sabbath). In Matt. 9:13, he goes on to say: 'For I have come to call not the righteous but sinners'. Jesus shows how powerful Hosea's message is, because it challenges deeply all religious vested interest. Religion does not consist in performance. There are no external signs or marks of genuine religion that can afford to sideline its essence: a love of mercy that comes from the heart.

This idea is so powerful because it is about the nature of God. That is why Hosea's insistence on mercy goes hand in hand with his insistence on the worship of Yahweh. So when Jesus quotes the saying in Hos. 6:6, it does not mean that Jesus has found an Old Testament text that conveniently writes off most Old Testament religion. Nor does it mean that he points to some abstract and universalizing 'religion' ('it doesn't matter what you believe as long as you show love'). The issue at stake is the right understanding of God.

This point can be taken a step further. Hosea, along with Jeremiah, illustrates the important concept of 'Incarnation'. (U. Mauser, in his treatment of 'Incarnation' [*Menschwerdung*], picks out these two prophets, along with Jesus, for his study.) This is because of what we have noticed already under Theological Themes ('No other gods' and Judgement and Love). The points have also been developed in Jeremiah in the Canon, where Hosea has been considered along with that prophet.

FURTHER READING

Items marked with * are considered suitable as first ports of call, while others are more complex, or relate to specific issues.

COMMENTARIES

*E. Achtemeier *Minor Prophets I*. NIBC. Peabody: Hendrickson, 1996.

F. I. Andersen and D. N. Freedman *Hosea*. AB. New York: Doubleday, 1980.

*G. I. Davies *Hosea*. NCB. Grand Rapids: Eerdmans/London; Marshall Pickering, 1992.

W. R. Harper *Amos and Hosea*. ICC. Edinburgh: T. & T. Clark, 1905.

P. J. King *Amos, Hosea and Micah: an Archaeological Commentary*. Philadelphia: Westminster, 1988.

F. Landy *Hosea*. Sheffield: Sheffield Academic Press, 1995.

A.A. Macintosh *Hosea*. ICC. Edinburgh: T. & T. Clark, 1967.

*J. L. Mays *Hosea*. OTL. London: SCM, 1969.

*D. Stuart *Hosea–Jonah*. WBC. Waco: Word Books, 1987.

H .W. Wolff *Hosea*. Hermeneia. Philadelphia: Fortress Press, 1974.

OTHER BOOKS AND ARTICLES

C. Bartholomew and T. Moritz eds *Christ and Consumerism: a Critical Analysis of the Spirit of the Age*. Carlisle: Paternoster, 2000.

B. S. Childs *Introduction to the Old Testament as Scripture*. London: SCM, 1979.

R. E. Clements *Prophecy and Tradition*. Oxford: Blackwell, 1975.

S. Dalley *Myths from Mesopotamia*. Oxford: OUP, 1991.

G. I. Davies *Hosea*. OTG. Sheffield: Sheffield Academic Press, 1993.

J. Day 'Pre-Deuteronomic Allusions to the Covenant in Hosea and Ps. lxxviii' *VT* 36. 1986, pp. 1–12.

*G. I. Emmerson *Hosea: an Israelite Prophet in Judaean Perspective*. JSOT Suppl. 28. Sheffield: JSOT Press, 1984.

J. C. L. Gibson *Canaanite Myths and Legends*. Edinburgh: T. & T. Clark, 1978, second edition.

U. W. Mauser *Gottesbild und Menschwerdung*. BHT 43. Tübingen: Mohr, 1971.

A. D. H. Mayes *Deuteronomy*. NCB. London: Oliphants, 1979.

J. G. McConville *Grace in the End: a Study in Deuteronomic Theology*. Carlisle: Paternoster/ Grand Rapids: Zondervan, 1993a.

J. G. McConville *Judgement and Promise: an Interpretation of Jeremiah*. Leicester: Apollos/Winona Lake: Eisenbrauns, 1993b.

G. Morris *Prophecy, Poetry and Hosea*. JSOT Suppl. 219. Sheffield: Sheffield Academic Press, 1996.

E. W. Nicholson *God and his People*. Oxford: Clarendon, 1986.

J. Nolland *Luke 9:21—18:34*. WBC. Dallas: Word Books, 1993).

L. Perlitt *Bundestheologie im Alten Testament*. WMANT 36. Neukirchen: Neukirchener Verlag, 1969.

*N. Snaith *Mercy and Sacrifice*. London: SCM, 1953.

J. M. Soskice *Metaphor and Religious Language*. Oxford: OUP, 1995.

M. Weinfeld *Deuteronomy and the Deuteronomic School*. Oxford: Clarendon Press, 1972.

R. R. Wilson *Prophecy and Society in Ancient Israel*. Philadelphia: Fortress, 1980.

Chapter 7

JOEL

DATE AND DESTINATION

The Book of Joel does not tell us its date in a heading, nor is it possible to be sure from its contents when it was written. Its position in second place in the Book of the Twelve may mean that in early Jewish tradition it was regarded as one of the older prophetic books, but even this is not certain. The lack of firm evidence about dating has meant that Joel has been thought to be one of the earliest books (see LaSor 1996, pp. 438–39), while others think it one of the latest. Arguments are often forced to rely on silences: the book mentions no king, nor identifies the nation whose army is pictured as coming to invade. The northern kingdom is not mentioned, only Judah.

On the positive side, the setting is clearly in the land, with the temple-worship in full swing, so the book is not exilic. Similarities between passages in Joel and parts of other prophetic books may give clues. For example, the accusation of Philistia and Tyre (Joel 3:4–8 [4:4–8]) is close to Amos 2:6–10, as is 2:1–11 to Isaiah 13 (see Outline). The 'day of the LORD' (2:1) has parallels in Amos (5:18), Isaiah (2:12), Zephaniah (1:14–15), Ezekiel (7:19) and Lamentations (1:12) (see

Wolff 1977, pp. 33–34, for further variations and texts). The metaphor of an army as locusts occurs in Nahum 3:15–16; Jer. 46:23; 51:14. And the idea of a decisive battle against 'the nations' (3:2 [4:2]) is like

INTERBIBLICAL QUOTATIONS

Joel's array of echoes of other prophetic books has led to theories as to how they came about. Nogalski thought there was a special 'Joel' redactional layer within the Book of the Twelve (1993). He thought this layer came at the end of the editing process of the whole Book of the Twelve. His theory is criticized by Coggins 1996, partly because Joel has connections with prophetic books outside the Twelve (cf. Joel 3:10 [4:10] and Isa. 2:4=Mic. 4:3; Coggins 1996, pp. 77–78). Each shows, however, the extent of the parallels between Joel and other prophetic books.

Allusions within the Old Testament are a well-known feature. The standard work on the subject is Fishbane (1985). Recently, Schultz has shifted the focus from inner-biblical exegesis to *quotation*. If the prophets, or prophetic books, quote each other, what does this mean for issues of authority and canon?

For an assessment of questions like this see Schultz 1999, pp. 62–114. See also the panel, Think about: Prophetic words in new contexts at 3:1–21 [4:1–21].

Ezekiel 38—39 and Zechariah 14. The imagery of 'signs and wonders', and disruption in the created order (2:30–31 [3:1–2]), is deep-rooted in biblical literature (Exodus 7—11; Deut. 6:22), and also found elsewhere in the prophets (Zeph. 1:14–16; Isa. 13:10; Ezek. 32:7–8). Finally, the idea of an escaped remnant in Jerusalem is found in Zech. 14:2. (See also Hubbard's table of similarities 1989, p. 24.)

The parallels come from books with a range of dates. While none of them is decisive in itself, the fact that Joel has echoes of a spectrum of other books may suggest dependence on them, and therefore a relatively late date (i.e. post-exilic). In any case we must imagine some situation in which the recipients of the book are under threat, and are encouraged by Joel both to repent and to believe that God will save them in the end.

CRITICAL INTERPRETATION OF JOEL

The main issue for critical interpretation of the book is what kind of situation Joel addresses. At the heart of this is whether he speaks about an actual plague of locusts, or whether the plague of locusts is a metaphor for an army's invasion. (See Outline, on 1:1—2:11.) Several points favour a literal interpretation (that is, that Joel refers to an actual plague of locusts). The invasion by locusts is mentioned right at the beginning, as the cause of the trouble the people face (1:4). They are also depicted in greater detail than in other uses of the locust image (see above), since several types of locust are named. This opening allusion is then returned to in 2:25, in a passage in which God is saying that he will overcome the problem the people face. In addition, some

of the imagery is very suitable for depicting a devastation by locusts (1:7; 2:3, 8, 10) (Stuart 1987, p. 232). Finally, it is also said that the invader is 'like an army' (2:4–5), which can be taken to mean that it is not itself an actual army (LaSor 1996, p. 440).

However, there are points in favour of taking the locusts as a metaphor for an army. First, as we saw (Date and Destination.), the locust-metaphor is used elsewhere for an invading army. It need not be surprising that the metaphor should be more fully developed than usual. In any case, the images used here resemble other passages where the picture is clearly military (Hab. 3:16–17; Jer. 50:41–46; 51:27–33, etc.; Stuart 1987, p. 233). Similarly in Exod. 10:3–20, the locust-plague is only a part of a bigger picture, namely the deliverance of Israel in a Holy War. Joel may have this exodus-plague in mind when he uses the words in Joel 1:2b (cf. Exod. 10:6, 14; Stuart, p. 234). In that case, the locusts would stand for the plagues in general, as part of God's Holy War (which in Joel's case, of course, is turned against God's own people). Finally, there is other imagery for the devastation of Judah besides the locust-metaphor, notably 'fire' (1:19–20). This suggests that the prophet is using a variety of metaphors to depict the disaster.

How does the image of the locusts work in the book as a whole? It begins with a problem (the suffering of Judah under a terrible invasion), and ends with a solution (God's deliverance). The solution, however, involves the judgement and defeat of nations that have oppressed Judah. This is like the movement within other prophetic books (Isaiah on Assyria, Jeremiah on Babylon). Like them, therefore, it seems likely that in Joel too the problem and the solution are closely related: the defeat of Judah's enemies in the end corresponds to their oppression by them in the beginning. The connection between the judgement on Judah and the final defeat of their enemies is brought out forcefully by the use of similar language in both cases (3:14–15 [4:14–15], cf. 1:6a; 2:2).

This last point raises the question of the book's unity. Some older scholars solved the problem of the locust-imagery by supposing that Joel consists of two originally separate prophecies, the first about a locust-plague, and the second an eschatological vision from the second century BC (Stuart, referring to B. Duhm, T. H. Robinson and others; Stuart 1987, pp. 234–35). Recent scholarship, however, favours the unity of the book (e.g. Wolff 1977, pp. 6–8). The idea of two original prophecies does not help explain why they could have been put together into a single prophecy.

Indeed, the two parts of the prophecy are combined in such a way as to unite them. Wolff sees the following correspondences. A first climax comes at 2:27, which is echoed near the end of the book (3:17 [4:17]). The natural disaster portrayed in 1:4–20 is reversed in 2:21–27. The military destruction in 2:1–11 is balanced by 3:1–3, 9–17 [4:1–3, 9–17]. The call to repent in 2:12–17 finds an echo in the giving of the spirit, and the calling on Yahweh in 2:28–32 [3:1–5] (Wolff 1977, pp. 7–8). Other structures besides Wolff's are also possible, because of the complex interplay of themes (see Hubbard 1989, pp. 31–34, for some of these).

If the book is a unity it remains to ask why the natural and military disasters have been brought into correspondence like this. That is a question for development below (Theological Themes and Rhetorical Intention).

Think about
THE METAPHOR OF LOCUSTS

Why do you think locusts are a suitable metaphor to depict the devastation of an army? If they do represent an army here, what do you learn about armies from the idea of an advancing locust-swarm? And what may we learn about locusts from the idea of an advancing army? (There is more on this in Rhetorical Intention, below.)

STRUCTURE AND OUTLINE

STRUCTURE

1:1—2:17   Laments and a call to repentance
2:18—3:21 [4:21] Promises of salvation

OUTLINE
1:1—2:17: Laments and a call to repentance
1:1—2:11 Joel's words in ch. 1 remind of the Psalm-form known as the lament, that is, where the psalmist prays about some calamity he or the community is enduring (e.g. Psalm 44). Joel is closest to this in 1:15–20, where he addresses God directly. His opening words are strictly a call to the people to lament (cf. Amos 5:16b; 1 Kgs 21:9). (Wolff describes what he calls the 'call to communal lamentation' form in detail; 1977, pp. 21–22.)

The laments are a response to a great disaster, portrayed as the devastation of the land by a plague of locusts. (The words in 1:2 recall Exod. 10:6, 14, which refer to the locust-plague in Egypt leading up to the exodus.) The rich locust-vocabulary (1:4) shows a terrible familiarity with this menace, and stresses the extent of the damage that such a plague can cause. The metaphor of a locust-swarm or plague for an invading army is well known in the Old Testament

(Jdg. 6:5; 7:12; Nah. 3:15–16; Jer. 46:23; 51:14). Here, it seems as if, in contrast, a locust-swarm is compared to an army (1:6; 2:1–9; cf. Prov. 30:27). (For the view that an army is being compared to locusts, see Critical Interpretation of Joel.)

Joel's lament is a wake-up call addressed to the people in general (elders and inhabitants of the land (1:2)), then calling in turn to 'drunkards' (1:5), 'farmers' (1:11) and 'priests' (1:13). He is picking out groups of people who suffer, or will suffer, because of the plague. Drinkers will have nothing to drink, farmers nothing to sell, priests nothing for the temple-service. 'Drunkards' (1:5) appears alongside value-neutral terms, but presumably implies the need for all the addressees to wake up, as if from a senseless stupor.

The catastrophe is described as the coming of the 'day of the LORD' (1:15; 2:1–2, 11). Joel's depiction of this is like that of Amos (Amos 5:18, cf. especially Joel 2:2), who had declared that the 'day of the LORD' would be one of disaster, not salvation (see Amos: Outline). Joel too uses the language of military destruction in depicting that terrible day.

The summons to 'blow the trumpet' (2:1) means to prepare for war (Num. 10:9). The words are as if in Yahweh's mouth ('my holy mountain'; cf. 3:17 [4:17]; that is, Mt Zion, cf. Ezek. 20:40). Yet 2:1–12 is a prophetic pronouncement of judgement. It resembles other prophetic pronouncements of judgement on a nation by the attack of an enemy. (Notice especially the oracle against Babylon in Isaiah 13; and against Judah in Jer. 4:5–8.) The picture is of Yahweh's Holy War, turned against his own people (2:1; cf. Jer. 21:3–7). (Wolff gives a number of further prophetic parallels to this text; 1977, p. 47.)

2:12–17 The lamentation is followed by an appeal to repent, explicitly said to be a word of Yahweh (v. 12). 'Rend your hearts and not your garments' is a typically prophetic internalization of external religious actions (cf. Isa. 58:3–9; Jer. 4:4; 31:33). The emphasis on the 'heart' is also deuteronomic (Deut. 6:5; 10:16). The portrayal of God as showing mercy, compassion and 'steadfast love' (*hesed*) is also familiar (most immediately from Hos. 11:8–11). The idea that he can be persuaded by prayer to change his mind about judgement is the basis of the prophetic intercession (Exod. 32:9–14; 2 Sam. 12:19–25).

It is assumed here that Israel has sinned, though the sin is never spelt out. This is unusual in the prophets, but close to Lamentations, where confession of sin also plays a minor part (Lam. 1:18). The motivation for Yahweh to act is that his name should not be mocked (cf. Pss 44:13–16 [14–17]; 79:10).

2:18—3:21 [4:21]: Promises of salvation
2:18–32[2:18—3:5] In 2:18, the prophecy turns from threat to promise. The specific judgements are now turned round. The 'northern' enemy (2:20, cf. Jer. 6:22) will be overthrown. (This hardly identifies the enemy, since most enemies came into Judah from that direction. In Jeremiah the 'foe from the north' turns out to be Babylon, but even there we do not know this immediately.) The famine caused by locusts will be turned to plenty (2:19, 25–26; cf. Amos 9:13–15). The prayer of 2:17 is answered in 2:26.

In this vision of a new age the relationship between God and his people will be restored. An aspect of this will be the pouring out of the spirit on 'all flesh'

(2:28–29 [3:1–2]; cf. Ezek. 36:26–29). 'Flesh' in this case is in opposition to spirit. 'Those days' (of salvation, v. 29 [3:2]) are in contrast to the 'day' that spelt punishment. The specific point is that everyone in the restored community will have this gift of the spirit to prophesy, so that even the social division between slave and free would be broken down. (Compare Num. 11:26–30, where the people expected this gift to be limited to certain people, but where Moses expresses the desire that all should have it.) The gift of the spirit also implies the power to live as God's people to the fullest extent (see also Theological Themes).

The vision is connected with terrible signs of the coming 'day of the LORD', and a turning to him by some for salvation in the coming crisis (2:30–32 [3:3–5]). It is this combination that is taken up in Acts 2:17–21 on the Day of Pentecost, when the gospel is proclaimed in many languages as a symbol of its universality.

3:1–21 [4:1–21] The restoration of Judah (or a 'remnant' of it) is expressed in words used elsewhere for restoration after exile (Jer. 29:14; 30:3 etc.). It leads into a picture of the judgement of all nations (3:2 [4:2]), because of how they have treated God's people (cf. Ezekiel 38—39). This is typical of prophetic reversals (for example, the oracles against Babylon in Jeremiah 50—51, after Babylon was first used as God's means of punishing Judah). The nearest echoes are with Amos, however, because Tyre, Sidon and Philistia are singled out, and the crime of selling the people as slaves is specially noted (3:4–6; cf. Amos 1:6–10).

The image of a final battle is developed, with some important reversals of images. The call to beat ploughshares into swords turns round the words of Isaiah and Micah (Joel 3:10 [4:10]; cf. Isa. 2:4; Mic. 4:3). The 'Day of the LORD' is now a day of salvation for God's people (3:14 [4:14]). When Joel says 'The LORD roars from Zion' (3:16) it is to declare that Yahweh will save Judah and Jerusalem, and take up his residence again on Mt Zion (in contrast to Amos's use of the phrase, Amos 1:2). The closing picture of plenty (3:18 [4:18], cf. Amos 9:13) again announces that Judah's enemies will be defeated for ever.

Think about
PROPHETIC WORDS IN NEW CONTEXTS

What does it tell us about the ministry of prophets that we find echoes of the words of one in the mouth (or book) of another? They may even be used to mean different things (cf. also Isa. 2:2–4 and Mic. 4:1–4). Did the prophets re-use the words of others in a kind of dialogue with them, or with the memory of what they had said? (The stories about the prophets in Ahab's day show that they watched and listened to each other, perhaps jealously; 1 Kgs 22:24.)

THEOLOGICAL THEMES

ALL-POWERFUL GOD
The Book of Joel follows a pattern that we find elsewhere in prophetic books: a proclamation of judgement, a call to repentance, a promise of salvation. Underlying this is the belief that Yahweh, the God of Israel, alone is powerful over all creation. When the disaster (or disasters) proclaimed in chs 1—2 falls on Judah it is because he has brought it (the destroying invader is '*his*' army'; 2:11; 'my great army'; 2:25). So far this accords with the theology

157

of Isaiah and Jeremiah (Isa. 10:5–12; Jer. 25:8–14). Joel goes further, with his vision of a great final judgement on 'all the nations' (3:2, 9, 11, 12 [4:2, 9, 11, 12]), in this respect like Ezekiel (38—39), and Zechariah (ch. 14). As is usual in the prophets, this means a challenge to other gods and their worship. Such gods are not named here. But the judgement falls heavily on Judah's *land* and its capacity to bear fruit, and this suggests a similar struggle for the heart of Judah that we saw in Hosea's conflict with Baal in the northern kingdom (Hosea 2), and indeed Elijah's back in the ninth century BC (2 Kgs 18).

THE 'DAY OF THE LORD'
Joel uses the image of the 'Day of the LORD' in each sub-section of the book (1:5; 2:1, 11; 2:31 [3:4]; 3:14 [4:14]). Stuart calls it 'an engine driving the prophecy' (Stuart 1987, p. 230). The 'Day of the LORD' may have its origin in the Holy War context (which was not only Israelite), and the idea that the god would win victory in a single day of battle (Stuart 1987, p. 231; and his reference there to G. von Rad 1959). What is interesting about Joel's application of this concept is that he uses it first (like other prophets; Amos, Zephaniah) to proclaim judgement on his people (that is, in a reversal of the traditional expectation); but secondly, he reverses it again, to declare that the 'Day of the LORD' will be one of victory in the end after all (Stuart 1987, p. 231).

REPENTANCE
The call to repentance (2:12–17) gives the impression that it offers a chance to avoid judgement late in the day ('Yet even now'; 2:12). The people seem to be already far along the path to judgement. In fact, there is little mention of their sin, nothing to tell us what it was or why the judgement is coming. Only the call to repent implies that they have sinned. Joel's appeals to lament and fast (1:8, 13–14) may do the same. They are called to repent from the heart, like other prophets who criticize the form of worship without substance (see Outline on 2:12–17). Here again (as in Hosea) this may mean, first, turning from other gods to Yahweh. But that is not enough, for the emphasis falls on true worship. And Yahweh responds in compassion, mercy and steadfast love (*hesed*, 2:13, cf. Hos. 2:19–20 [21–22]). Due judgement can be overcome by the mercy of God (cf. Hos. 11:8–11).

NATURE AND HISTORY
Joel's depiction of Yahweh's control over natural forces is one of his key contributions to the theology of the prophets. It is not that the idea is new in itself. We have seen it in Hosea, and also in the covenantal curses in the Pentateuch (Lev. 26:16, 20; Deut. 28:23–24, 38; cf. Ps. 105:34). The interesting thing in Joel is how he fuses together the destruction by locusts with destruction by foreign invaders (as we saw above, Critical Interpretation of Joel).

Joel's use of the locust-metaphor for an army is significant in itself, for it signals that Yahweh is *also* in control of natural forces: these too have been and could be used by him in judgement. In this way, Joel shows that Yahweh's power extends to both nature and history. Indeed, it is difficult in the end to distinguish between the two. (See Rhetorical Intention for more on this.)

THE SPIRIT
Joel is also, finally, the prophet of the spirit of God. Here again he is not actually unique (cf. Ezek. 36:26–27). But his prophecy is important because he sees the giving of the spirit to all God's people without distinction.

While the spirit in the past may have been given to specially gifted individuals (like Samson, Jdg. 14:19), or prophets (Ezek. 8:3), it will then be given to all. This means that Joel's prophecy is rather like Jeremiah's New Covenant prophecy, where there will be no need for teachers, because all will know the LORD (Jer. 31:34). (Compare Num. 11:26–30 and the comment in Outline.)

The 'spirit' refers basically to the very power to live (Isa. 42:5), and especially to the power of God given to people for a purpose. The picture should not be separated from the preceding verses (2:26–27), in which God promises his presence among his people and that they will enjoy plenty, as

they worship him, recalling all he has done for them. The vision of the spirit given to the members of this people is one of a society enjoying the full, liberated life in a community bound together in God's presence (cf. Deut. 16:13–15).

Finally Joel links the spirit with 'the latter days', by which he means an unspecified future time. And he links it with the salvation of God's faithful people in a judgement on all the nations. All these aspects of the prophecy explain why it was taken up in the Acts of the Apostles (Acts 2:17–21).

Think about
THE SPIRIT

The 'spirit' in the Old Testament is often qualified by a characteristic (e.g. Jdg. 9:23, 'an evil spirit'; 1 Kgs 22:22, 'a lying spirit'). Joshua, Moses' successor, is described as 'full of the spirit of wisdom' (Deut. 34:9). The messianic figure in Isa. 11:2 has the 'spirit of the Lord', that is, 'the spirit of wisdom and understanding, the spirit of counsel and might, the spirit of knowledge and the fear of the LORD'. The spirit of God means in some sense a spirit like God's.

The spirit of God in the Old Testament has been called 'Yahweh's life-giving, chaos-ordering, exile-resisting, death-overcoming force' (Brueggemann 1997, p. 648). The spirit is not yet understood as the Holy Spirit, the third person of the Trinity (either here or elsewhere in the Old Testament). Even so, can you see connections between the spirit in the Old Testament and the Holy Spirit in the New?

RHETORICAL INTENTION

The final line in Joel, 'The LORD dwells in Zion', gives a clue to the orientation of the book. The worship of God in Jerusalem is an undertone of the whole prophecy. Judah is portrayed as a rural society with Jerusalem at its centre, its farmers producing food, and the people bringing offerings to the temple (1:8–12). All this has been disrupted by the judgement brought upon the land (ch. 1). So the priests are called to repent, and to lead the people in repenting (1:13–14; 2:15–17). When the grain is restored the people shall not only eat but worship (2:26–27).

The vision of salvation also focuses on Jerusalem (2:32—3:1 [3:5—4:1]), the last section (3:16–21 [4:16–21]) with increasing intensity. The specific concept is that the presence of Yahweh is there. This notion, as we have seen, is deep in the tradition inherited by Israel (see Isaiah: Theological Themes: Zion City of God). The way in which it is received and understood is a recurring issue among the prophets (recall Jer. 7:1–15, for example, who criticizes futile worship in Jerusalem). Joel's attitude is not far from that of Ezekiel in the closing chapters of his book. That is, he holds out a hope for a renewed Zion, in which the people worship in a genuine way. The Rhetorical Intention is to call people to this kind of worship, and to reassure them that if they respond they will enjoy God's presence and peace from enemies.

The rhetorical means include appeals to respond to the crisis (1:2–14), images of coming disaster (2:1–11), the positive inducement of a merciful God (2:12–17), promises of plenty and peace, based upon the belief in God's permanent commitment to his people (2:26–27; 2:28—3:3 [3:1–8]), promises of judgement on nations that have oppressed Judah (3:4–8 [4:4–8]; 3:19–21 [4:19–21]).

In all the vivid poetic imagery, the most striking effect is created by the locust-metaphor. The metaphor is pursued so rigorously that, as we have seen (Critical Interpretation of Joel), there has been uncertainty about whether it is a metaphor at all. I think it is better to see a close connection between the locusts (the 'vehicle' of the metaphor) and the armies they represent (the 'tenor' of the metaphor). (For these terms, see Cotterell and Turner 1989, p. 300. This is part of their helpful explanation of metaphor on pp. 299–307.) As often with metaphors, there is a kind of 'exchange' between 'vehicle' and 'tenor'. The image of the locusts aims to portray the voracious, mindless, ruthless devastation of an invading army. At the same time, the image of a locust-swarm itself gains strength from the discipline and purpose of an army. The metaphorizing becomes rampant in a text like 1:6 (where, if I am right, a 'nation' is portrayed by a locust-swarm, which is then thought of itself as a 'nation', whose teeth are like those of

lions!). (We are not far here from the type of 'beastly' imagery found in Ezekiel 1 or Daniel 7, which defies logic, but symbolizes various characteristics.) Again in 2:4–5, the invading army is like locusts – like an army!

I am suggesting a view of the metaphor that is a bit more complicated than that of Stuart, for example, who thinks that if we simply took away the locust-images in 1:4; 2:25 we would be left with a rather straightforward picture of an invading army (Stuart 1987, p. 233). The advantage of what I am suggesting is that God can be depicted as, at one and the same time, Lord of both nature and history (see Theological Themes).

JOEL IN THE CANON

Joel's prominent place in the Book of the Twelve may be intended to give prominence to his portrayal of a restored people dwelling on Mt Zion, their enemies defeated and all threats removed. Placed before Amos (as it is in MT) it draws the sting of Amos's use of the motif 'the LORD roars from Zion' to introduce a prophecy of judgement (Amos 1:2; Joel 3:16). However, Joel is placed in fourth position in LXX (after Hosea, Amos and Micah). This canonical point should not be overstressed, therefore. The ordering of the books in the Twelve may have been for reasons that we no longer know. However, its position in MT may represent one perception at the time when the biblical books were being brought into their present order.

In the wider canon, Joel has contributed to the language of the end-times taken up in several New Testament books (e.g. the darkening of sun and stars (2:30–31 [3:3–4]; 3:15 [4:15]; cf. Luke 21:25; Rev. 8:12);

putting in the sickle when the harvest is ripe (3:13 [4:13]; Mark 4:29); the locust-swarm as an army appointed to punish the wicked (2:4–5; Rev. 9:7, 9). (For further echoes, see Hubbard 1989, p. 38.)

The most famous echo of Joel in the New Testament is the outpouring of the Spirit in Acts 2:17–21. There, the vision of Joel has been reinterpreted to apply to the new era that has been brought in by the coming of Christ. The 'afterward' in Joel 3:1 is re-expressed as 'in the last days', which in Acts means the new era that has begun with the coming of Christ. The 'Day of the LORD' is a later time, not yet arrived (cf. Luke 21:9; L. Alexander 2001, p. 1032). The gift of tongues is presented as in line with Old Testament prophecy. The Spirit is now given not just to Jews, but to people of all nations and tongues ('all flesh' is given a sense in keeping with the new international scope of the gospel). And calling on the name of the LORD means believing in Christ.

FURTHER READING

Items marked with * are considered suitable as first ports of call, while others are more complex, or relate to specific issues.

COMMENTARIES

*D. A. Hubbard *Joel and Amos*. TOTC. Leicester; IVP, 1989.

D. Stuart *Hosea–Jonah*. WBC. Waco: Word Books, 1987.

*J. D. W. Watts *The Books of Joel, Obadiah, Jonah, Nahum, Habakkuk and Zephaniah*. CBC. Cambridge: CUP, 1975.

H. W. Wolff *Joel and Amos*. Hermeneia. Philadelphia; Fortress Press, 1977.

OTHER BOOKS AND ARTICLES

L. Alexander 'Acts' in *Oxford Bible Commentary*. Oxford: OUP, 2001, pp. 1028–61.

W. Brueggemann *Theology of the Old Testament*. Minneapolis: Fortress, 1997.

P. Cotterell and M. Turner *Linguistics and Biblical Interpretation*. London: SPCK, 1989.

R. Coggins 'Interbiblical Quotations in Joel' in J. Barton and D. Reimer eds *After the Exile: Essays in Honour of Rex Mason*. Macon, Ga.: Mercer University Press, 1996, pp. 75–84.

M. Fishbane *Biblical Interpretation in Ancient Israel*. Oxford: Clarendon Press, 1985.

W. LaSor, D. A. Hubbard and F. W. Bush *Old Testament Survey: the Message, Form, and Background of the Old Testament*. Grand Rapids: Eerdmans, 1996, second edition.

J. Nogalski *Redactional Processes in the Book of the Twelve*. BZAW 218. Berlin: de Gruyter, 1993.

G. von Rad 'The Origin of the Concept of the Day of Yahweh' *JSS* 4. 1959, pp. 97–108.

R. Schultz *The Search for Quotation: Verbal parallels in the Prophets*. JSOT Suppl. 180. Sheffield: Sheffield Academic Press, 1999.

The accusation is followed (vv. 9–10) by a memory of Israel being brought by God out of slavery in Egypt (Exodus) and into the promised land (Joshua; 'Amorite is similar to 'Canaanite', cf. Deut. 1:7). But they rebelled by suppressing prophet and nazirite (2:11–12; cf. Num. 6:13–21). So they will suffer judgement, in spite of the strength that they think they have (vv. 13–16).

3:1—6:14: Judgement speeches and woe-oracles against elect Israel

3:1–15 The thought in 2:9–10 continues with another reference to Israel as God's elect people, which he saved from Egypt (3:1–2). The word 'chosen' (NIV) in v. 2 is strictly 'known' (NRSV). The sense is close to 'chosen', but the personal aspect is strong. (Compare the similar phrase about Abraham in Gen. 18:19; and for the 'families of the earth' see Gen. 12:3b. It seems that a memory of Abraham is in the prophet's mind.) The point of v. 2 is that Israel, as God's elect people, is all the more liable to his judgement, because the privilege involved responsibility.

Think about
ELECTION

How useful is the idea of a 'chosen people' in modern church life? It is used of the Church in 2 Peter 2:9. What sort of encouragement and challenge should it bring?

The accusation proceeds by an argument built with rhetorical questions (3:3–8). The series culminates in v. 6b, and the point is that when disaster befalls a city, it is certainly the LORD who has done it. This is confirmed by the sayings about the prophets (vv. 7–8). The accusation against Samaria (oppression,

robbery, 3:9–10) is repeated in a style like a court-judgement, with Egypt and Ashdod called as witnesses. The verdict is pronounced in v. 11. The 'adversary' may be Assyria (but see Date and Destination). A final saying pictures a great punishment, which will be barely survived by a tiny remnant (vv. 12–15). On Bethel see Date and Destination.

4:1–13 Wealthy women of Israel (like 'cows of Bashan' only in the sense that these are an image of wellbeing because of the rich pastures there!) will be brought low by the coming disaster (4:1–3, cf. Isa. 3:16—4:1. Removal with hooks may refer to the disposal of corpses; Hayes 1988, p. 141). Verse 4 ironically imitates a call to worship, in order to proclaim scathingly that the carefully observed worship at Bethel and Gilgal is empty and self-indulgent. In this rejection of futile worship Amos is close to Hosea (Hos. 6:6).

The horrific pictures in 4:6–11 are mainly based on famine, plague and war, the common coin of divine judgement (cf. Jeremiah's use of this trio, e.g. Jer. 14:12), and covenantal curse (cf. Deut. 28:22, for 'blight and mildew', Amos 4:9). Amos apparently has instances in mind, which had the aim of bringing the people to repentance, but had not had that effect (note the refrain in vv. 6c etc.). The backward look at failure to repent is a common prophetic theme (cf. Hos. 6:1–3, and the comment there). The chapter closes with a warning of judgement, based on God's power shown in creation (4:12–13).

5:1–7 Chapter 5 opens with a lamentation for a young woman who has died (vv. 1–2), usually identified as Israel ('virgin Israel'; literally 'virgin of Israel'). Feminine personification is known elsewhere for cities and peoples (cf. Lam. 1:1, 15, and especially Hosea). This 'virgin'-image is the more poignant because it suggests a relationship not yet even begun.

The command to 'seek Yahweh and live' (v. 4) means that Israel will find its life in true worship of Yahweh. 'Life' means, first, being spared from destruction by an enemy, as is clear from the dreadful alternative in v. 6. But it also means the life that comes from true worship itself. This is the point of the contrast with 'seeking' Bethel, Gilgal and Beersheba. Of course, to 'seek Bethel' is a kind of shorthand for 'to seek the LORD at Bethel', which people thought they were doing. But as the worship in those places is corrupt (4:4), they will not find him there. It is repugnant because the people despise justice and righteousness (v. 7; cf. *mishpat* and *sedaqah*; cf. Isa. 1:27; 9:7 [6]; 33:5).

5:8–27 After a hymn to God as creator (5:8–9), the call to practise 'justice and righteousness' now becomes the dominant theme of chs 5—6 (5:15, 24; 6:12). The combination means the right relations between people *and* the action needed to bring it about. The setting of justice is in the courts (vv. 10, 15). To do this is to 'seek good, not evil', which leads to life (v. 14). As the phrase is like 5:4, 'seeking good' is another explanation of what it means to 'seek Yahweh'. Amos once again makes his basic accusation, that worship without justice is false. God's desire for justice, moreover, is rooted in the order he has created (vv. 8–9). He will maintain his standards with due penalties (v. 3, cf. Deut. 28:25; v. 11, cf. Deut. 20:5–6; 28:30).

A 'Woe!'-saying proclaims that the 'day of the LORD' will be darkness and not light (5:18). The basic imagery is of creation (cf. 5:8; Gen. 1:3–4). Light can also mean salvation (Isa. 9:2 [1]). The oracle may imply some expectation of a 'day of the LORD' that would bring salvation. Instead it will be a day of judgement (the theme is taken up by Isaiah in Isa. 2:11, 12, 17). (For particular theories of the meaning of the 'day of the LORD', see Hayes 1988, p. 171.) Amos challenges false hopes of security, here as elsewhere (1—2; 6:1–7). The accusation continues with more criticisms of falsely based worship (5:21–25), with a renewed call for 'justice and righteousness' (v. 24, cf. 7). The result of their disobedience will be exile (vv. 26–27).

6:1–14 A further 'Woe!' aims at complacency in both Israel (Samaria) and Judah (Jerusalem) (6:1–6), clearly in a prosperous time (at least for the rich). Samaria and Zion will be like other cities that have been (or are about to be) conquered (v. 2). (For the situation presupposed here, see Date and Destination). The chapter continues with pronouncements of thoroughgoing destruction. The difficult vv. 9–10 imply that in the overwhelming catastrophe burial rites are not being properly carried out. Once again, the flouting of 'justice and righteousness' is cited as the root cause (6:12).

7:1—9:15: Visions
A series of symbolic visions in chs 7 and 8 leads up to a vision of God himself (9:1).

7:1–17 The first two visions (locusts and flood, 7:1–6) obviously imply a threat to the land and people. Amos acts in the prophet's traditional role as intercessor, and God relents (cf. Moses in Exod. 32:11–14). The third vision (7:7–9) is not so clear and needs an explanation, and Amos makes no protest (rather as Jeremiah is forbidden from interceding when God is set on judgement; Jer. 7:16; 15:1).

In a rare glimpse of the prophet Amos himself (vv. 10–17), Amaziah, the 'priest of Bethel' (which Amos had attacked; 4:4; 5:4–5) denounces him to the king. He calls him a *hozeh* or 'seer' (appropriately in this 'visions' context), a synonym of *nabi'* (prophet), and implies that he is plying his prophetic trade for gain. Amos denies that he is a professional prophet ('prophet' and 'son of a prophet' are two ways of saying the same thing, in a typical Hebrew parallelism; cf. 2 Kgs 4:1; 6:1 for 'sons of the prophets' as a name for 'prophets'). NIV's 'I was not a prophet' is unjustified by the Hebrew. Amos has been called to 'prophesy' (*hinnabe'*) though not a *nabi'*. He points to his professional interests (see on Date and Destination) to refute the charge of

Think about
WHAT'S IN A (PROPHET'S) NAME?

Prophets were often unwelcome because of their message. Like Amos, Isaiah was accused of 'conspiracy' (effectively treason), v. 10, cf. Isa. 8:12 (also Jer. 37:13). And there were attempts to silence Jeremiah and the effect of his words; Jer. 11:18–20; 36.

How important do you think it is that Amos was not an 'official' prophet? Jeremiah opposes 'the prophets' (Jer. 23:9), but these were not necessarily official prophets by definition (see Introduction: The Prophet). Micaiah is an example of an official prophet who speaks a true word of God (1 Kgs 22:8–36). Does this tell us anything about 'charismatic' and 'traditional' forms of leadership in modern religious life?

Digging deeper:
WHAT DO NAMES TELL US ABOUT THE PROPHETS?

Hozeh ('seer') is sometimes thought to be a southern term, while *nabi'* ('prophet') is northern. This might explain Amaziah's scathing use of it. R. R. Wilson argues that the term 'seer' actually tells us something about how the prophet received his message, that is, by vision (1980, pp. 260–61). This might be supported by the visions of Amos in the present context, and by Isaiah, whose prophecy is called a 'vision . . . which he *saw*' (*hazon . . . hazah*, Isa. 1:1), and who had an important vision early in his ministry (Isaiah 6).

But the theory depends on *hozeh* and *nabi'* having different meanings in particular passages. Look at the following passages and see if you think they do: (Mic. 3:5–8; Isa. 29:10). Then ask what makes best sense of the present passage, when Amos replies to Amaziah's 'O seer', by saying, 'I am not a *nabi'*.

For discussions see Wilson 1980, pp. 254–57; D. L. Petersen 1981, pp. 52–63. Note Petersen's caution about putting undue emphasis on the derivation of words (pp. 35–38). See also McConville 1993, pp. 163–67.

prophesying for gain. (For a review of other translation possibilities of 7:14, see Stuart 1987, pp. 376–77.)

Amaziah is trying to prevent Amos from speaking the prophetic word (v. 16). (Compare the attempt of the temple-official Pashhur to stop Jeremiah doing the same; Jer. 20:1–2.) Amos responds by saying he has been called and cannot be stopped (v. 15); and his word against Amaziah follows (v. 17).

8:1–14 The sequence of visions resumes (from 7:1–9). The vision of the basket of ripe fruit (8:1–3) needs explanation, as did the third vision (7:7–9). It is based on a wordplay (*qayis*, 'summer fruit') and *qes* ('end'). There is a sharp contrast between the symbol (suggesting plenty) and the meaning given (destruction), which makes this vision highly ironic and disturbing (see Sherwood 2001). (NIV's 'ripe' for both *qayis* and *qes* tries too hard to make this image rational.)

The accusation returns (8:4–6) to Amos's main theme of social injustice and oppression (cf. vv. 4 and 6 with 2:6–7). Disrespect for the sabbath and feast days (8:5) is a mark of the unscrupulous greed of the wealthy classes. (New moons were marked with special observances; Num. 10:10; 28:11–15; 1 Sam. 20:5.) The pronouncements of judgement that follow are solemnly introduced with Yahweh's oath by the 'pride of Jacob' (v. 7, cf. 6:8, perhaps ironically, Wolff 1977, p. 328). Pictures of disruption in the natural world, and of famine and mourning are mixed with the idea of a famine of God's word (8:11–12). (For famine and the land mourning, v. 8, see also Jeremiah 14.) Religious feasts, which should be the occasion of rejoicing, also bring only mourning (8:10; and see note on Hos. 9:1).

9:1–10 The final vision, different in form from the others, simply pictures God poised to judge. The setting is a temple, but this temple-presence of God is no comfort, rather the reverse. The point of vv. 1–4 is that there is no escape from the judgement of God. Verses 2–3 are a dreadful reversal of the confidence of Ps. 139:7–12. Yahweh rules in heaven and on earth, and it is he who brings judgement (vv. 5–6).

The final word of judgement (9:7–10) makes the election of Israel null and void, by declaring that there was nothing special about its being brought out of Egypt, since God had also brought other nations from other places to their present homes (v. 7). There is an echo of the unexpected outcome of the OAN (chs 1—2). However, the pictures of total and unavoidable doom in this chapter are modified by the thought of a remnant that might escape, destruction falling only on the *sinners* among the people (cf. Isa. 1:27–28).

9:11–15 This is the most controversial passage in Amos (see Critical Interpretation). It suddenly turns the direction of the prophecy around, and promises a future salvation. 'In that day' recalls the 'day of the LORD' in 5:18, but now it *is* a day of salvation. The promised restoration of 'David's fallen booth' is the first allusion to a Davidic hope in the book, and refers to a renewed Davidic kingdom, probably uniting the two kingdoms into which the historic Davidic empire had split (though this is not explicitly said). In the context of Amos this points to a time after the exile that he foresees for Israel (9:4). This salvation will also involve Edom and other nations 'that are called by my name' (v. 12), in a reversal of the OAN (1:1—2:3).

The book closes with images of Israel restored to a fertile land, recalling the plenty that was promised to it at the beginning of its life (e.g. Deut. 8:7–10). It also reverses the judgement of 5:11 (Andersen and Freedman 1980, p. 887). The phrase 'restore its fortunes' (9:14) is found once each in Hosea (6:11), Zechariah (3:20) and Deuteronomy (30:3), but is commonest in Ezekiel and above all Jeremiah (in Jer. 29:14 and eight times in his Book of Consolation, Jer. 30—33; see on those chapters). It means specifically a restoration after exile. Paul, commenting on the sudden transition from judgement to salvation in these verses says: 'Punishment for punishment's sake is not the prophetic ideal. The prophet's chastisement is meant to serve as a transitional stage to a period of future restoration' (Paul 1991, p. 289).

THEOLOGICAL THEMES

JUSTICE AND RIGHTEOUSNESS, AND THE 'GOOD' OF GOD'S PEOPLE

In the prophetic literature, Amos is the key exponent of this theme. The heart of his message about it is in ch. 5, where the worship of God is forged together with a love of justice. Equally, worship without such love is exposed as utterly vain. The message is developed in 5:4–5, 6–7, 14–15, 21–24. On the key combination 'justice and righteousness' (5:7) see Outline on ch. 5. There is another important parallel between 'justice' and 'good' (5:14–15). 'Good' refers to a condition similar to blessing. It is what God seeks to bring about for his people. And the practice of justice and righteousness is inseparable from it.

So justice and righteousness lead to life. Note the threefold appeal in ch. 5: 'seek me/the LORD and live' (vv. 4, 6); 'Seek good and not evil, so that you may live' (v. 14). 'Justice and righteousness', 'good' and 'life' amount to a picture of the covenant life of the people of God. However, there is no mechanical connection between good acts and personal blessing. Rather, the combination of these things is a picture of God's order that lies behind his creation of the world. The same combination of 'good' (*tob*), 'righteousness' (*sedaqah*) and life is also found in Deuteronomy, the Old Testament's greatest book on the covenant (Deut. 6:24–25).

This vision for the life of the covenant is closely bound up with the nature of God. 'Seek me/seek the LORD' (5:4, 6) is echoed by 'Seek good and not evil' (v. 14). This corresponds to an important strand in the Old Testament's thinking about ethics: that it is a response to God by imitating what he is like. This is expressed in the call to holiness ('You shall be holy, for I the LORD your God am holy'; Lev. 19:2), and the appeal for compassion on the poor, in imitation of God's compassion in bringing Israel out of slavery in Egypt (Deut. 15:12–18, note v. 15).

This grounding of Amos's ethics in God himself explains why the call to righteousness is made with such strong condemnation of false worship, perhaps the most severe in the Bible:

> 'I hate, I despise your festivals
> and I take no delight in your solemn
>   assemblies' (Amos 5:21)

Surprisingly, this is from God who ordained festivals and solemn assemblies (Leviticus 23; Deuteronomy 16)! But those Pentateuchal texts that commanded regular observances meshed them completely with visions of a people in harmony and mutual service (Lev. 25:8–17; Deut. 14:28–29; 16:13–15). Amos's anger is based on what the people should have known. The covenant people knew well that God is denied and even blasphemed when there is a form of worship apart from the love of neighbour, which desires to do justice. In that case, the worship becomes, not merely irrelevant, but offensive to God. To this perversion of truth is opposed the most beautiful poetic exhortation to right living:

> But let justice roll down like waters
> and righteousness like an ever-flowing
>   stream (5:24).

This seeking of justice and righteousness has the most concrete forms. Its setting is the court, as is clear from 5:10–15. The love of God in the Old Testament is tested and demonstrated in the most practical ways, that stretch to the political and administrative. Once again Deuteronomy illustrates the point, in its establishment of a system for ensuring justice, with judges, and officials, local and central courts (Deut. 16:18—17:13).

Amos's rejection of false worship is similar to Hosea's 'I desire mercy and not sacrifice',

Think about
JUSTICE AND RIGHTEOUSNESS

What do you think Amos has to say to those who say that religion is a 'private matter'? How can his passionate desire for justice and righteousness be realized in practical ways today? Does the Christian church have a special role to play in campaigns and programmes to combat poverty and unjust economic systems? (The British Chancellor of the Exchequer at the time of writing, Gordon Brown, acknowledges the role of the churches in the UK in promoting the movement for debt-relief, which was subsequently supported by a number of governments.) Does Amos help us understand the New Testament's emphasis on love of neighbour? Consider 1 John 2:3–11, and ask if it is illuminated by Amos.

For Amos, justice issues were on his doorstep. In the 'global village' our horizons are much wider. Do scale and distance make any difference in principle to Amos's vision for a just society? Can a rich world be comfortable while children die in their thousands for lack of basic resources?

and his critique of it should be understood in the same way (i.e. not the abolition of formal worship as such; see Hosea: Theological Themes, 'Steadfast love, not sacrifice'). But Amos goes beyond Hosea in his insistence that out of the love of righteousness should come the practical implementation of justice.

JUSTICE AND CREATION
If justice is rooted in God's character, it is not surprising to find it directly connected with his creation. The creation-hymn in 5:8–9 is inserted into the accusations of injustice. God who made the day and night and governs the rhythms of nature also acts in power against 'the strong' (v. 9). (Compare 4:13 where another creation-praise follows a judgement-speech.) This connection between creation-power and the law of God is also made in certain psalms (cf. Psalms 19; 93). The laws of God are not meaningless, but are written in the order that God has imprinted on the whole world. In the context this means that God's action against 'the strong' will be a punishment of those in Israel who use their strength to oppress the weak. (The same idea is present in 8:9–10, following the accusations in 8:4–8.)

It is important to understand the relation between creation and the religious and ethical life correctly. We have seen that it can be misunderstood in a deterministic way (see Hosea: Theological Themes: Steadfast love, not sacrifice, and the 'disenchantment' of the world). The idea of a creation *order* leads to the ethical responsibility of free creatures to keep the commands of God.

THE UNIVERSAL GOD AND THE ELECTION OF ISRAEL
Amos puts his ethical message to Israel in the context of God's rule over the whole

world. The first expression of this is in the OAN, that dramatic opening of the book, which implies that all nations have an obligation to obey God's laws (see on the OAN in Outline). At the end of the book too (9:7), the election of Israel is put in the bigger context of God's rule over the history of all nations. These indications of universality are what led an older generation of scholars to think of the prophets as the founders of 'ethical monotheism', that is, a belief in one creator God whose standards applied to all humanity. It is true, in a paradoxical way, that the pronouncements of judgement on the nations in 1:1—2:3 imply a kind of 'universalism'. If the nations are responsible to God it must mean that in principle they come under his care, and could be saved. Amos does not develop this as Isaiah 40—55 does. But the seeds are there.

It is wrong, however, to think of a universal 'ethical monotheism' as a stage in Israel's development, leaving behind its older election traditions. This is because Amos does not deny Israel's election in theological principle. He declares instead that Israel's election does not mean that it cannot be punished (a theme common to the prophets; cf. Jeremiah 21, for example, where the Holy War traditions are turned on their head and directed against Israel). But Amos is like other important Old Testament texts, which stress that Israel's election is for the purpose of bringing salvation to the nations (Gen. 12:1–3). Close to Amos in this respect (especially Amos 9:7) is Deuteronomy 2. Deuteronomy has a strong doctrine of Israel's election (Deut. 7:6; 26:18–19). Yet in Deuteronomy 2 God marks out the land he is giving to Israel, carefully demarcating it from lands that he himself has given to other peoples (2:5, 9, 19–23).

In fact, the idea of election itself already presupposes God's universal rule. God can only 'choose' Israel if he *could* have chosen others! The election of Israel is not a contradiction of God's universal rule. Rather, it confers both responsibility and privilege. This is the point of the key election text in 3:2. An elect people are called to witness to the reality and character of God in the whole world that he has made (cf. Deut. 4:5–8).

RHETORICAL INTENTION

RHETORICAL DEVICES

I have distinguished already between Amos's rhetorical intention in a passage like 9:7 and his theological intention. Like all the prophets, Amos uses powerful rhetorical effects in order to press home his message. The argument about election in 9:7, as we have seen, is not to deny that Israel is elect, but is designed to shake his hearers out of complacency. The same is true of the OAN, followed as they are by the swingeing criticism of Israel. The thought in the OAN might appeal to an exclusivist understanding of election, but this is quickly dashed by what comes immediately after. The criticisms of worship in places like Bethel, Gilgal and Beersheba also intend to shock, since these places are full of significance in Israel's memory of its origins. Bethel and Beersheba recall the patriarchal stories (e.g. Gen. 12:8; 13:3; 21:25–34; 26:23–25; 46:1). Bethel is especially associated with Jacob in Gen. 28:10–22; 35:1–8, so the Jacob-Bethel link in the judgement-speech in 3:13–14 is strongly ironic. And Gilgal is the place where Israel crossed the Jordan and entered the promised land (Josh. 4:19). The language of covenantal curse (4:6–9), the ironic allusion to the plague in Egypt (4:10) which was part of the story of the exodus (Exod. 9:3–7, cf. vv. 14–15), the comparison of Israel with Sodom and Gomorrah (4:11), the devastating wordplay of *qayis/qes* ('summer-fruit'/'end'!; 8:2) are further examples of Amos using rhetorical means to persuade his hearers' of their false beliefs about themselves because of their well-known traditions.

Amos is shot through with allusions designed to arrest the hearer by their bold unexpectedness. How can there be 'Woe' for those who are 'at ease in Zion' (6:1)? How can the likes of Calneh, Hamath and Gath be mentioned in the same breath as Jerusalem or Samaria (6:2)? How can the great King David and his musical prowess, which fed Israel's worship, be invoked merely to pour scorn on the leading people of Israel, portraying them as decadent idlers who care nothing for the heart of God's covenant (6:4–6)? How, indeed, can this successful people, basking in the blessings of the land God has given them, be supposed to take seriously the threat of exile (6:7)!

He also uses a variety of techniques to make his points. Alongside the bold proclamation of judgement (e.g. 3:13–15) we find a rational argument (3:3–8), designed to carry the hearer along in agreement, until a devastating climax makes the critical point. The technique is found in Job (Job 6:22–28; 41:1–8 [40:25–32]; Wolff 1977, pp. 182–83). (On this text see also Möller 1999, pp. 140–44.) The review of history (2:9–11) is designed to elicit gratitude and penitence. The image of the fallen virgin (5:1) makes an emotive appeal. The savage parody of a call to worship (4:4–5) taunts the hearers to react. The exhortations to 'seek me/the LORD and *live*' (5:4, 6) offer life while forcefully claiming that the people's current

lifestyle can bring only death (cf. Jer. 7:5–7). Amos is sometimes misunderstood because his sayings are not heard for what they are, namely parts of a network of persuasive exhortations. Declarations of judgement have therefore been wrongly detached from appeals to repent, and also from the glimpse of hope held out in the final paragraph (9:11–15). Wellhausen thought that the prophet who promised 'blood and iron' could not suddenly have held out 'roses and lavender'. But the prospect offered in 9:11–15 is only properly heard *after* the full message that precedes it. The picture of a restored Israel is intended to show Israel in its true colours, the people as its covenantal God intended it to be. Here is the 'good' that it is pressed to seek (5:14). This image of a renewed Israel and Davidic dynasty (cf. 2 Sam. 7:13–17) functions as one more critique of Israel as it currently is (having departed from the standards expected of 'David', and abandoned the call to establish 'good' in the land). And yet it also does what it plainly does, it states finally that God is indeed the faithful God of Israel, and that in spite of his severe accusation and pronouncements of judgement, he will not cast them off forever.

RHETORICAL LEVELS

We are getting used to the idea that a prophet's words operated at a number of levels. They had their meaning and effect first of all in the prophet's own situation, but they were later heard in new ways by successive 'audiences'. These new hearers were able to see them in their totality, understand how they had begun to be fulfilled, and apply them to their own situations in life. This means that audiences could tell the difference between what a word might have meant in the past and what it meant for them. They could also tell what it might mean in the future. As we have seen (Critical Interpretation of Amos), Andersen and Freedman think the prophet too was capable of this kind of reflection, going beyond the stage of his prophecy that he was engaged in at any particular time.

The most obvious 'after-life' of the words Amos spoke in the northern kingdom is in its reception in Judah. It is clear from the start, in 1:1, that such a secondary level of reception took place, because the author of that verse dates the prophecy first in the time of the Judean King Uzziah, and only then by referring to Jeroboam II of Israel. This recognition of a Judean stage following the original 'Israelite' stage is only a simple distinction, however. Wolff finds four of his six redactional levels in Judah, ranging from the 'old school' of Amos's disciples (760–730 BC) to his post-exilic eschatological layer (see Critical Interpretation of Amos).

As we have seen, many commentators now think that much more of the book can be attributed to Amos than Wolff thought. On this view, there are few handles on the way in which the prophecy was received in Judah. Ultimately what was heard in Judah was the Book of Amos in its finished form. A quest for the rhetorical intention, therefore, has to deal in the end with the various kinds of sayings as they stand together.

The God who chose Israel still dwells in Zion (1:2). However, this is no guarantee of salvation (as it may have seemed in Joel 3:16). On the contrary, God is never to be taken for granted, since Judah like Israel can be accused of covenant breach, and stand under judgement as a result (2:4–5). The judgement that fell on Israel (in 722 BC) confirms to Judah after that time that the threats of Amos can come to an all too real fulfilment. However, God's covenant intention for his people remains as it always was. In 9:11–15, Judah has a testimony that what has befallen Israel is not (or need not be) God's last word.

AMOS IN THE CANON

Amos's prominent place in the Book of the Twelve is owed to the lead he gave on 'justice and righteousness' as an imperative in the life of God's people. We have also found it impossible to explain his meaning without reference to large parts of the Old Testament, especially Genesis–Deuteronomy. Amos shows that Israel's obligations to the poor arise out of their creation and covenant traditions.

Amos's importance in the Canon of Scripture is well illustrated by the fact that it is almost always cited first when anyone wants to say that biblical religion has a strong social ethic. Amos is a bulwark against the notion of a spiritualized or privatized religion. His insistence that the people of God have a responsibility for the poor finds echoes in the New Testament (Gal. 2:10; Acts 11:27–30), and invites modern applications. (See Think about: Justice and righteousness.) In certain times and places in the church's history, the severe words of Amos have been overlooked, in favour of an internalized individualistic spirituality.

The Book of Acts has a direct quotation of Amos 9:11–12, based on LXX. In it, the original promise of the rebuilding of the 'booth' of David (which to its first hearers meant a restoration of the Davidic kingdom, whether Judean or all-Israel) is reinterpreted. Edom is no longer singled out, rather the focus falls on the 'other nations', and the prophecy becomes a prophecy of the world-salvation in Christ (cf. Wolff 1977, p. 355).

FURTHER READING

* Items marked with * are considered suitable as first ports of call, while others are more complex, or relate to specific issues.

COMMENTARIES

*E. Achtemeier *Minor Prophets I*. NIBC. Peabody: Hendrickson, 1996.

F. I. Andersen and D. N. Freedman *Hosea*. AB. New York: Doubleday, 1980.

F. I. Andersen and D. N. Freedman *Amos*. AB. New York: Doubleday, 1989.

*J. Barton *Isaiah 1–39*. OTG. Sheffield: Sheffield Academic Press, 1995.

*G. F. Hasel *Understanding the Book of Amos*. Grand Rapids: Baker, 1991.

*J. H. Hayes *Amos the Eighth-Century Prophet: His Times and His Preaching*. Nashville: Abingdon, 1988.

*D. A. Hubbard *Joel and Amos*. TOTC. Leicester: IVP, 1989.

*J. A. Motyer *The Day of the Lion: the Message of Amos*. London: IVP, 1974.

S. Paul *Amos*. Hermeneia. Minneapolis: Fortress Press, 1991.

D. Stuart *Hosea–Jonah*. WBC. Waco: Word Books, 1987.

H. W. Wolff *Joel and Amos*. Hermeneia. Philadelphia: Fortress, 1977.

OTHER BOOKS AND ARTICLES

*A. G. Auld *Amos*. OTG. Sheffield: JSOT Press, 1986.

H. Barstad *The Religious Polemics of Am 2, 7B–8; 4,1–13; 5,1–27; 6,4–7; 8,14*. SVT 34. Leiden: Brill, 1984.

J. Barton *Amos's Oracles against the Nations*. Cambridge: CUP, 1980.

M. D. Carroll *Contexts for Amos: Prophetic Poetics in Latin American Perspective*. JSOT Suppl. 132. Sheffield: JSOT Press, 1992.

G. Chirichigno *Debt-Slavery in Israel and the Ancient Near East*. JSOT Suppl. 141. Sheffield: Sheffield Academic Press, 1993.

R. P. Knierim '"I will Not Cause it to Return" in Amos 1–2' in G. W. Coats and B. O. Long, eds *Canon and Authority*. Philadelphia: Fortress Press, 1977, pp. 163–75.

J. G. McConville *Judgement and Promise: an Interpretation of Jeremiah*. Leicester: Apollos; Winona Lake: Eisenbrauns, 1993.

K. Möller *Presenting a Prophet in Debate: An Investigation of the Literary Structure and the Rhetoric of Persuasion in the Book of Amos*. Dissertation, University of Gloucestershire, 1999 (Sheffield: JSOT Press, forthcoming, 2002); cited here in unpubl. version.

S. Niditch *The Symbolic Vision in Biblical Tradition*. HSM 30. Chico: Scholars Press, 1983.

D. L. Petersen, *The Roles of Israel's Prophets*. JSOT Suppl. 17. Sheffield; JSOT Press, 1981.

M. E. Polley *Amos and the Davidic Empire*. Oxford, New York: OUP, 1989.

Y. Sherwood 'Of Fruit and Corpses and Wordplay Visions' *JSOT* 92. 2001, pp. 5–27.

R. R. Wilson *Prophecy and Society in Ancient Israel*. Philadelphia: Fortress, 1980.

Chapter 9

OBADIAH

DATE AND DESTINATION

Obadiah, the shortest book in the Old Testament, is an oracle against a single nation, Edom. It gives us few clues about its dating. The bare title ('The vision of Obadiah'), mentions no king or event to help the reader. So we have to try to work it out from the contents.

The clues are a) the subject matter itself and b) vocabulary and ideas that suggest links with other books.

SUBJECT MATTER

The oracle against Edom contains some hints. Edom and Israel had a long history together, going back to patriarchal times, for Israel is Jacob and Edom is Esau (Gen. 25:25–26, 30). Edom was a neighbour to Judah, below the Dead Sea and to the east. Its land was mountainous and difficult. When Esau had retreated to leave Jacob to his ill-gotten birthright he had chosen a harder lot (Gen. 36:6–8).

From time to time there was conflict between the two nations. This went back as far as Israel's approach to the promised land, when Edom barred its way (Num. 20:14–21). Edom was vassal to Judah in the ninth century, until it rebelled against King Joram, leading to a period of war between them (2 Kgs 8:20–22). In the eighth century Judah again dominated Edom for a time, but Edom was able to attack Judah in return (2 Kgs 14:7; 2 Chr. 28:17). In the same century, Amos accused Edom of attacking 'his brother' (Israel–Judah) (Amos 1:11–12). It was also a willing trader of Israelite slaves (1:6, 9). Then in 587 BC Edomites apparently joined in the destruction of Judah by the Babylonians (Ps. 137:7; Lam. 4:21–22; Ezek. 25:12–14).

So there was long-running enmity between the two. An oracle against Edom could fit a number of historical occasions. However, vv. 11–14 picture Edom rejoicing and taking advantage of an enemy attack on Jerusalem, to join in the plunder, and to ambush those who were fleeing. This perhaps fits best with the situation in 587 BC.

Obadiah 7 contains an allusion to a specific event, but again it does not give enough information to pin it down to a known situation.

VOCABULARY AND IDEAS

Obadiah 1–9 has striking similarities with

another oracle against Edom, Jer. 49:7–16 (cf. Obad. 1–4 with Jer. 49:14–16; Obad. 5 with Jer. 49:9; the allusions to Edom's 'wisdom' in Obad. 8 and Jer. 49:7). It may be that one of these oracles is partly dependent on the other, or that each has made use of known phrases and ideas in a tradition of Edom-sayings. Either way it is very difficult to know which came first (see Allen 1976, pp. 131–33; Stuart 1987, pp. 414–16).

There are also links between v. 17 and Joel 2:32 [3:5]; 3:17 [4:17] (in the latter case just the phrase 'it/Jerusalem shall be a holy place'. Here too it is not certain which way the influence runs. (See Allen 1976, pp. 164–65, n. 20, for the view that Joel depends on Obadiah in both cases; cf. Baker 1988, p. 39.)

Obadiah echoes Lamentations in its belief (vv. 15–16) that, while the Day of the LORD has come for Judah (Lam. 2:21–22), it still lies in the future for its enemies (Lam. 1:21b; Gottwald 1954, pp. 84–85).

One way of thinking about these connections would be to suppose that Obadiah draws on Lamentations, and that Joel in turn draws on Obadiah. This would mean dating Obadiah in the sixth century, but it is not possible to date it closely within that period.

CRITICAL INTERPRETATION OF OBADIAH

The short book basically falls into two parts: vv. 1–14, accusations of Edom and pronouncements of punishment; and vv. 15–21, pronouncement of future punishment of all nations that have oppressed Israel, and of Israel's regaining its historic land.

Commentators have often assigned the later part to a different author (or authors) than vv. 1–14 (v. 15b was sometimes included with this first section). This was for the familiar critical reason that prophets were thought to address immediate situations and did not look to the remote future. We have dealt with this point of view elsewhere, and will not repeat the general points made there (Isaiah: Is prophecy predictive?).

It is sufficient to say that Edom provides a unity of theme throughout the book. A unity is achieved too by the motif of the 'Day of the LORD' (v. 15 – familiar now from Amos, Lamentations and Joel). The 'day' motif comes first at v. 8, then several times in vv. 11–14 to refer to the day when Judah was overcome and Edom took advantage. Verse 15, which uses the full expression, then uses it to make a dramatic contrast with the previous verses: instead of Judah's 'day of calamity', there will be the 'Day of the LORD' against all who oppressed her, especially Edom.

STRUCTURE AND OUTLINE

STRUCTURE
The sayings against Edom go through distinct stages:

1–4 A declaration of God's judgement on Edom's pride
5–10 An argument showing that the destruction of Edom will be complete.
11–14 The central accusation about Edom's plundering of Judah.
15–21 The Day of the LORD against the nations and Edom; Israel regains the land

OUTLINE
1–4: A declaration of God's judgement on Edom's pride
The book opens briefly with the 'The vision of Obadiah'. Isaiah's prophecy is also called

a 'vision' (Isa. 1:1; 2:1). As elsewhere, this does not necessarily mean that the message has been received by visual means (see Amos: Outline, 7:1-17).

The accusation of pride is a well-known prophetic topic (cf. Isaiah 2; Ezek. 28:17). Here it is poetically depicted with images of Edom's high mountains. The lofty Edom will be 'brought down' and made small.

5–10: An argument showing that the destruction of Edom will be complete

Edom in its secret, inaccessible places has been fully invaded and exposed (v. 6). There is emphasis on total destruction (cf. v. 18; and Isa. 34:8–17). They have been betrayed in an alliance, or 'covenant' (*berit*) (v. 7; NRSV 'your confederates' is literally 'men of your covenant'). (Prophets warned elsewhere against such misplaced trust; Isaiah 7; 30: 1–5.) Edom's pretensions to great wisdom are mocked, since it could not see the folly of its policy in this respect (vv. 7c–8). Its violence against Israel will come back on its own head (v. 10).

11–14: The central accusation about Edom's plundering of Judah

These verses have a regular parallel structure, each line accusing Edom of enjoying the 'day' of Judah's ruin (the word 'day' occurs nine times in this refrain). There is a progression in the accusation from gloating to participation, so that finally Edomites 'handed over his (Judah's) survivors' (v. 14), in the hope of destroying them completely.

15–21: The Day of the LORD against the nations and Edom; Israel regains the land

Verse 15 contains a double blow to Edom. As they took part in a 'day' of Judah's ruin, so there will be an even greater 'day' of judgement against them (15a). And in poetic justice, what they tried to do to Judah will be done to them (v. 15b). Verses 17–18 press home this idea of a turning of the tables. As Edom cut off the 'escape' of Judah's 'survivors', there *will* be 'escapees' in Jerusalem, and they shall turn on Edom, so that 'there shall be no "survivor" of the house of Esau' (v. 18).

The judgement on Edom is extended to 'all the nations' in vv. 15–16 and in vv. 19–20. (On drinking the 'cup' of God's anger see Jer. 25:15–16, 27.) The theme in these verses is the retaking of the historic land of Israel, from the Negeb in the south to Phoenicia in the far north. Israelites will drive out others who have occupied the territory, as Joshua once did (Sidon in Phoenicia was on the border of the tribal territory of Asher; Josh. 19:28; cf. 1 Kgs 17:9, 'Zarephath, which belongs to Sidon').

Obadiah is, in the first place, an oracle against a particular nation, Edom, because of some hostile act against Judah. But, like other prophetic books, it extends its view beyond the immediate judgement on that nation, to take in God's greater judgement on all nations, and his final salvation of his people.

THEOLOGICAL THEMES

Underlying Oracles Against the Nations (OAN) generally is the theme of the judgement of God against all wickedness. However, they often have a special twist. In God's providence, he brings judgement in due course on those who have caused his people to suffer – even if he used their oppression as a punishment for a while on his own people (this is quite clear in Isaiah and Jeremiah). The larger point is that

God's providence has a broader horizon than the immediate events that Israel–Judah has to endure.

The special twist in relation to Edom lies in its close relationship with Israel. This is recognized in Deut. 23:7–8 [8–9], where Edomites may be admitted to membership of Israel's religious assembly in the third generation because they are 'brothers' (NRSV 'kin'). It is also recognized by Amos when he condemns them the more strongly because of this relationship (Amos 1:11). (See Obadiah in the Canon, where you are asked to think about the fact that Obadiah is placed next to Amos in the order of the Book of the Twelve.)

The punishment of Edom fits the crime. Its pretension to great wisdom is exposed in the unravelling of its clever foreign policy (v. 7), and its high and mighty fortresses are

---

Think about
THE JUSTNESS OF JUDGEMENT

The matching of punishment to crime says something important about judgement itself. It goes to the heart of the evil that Edom is guilty of. Obadiah is not saying: 'Just you wait, my God is bigger than your God, and you'll be sorry!' This is not a charter for revenge. Instead it expresses the rightness of God's judgement on human corruption. Behind it is a sense of sin against God (pride is the fundamental sin, Genesis 3), and also a concept of what human relationships should be like.

Think about v. 15a. Does it have a flip side in a positive ethic for human relationships? (See what Jesus says in Matt. 7:12.)

---

levelled. But more than that, the very things Edom wished to happen to Judah now fall on its own head. This is clearly expressed in vv. 15b, 17–18 (see above, Outline). There is an echo of this in a Pentateuchal law about false witness (Deut. 19:16–19), where the false witness must suffer the punishment he or she had hoped to bring on the accused.

RHETORICAL INTENTION

The intention of Obadiah is to encourage post-exilic Judah, in the same way that other OAN do in, for example, Jeremiah. After 587 BC, the people of Judah were keenly aware that they had suffered at the hands of God. The prophetic warnings of generations had come to pass. They could no longer pretend that their God would never act against them. A whole segment of Old Testament literature now reckoned with this fact.

However, the acceptance of their own guilt did not stop them from feeling outrage at the injustices and cruelties of others. Obadiah speaks to the need to see justice. It takes its place alongside other prophetic texts that warn God's people of their own continuing need to be faithful (e.g. Joel 2:32 [3:5]).

OBADIAH IN THE CANON

Obadiah shares with other prophetic books its teaching about judgement on the nations and the vindication of God's people Judah. In doing so it has penetrating insight into the nature of human evil. It does not yet have a truly universal vision. But the re-establishment of God's rule on Zion (v. 21) provides a typology of God's universal kingdom, established after the defeat of the powers of evil.

Think about
OBADIAH IN RELATION TO AMOS

Why do you think Edom is the subject of a separate book (even if it is a short one)? Think about Obadiah's place in the canonical order, placed after Amos. What role does Edom have in Amos? Remember Amos 9:12 as well as 1:6, 9, 11–12. Could the canonizers have wanted to redress a balance? Do you see an irony in its suffering from a broken 'covenant' (Obad. 7), when you consider how Amos stresses the duty owed by Edom to Israel because of the bond of blood between them (1:11)? Note also the 'covenant (*berit*) of brothers' (NRSV 'kinship') in Amos 1:9 – is this Edom's or Tyre's (see Stuart 1987, p. 313)?

FURTHER READING

Items marked with * are considered suitable as first ports of call, while others are more complex, or relate to specific issues.

COMMENTARIES

*E. Achtemeier *Minor Prophets I*. NIBC. Peabody, Mass.: Hendrickson, 1996.

L. C. Allen *The Books of Joel, Obadiah, Jonah and Micah*. NICOT. Grand Rapids: Eerdmans, 1976; London: Hodder and Stoughton, 1978.

*D. W. Baker 'Obadiah' in D. W. Baker, T. D. Alexander and B. K. Waltke *Obadiah, Jonah, and Micah*. TOTC. Leicester: IVP, 1988.

P. R. Raabe *Obadiah*. AB. New York: Doubleday, 1996.

D. Stuart *Hosea–Jonah*. WBC. Waco: Word Books, 1987.

*J. D. W. Watts *The Books of Joel, Obadiah, Jonah, Nahum, Habakkuk and Zephaniah*. CBC. Cambridge: CUP, 1975.

OTHER BOOKS AND ARTICLES

B. Dicou *Edom: Israel's Brother and Antagonist*. JSOT Suppl. 169. Sheffield: Sheffield Academic Press, 1994.

N. K. Gottwald *Studies in the Book of Lamentations*. SBT 14. London: SCM, 1954.

*R. A. Mason *Micah, Nahum, Obadiah*. OTG. Sheffield: Sheffield Academic Press, 1991.

Chapter 10

JONAH

DATE AND DESTINATION

Unlike Hosea and Amos, Jonah does not give definite clues either to its dating or to its intended audience. This is because of the nature of the book. There is no other like it among the prophetic books. In its four chapters, the prophet utters only one line of prophetic speech, not even a whole verse: 'Forty days more and Nineveh shall be overthrown!' (Jonah 3:4b). The other prophetic books (Daniel apart) are dominated by sayings of the prophet, which give us something to go on when working out the situations addressed. In Jonah, the prophetic word itself plays only a tiny role in the story. Many of the other books also give dates when the prophet is said to have worked. But Jonah is silent about this. Finally, Jonah himself is never called a 'prophet' in the book.

Jonah was no doubt included in the 'Latter Prophets' because 'Jonah son of Amittai' is also named in 2 Kgs 14:25. He came from Gath-hepher, in the territory of Zebulon, near the Sea of Galilee (Josh. 19:13). This means he was known as a prophet of the northern kingdom in the reign of Jeroboam II (786–746 BC), which puts him close in time to Amos and Hosea. Nothing is said

there about a mission to Nineveh. However, the allusion to Jonah in Kings means that a historical setting can be imagined for the events reported. Nineveh itself, a great Assyrian city, also makes us think of that time, since it was then that Assyria was rising to new dominance in the region.

The book itself, however, much more than other prophetic books, is a narrative. This might make us expect information about the time and place, and about the society and politics that usually made prophets speak out. But there is nothing of the sort. The story tells of Jonah's commission to go and preach to Nineveh, of how he fled from this task, but was compelled to go in the end, how he carried out his mission, and how Nineveh repented and was saved. But the focus seems to be much more on Jonah and his relationship with God than on the events. Nineveh as a city is not fleshed out. We hear only about its great size (3:3), and of the 'King of Nineveh' (3:6). But the king is not named, and even the expression 'King of Nineveh', is not used elsewhere (we normally read of the King of Assyria).

DATING AND GENRE

All this makes us wonder if we are reading a

historical narrative at all. So the question about dating turns out to be a question about the kind of literature. If we are reading about historical events, then we might expect that the book would have been written fairly close in time to those events. If we are reading a fictional story, which has adopted the name of an obscure prophet mentioned only once in the history books, then the date could be much later.

It is, in fact, very common to suppose that the narrative is fiction. This is partly for historical reasons. No repentance of Nineveh at the preaching of a Hebrew prophet is known from any other source. The impression that Nineveh is the chief city of Assyria at the time (having a 'king') is out of keeping with what is known of Assyrian history (Nineveh was made capital only by Sennacherib in 701 BC; however, Stuart 1987, pp. 441–42, argues that it was a royal residence in Jonah's time). The detail that it took three days to go through the city (3:3) is hard to square with its dimensions as known from archaeology (about seven miles across).

But the belief that it is fiction is partly due also to the nature of the book itself. Not only does it seem uninterested in real events of the time in which it is set, but it tells of very strange happenings. Jonah is saved from drowning by being swallowed by a great fish, which vomits him out on dry land after three days (1:17 [2:1]; 2:10 [11]). A strange plant grows quickly to give Jonah shade, and as quickly dies, because God sends a worm to destroy it (4:6–7). There is even a humorous side to all this, with the peevish Jonah outraged because God has saved Nineveh (4:1–2), and God's unexpected parting shot: ' . . . and also many animals' (4:11)!

Think about
WHAT IS JONAH LIKE?

If Jonah is a story, might it not have been better placed in the Writings section of the Hebrew canon, alongside Esther and Ruth? Rofé says in his *Introduction to the Prophetic Literature*: 'The Book of Jonah, however, should not be included, as it is a story about a prophet and not a collection of speeches actually spoken by him' (p. 11). If it had been classed with the Apocrypha, it might have stood alongside Tobit, which is set partly in Nineveh, and (according to some ancient texts) mentions Jonah twice (Tob. 14:4, 8 RSV; see Limburg 1993, pp. 19, 80). There are also stories about prophets, however (1 Kgs 17-19; 2 Kgs 2–9; Jer. 32–44), and some of these tell of strange miracles (2 Kgs 2:19–22; 4:42–44). Indeed there are a number of echoes of the Elijah stories in Jonah (e.g. 1 Kgs 19:4; Jonah 4:8; and see Limburg, pp. 29–30; and Dell, 1996).

For more on genre, see below, Rhetorical Intention.

The oddnesses of the story do not mean, in themselves, that Jonah is unhistorical. But the fact that it is a narrative does not make it historical either. The reader will make up his or her own mind based on several factors. The historicity of the narrative is accepted by some modern writers (Alexander 1988, pp. 51–63; Stuart 1987, pp. 440–43).

CRITICAL INTERPRETATION OF JONAH

The Book of Jonah is a continuous narrative, which incorporates a Psalm of Thanksgiving (2:2–9 [3–10]). Scholars have often thought that the Psalm was not an original part of the story (e.g. Wolff 1986,

Think about
JONAH AS HISTORY?

Stuart explains why he thinks it important to believe Jonah is historical in this way:

> If the events described in the book actually happened, the audience's existential identification with the characters and circumstances is invariably heightened. People act more surely upon what they believe to be true in fact, than merely what they consider likely in theory. (Stuart 1987, p. 440)

Do you agree with this judgement as it is applied to Jonah? To answer the question you should decide what the *point* of the book is. Then you can ask: Does it make a difference to the point whether the book is historical or not? (You may need to read on before you answer.)

pp. 78–79). It seemed odd that Jonah should pray a prayer of thanksgiving while still in the belly of the fish. Jonah appears faithful and grateful here, while in the rest of the story he is rebellious and churlish. In the story he wants to die (4:8–9), while in the Psalm he does not! Certain differences in vocabulary are also pointed out (see Alexander 1988, p. 65).

However, the modern tendency is to see the Psalm as integral. The main reason is that the story needs it. The fish-episode would be more bizarre if it were not the occasion of Jonah's experience of great distress and deliverance. Certain elements are carried on from ch. 1 into the Psalm (Jonah 'goes down'; 1:3, 5; 2:6 [7]; he 'calls on the LORD', 2:2 [3], cf. 1:6). And the difference between the thankful Jonah in the Psalm and the rebellious Jonah in the story simply adds a

certain richness to the portrayal of the character (see also Limburg 1993, pp. 31–33; or Alexander 1988, pp. 63–69).

STRUCTURE AND OUTLINE

STRUCTURE
Alexander, following Magonet, offers a structure of the book in parallel panels as follows:

A	1:1–16	The first call – flight. Sailors
B	1:17 [2:1]	Transition
C	2:1–10 [2:2–11]	Prayer – 'discussion with God'
A'	3:1–10	The second call. Obedience. Nineveh
B'	4:1	Transition
C'	4:2–11	Prayer – 'discussion with God' (Magonet 1983, p. 55; Alexander 1988, p. 68)

This nicely brings out the contrasts in the story, especially between Jonah's gratitude in ch. 2 and his anger in ch. 4.

OUTLINE
1:1–17 [2:1]
The book opens with a familiar way of saying that God's word came to a prophet, or other important figure (cf. 1 Sam. 15:10; 1 Kgs 17:2). Nineveh was historically one of the three great cities of Assyria (with Assur and Calah). In the time of Jeroboam II (see Date and Destination) it was, by most accounts, not yet the capital of Assyria.

Other prophets gave oracles against Assyria (cf. Isa. 10:12–19; Nahum; Zeph. 2:13–15). But it is unusual to read that a prophet should be sent to a foreign city to preach against it. Does Jonah know immediately what he knows in 4:2 – that God's intention in sending him was to save Nineveh? That is the reason he gives there for trying to escape the call of God.

The story in ch. 1 is remarkable because it portrays the foreign (pagan) sailors rather sympathetically, while Jonah appears in a bad light. Though they worship other gods they are afraid of Yahweh because his follower Jonah has offended him. Both Jonah and the sailors accept that Jonah must be thrown overboard in order to appease the angry God. Yet the sailors are afraid too, because of their act in doing so, and worship Yahweh all the more.

God is portrayed as in control of the wind, the sea, the creatures and the events. In the midst of the storm and the human anxiety, his purpose goes calmly forward (he stills the sea, 1:15, and provides the fish for Jonah, 1:17 [2:1]).

(Note. In this chapter and throughout Jonah, the name 'God' alternates with the name 'Yahweh'. See Theological Themes for comment).

2:1–10 [2:2–11]

Jonah's prayer is a thanksgiving (cf. Psalms 18; 30; 32; 116; 118. Limburg gives a useful comparison of it and Psalm 30; 1993, pp. 65–66). The experience of deep distress is fully expressed, but the note of thanksgiving is established at the beginning (v. 2 [3]), and emerges strongly in the end (vv. 6c–9 [7c–10]). Distress is often expressed by the Psalmists in watery terms (Ps. 18:16 [17]). Here, of course, it is especially appropriate. The Psalm speaks of the experience in general terms ('I am driven away from your sight. You brought up my life from the Pit'). That is, the specific points of the story are not mentioned. This is why the Psalm has often been thought secondary (but see Critical Interpretation). It is remarkable, perhaps, that Jonah longs to see 'your holy temple' (vv. 4, 7 [5, 8]), and vows to sacrifice there to Yahweh once again (v. 9 [10]). The plain sense of this is

Jerusalem, and that might seem odd in a prophet from Gath-Hepher, since the royal sanctuary of Jeroboam II was Bethel (Amos 7:13). This no doubt reflects the perspective of those who heard the Book of Jonah.

The narrative continues with Jonah arriving on land (2:10 [11]), and so does the sense of movement towards God's purpose.

3:1–10

The second call of Jonah (3:2) echoes the first (1:2). The wording may imply that Jonah knows very well what it is! He now obeys. We should imagine Jonah spending time going through the great city, giving the message repeatedly as he went. Even so, the telling of the message, and of the immediate and unexpected response to it, is remarkably brief (3:4–5). The King of Nineveh then expresses a key theological point of the story: 'Who knows? God may relent and change his mind; he may turn from his fierce anger so that we do not perish' (3:9). This is echoed in other texts: Joel 2:13–14; 2 Sam. 12:22 ('Who knows?' + 'gracious' + 'God turning'). A number of other texts have the idea of God changing his mind (Gen. 6:6–7; 1 Sam. 15:11). So the king seems to be expressing something commonly accepted, that God may have mercy if people repent.

4:1–11

Jonah's angry reaction contains the theological heart of the book: that God is 'gracious and merciful, slow to anger and abounding in steadfast love, and ready to relent from punishing' (4:2). Because of its similarity to Exod. 34:6 the Book of Jonah has even been called a 'midrash' on that text. ('Midrashim' were theological expositions of biblical texts in post-biblical Judaism; see Salters 1994, p. 47, for a comment on the term's application to Jonah.)

The narrative closes with a dialogue between God and Jonah in which God justifies his merciful act. The incident of the strange plant, and the worm that killed it, serves this purpose. But Jonah's last word is a wish for death (4:8–9). God's last word is an affirmation of his mercy, and the author allows no more contradiction of it. (Note. The plant that shaded Jonah cannot be exactly identified. See Sasson 1990, pp. 291–92, for caution on this.)

THEOLOGICAL THEMES

It is part of the puzzle of Jonah to discover what its theological concerns really are. It is important to distinguish between what is merely assumed to be true in the book, and what it might actually want to teach. This is generally a challenge of reading narrative, more than reading other prophetic books, where the purpose of prophet and author lie closer to hand.

WORKING OUT THE SOVEREIGNTY OF GOD

For example, we might say that the sovereignty of God is a theme of the book. God clearly controls events. Jonah's attempt to run away from him is a hopeless failure. The 'odd' events emphasize that God is in control – in fact, for that purpose, the odder the better! Notice how the word 'appointed' brings this out: God 'appointed' the great fish (1:17 [2:1]), the strange plant (4:6), the worm (4:7) and the east wind (4:8) (NRSV obscures this by using different words for the same Hebrew verb).

Jonah is hardly teaching this view of God to its hearers for the first time. Most Old Testament books take it for granted, or work out what it means in certain respects (like Genesis, in its dialogue with the mythologies of the ancient world). God is certainly sovereign in Jonah, but this is something that the author and readers already share, and of course Jonah. The more interesting question is how the idea is applied.

We see how it works in ch. 1. Here we have some characters who are *not* worshippers of Yahweh (the sailors). They quiz Jonah about his God, and Jonah answers with a confession of faith: Yahweh is 'the God of heaven, who made the sea and the dry land' (1:9; note how the names Yahweh and 'Elohim are both used; see below). This may come as a challenge to the sailors, who are no doubt polytheists. We wonder what they make of this claim about a God they do not know. We see their fear because they may be in danger from this God (1:10, 16), and their prayer to him not to hold them responsible for Jonah's death (1:15).

In all this we are not being taught monotheism by the book of Jonah. Rather we know that author and readers share that belief, and view the events from that point of view. And we, as later readers, know that those assumptions were made. It may be, however, that Jonah is working out issues connected with the Jewish claim about the one sovereign God. Can worshippers of other gods come to faith in Yahweh? Does not their belief in God as creator imply that all people owe him the same allegiance that they do? This may be intended by the worship offered by the sailors, by the line about 'vain idols' in the Psalm (2:8 [9]), and by the repentance of the Ninevites.

WORSHIP AND THANKSGIVING

Jonah's Psalm of thanks must be taken as an example of the true devotion of a grateful worshipper. The similarities with other known Psalms of thanks make it clear that this is the right response and an example of proper worship. But again, the Book of Jonah does not teach us this for the first time; the important thing is that *Jonah* behaves in this way. The one who was disobedient now gives thanks. He has been tried and tested, and his confession of faith and his desire to worship again in the temple show that his time of disobedience is past, he will now fulfil his prophetic mission.

RETRIBUTION?

What do we make of 1:12? Jonah says that the storm is all his fault, and if the sailors throw him overboard the sea will become calm and they will be saved. In this he turns out to be a true prophet! But are we to suppose that Jonah is theologically correct here? Does God punish the disobedient by killing them? In this case we have to ask what Jonah may have intended by saying it. Some have said it was his last desperate attempt to get out of the dreaded mission to Nineveh, and others that it was a noble act of self-sacrifice. Perhaps Jonah did think that God meant to kill him for his disobedience. Jonah will hardly have seen the fish coming! In any case, it turns out that God does not mean to punish Jonah for his disobedience by drowning him. So here is a case where the things that a character says in the book (even a prophet of God) are not necessarily a guide to what the book teaches.

GOD'S FORGIVENESS EXTENDED TO ALL?

Here we have a candidate for a major theme of the book. This is because the dialogue between God and Jonah in the final chapter focuses on God's compassion and forgiveness. So too does the narrative method, for it is introduced in the most unexpected way. Jonah has seen the Ninevites repent, and now fears that his prophecy of judgement will not come true! And why? Because he knows that God is 'gracious, merciful, slow to anger, abounding in steadfast love, and ready to relent from punishing' (4:2). The statement is theologically significant in itself, and has links with other important texts (Exod. 34:6; Joel 2:13).

But in the context it is especially striking, because what Jonah is saying contrasts so sharply with his state of mind when he says it. (We have already noticed that this verse has been thought the theological centre of the book; see Outline on 4:1–11.) What does the book teach here? Not this theological affirmation in itself, since that is already known. Rather, it says that if God is compassionate, surely this must apply to people other than Israelites. The narrative extends the meaning of what is already known. The teaching is made effective to Israelites because it is so shocking to this Israelite prophet! It might even be a deliberate response to Joel, who knew of God's compassion in return for repentance, but applied it only to Israelites (Salters 1994, p. 55). It has equally been thought to be a reaction against the exclusivism of Ezra-Nehemiah (Salters 1994).

CAN GOD 'REPENT'?

Some have found the main weight of the story to fall on the idea of repentance itself (Clements 1975). The key in this interpretation is Jonah's reaction to the repentance of the Ninevites (3:10) in 4:2–5. Why did Jonah sit down outside Nineveh 'waiting to see what would become of the city'? After all, he has seen the Ninevites repent, and he knows that God in his mercy is 'ready to relent [or 'repent'] from punishing'. One answer is that Jonah is worried that he may be proved a false prophet. According to some texts, prophets were judged by whether their words came true (Deut. 18:21–22). Jonah had said that

Think about
'UNIVERSALISM' AND JUDAISM

Sherwood has written forcefully about how Christians may be over-zealous in finding universalism in Old Testament texts, and that they are influenced in doing so by a 'supersessionist' theology. She also argues that even modern critical readings of Jonah can display deep-seated prejudice against Jews when they bring out the weaknesses of the prophet's personality in the course of their interpretation (Sherwood 2000, pp. 48–87, note pp. 55–56, 64–66; cf. pp. 26–27). The following passage, which contains a notable concession, expresses her main concern:

> For while I have no objections to the reading of Jonah in the context of Christian theology – at least in works that consciously foreground themselves as such – there is something profoundly disturbing about the habitual and relentless assumption of a Eurocentric, Christian, critical standard, by which the primitive Hebrew text, and the primitive Hebrew, are judged. (Sherwood 2000, p. 79)

What do you think are the dangers to which she draws attention, and in what ways do you think Christian interpretation and theology should take note of them?

Nineveh would be destroyed in forty days (3:4). What if it didn't happen? The Book of Jonah makes sure we know that Jonah was a true prophet, by telling how God compelled him to give the message he sent him to give. Then it shows that, if people repent when they hear a word of judgement, God may change his mind too. Jonah himself may have had to learn this, as well as the readers of the book. The same point is made in Jer. 18:7–8.

Think about
IS THERE ONLY ONE POINT?

Should we expect to find that a story like Jonah has only one point? If Jonah is meant to teach that God may repent of his intention to judge, what is the point of it being a story about *Nineveh*? Is that just incidental? Clements and Emmerson think it may be. But is not the idea of *Assyrians* turning to Yahweh the God of Israel bound to make an impact on Israelite or Jewish hearers? (see Salters, p. 56). Good stories rarely have just one point. (See Jenson 1999, pp. 17–18.)

'GOD' AND 'YAHWEH'
The alternation of the two names for God, 'Elohim and Yahweh, is one of the curious features of the book. 'Elohim is the general word for God (also 'god', or 'gods'), and Yahweh is the personal name of the God of Israel (Exod. 3:15). The two occur together in combination four times (1:9; 2:1 [2], 6 [7]; 4:6). Their appearance in different passages in the Pentateuch was one factor in the critical identification of sources there. Some scholars have suggested a similar explanation for the two names in Jonah.

An alternative explanation is a theological one, that Yahweh God of Israel is the God of the whole world. This would fit with the idea of a 'universalistic' message of the book. The combination Yahweh-'elohim (e.g. 4:6) could point in this direction (cf. Gen. 2:4). Limburg (1993, pp. 45–46) and Magonet (1983, pp. 33–38) have argued that the distribution of the names is deliberate and is theologically significant. Others are less convinced and think it is hard to see a clear pattern (Sasson 1990, p. 18).

RHETORICAL INTENTION

Interpretation of Jonah revolves around the question of the audience. The book hardly functions at all at the 'first level' of rhetorical persuasion that we have observed in other books. The words that Amos or Micah actually spoke to their contemporaries still have persuasive power because of the powerful means of expression they used. But Jonah hardly preaches at all. The issues are played out between author, narrative and audience.

This means that rhetorical aims are met by narrative techniques. These include:

i. Literary structures, e.g. a concentric pattern of vocabulary and ideas in 1:4–16, highlighting Jonah's confession of faith in Yahweh (v. 9; Limburg, p. 47); the extended parallel between the two commissionings of Jonah and their consequences (chs 1—2; 3—4; see Structure and Outline). This allows a contrast between Jonah in his disobedience and in his obedience.

ii. The repetition of key words ('go down', 1:3 [twice; NRSV has 'went on board' for the second]; 2:5; 2:6 [7]); 'appointed' (1:17 [2:1]; 4:6, 7, 8). The first of these connects the story with the Psalm, and charts the decline of Jonah to a place of deep distress; the second helps express God's entire control of the events.

iii. The use of exaggerated, unlikely or comic events (the great fish, the huge city of Nineveh; the brief announcement of punishment followed by immediate repentance – the only such effect of prophetic preaching in the Old Testament; Jonah's anger; the strange plant; the curious interest in animals (3:8; 4:11). On one level, these are entertaining. On another, they help to bring out the difference between Jonah's small view of things and God's large view.

iv. Depiction of character. The main character, Jonah, develops because of what he learns the hard way, yet is still left open at the end (we do not know how he responds to God's last appeal). The portrayal of the sailors is, as Sasson puts it, 'surprisingly nuanced' (Sasson 1990, p. 340). Their curiosity about the stranger among them (1:7–10) first, shows that foreigners may display a suitable reverence for Yahweh, God of Israel, and second, carries over to ch. 4, so that we do not need to go through the same motions for the people of Nineveh (Sasson 1990, pp. 340–41).

As for what the author wanted to persuade the audience about, there is little to add, because of the way in which we have dealt with the Theological Themes of Jonah. We saw there that the theology of the book had to be worked out carefully by thinking about what the author might have been trying to convey to his audience. It is almost impossible to know what the concerns of that audience might have been, and therefore what the author might have been trying to achieve. It is highly speculative to suggest that he was responding to Ezra–Nehemiah, for example, or to Joel. What we have tried to do above is work out an intention of the author by considering possible theological aims that he might have had. But these are derived almost entirely from the story itself.

JONAH IN THE CANON

The canonical function of Jonah depends on a recognition of the kind of thing it is. Its purpose is not to contribute to a full biblical understanding of Assyria. Rather it makes

Digging deeper:
LITERARY TECHNIQUES; MORE ON GENRE

Sasson employs literary analysis generally in his commentary. He also has a useful final section on 'Interpretations'. Here he looks in turn at Narrator, Audience and Character Roles. In the course of this he considers categories like satire, parody, farce, parable, fable, didactic fiction and allegory. (On satire, see also Holbert, 1996.)

In exploring this, consider how your idea about the genre of the narrative affects how you read it. Take the point about Jonah as 'comedy': if an audience identifies the genre as comedy, it will know immediately that it does not have to ask questions about historical consequences (how did the Ninevites' repentance affect Assyria's later history? Did the sailors remain Yahwists? Sasson 1990, pp. 333–34, citing Mather).

The student might also try Person's *Conversation with Jonah* (1996), an application of 'conversation analysis' to the book. Or they might find the theological-psychological analysis of Lacocque and Lacocque (1981) stimulating. A sample of this gives an idea of how it reads the text (incidentally taking it as a unity). Making an analogy with psychotherapy, in which patients 'break the cyclical patterns from which escape was previously impossible', they go on:

> This is not to say that there is a radical break in the personality (or in the Jonah narrative). Jonah does not leave a sinful condition to adopt a saintly one. There is no Ovidean 'metamorphosis' from a former stiff-necked, stubborn and hard-hearted sinner into a broad-minded, radiant and successful 'P. R.-person'. For it is the same Jonah of chapter 1 who now prays in chapter 2. (Lacocque and Lacocque 1981, p. 60)

echoes with other books of the Bible. In its discussion of the uniqueness and sovereignty of God, it shows that non-Israelites come within the range of his compassion. They too may repent and experience divine mercy. This same point bears on the concept of Israel's election (Jonah is 'a genuine Old Testament witness directed against a misunderstanding of the election of Israel' (Childs 1979, p. 427). There is a reflection too on prophecy itself: an oracle of doom may have its proper and desired effect by turning people to repentance and thus avoiding the promised judgement. This has echoes within the Book of the Twelve, since it shows how the words of Amos, for example, may be heard.

The 'sign of the prophet Jonah' is mentioned in three New Testament texts: Matt. 12:38–41; 16:1–4; Luke 11:29–32. It is adopted in slightly different ways. In Matt. 12:38–41 it sees a link between Jonah's three days and nights in the belly of the great fish and Jesus' three days and three nights 'in the heart of the earth'. In Luke, Jonah himself is the sign to the Ninevites (presumably in his preaching), and is thus like 'the Son of Man' to his generation. The Gospel writers, or Jesus himself, have seen more than one way in which the story of Jonah could be used to reinforce Jesus' message (see Alexander 1988, pp. 91–94; Allen 1976, pp. 194–97). This openness to various possibilities led to great divergence in Christian interpretation over the centuries. Sherwood documents this fully and entertainingly. For example, Jonah was early seen as a Christ-figure, but this was largely overtaken by readings that focused on Jonah, the Jew who struggled against the call of God (Sherwood 2000, pp. 11–32).

The interpretation of Jonah, therefore, both in the Canon and afterwards, does not finally determine its meaning for modern readers.

FURTHER READING

Items marked with * are considered suitable as first ports of call, while others are more complex, or relate to specific issues.

COMMENTARIES

*E. Achtemeier *Minor Prophets I*. NIBC. Peabody; Hendrickson/Carlisle: Paternoster, 1996.

*T. D. Alexander *Jonah* in D. W. Baker, T. D. Alexander and B. K. Waltke *Obadiah, Jonah and Micah*. TOTC. Leicester; IVP, 1988.

L. C. Allen *The Books of Joel, Obadiah, Jonah and Micah*. NICOT. London: Hodder and Stoughton, 1976.

B. S. Childs *Introduction to the Old Testament as Scripture*. London: SCM, 1979.

*J. Limburg *Jonah*. OTL. London: SCM, 1993.

J. Sasson *Jonah – a New Translation, with Introduction, Commentary and Interpretation*. AB. New York: Doubleday, 1990.

*D. Stuart *Hosea–Jonah*. WBC. Waco: Word Books, 1987.

J. D. W. Watts *The Books of Joel, Obadiah, Jonah, Nahum, Habakkuk and Zephaniah*. CBC. Cambridge: CUP, 1975.

H. W. Wolff *Obadiah and Jonah*. London: SPCK. Minneapolis: Augsburg, 1986.

OTHER BOOKS AND ARTICLES

T. D. Alexander 'Jonah and Genre' *TB* 36. 1985, pp. 175–81.

T. M. Bolin *Freedom Beyond Forgiveness: The Book of Jonah Re-examined*. JSOTS 236. Sheffield: Sheffield Academic Press, 1997.

R. E. Clements 'The Purpose of the Book of Jonah' in J. A. Emerton et al eds *Congress Volume Edinburgh 1974*. VT Suppl. 28. Leiden: Brill, 1975, pp. 16–28.

J. Day 'Problems in the Interpretation of the Book of Jonah' *OS* 26. 1990, pp. 32–37.

K. J. Dell 'Reinventing the Wheel: The Shaping of the Book of Jonah' in J. Barton and D. Reimer eds *After the Exile: Essays in Honour of Rex Mason*. Macon, Ga. Mercer University Press, 1996, pp. 85–101.

J. Ellul *The Judgment of Jonah*. Grand Rapids: Eerdmans, 1971.

G. I. Emmerson 'Another Look at the Book of Jonah' *ExpTim* 88. 1976, pp. 86–87.

T. E. Fretheim *The Message of Jonah*. Minneapolis: Augsburg, 1977.

J. C. Holbert '"Deliverance Belongs to Yahweh": Satire in the Book of Jonah' in P. R. Davies ed. *The Prophets: a Sheffield Reader*. The Biblical Seminar 42. Sheffield: Sheffield Academic Press, 1996, pp. 334–54.

P. P. Jenson *Reading Jonah*. Cambridge: Grove Books, 1999.

A. Lacocque and P.-E. Lacocque *The Jonah Complex*. Atlanta: John Knox Press, 1981.

J. Magonet *Form and Meaning: Studies in Literary Techniques in the Book of Jonah*. Sheffield: Almond Press, 1983.

J. Mather 'The Comic Art of the Book of Jonah' *Soundings* 65. 1982, pp. 280–91.

D. F. Payne 'Jonah from the Perspective of its Audience' *JSOT* 13. 1979, pp. 3–12.

R. F. Person *Conversation with Jonah: Conversation Analysis, Literary Criticism and the Book of Jonah*. JSOT Suppl. 220. Sheffield: Sheffield Academic Press, 1996.

A. Rofé *Introduction to the Prophetic Literature*. Sheffield: Sheffield Academic Press, 1997.

*R. B. Salters *Jonah and Lamentations*. OTG. Sheffield: JSOT Press, 1994.

Y. Sherwood *A Biblical Text and its Afterlives: the Survival of Jonah in Western Culture*. Cambridge: CUP, 2000.

Chapter 11

MICAH

DATE AND DESTINATION

Micah is known only from his book, and from the allusion to him in Jer. 26:18–19. His name is a contraction of *mi ka'el*, 'Who is like God?', or *mikayahu*, 'Who is like Yahweh?' (see 7:18). The heading of the book, its content (e.g. 1:10–16) and the Jeremiah allusion all point to his having worked at least in the time of King Hezekiah (715–687). The heading also mentions Jotham (742–735) and Ahaz (735–715). These dates span the fall of the northern kingdom (722 BC) and the crisis of Sennacherib's attack on Judah in 701 BC. (On the earlier chronology for Hezekiah, which some scholars adopt and which puts his accession at 627 or 625 BC (see Andersen and Freedman 2000, p. xvi), there would be no clear evidence of him having worked earlier than that king, though it is perfectly possible that some of the oracles we have could have originated in an earlier time.) His period is similar to that of Isaiah (cf. Isa. 1:1).

The place of his activity (also like Isaiah) is Jerusalem and Judah. Micah is the first prophetic book in the Twelve to focus its criticism on these (since Hosea and Amos are spoken mainly to the northern kingdom,

Joel contains hardly any criticism of its addressees, Obadiah is a salvation-oracle, and Jonah has no obvious political setting). His home town, Moresheth, was probably Moresheth-Gath, not to be confused with Philistine Gath mentioned in 1:10 (see Andersen and Freedman 2000, p. 110, for a discussion). It was probably a fortified city in the Shephelah, the low hills west of Jerusalem, bordering on Philistine country. The places named in 1:10–16, therefore, must have been familiar to him. And he will have felt acutely the danger to his homeland (whether or not that text has in mind the Assyrian armies that brutally overran Judah in 701 BC).

His message is designed to avoid the worst disaster by turning people from their sins. He is remembered as having been successful in this, at least as far as Jerusalem was concerned, in Jer. 26:18–19. The deliverance of Jerusalem is recorded in 2 Kings 18—19; Isaiah 36—37.

CRITICAL INTERPRETATION OF MICAH

Because certain passages seem to presuppose an exile, it is usually held by commentators that the book contains

PROPHETIC TRADITION: HOW ORACLES GOT INTO BOOKS

Micah has two cases that give us some idea of how prophetic oracles might have been passed on, and finally taken their place in books.

First, the memory of Mic. 3:12 in Jer. 26:18 has led scholars to ask how such a memory might have been preserved. Did the elders who remembered Micah in Jeremiah's day know the text in written form? The elders do not seem to be quoting a book. Rather, they know more about Micah than is written in the book. (They know that Hezekiah did not kill him, a fact that we do not know from any other biblical source.) It may be that the sayings of Micah were passed on in more than one form, perhaps both oral and written. The oracles may have been attached at one time to stories about the prophet, of the sort that we find in Amos 7 and Hosea 1—3. If so, it seems as if only some of these have been preserved as the sayings of the prophets that became fixed into the book-forms that we now know. (See Andersen and Freedman 2000, pp. 111–16, for more detailed discussion of this issue.)

Second, Mic. 4:1–4 raises a similar question. How did it come about that two almost identical oracles could find their way into two different prophetic books? Perhaps the least likely answer is that God inspired the two prophets separately to say identical things. Therefore the main options are:

i. the saying originated with one of the prophets, and was taken over by the other (or it has been introduced into the other's book by redactors);
ii. the saying was already known to both;
iii. the oracle is original to neither prophet but was introduced into both books by later redactors.

The last of these options is commonly adopted, because the thought in the passage is similar to Second Isaiah, and because it is supposed that eschatological sayings are likely to be post-exilic. Mason, for example, states this categorically:

It is . . . idle to ask whether 4:1–4 (= Isa. 2:2–4) is 'originally' by either Isaiah or Micah. It is by neither; but its presence in both books shows how the prophetic collections were treated in order to make them relevant to later generations. (Mason 1991, p. 49)

The placement of 4:1–4 immediately after 3:9–12, reversing the words of judgement there point by point, he thinks is the work of post-exilic editors who are convinced that the time of judgement is past and the time of salvation has come.

This point about the structure of Mic. 3:9—4:4 is perfectly valid. However, each of the other possibilities above can be taken seriously too. The second (ii) is perhaps weaker than the first (i), since there is no evidence for it, and (i) is simpler. As we have already seen (Isaiah: Is prophecy predictive?), the saying is attributed by at least some scholars these days to Isaiah. And, as Andersen and Freedman point out, neither the language nor the ideas in the passage are demonstrably post-exilic (2000, p. 424). On the basis of a detailed comparison of the textual differences between the two, they cautiously favour the view that Micah is the original (p. 423). Waltke comes to the same conclusion (1988, pp. 170–75).

Like the case of Mic. 3:12, this text also suggests that prophetic oracles had an existence apart from the books in which they found a place. Oracles were collected into books in a way that is not fully known to us. This unique occurrence of the same oracle in two books gives some indirect evidence of the process. It is an instance of an oracle that was presumably originally associated with one prophet being included also in the book of another. This was hardly accidental, since in both Isaiah and Micah it has a function in the structure and theology of that book.

See also Introduction: The prophets: Did they write?

additions to the words of Micah. It is common to date 4:1–4 to a post-exilic period, for example. (We will come back to this in a moment.) Indeed, there is a tendency to find genuine words of Micah in chs 1—3 and additions from later times in chs 4—7. Micah 7:11–20, for example, seems to presuppose an exile and also has some similarities with Isaiah 40—55. Achtemeier concludes that Micah's words were 'incorporated into a Micah book that found its final form sometime after 515 BC' (Achtemeier 1996, p. 290). This judgement, however, is subject to the same qualifications that we made about Isaiah; that is, it is not absolutely clear what kind of sayings are definitely 'late'. (Isaiah: Is prophecy predictive?)

STRUCTURE AND OUTLINE

Commentators find that Micah is difficult to break down into satisfactory sub-sections. Most divide it into three: either: chs 1—2; 3—5; 6—7 (Smith 1984, p. 8; cf. Allen 1976, pp. 257–61); or 1—3; 4—5; 6—7 (Andersen and Freedman 2000, p. 7; Mason 1991, pp. 13–14). The former may be refined in order to produce three sections, each consisting of a judgement passage followed by an assurance of salvation (1:1—2:11 and 2:12–13; 3:1–12 and 4:1—5:15; and 6:1—7:7 and 7:8–20 (Achtemeier 1996, p. 288; see also Hillers 1984, p. 8). The latter produces a slightly different structure: 1—3 (judgement); 4—5 (hope); 6—7 (judgement and hope).

Differences like this can depend on how a particular passage is interpreted. For example, 2:12–13 has been read either as an oracle of salvation, or of judgement, or has even been moved to a different point in the book because it is seen as out of place.

No structure of Micah is perfect, or commands agreement. However, the two main approaches mentioned both show an alternation of oracles of judgement and of hope. In the Outline, we follow the first pattern given above (with Smith, Allen, Achtemeier).

STRUCTURE
1:1—2:13	Witnessing the just judgement on Samaria and Judah – but a 'gathering'
3:1—5:15 [14]	Zion condemned – but redeemed!
6:1—7:20	Controversy and lament – but pardon!

OUTLINE
1:1—2:13: Witnessing the just judgement on Samaria and Judah – but a 'gathering'
1:2 Micah's words begin with an appeal to the nations to witness God's judgement (cf. Deut. 32:1). This affirms that the whole earth belongs to him (cf. Ps. 24:1). Curiously, the judgement is directed 'against you', that is, the nations themselves. The point seems to be that in God's judgement on his own people all the nations are somehow involved. This fits with the vision in 4:1–4, where the nations come to a restored Zion to see Yahweh there. Yet in other texts they are clearly under his judgement (7:16–17; cf. 4:11–12; and see Theological Themes).

Micah thinks of God as speaking 'from his holy temple', that is, in Jerusalem (cf. Amos 1:2). Yet Jerusalem and Judah themselves are accused, and under threat from invasion by an enemy as a punishment from God.

1:3–16 The background is the Assyrian attacks in the late eighth century, including the fall of Samaria (the northern kingdom) in 722 BC and the destruction of many of the cities of Judah by Sennacherib in 701 BC. There is an oracle against Samaria in 1:6–7.

Then attention turns to Jerusalem in vv. 10–16, as the enemy closes in by a western route. This could be the attack recorded in 2 Kgs 18:13–16, which forced King Hezekiah to pay tribute. But there is not enough detail to make this certain, and it could come from a time before the fall of Samaria (Andersen and Freedman 2000, p. 113).

As a cause of the judgement, the religious sins of the people are emphasized, and the same prostitution metaphor is used as in Hosea (1:7).

2:1–11 Micah takes further the reason for God's judgement, now mainly oppression of the poor. The powerful are accused of ruthless greed, as well as pride (like Isaiah 2), and falsehood (like Jeremiah 9). God's judgement meets the sin point by point: the powerful rob others of their 'inheritance' (as Ahab robbed Naboth; 1 Kings 21); so God will destroy the 'inheritance' that is Israel itself (v. 4 – a different Hebrew word from v. 2, yet close in meaning. The two are used

---

PROPHETIC SAYINGS AND THEIR BACKGROUNDS

Scholars often try hard to find particular situations that a saying fits, and sometimes this can be done (e.g. 1:10–16). In this case the 'gathering in' to the safety of a sheepfold in v. 12 is hard to relate to the 'breaking out' in v. 13. Is it the same shepherd-image, or is the picture now a military one? And does it relate to the 'breaking out' of a siege, or more generally to God's rule in a future time?

Commentators try to make sense of passages like this in terms of their view of the prophecy as a whole. Contrast the comments of Smith 1984, pp. 28–29, and Hillers 1984, p. 39, who advises not to attempt to be too specific.

---

in parallel in Deut. 18:1). Verse 11 is a savage indictment of falsehood.

2:12–13 This is surprising after vv. 1–11. Some put it after 4:7. But we find words of salvation coming at early stages in other prophetic books, before the full message of doom has been unfolded (e.g. in Hosea 1—3; Isa. 2:2–4; Jer. 3:12–18). The imagery itself is hard to pin down (see note). But the passage is part of the pattern of alternation of judgement and salvation sayings.

3:1—5:15 [14]: Zion condemned – but redeemed!
3:1–12 'Heads', 'rulers', 'prophets', 'seers', diviners' and 'priests' come under attack here, that is, all who exercise power. They are accused of savage oppression. When the poor are denied the justice they should receive from those in authority it is as good as committing the worst kind of violence against them (vv. 2–3). (For denial of justice in the courts, see also Amos 5:7, 15.)

As a result, Zion itself stands under judgement (v. 12). This was shocking to people who believed that Yahweh dwelt in the temple in Jerusalem, and would not abandon his people (v. 11b). It is the first full-frontal attack on Jerusalem and the temple in the Book of the Twelve. And it comes from a prophet who began with Yahweh speaking 'from his holy temple' (1:2). Micah's words in the eighth century made such an impression that they were remembered and quoted a century later by some elders (Jer. 26:16–19). This was to defend Jeremiah, who made a similar attack on the temple at that time (Jer. 26:2–6).

4:1–13 The theme changes abruptly again to salvation. Mic. 4:1–4 is very similar to Isa. 2:2–4 (see comment on that passage). Micah looks beyond the present crisis to a time when nations shall come to Jerusalem to learn the laws of Yahweh, and there will be peace between them. In Micah, the passage makes a stark contrast with ch. 3, especially vv. 9–12. In Mason's words, this is 'no coincidence'. The condemnation in 3:9–12 'is followed immediately by a promise that this judgement will be reversed in every particular' (Mason 1991, p. 49).

Think about
'THE MOUNTAIN OF THE LORD'S HOUSE'

Compare closely how this passage (4:1–4) contrasts with 3:9–12. Topics to consider are: what happens to Jerusalem and the temple; justice; teaching; God's presence; poverty-plenty (cf. also 3:1–3); God speaking (cf. also 3:4).

Verse 5 sounds a change in direction, where the nations are still worshipping their own gods. The continuation (4:6–13) is in contrast to the vision of nations at peace, for now the image is of the people of Zion rescued from exile in Babylon, and their conquerors defeated. 4:13 contrasts with v. 3. The picture is of a 'remnant' (v. 7) returning after exile. The thought here is a little like Isaiah 40—55.

5:1–15 [4:14—5:14] 5:1 is obscure, but seems to refer to a siege in which the ruler of Judah is humiliated (Achtemeier 1996, p. 338). This image is immediately reversed with a prophecy of a future ruler (vv. 2–4 [1–3]). The word 'king' is avoided here (Mason 1991, p. 52), yet the reference to Bethlehem makes us think of David (1 Sam. 16:1, 18; cf. Gen. 35:19). The historic line of kings will come to an end, but God will raise up a new king. This will be after a period of suffering (v. 3 [2], probably referring to the exile).

This ruler will be a true shepherd, who will feed his flock, and bring peace (for peace as a feature of the messianic kingdom, see also Isa. 9:7 [6]).

SHEPHERD-MESSIAH

We have met the image of shepherding for leadership already in the prophets, where false 'shepherds' are contrasted with the shepherd(s) whom God will raise up in the future. See Jer. 23:1–6; and especially Ezekiel 34, where the metaphor is developed at length (note vv. 7, 12, 23).

The restoration of Judah (or its 'remnant', 5:7 [6]) will mean that it will prevail over the nations that had oppressed it (vv. 5–9 [4–8]). Verses 10–15 are a direct word of judgement against those nations.

6:1—7:20: Controversy and lament – but pardon!
6:1–5 The final section of the prophecy turns back to judgement. It opens with a saying in the familiar style that we have found in other prophetic texts (cf. Hos. 4:1–10; Isa. 3:13–15; Jer. 2:4–13). The form is sometimes called the 'controversy'- or 'lawsuit'-pattern, because of the dominant word, here in vv. 1–2 (*rîb*). It is better termed a 'covenant accusation'. It is not a rigid form, but used freely by the prophet (Andersen and Freedman 2000, pp. 510–11). Yahweh recalls the exodus from Egypt itself, and Israel's leaders whom he appointed (cf. Amos 2:9–10). He then mentions Balaam, a sort of opposite of Moses. Together they stand for true and false prophecy. The Balaam incident shows that God was determined to save Israel, and that he could not be stopped by any other power (in this case an enchanter's spell

(Numbers 22—24). 'Shittim to Gilgal' is the last stage of Israel's journey to the promised land. Shittim was a place where Israel sinned (Num. 25:1), so here too God hints that he brought them to the land even in spite of their sin. He argues for these reasons that they should have kept faith with him.

Digging deeper:
THE 'COVENANT ACCUSATION'

The 'covenant accusation' has often been thought to have a special form with a legal or cultic background. Mic. 6:1–4 may be compared with Psalm 50, which is said to be a fuller example of the form. Important treatments are found in Huffmon 1959; Clements 1965; Nielsen 1978. See also Andersen and Freedman (2000, pp. 508–11) for a cautious review of this approach to *rîb*-texts, in which he argues that the prophets used traditions freely, rather than reproducing rigid forms.

Another approach to this issue finds that the *rîb* texts do not have a covenant background, but are based on more general criteria. This was in line with the belief of many scholars that the concept of 'covenant' is a late (deuteronomistic) idea in Israel, and has only been imposed on Israel's traditions at a late stage. Clements came to hold this view (1975).

See also below, Theological Themes.

6:6–8 Micah poses questions rhetorically as if from would-be worshippers. Yet the tone is ironic, and the way the questions are asked suggests the answers: 'Will the LORD be pleased with thousands of rams?' – of course not! The thought behind these questions is the same one that we find in Hos. 6:6; Amos 5:21–24, as well as Pss 40:6 [7]; 50:7–15. The point is that the formalities of worship are nothing in themselves.

Micah's summary of true religion (v. 8), in contrast, is famous. It does not consist in any kind of religious performance. Instead, it stresses doing justice (like Amos 5:24), showing 'kindness' (*hesed*) (like Hos. 6:6), and it adds a touch of Micah's own, a humble walk with God. (See the little jewel of a humility-Psalm, Psalm 131.) There is a particular echo of Micah's language in Deut. 10:12–13. Verse 8a implies that the people had enough knowledge already to know what true religion was. The form of address, 'O mortal' (NRSV, that is, 'man', in the sense of 'human being', *'adam*) suggests that human beings in general have a knowledge of God's basic commands, and are subject to them.

TOO MUCH SACRIFICE

Misguided and over-enthusiastic sacrificial worship was criticized by both prophets and psalmists. Amos condemned the worship at Bethel and Gilgal (Amos 4:4–5). But the temple at Jerusalem was not exempt (cf. Isa. 1:10–17). Psalmists too could show that God wanted true worship and obedience: see Ps. 40:6–8 [7–9]; 50:7–15. This prophetic concern continued into the post-exilic time: Zech. 7:2–4, 9–10; cf. Hag. 2:10–14 (Mason 1991, pp. 47–48).

6:9–16 A renewed accusation of injustice leads to a threat of 'desolation' (vv. 13, 16; cf. Jer. 19:8). Other threatened punishments have an ironic ring about them (like Hag. 1:6), that remind of certain covenantal curses (vv. 14–15, cf. Deut. 28:38–44).

7:1–7 The last accusation in the book is a lament, in which Micah expresses his own anguish at the falsehood in the land (7:1, 7). He paints a picture of penetrating falsehood among the people (cf. Jer. 8:22—9:9 [8]). In doing so, he gives a glimpse of the prophet's faithfulness, and his rejection of his people's sin (cf. Hos. 9:14). (This strand in prophetic thinking reaches its height in Jeremiah's 'confessions'; see at Jeremiah: Outline: 11:18–23.) His attitude of 'waiting' for the LORD is exemplary for a people who look for deliverance (v. 7). (Compare Hab. 2:1–4.)

7:8–20 The final turn in the book is again to salvation. The voice in vv. 8–10 appears to come from one who is in exile (Achtemeier 1996, p. 287), but who knows that deliverance will come. Return from exile is assured (vv. 11–13). A prayer for Yahweh to 'shepherd' his people (v. 14) echoes the 'shepherding ' of the messianic ruler (5:4 [3]). The nations who opposed Israel shall be brought low (vv. 15–17; cf. Isa. 2:9–10). Yet there is a hint of them turning to the LORD (v. 17). Here again there are similarities to Isaiah 40—55, which also had visions of salvation for the nations (Achtemeier 1996, p. 290). But the passage must also be understood within the structure of Micah. In 1:2, the nations' 'seeing' was

---

Think about
WAITING FOR SALVATION

People in parts of the modern world suffer all the kinds of torment experienced by people in ancient times: economic oppression, displacement, war, famine and disease. Think about situations today (or in the recent past) in which people might feel the need of salvation. When might it be right to 'wait'? And when might prophetic anger lead to action?

---

there a witness to judgement on Israel; now they witness God's salvation of his people. They in turn are judged, but turn to Yahweh for salvation.

The book closes with a praise to Yahweh. The rhetorical question, 'Who is a god like you' (v. 18) is a play on Micah's name (see Date and Destination). The uniqueness of Yahweh, also a major theme of Isaiah 40—55, is in his willingness to forgive and show compassion (vv. 18–20). This theological high point in the book puts Micah close to Hosea (Hos. 11:8–11).

THEOLOGICAL THEMES

JUDGEMENT AND SALVATION
The Book of Micah proclaims both judgement and salvation. This, as is now familiar to us, is typical of the prophetic books (see, for example, Hosea: Theological Themes). The turn from the one to the other can be abrupt, as in 2:12–13, or 4:1–4. This has led interpreters to question whether such texts are original to the writer, or in their original place. But in fact these abrupt turns say something important: that God's grace has the last word in his dilemma over judgement on sin and his desire to save (cf. Hos. 11:8–11; 14; Amos 9:11–15).

EXODUS AND COVENANT TRADITIONS
The theme of 'covenant' rarely emerges clearly in the eighth-century prophets. However, we have seen in different ways in both Hosea and Amos that some of their theological themes made sense against the background of the traditions that we also meet in the Pentateuch (look again at Hosea: Theological Themes, on the First Commandment and Deuteronomy 32; and Amos in the Canon). Micah calls on Israel's

past traditions in one specific way, namely the 'covenant accusation' in 6:1–5 (see Outline). God's 'controversy' with his people depends on an assumption that they owed him something (6:1–2). That obligation goes back to the fact that he saved them from slavery in Egypt (Exod. 19:4–6; 20:2). The phrase 'my people' itself (v. 3) has echoes in the Exodus narrative, 3:7; 5:1. And Micah refers to another incident in the story of salvation, how Balak king of Moab hired the enchanter Balaam to curse Israel, only to find that Yahweh was determined to save them, and his will could not be resisted by any spell (Numbers 22—24).

PROPHETIC ETHICS

We have seen how the ethics of the prophets are rooted in their theology (e.g. on Amos: Theological Themes: Justice and righteousness). Right behaviour depends on knowing God, and showing his own concerns in the life of the community. Micah's preaching of justice is as vivid as any other prophet (Mic. 3:1–3). One point may be highlighted, however. For Micah knows the close link between the thought of sin and the sin itself (2:1–2).

This connection is made at other places in the Old Testament's thinking about ethics. The Tenth Commandment itself shows that the other commandments need to be backed up by another that appeals to the heart (Exod. 20:17). The desire to sin can bear fruit in theft, adultery or murder. Jesus expounded this truth about human nature in the Sermon on the Mount (Matt. 5:21–32).

A story illustrates it. King Ahab thinks sulkily about how he wants his neighbour's vineyard, because it would make such a nice extension to his own property. And egged on by his wife Jezebel he allows the man to be conspired against and murdered, and then takes his chance to get what he wanted (1 Kgs 21:1–16). The story of how Ahab's sullen resentment (v. 4) gave birth to the deed shows that the concern expressed by the commandment has a real basis in human nature. Micah's words could easily have had Ahab in mind. It seems that there were many 'Ahabs' in his own day.

THE NATIONS

The place of the nations in Yahweh's purposes has come up in a number of the prophetic books (e.g. Isaiah, Amos, Jonah). Within the Book of the Twelve, Micah, following Jonah's record of the salvation of Nineveh, opens with an address to the nations as witnesses of God's judgement, which involves themselves as well as Israel and Judah (1:2). This picks up an important covenantal theme, developed in Deuteronomy (Deut. 4:6–8; 26:19; and see Millar 1998). Micah contains the saying about the nations coming to Zion to learn the torah (4:1–4 = Isa. 2:2–4). In Isaiah, this was an important part of that book's teaching about the salvation of the nations. Yet in Micah that emphasis is not so strong. More important here is the idea that the judgement of Israel *affects* the nations, which is an election theme (cf. Gen. 12:1–3).

RHETORICAL INTENTION

Micah uses a number of types of speech to create his rhetorical effects. He vividly portrays people leaving towns in his home region to go into exile (1:10–16). He accuses people of sin with great insight (2:1–2), and sometimes with savage imagery (3:1–3), or irony (2:11). He thinks the unthinkable, that Zion itself should be razed to the ground, as if there had never been a city there (3:12).

He appeals to reason, with his 'covenant accusation' (4:1–4). He conducts rhetorical 'dialogues' with his hearers, in order to arrest attention and then drive home a point (6:6–8). And he utters a lament (7:1–7). Like Jeremiah's 'confessions', this lament no doubt reflects his own anguish at the terrible message he is proclaiming, but yet it is also part of his proclamation. His grief over sin is at the same time an accusation of sin. Yet the factor of personal lamentation is a powerful persuasive device. It also says something important about the role and influence of the prophet – to be one who embodies and reminds of the true path of covenant obedience.

Micah's rhetoric also includes the abrupt changes from judgement sayings to salvation sayings that we noticed under Critical Interpretation. Whether this was part of his method in spoken prophecy we do not know. However, it is now widely accepted that, like other eighth-century prophets, he did speak words of salvation as well as of judgement. And the alternation of the two types of message has been carefully built into the written record of his work. The salvation-oracles did not 'trump' the judgement-oracles. The form of the prophecy is too balanced for that (since, except for 7:8–20, the salvation-oracles not only follow judgement-oracles but are also followed by them). The two-sided view that results knows that God is God of blessing as well as of curse (to borrow the terms of covenantal theology).

Even in his judgement-prophecy, Micah's intention was almost certainly to bring people to repentance and avoid judgement. This is in spite of the fact that Micah nowhere expressly calls his hearers to repent. But his intention to avoid judgement is exactly what is remembered about him in Jeremiah's time: that as a result of his preaching King Hezekiah had turned to Yahweh and the promised disaster did not come to pass (Jer. 26:18).

The 'rhetorical intention' of the Book of Micah after the time of the prophet may be considered in relation to the post-exilic community in Judah. What was the effect of a prophecy threatening Jerusalem on a community that had seen the destruction of the city and had now rebuilt the temple? Perhaps the balance between judgement and salvation must now be seen in reverse. The post-exilic community knows that the salvation did come after the judgement, but needs to go on hearing the words of judgement in order to keep it from falling back into false trust – a big part of the problem Micah (and others) addressed in the first place. The salvation-oracles also continue to be needed, for even after the temple was rebuilt, the community had trying times when God's promises seemed to have been only partially fulfilled. Mason compares post-exilic Micah with Chronicles:

> So, after the exile, the faith of the people was stimulated by a renewal of the prophetic promises of old, but with a pastoral call to the community to keep the faith during the present time of waiting. (Mason 1991, p. 50).

Indeed, in its reversal of judgement theme, 'Micah's preaching has thus provided a basis for a more general eschatological hope' (p. 51).

MICAH IN THE CANON

Micah stands sixth in the Book of the Twelve in the MT form, but third in LXX (after Hosea and Amos). It is, perhaps surprisingly, the first of the Twelve to turn the spotlight of prophetic criticism directly on Judah and Jerusalem. Micah's realization that even the Jerusalem temple was not immune to divine punishment (3:12) is the primary canonical example of this, as is shown by the citation of this prophecy in Jer. 26:18.

The importance of Micah for Jeremiah may be seen from other echoes in the later book (following Andersen and Freedman 2000, p. 27, who draw on Cha 1996): e.g. 1:8 (Jer. 4:8); 1:9, 14 (Jer. 15:18); 1:10, 16 (Jer. 6:26; 7:29); 2:4 (Jer. 9:18); 3:5 (Jer. 6:14); 3:11–12 (Jer. 7:4–15); 4:9–10a (Jer. 4:31; 6:24); 7:1–2 (Jer. 5:1); 7:5–6 (Jer. 9:4–5 [3–4]; 12:6). It is also possible that Micah influenced Isaiah (but this depends on the assumption that 4:1–4 originated with him).

Micah's roots in the exodus and covenant traditions have been noted above, as also his ethical preaching, which touches a chord that is later developed by Jesus (Matthew 5).

FURTHER READING

Items marked with * are considered suitable as first ports of call, while others are more complex, or relate to specific issues.

COMMENTARIES

*E. Achtemeier *Minor Prophets I*. NIBC. Peabody: Hendrickson, 1996.

L. C. Allen *The Books of Joel, Obadiah, Jonah and Micah*. NICOT. Grand Rapids: Eerdmans, 1976.

F. I. Andersen and D. N. Freedman *Micah*. AB. New York: Doubleday, 2000.

D. R. Hillers *Micah*. Hermeneia. Philadelphia: Fortress Press, 1984.

W. McKane *Micah*. Edinburgh: T. & T. Clark, 1998.

R. L. Smith *Micah–Malachi*. WBC. Waco: Word Books, 1984.

*B. Waltke 'Micah' in D. W. Baker, T. D. Alexander and B. Waltke *Obadiah, Jonah and Micah*. TOTC. Leicester: IVP, 1988, pp. 135–207.

OTHER BOOKS AND ARTICLES

J. H. Cha *Micha und Jeremiah*. BBB 107. Weinheim: Beltz Athenäum, 1996.

R. E. Clements *Prophecy and Covenant*. SBT 43. London: SCM, 1965.

R. E. Clements *Prophecy and Tradition*. Oxford: Blackwell, 1975.

M. Cogan and H. Tadmor *II Kings*. AB. New York: Doubleday, 1988.

H. B. Huffmon 'The Covenant Lawsuit in the Prophets' *JBL* 78. 1959, pp. 285–95.

*R. Mason *Micah, Nahum, Obadiah*. OTG. Sheffield: JSOT Press, 1991.

R. Mason *Preaching the Tradition*. Cambridge: CUP, 1990.

J. G. Millar *Now Choose Life: Theology and Ethics in Deuteronomy*. Leicester: IVP, 1998.

K. Nielsen *Yahweh as Prosecutor and Judge*. JSOT Suppl. 9. Sheffield: JSOT Press, 1978.

C. S. Shaw *The Speeches of Micah: a Rhetorical-Historical Analysis*. JSOT Suppl. 145. Sheffield: JSOT Press, 1993.

Chapter 12

NAHUM

DATE AND DESTINATION

The Book of Nahum is a series of oracles against Assyria, or more precisely Nineveh, capital of Assyria from 701 BC. Nahum appears to know that the Assyrian king Ashurbanipal attacked and destroyed Thebes, the capital of Egypt (Nah. 3:8). (Smith 1984, p. 63, puts this in 663 BC, Mason 1991, pp. 59–60, in 661 BC.) So it is likely that the prophecy was made between that event and the fall of Nineveh in 612 BC, which marked the collapse of Assyrian power in the region. The things said about Assyria presuppose that it has committed great atrocities.

Nahum may have in mind a history of Assyrian oppression, going back perhaps a century, since the rise of its power in the mid-eighth century. But there may have been a specific occasion. According to the Chronicler, the Assyrians attacked Jerusalem in the time of King Manasseh (687–642 BC), and took him in chains to Babylon (which they then controlled) (2 Chr. 33:10–13). Assyria's last major campaign in the west took place in 639–637 BC, and this might have been another occasion for an oracle against Assyria. But any time up to 612 is possible (Christensen 1975).

Of course, we do not know whether a prophecy like this could only have been given in or after a particular attack. Nahum opens with a passage on the nature of God, who punishes his enemies and can be trusted by the faithful. One view of Nahum is that it was used in a liturgical (worship) setting (Watts 1975). If so, it might be impossible to pin it down to any particular date. It is possible too that a basic liturgy could have been expanded in a particular crisis. It is even possible that 'Nineveh' stands symbolically for an altogether different enemy, as Babylon stands for Rome in Revelation (Mason 1991, p. 60).

Older critics sometimes tried to separate genuine oracles of Nahum from later additions. Chapter 1, with its partial acrostic poem in vv. 2–8 (see Critical Interpretation of Nahum), was thought to be post-exilic (Smith 1984, p. 65). Nowadays the interest focuses more on how the book as a whole might have spoken to people in Judah about the fate of Assyria.

Nahum himself is unknown apart from his prophecy. His name means 'comfort', and is reminiscent of the opening line of Isaiah 40: 'Comfort, comfort my people, says the

LORD'. This has a bearing on the meaning of the prophecy for Judah. His home town Elkosh (1:1) is also unknown. One ancient tradition puts it in Galilee, and some have thought it may have been Capernaum ('village of Nahum'). But another tradition, pointing to modern Beit-Jebrin, south-west of Jerusalem, is more probable. Nahum is likely to be a southerner, since the prophecy must be dated well after the fall of the northern kingdom.

CRITICAL INTERPRETATION OF NAHUM

Nahum contains a variety of types of sayings. It opens with a partial acrostic poem (1:2–8). (An acrostic poem is one in which each poetic line begin with the next letter of the Hebrew alphabet, as in Lamentations and a number of Psalms, e.g. Psalms 25; 119.) As the acrostic is neither quite clear nor complete, there have been attempts to restore it to an original form, and to extend it beyond v. 8 by making emendations to the text. These attempts are probably unreliable.

Beyond this, it is not easy to break the book up into definite sections. It is possible that a number of sayings have been deliberately combined into the form that we now have, resulting in a kind of medley on a single theme. There are some abrupt changes, which means the flow is sometimes a bit jerky (as in the alternation of direct address and third-person sayings in 1:9–14).

However, it is interesting to note that, alone of the prophetic books, Nahum is actually called a 'book' (1:1). This may tell us more about the stage at which the heading was written than about the actual process by which Nahum became a book. That is, it

may not be much different from other prophetic books in practice. But the heading represents a point when it was known that the prophetic oracles were being or had been collected into books. The Book of Daniel, of course, knows that the prophetic message was transmitted in books (Dan. 9:2).

For more on the types of sayings, see Rhetorical Intention.

STRUCTURE AND OUTLINE

STRUCTURE

1:1—2:2 [2:3]	God, jealous and faithful, will redeem his people
2:3–13 [4–14]	Nineveh overcome, its pretensions mocked
3:1–19	Judgement pronounced, and complete destruction

OUTLINE

1:1—2:2 [2:3]: God, jealous and faithful, will redeem his people

1:1 The Book of Nahum is headed with the term 'the burden of Nineveh' (1:1), 'burden' being a technical word for an oracle. In this respect it is similar to other Oracles Against Nations (OAN; e.g. Isa. 13:1). The book is called both a 'book' (see Critical Interpretation) and a 'vision' (cf. Isa. 1:1; 2:1).

1:2–8 The sayings begin with a 'theophany', that is, a description of God appearing in power (1:1–8). The theme is the certainty of his vengeance on his enemies (vv. 2–3a), also called his 'jealousy' (Exod. 20:5). God's powerful presence is often marked by storm, cloud, whirlwind and the drying up of the sea in the Old Testament (vv. 3b–5; cf. Exod. 19:16; Ps. 18:7–15 [8–16]; cf. Exod. 15:4–10).

His wrath against his enemies is a reason for trust in him by those who have faith (v. 7).

'The LORD is good, a stronghold' may be better taken as 'the LORD is better than a stronghold' (Smith 1984, p. 75–76, citing Cathcart 1973).

1:9—2:2 [3] Assyria, or its leaders, is now directly addressed. The 'one who has gone out' (v. 11) could be Sennacherib. The enmity against Yahweh is emphasized by the terms 'plotting' and 'counselling' wickedness (v. 11). ('Wickedness' is Belial (*beliyya'al*), cf. 1 Kgs 21:10, 'sons of Belial'; Belial could be the name of a demon; Smith 1984, p. 76.)

The power of Assyria will be broken, with its gods, and Judah will once more be able to worship Yahweh in peace (1:15 [2:1]). The picture of the messenger bringing good news is very like Isa. 52:7.

2:3–13 [4–14]: Nineveh overcome, its pretensions mocked

The sack of Nineveh is pictured vividly, destroyed by a well-organized army, its people led away in humiliation (v. 7 [8]; there might be a reference to a goddess-idol and its attendants here, but the line is difficult). The 'lion' that had savaged so many others is now savaged in turn. Nineveh fell to a coalition of Medes, Babylonians and Scythians in 612 BC.

3:1–19: Judgement pronounced, and complete destruction

The pictures of terrible destruction continue. Nineveh's enslavement of other nations is likened to the false allure of a prostitute, and she will be treated like a prostitute in turn (3:4–5). As Assyria had destroyed proud, powerful Thebes, capital of Egypt, with its allies (3:8–9), so its own power would be ended for ever. What had seemed strong would suddenly be shown to be weak (vv. 12–13), and simply evaporate (v. 17). The final note (v. 17c) recalls why the nation has suffered this deserved fate.

THEOLOGICAL THEMES

Scholars have often thought little of Nahum's prophecy because it lacks the ethical themes of the great prophets (see Mason 1991, pp. 57–58, referring to J. M. P. Smith 1911). However, this may apply too narrow a measure. OAN are an important feature of Old Testament prophecy. They show the universality of God's rule, and that his judgement reaches all nations. This is fundamental to Old Testament theology: God could hardly choose and care for Israel, or judge them by bringing other nations against them, or save them from those nations, if he were not Lord of all the world. There are times, then, when this message comes to the fore, to show God's reliability to those who believe in him. God can be trusted (1:7); he sent the oppressor; the present suffering is not the last word, but Judah will again be saved.

Admittedly, in certain contexts, Nahum would have been regarded as a 'false prophet', since he had no word of criticism for Judah, but only an assurance of salvation. This should alert us to the need to pay attention to the context of a prophecy. We can only know imprecisely what that context might have been for Nahum's first hearers (or readers). But it comes to us in the Book of the Twelve, following Jonah and Micah (see more about this important point in Nahum in the Canon). Nahum comes to us with some safeguards, in case we are tempted by him into vengeful or self-satisfied theology.

And Nahum does have an ethical basis for his prophecy. This comes out in the judgement on Assyria. As with Edom in Obadiah, the depth of Assyria's sin is exposed in this condemnation. Its typical sin is its cruelty. Its shedding of blood is at the heart of the accusation (3:1), and the last word of the book returns to the theme. Further, its 'evil' (ra'ah) towards other nations is in effect 'evil' (ra'ah) plotted against God (1:11). Assyria's inhumanity condemns it in the eyes of God, as it condemned the nations opposed by Amos (Amos 1:1—2:3).

The little link between Nahum and Second Isaiah (1:15 [2:1]; Isa. 52:7) puts the oracles against Assyria in the context of a word of salvation to Judah (see Nahum in the Canon for more on this too).

RHETORICAL INTENTION

We only guess at the situation of Nahum's first hearers. The intention could have been to encourage people who were suffering acutely under Assyrian oppression, by promising that the tyrant would certainly meet its end. Or it could be a celebration because its end had already come.

The power of the prophecy as rhetoric lies in its effective use of poetry and metaphor. There is tremendous variety in it. The theophany in 1:2–8 is in the form of a partial acrostic, as we have already noted. The point of an acrostic is often to give the impression of a complete treatment of a theme (in this case that God can be trusted to overcome his – and his people's – enemies). (See on Lamentations for the effectiveness of acrostics.) The sayings switch from direct address to speech in the third person (e.g. 1:12–14). The words of judgement against Assyria are suddenly interrupted with a cry of peace to Judah

(1:15 [2:1]). Visual imagery is vivid in 2:1–13 [2–14]. The rhetorical questioning of 3:8–9 is designed to bring home the folly of false pretension. And there is a wealth of metaphors, often used in striking ways. For example, the image of locusts and grasshoppers is used in other books to depict the might of a vast army (Joel 1:4; 2:25). But here it gets an unexpected twist, when Assyria's locust-army suddenly just flies away and disappears (3:17). The power of prophetic poetry to evoke the fine line between great strength and utter weakness is nowhere greater than here.

Think about
POWER AND WEAKNESS

If you had been a Judean, or indeed a Syrian or an Egyptian, when Assyria was overrunning its neighbours, it might have seemed as if its power would never come to an end. Are there oppressive situations today that seem as if they can never change? Or have you seen such situations change? What might we learn from Nahum's image of the locust-swarm that simply vanishes?

Compare what the apostle Paul says about power and weakness (1 Cor. 1:25, 27; 2 Cor. 12:9–10).

NAHUM IN THE CANON

Nahum's place in the Canon depends on it being weighed together with prophecies that put the balance differently (as we have already seen). Though it echoes Second Isaiah's glorious promises of deliverance (1:15 [2:1]), it does not have the corresponding theology of judgement on Judah's own sin. This may be regarded as a defect in its theology. But Nahum's effectiveness comes in part from our knowledge that Assyria was the great oppressor of Israel and Judah in the period of the pre-exilic prophets. If we take the link with Isaiah as a clue to the reading of Nahum, we recall that Assyria was once the 'rod of God's anger', because of Israel and Judah's sin. However, since it pursued its own greedy ambition, it came in turn to judgement (Isa. 10:12–19). This gives the full context of the message of salvation to Judah. (Remember also that Nahum's name, 'comfort', recalls Isa. 40:1.)

Nahum's immediate context in the Book of the Twelve is also important. Nahum follows Micah (in MT), which contains a direct warning to Jerusalem that it is liable to judgement (Mic. 3:12). This too redresses the balance somewhat as we read Nahum's attack on Assyria.

At the same time, we still have the unexpected message of Jonah ringing in our ears. The LXX canonical order puts Jonah right before Nahum, so the tremendous contrast between these two books, which have Nineveh in common, is all the more striking. In Jonah, Nineveh turns from its evil (the sort of evil that is catalogued so colourfully in Nahum), and is spared from judgement. In Nahum, no warnings are given, and it is thoroughly destroyed.

What do we make of this strange contrast? We could be quite literal about it and say: Well, Nineveh showed its true colours in the end, and finally got what it deserved. History bears it out; after its levelling in 612 BC it never rose again. Nahum wins hands down. Yet this may not do justice to the contrast between Jonah and Nahum. We saw on Jonah that it was best not to push the literal questions too far (e.g. by asking questions

like: Did Nineveh's repentance last?). And we have also suggested that Nineveh may be meant symbolically in Nahum also (Date and Destination). That is, Nineveh, because of its well-known cruelty and oppression, may stand for any nation or individual that is bent on evil and shows enmity to God.

In that case, Jonah and Nahum together hold out two ways. Neither contains an accusation or condemnation of Israel–Judah. Yet both speak to Israel–Judah and also to other readers because they portray abiding possibilities in relationships between God and human beings.

FURTHER READING

Items marked with * are considered suitable as first ports of call, while others are more complex, or relate to specific issues.

COMMENTARIES

*D. W. Baker *Nahum, Habakkuk and Zephaniah*. TOTC. Leicester: IVP, 1988.

O. P. Robertson *The Books of Nahum, Habakkuk and Zephaniah*. NICOT. Grand Rapids: Eerdmans, 1990.

J. M. P. Smith, W. H. Ward, J. A. Brewer *Micah, Zephaniah, Nahum, Habakkuk, Obadiah, Joel*. ICC. Edinburgh: T. & T. Clark, 1911.

R. L. Smith *Micah–Malachi*. WBC. Waco: Word Books, 1984.

*J. D. W. Watts *Joel, Obadiah, Jonah, Nahum, Habakkuk, Zephaniah*. CBC. Cambridge: CUP, 1975.

OTHER BOOKS AND ARTICLES

K. Cathcart *Nahum in the Light of Northwest Semitic*. Rome: Biblical Institute Press, 1973.

D. L. Christensen 'The Acrostic of Nahum Reconsidered' *ZAW* 87. 1975, pp. 17–30.

*R. Mason *Micah, Nahum, Obadiah*. OTG. Sheffield: JSOT Press, 1991.

of his reforming father King Josiah (609 BC), returned to the worship of other gods than Yahweh (see Mason 1994, pp. 82–83). However, this theory cannot be carried through consistently, since one has to allow for certain 'anti-Babylonian' additions (that is, texts that speak of the conquest of nations, such as 1:14, 17; 2:5b, 8; see Mason 1994, p. 83).

The simplest theory of date and authorship is that Habakkuk laments injustice in Judah, prophesies that it will be punished by Babylon, and also that Babylon will be punished in turn for its own crimes. This sequence of ideas is similar to that which we found in Jeremiah. The twist in Habakkuk is in his questioning the justice of this answer, since the Babylonians will thereby overrun 'those more righteous than they' (which presumably refers to the righteous within Judah). God's answer to Habakkuk's question comes in 2:1–5. This encourages the faithful to be patient, because Babylon will be overthrown in due course. The famous statement in 2:4b ('the righteous will live by their faith') is part of this answer.

A further question concerns ch. 3. This is sometimes thought to be a late addition, because the commentary on Habakkuk found at Qumran (1QpHab) comments only on chs 1—2 (see Vermes 1997, pp. 478–85). Formally too ch. 3 is distinct, having a separate heading, and being a self-contained Psalm-like prayer of praise and confidence.

It is not possible to be sure whether the Book of Habakkuk as a whole comes originally from the prophet. However, the book as it stands has a unity of theme, which we have begun to see. Chapter 3 fits well with that theme, as it affirms in a new way the need to wait for God's salvation.

The period addressed by the book may stretch as far as 597 BC, to include Babylon's overrunning of nations in the region (reflected in the 'Woes', 2:6–20), and its first attack on Judah and Jerusalem.

CRITICAL INTERPRETATION OF HABAKKUK

We have begun to see a way of thinking of the book as a unity. One variation of the view outlined above is to see the sequence of oracles as set in the temple worship. That is, the prophet is a cultic prophet ('certainly a cultic prophet at the temple of Jerusalem', Lindblom 1962, p. 154; cf. Sweeney 1991). He puts the questions to Yahweh in a worship setting and receives oracular answers in the same context.

The cult-prophet idea could account for some features of ch. 3. The prophet's words there are called a 'prayer', like certain Psalms (Ps. 17:1; 86:1; 90:1; 102:1; 142:1). The musical reference in 3:1 ('according to Shigionoth'), occurs in Ps. 7:1. The 'choirmaster' (3:19c) is familiar from a number of Psalms headings, some of them also having the phrase 'with stringed instruments' (e.g. 4:1; 6:1; 54:1). The line before the final prayer declares that 'the LORD is in his holy temple' (2:20), which may be an indication of a temple setting. More generally, the structure of petition or lament (1:2–4) and response in salvation-oracle corresponds to the concept of cult-prophecy as accepted by many scholars (for example, Bellinger 1984, pp. 32–59; see also Murray 1982).

However, the cult-prophet theory is by no means accepted by all. It is not certain that salvation-oracles were delivered at all in cultic settings. And there is not enough evidence that the Book of Habakkuk as a whole conforms to such a pattern.

The book may be considered a unity nevertheless. The unity is supplied by the theme of waiting patiently for deliverance from present distress. In this respect 3:16–19 corresponds to 2:1–5. The vision of Yahweh coming in power over the earth and the nations (ch. 3) is in contrast to the false pretensions of Babylon to exercise such power (1:5–11; 2:6–20). It is this power that justifies the faithfulness of the believer.

STRUCTURE AND OUTLINE

The structure of Habakkuk is widely agreed. After the heading, Habakkuk makes two complaints to Yahweh (1:2–4; 1:12–17), each followed by a response from Yahweh (1:5–11; 2:2–5). Habakkuk then pronounces a series of five 'Woes' against Babylon (2:6–20). The prophecy ends with the psalm in ch. 3. This itself subdivides into 3:1–2 (heading and petition); 3:3–7 (Yahweh's victory march); 3:8–15 (a hymn of salvation); 3:16–19 (the poet's renewed confidence).

STRUCTURE
1:1   Heading
1:2–4   Habakkuk's first complaint
1:5–11   Yahweh's first response
1:12–17   Habakkuk's second complaint
2:1–5   Habakkuk waits, and Yahweh's second response
2:6–20   Five 'woes' against Babylon
3:1–19   Yahweh's victory and salvation; the prophet's quiet trust

OUTLINE
1:1: Heading
The prophecy is described as an 'oracle', or 'burden', that Habakkuk 'saw' (cf. on Nahum 1:1).

1:2–4: Habakkuk's first complaint
Habakkuk utters a 'lament'. The exclamation 'How long?' is typical of this form (cf. Ps. 13:1 [2]). There are echoes of Jeremiah in the language used (cf. Jer. 20:8; 15:10), and in the picture of a society which has lost its true basis (cf. Jer. 8:22—9:9 [9:8]). Habakkuk sees that *torah* is not practised. *Torah* may refer here to the body of law, as in Deuteronomy (so Baker 1988, p. 52). In parallel with *mishpat*, justice, it means that the process of law is being perverted by the powerful (cf. Amos 2:6–8).

1:5–11: Yahweh's first response
Yahweh's answer is that he is raising up the Babylonians, who are depicted as ruthless and powerful. The curious thing about this response is that they immediately appear as a wicked nation, rather than as a 'rod of God's anger' (Isa. 10:5). They are the source of their own 'justice' (v. 7, NRSV, better than 'law', NIV), that is, they do not find it in God. They are 'guilty'. For this reason some have thought that Habakkuk is really complaining about Babylon's evil in 1:2–11 (as we saw above, Date and Destination).

1:12–17: Habakkuk's second complaint
Habakkuk turns again to lament and petition. Prophetic prayer often aims to persuade God to act by appealing to his own character. The word 'pure' (*tahor*, v. 13), is taken from the sphere of ritual holiness (meaning ritually 'clean'). It is unusual here in referring to God himself.

Habakkuk's complaint is essentially the same as before, but now the 'wicked' who are oppressing the 'righteous' are the Babylonians. The prophet's second complaint follows directly from Yahweh's response to his first, therefore. The 'righteous' must now refer to the righteous within Judah, who were formerly oppressed by other more powerful Judeans. It is clear from 2:4b that Habakkuk defines the righteous among his people. His problem here is to know how God can allow the idolatrous, self-obsessed Babylonians to come in judgement against innocent Judeans.

This oppression by the Babylonians brings a kind of disorder into the world. In 1:14 we find an allusion to the creation narratives in Genesis. The word for 'people' (NRSV), 'men' (NIV), is 'adam, which means 'humanity' in Gen. 1—3. Whereas 'adam was made to rule over the other creatures in Gen. 1:26–28, here humanity has been reduced to the same level as the 'fish' and 'creeping things'. There is no order or rule that would mark humanity out from the mass of creatures.

2:1–5: Habakkuk waits, and Yahweh's second response

The ideas of the prophet as a 'watcher', and of a written prophecy that points to a future fulfilment, are familiar from the prophetic books (vv. 1–3; cf. Ezek. 3:16–21; Isa. 8:1–4). The point is that God has fixed a definite time for salvation, though it is not yet.

In the saying about the 'righteous' (2:4b), a contrast is made with the 'proud'. Their *nephesh* is not upright. (*Nephesh* is translated 'spirit' (NRSV), 'desires' (NIV). It is traditionally 'soul'. The point is about the essential being of the proud.) The 'proud' seem to be the Babylonians, because of v. 5, which refers to the conquest of nations.

The 'righteous' (always singular in Habakkuk) will live because of 'his faithfulness'. Though it is not specified, this probably refers to his own faithfulness (rather than God's), because of the contrast in the line with the proud (but see Theological Themes for

alternatives). The thought then is that the righteous will be saved from the dangers that are coming by remaining faithful, because God will overcome the tyrant in the end.

2:6–20: Five 'Woes' against Babylon

These sayings contain typical accusations against ruthless, powerful people (e.g. 2:6–7, 9). But the dominant note is about the oppression of nations by a more powerful nation (vv. 8, 10, 12–13, 16–17. Their crime is violence and bloodshed (cf. Nah. 3:1–4; Amos 1:1—2:3). The metaphor of the 'cup' coming to the oppressor in his turn (v. 16) is also applied to Babylon by Jeremiah (Jer. 25:15–26, note v. 26b).

In the midst of the oracles of judgement on Babylon comes a fleeting vision of a time in the future when the whole earth will know the glory of Yahweh (2:14). This closely resembles the paradisal vision of Isaiah (11:9) (the word 'glory' is added in Habakkuk, perhaps to contrast with the self-glorying of Babylon).

A word on the folly of idolatry (2:18–19) reminds of the critique of Babylonian idolatry in Isa. 44:9–20. This is followed by a declaration that Yahweh is in his temple (v. 20). The section closes with this contrast between futile worship and a call to reverence in the presence of the true God (Baker 1988, pp. 67–68).

3:1–19: Yahweh's victory and salvation; the prophet's quiet trust

The last chapter is framed with notices that remind of the Psalms (see Critical Interpretation). It is a prayer of Habakkuk, beginning with a petition (v. 2) and ending in an expression of trust (vv. 16–19). The body of the Psalm falls into two parts. Verses 3–7 are a theophany, that is, an appearance

214

of God in his power (like Nah. 1:2–8). The idea of a march of God from desert places in the south is known also in Jdg. 5:4–5; Ps. 68:7–10, 17–18 [8–11, 18–19]. The nations, trembling as he passes, know his power.

In vv. 8–15 Habakkuk addresses a hymn directly to God. It is about God's victory over nations, with echoes of the exodus from Egypt (vv. 8, 12–15). The victory language is mixed with the language of creation (v. 8 – the idea of a victory over 'rivers' and the 'sea' recalls the Canaanite creation myth, in which River and Sea are personified as forces opposed to Baal). The imagery develops to depict the earth trembling at God's action against his enemies (vv. 10–11).

Verse 13 is the heart of this passage, with its promise of salvation to God's people ('your people', recalling the covenant language of Exodus, e.g. Exod. 3:7). 'Your anointed' is (unusually) a way of referring to the people as a whole.

The book closes (vv. 16–19) with Habakkuk waiting quietly for the oppressor to be overcome (v. 16). He will wait in faithful trust, even though there are no immediate signs of salvation (vv. 17–18).

THEOLOGICAL THEMES

HOW CAN A JUST GOD TOLERATE EVIL?

The theological foundation of Habakkuk's prophecy is a concern for 'justice and righteousness'. The main exposition of this is in Amos (see Theological Themes there). Habakkuk shares with Amos a dismay that justice is not being done among his people (1:2–4). He knows too that this is offensive to God, because God's demand for righteousness lies in God's own character. This is why his desire for righteousness can be expressed in such emotive terms ('I hate, I despise your festivals . . . but let justice roll down like waters, and righteousness like an everflowing stream', Amos 5:21, 24; 'I desire steadfast love and not sacrifice', Hos. 6:6).

The Old Testament writers expect God's judgement when justice is neglected. So Amos declares that judgement will come. The author of Kings shows that it *has* come. The Old Testament writers expect God to judge evil. There would be something wrong if he did not (this 'justification of God' is called 'theodicy').

The new thing in Habakkuk is the element of lament or protest. Since God is righteous, how can he tolerate evil? Habakkuk's question borders on the questioning of some psalmists and Wisdom writers (Psalm 73; Job). These in their different ways ask how God's justice can be reconciled with the things the authors see and experience in the world.

So Habakkuk, instead of declaring that judgement is coming, takes the role of one who laments or petitions. That is, he addresses God and asks why his judgement does not come. God answers that it is indeed coming, in the shape of Babylon. However, this answer just prompts the next question. For the picture of Babylon from the start shows that it cannot establish true justice. Their 'justice' is of their own making (1:7), a mockery of true justice. 'They all come for violence' (1:9), and glory in their destructive might (1:15–17).

If Babylon is 'appointed for judgement' (1:12), this judgement does not produce justice. Other prophets saw and dealt with this problem. Both Isaiah and Jeremiah portrayed the imperial power (Assyria,

Babylon) as God's instrument of punishment, and carefully showed that they in turn would be judged because of their arrogance (Isa. 10:12–19; Jer. 25:12; 50—51). In other places the foreign power can even be shown to exercise rule benevolently (briefly Nebuchadnezzar in Daniel 4; Cyrus in Isaiah 40—55). But here the accent falls on the wickedness of the agent appointed by God to do justice. Habakkuk is disturbed by this in itself.

So his protest, that righteousness is betrayed, simply moves on. How can God use a wicked agent against his own people, and especially against the righteous among them (1:12–14)? Here Habakkuk takes up another theme we have met, that among God's rebellious people there are some who are righteous (cf. Isa. 1:27–28).

'THE RIGHTEOUS SHALL LIVE BY (WHOSE?) FAITHFULNESS'

 God's answer to this produces the best-known passage in Habakkuk: 'the righteous shall live by his faithfulness', or 'by his faithfulness shall live'. The 'righteous' (singular) stands for any and every righteous person. God's answer in 2:4 is a Wisdom answer to a Wisdom question. Though the powerful prevail for now, their life is falsely based; the point about pride is that it leads to death (cf. Prov. 14:12; 16:25; Baker 1988, p. 60). The righteous, on the other hand, will have life (the verb 'shall live' comes in the climactic final position, bringing out the contrast with what is said about the proud). The point is very like Ps. 73:15–20, 27, where the psalmist realizes that the powerful wicked are in mortal danger, while the innocent have true life and security (vv. 23–28).

By *whose* faith(fulness) shall the righteous live? As we saw above (Outline), 'his' could refer to either the righteous person's own faithfulness or to God's. The Greek Old Testament (LXX) has 'the righteous shall live by *my* faith(fulness)' (that is, God's). This makes good sense. We know that faithfulness is one of God's important characteristics (a major topic in Hosea; see Theological Themes there). In this context it would mean: 'In spite of the present crisis God will save the righteous because he (God) is faithful'.

The New Testament readings of Habakkuk appear to preserve some of the ambiguity in the textual tradition of Hab. 2:4. Hebrews 10:37–38 is very close to the sense of Habakkuk (in the MT, Hebrew, form). The readers of that letter are called to 'endurance' in whatever crisis they are in (v. 36), because the salvation of Christ is coming (v. 37), and 'my righteous one will live by faith' (v. 38). That this faith is the believer's own is the natural reading of v. 38, and also clear from v. 39. (For the readings of Hab. 2:4 that lie behind the Hebrews text see Baker 1988, pp. 60–61).

Paul's reading of Hab. 2:4 in Rom. 1:17 is more complicated. Here it is possible that he has dropped the 'his' from Hab. 2:4 in order to leave the possibility open that it might be the believer's or God's. This openness also affects how we understand 'faith(fulness)' (*pistis*). Which is it to be in the end: faith or faithfulness? Here too it may be best to embrace all the possibilities: the faith of the believer amounts to belief in the faithfulness of God. It is therefore close to *trust*, and not far after all from *faithfulness* (see J. D. G. Dunn 1988, pp. 44–46).

The connection between Habakkuk and the interpretations of him in the NT lies in the belief that God will finally demonstrate his righteousness and vindicate it in faithful people. Habakkuk moves in this direction when he uses the imagery of creation and the Divine Warrior in order to confirm that God will save (ch. 3). The NT puts salvation for the faithful in the context of Christ's revelation of God's righteousness (Rom. 3:21). The 'life' that is promised the righteous now means life in Christ, and is ultimately eschatological (1 Thess. 5:9–10).

RHETORICAL INTENTION

The rhetorical force of Habakkuk is implicit in the above: it aims to persuade people who are being oppressed by a cruel overlord that their sufferings will not last and they should endure. The argument that we have unfolded is not a theological treatise, but aims to have an effect on an audience. Habakkuk's laments are not just for himself, but carry a message (as Jeremiah's 'confessions' were not just his private prayers). The dominant appeal is to wait patiently, and to believe in God's power to save even though there is no immediate evidence of it. The rhetorical purpose is thus borne by two key passages, 2:1–5 and 3:16–19. It is possible that the proclamation came in a cultic setting.

The power of Habakkuk to address new audiences is clear from its reception in the New Testament (which we have observed), and also at Qumran. An important document of the Dead Sea community was the so-called *pesher* (interpretation) on Habakkuk (1QpHab; see Vermes 1997, pp. 478–85). The sectarians at Qumran saw themselves as 'the righteous', God's eschatological elect community. Their reading of Habakkuk may seem bizarre to us. However, it is an example of a fresh hearing of the prophetic book, according to accepted methods of interpretation in its

day. The underlying message – the need to wait patiently for God's salvation in a period of oppression that has no visible end – is very powerful.

Think about
WAITING FOR GOD TO ACT

On this topic, see the panel at Mic. 7:8–20.

HABAKKUK IN THE CANON

Our study of Theological Themes in this book has already put Habakkuk in a canonical context, since its theological high point was taken up in the New Testament, as well as at Qumran. We have also seen how the message of Habakkuk was distinguished from other prophetic books by drawing in a Wisdom emphasis (the question of why the unjust get away with oppressing the just). Following Nahum, a 'correction' may be observed in this sense, that the divine punishment of cruel powers may not come immediately. Habakkuk teaches what is involved in faithfulness when God does not yet act.

FURTHER READING

Items marked with * are considered suitable as first ports of call, while others are more complex, or relate to specific issues.

COMMENTARIES
*E. Achtemeier *Nahum–Malachi*. Interpretation. Atlanta: John Knox, 1986.
*D. W. Baker *Nahum, Habakkuk and Zephaniah*. TOTC. Leicester: IVP, 1988.
O. P. Robertson *The Books of Nahum, Habakkuk and Zephaniah*. NICOT. Grand Rapids: Eerdmans, 1990.

ZEPHANIAH AND JEREMIAH

The parallels between the two prophets, documented in detail by Holladay, involve individual phrases, which are not easily picked up when comparing the two books, because the English versions give different translations in different passages. For example, Zeph. 1:9, '(those) who fill their master's house with violence and fraud', is echoed in Jer. 5:27; 'Their houses are full of treachery (fraud)'. And the phrase 'great destruction' (Jer. 4:6; 6:1) may depend on the same phrase in Zeph. 1:10 (where NRSV translates 'loud crash') (Holladay 2001, p. 674).

It is quite likely that prophets did influence each other in their use of language (see note on this at Joel: Date and Destination: Interbiblical quotations). The influence may even run through a number of prophets. For example, behind the phrase in Zeph. 1:9 and Jer. 5:27 may lie Isa. 3:14; Amos 3:10 (as Holladay points out, p. 674).

However, since the dates of both Jeremiah's and Zephaniah's individual oracles are uncertain, it is unclear which way the influence goes. So once again we are left without a sure way of knowing when Zephaniah spoke.

enemy if, as some think, the threats of attack by invaders are conventional, perhaps used in worship settings. As for the practices that Zephaniah criticizes, these may well have returned quickly after the reform, and indeed the reform may not have been as far-reaching or permanent as we may think from a reading of Kings.

We should also bear in mind that there is little evidence of the reform in Jeremiah either, even though Jeremiah certainly preached after that event, so this could be an unreliable guide. The great Reformation commentator, John Calvin, placed Zephaniah's work *after* the reform, on the grounds that the people of Israel were habitually unfaithful to Yahweh. Calvin was followed by some nineteenth-century scholars (House 1988, pp. 10–11). It is probably safer to say that Zephaniah prophesied before 612 BC, since the city of Nineveh fell in that year, but this seems not yet to have happened in 2:13.

As always, the date of the prophet's own ministry must be distinguished from the date of the book. However, there is little in the book that points to a particular date, except for the superscription, which looks back to the reign of Josiah. Scholars sometimes assign certain passages to the post-exilic period (see next). In any case the book as it stands has a message of both judgement and future salvation, and its audience is therefore in some setting (exilic or post-exilic) in which it can be asked to reflect on this.

Hyatt 1949, and Williams 1963, pp. 122–3.) Part of the reason for this later dating is that it is not clear what enemy might be a threat in 626 BC. Assyria was weak by then, and Babylon had not yet become a force. Older critics pointed to the invasion of Egypt by Scythians (from Russia) at about that time, and see this is as an occasion for the book (House 1988, p. 12). (Some had seen this Scythian invasion behind Jeremiah's allusions to a 'foe from the north' also; Jer. 4:6; 6:1.) This theory is not so popular today.

This kind of evidence is difficult to evaluate. We may not need to be able to identify an

CRITICAL INTERPRETATION OF ZEPHANIAH

There are the usual discussions of 'authenticity'. Some think Zephaniah uttered almost all the oracles in the book (e.g. Baker 1988). Kapelrud writes: 'The short and concise form we find in the Book of Zephaniah indicates that we have here the words of the prophet mainly as they were spoken' (1975, p. 13). Others, however, think there is almost nothing of the prophet's left (Ben Zvi 1991). And there are shades in between.

Scholars often think that they can trace a shift of perspective in the book. Kapelrud, in spite of his rather conservative view just mentioned, thinks that further comments were added. For example, 1:8, 12 deliberately change the focus from 1:7, 14–16. While 1:7, 14–16 speaks of a 'day' that is to come soon, vv. 8, 12 make the 'day' refer to a future event. This is to 'take the sting' out of Zephaniah's words, and make them less dangerous (Kapelrud 1975, pp. 17–19). (That is, it was politically dangerous to accuse rulers, and claim judgement was about to fall on them. Both Jeremiah and the even unluckier Uriah discovered this; Jeremiah 26.)

Parts of the book are given late dates because of their developed eschatology, that is, ideas of a future victory of Yahweh over all the nations, and a restoration of Judah after a time of judgement. Zeph. 3:14–20 has been widely doubted (Driver 1891, pp. 342–43). Mason points to similarities between 3:14–20 and Second Isaiah and the Enthronement Psalms, as evidence of lateness (Mason 1994, p. 46). Zephaniah 3:19–20 in particular, with its echoes of Jer. 29:14; 30—33, is thought to be typically exilic or post-exilic. The very structure of the book (judgement followed by salvation) is often taken as evidence for composition a long time after the prophet's own work (Childs 1979, p. 459). (See further Mason 1994, pp. 44–54.)

ZEPHANIAH A 'DRAMA'?

An unusual view is taken by House. He believes that historical criticism has not enough information to go on in trying to uncover the history behind the text, and proposes a holistic study of the book as a 'drama'. House insists on reading the text in the form in which we have it, and as a unity, rather than breaking it up into disconnected parts, and always asking historical questions (1988, pp. 19–20). He finds that Zephaniah's structure is created by a dialogue between the prophet and Yahweh in seven sets of speeches (pp. 56–61). These speeches unfold a plot, with a 'conflict' and a 'resolution'. The conflict consists in the intention of Yahweh to judge Judah and the world. The idea of a 'remnant' (3:11–13) then becomes a step on the way to a declaration of final victory (3:14–20; pp. 61–68). The prophet himself changes in the course of the plot. The prophet who once warned of judgement becomes one who encourages and exhorts, a preacher of restoration (pp. 60, 72–73).

House rightly puts the question of composition in a frame that directs us to the impact of the text as a whole, and his plot-line is helpful. It is a quite different way of resolving some of the tensions in Zephaniah, and perhaps other prophetic books (such as God's anger and his mercy; immediate and future judgement; Israel and the nations) than the historical-critical one. It only needs to be asked why 'drama' applies particularly here, when other prophetic books have a variety of speakers in their discourse too. And we have seen that a resolution of conflict into a pattern of judgement and salvation is typical of prophetic books. To say that Zephaniah is a 'drama' does not avoid the question of who was the dramatist (Zephaniah or some other? See Mason 1994, pp. 50–51).

ZEPHANIAH A 'CULT-PROPHET'?

If 'drama' is one way to try to hold together the diverse elements in the prophecy, another way of doing this is to suppose that Zephaniah was a 'cult-prophet'. A clue is found in references to Jerusalem and worship in the book (e.g. 1:7b–8a; 3:11, 14–18). If the book contains types of saying that are quite different from each other, maybe this is because it is a collection of kinds of hymns and songs that were used in Israel's temple-worship, like the Psalms. The diversity would simply reflect the different kinds of belief about God in Israel's religion (Mason 1994, p. 30).

CULTIC PROPHETS

See Introduction: Prophets and Psalms, and panel.

The limitation of this approach to Zephaniah is that it does not account for the progression of thought that is uncovered, for example, by House. The progression of thought is similar to that of other prophetic books, and there is little indication that this is due to a temple setting.

STRUCTURE AND OUTLINE

STRUCTURE

1:1	Superscription
1:2—2:3	The Day of the LORD
2:4–15	Oracles against the Nations
3:1–8	Accusation of Jerusalem
3:9–13	Salvation of the nations and Jerusalem
3:14–20	Yahweh's universal reign in Jerusalem

OUTLINE

1:1: Superscription

The superscription, with its rare four-generation genealogy, places Zephaniah's prophecy in the reign of King Josiah (see on Date and Destination).

1:2—2:3: The Day of the LORD

1:2–6 The sayings about Judah in this chapter are enclosed by words about the whole world. The prophecy opens, like Micah's, with a word of judgement on the nations (vv. 2–3), and the chapter closes with another (v. 18). This stylistic feature of 'enclosing' is called an 'inclusio'. It shows a connection between themes (in this case judgement on the nations and on Judah).

Zephaniah proclaims God's judgement on all creation (vv. 2–3). The language reminds us of Genesis 1, with even the same play on words (*'adam/'adamah*, humans/earth), as well as other terms (animals, birds of the air, fish of the sea). The judgement is a kind of undoing of creation.

This belongs closely with the first judgement saying against Judah, for the speech runs on without interruption (note: 'I will cut off humanity', v. 3; then 'I will cut off from this place [= Jerusalem]', v. 4). The first sin of Jerusalem is religious. Its priests are 'idolatrous priests' (*kemarim* – only here and in 2 Kgs 23:5; Hos. 10:5). People worship Baal, the stars (cf. Deut. 4:19; 2 Kgs 21:3, 5), and Milcom (an Ammonite god; cf. 1 Kgs 11:5; 2 Kgs 23:13. The Hebrew word 'Milcom' could also be 'their king'; NRSV (margin), and Smith 1984, pp. 126–27, who thinks 'their king' refers to Baal). The worship in Jerusalem is syncretistic, that is, the people worship these gods *as well as* Yahweh (v. 5). This is the same as rejection of Yahweh altogether (v. 6).

1:7—2:3 Zephaniah proclaims a day of judgement against the sins of Judah. The chief offenders are the leaders (1:8). The sins now extend to social oppression ('violence and fraud', v. 9). The target group is wealthy and complacent (vv. 12–13, 18).

The wrath of God on the 'day' itself is carried by an unnamed enemy army (vv. 14–16). The 'darkness' imagery is like the descriptions of the 'day' in Amos (Amos 5:18, 20) and Joel (Joel 2:2), and implies chaos (a bit like vv. 1–2). Clouds and thick darkness also speak of God's presence in 'theophany' (cf. Exod. 20:21; Deut. 4:11; 5:22). But the presence is now for judgement. The 'day' is 'near' (vv. 7, 14), yet the perspective is also extended to a future time (vv. 8, 12), and even to a judgement on the whole earth (v. 18), as in other prophets (Ezekiel 38—39; Joel 3:9–15 [4:9–15]).

The punishment is called a 'sacrifice' (1:7–8; cf. Jer. 46:10; Ezek. 39:17–20 for this image). The language also reminds of the curses of the covenant in Deuteronomy (Zeph. 1:13, cf. Deut. 28:30). There are also a number of parallels between 1:14–18 and Deut. 28 (Mason 1994, p. 32; see also Robertson 1990).

2:1–3 As with Amos, the pronouncement of judgement goes hand in hand with a call to repent (cf. Amos 5:6–7). Zephaniah echoes Amos's call for righteousness, but he adds the virtue of *humility*, the opposite of the pride that the prophets so often condemn. If the people repent they may avoid the *anger* of the LORD (v. 2, cf. Deut. 29:20, 23–24 [19, 22–23]).

2:4–15: Oracles Against the Nations
Zephaniah's Oracles Against the Nations (OAN) are directed against the Philistines, Moab, Ammon, the 'Cushites' (2:12) and finally Assyria. The Philistines, Moab and Ammon often feature in OAN (Isa. 14:28—16:14; Amos 1:6–8, 13–15; 2:1–3; Jer. 47:1—49:6; Ezek. 25:1–11, 15–17). Here they are condemned to be overrun and have their land possessed by Judah (2:7, 9). The Cushites are Nubians, or Ethiopians, but the reference may be to Egypt. The OAN climax in judgement on Assyria, still the power in the region in Josiah's day, though declining. Its false trust in its own power is exposed. 'Living securely' (2:15) is a great blessing in Old Testament thought (Lev. 25:18–19; 26:5; Deut. 12:10; Jer. 23:6; 32:37; 33:16), but the term often refers to a false security before a terrible disaster (cf. Jdg. 18:7, of Laish; Isa. 47:8, of Babylon; Jer. 49:31, of Kedar).

3:1–8: Accusation of Jerusalem
3:1–5 The 'city' in 3:1 is now Jerusalem. This makes a sharp, ironic contrast to the 'city' in 2:13–15, which was Nineveh. Jerusalem too is under judgement. (This surprising transition is like the one in Amos 2:4–8, following the OAN.)

While the officials and judges 'within it' are corrupt (3:3), Yahweh alone 'within it' (3:5) is just (*saddiq*) and gives true judgement.

3:6–8 As in 1:2–6, the judgement on Jerusalem is now bound up with judgement on the nations. Before God, Judah is part of his whole creation, and as liable to judgement as all the rest.

3:9–13: Salvation of the nations and Jerusalem
The turn to a promise of salvation is a mirror-image of the foregoing, because it applies first to the nations (3:9–12) then to Jerusalem. The phrase 'my holy mountain' (= Mt Zion, 3:11) shows that vv. 11–13 refer to Judah. It is a 'remnant' that will be left there, a 'humble' people (cf. 2:3) that speaks truth (note how speaking truth is a theme of vv. 9–13, as is highlighted by its appearance in vv. 9, 13, making an 'inclusio' – or envelope-structure; see above on 1:2–18).

The salvation of Jerusalem is a kind of purging, rather like Isa. 1:21–26. But it now embraces all the nations.

3:14–20: Yahweh's universal reign in Jerusalem

The prophecy closes with a call to Zion to celebrate Judah's salvation (for the feminine image, v. 14, cf. Lam. 2:1). Like the earlier 'Day of the LORD' passages, this hymn now speaks of a future 'day'/'time' (vv. 16, 18–20) when Judah's 'fortunes will be restored' (v. 20). This phrase is familiar from Deut. 30:3 and its repeated occurrence in Jeremiah 30—33 as a way of speaking of salvation after exile. The 'Day of the LORD' motif finishes on this high note: God's final word will be salvation for his people.

The key to the theology is the idea of God's presence in Jerusalem, especially as a warrior who gives victory (vv. 15, 17). Judah will no more suffer humiliation at the hands of enemies, but be restored to its position of fame and praise among the nations (3:20, cf. Deut. 26:19).

Most notably, Yahweh is called the 'king of Israel'. This title is given to no one else in Zephaniah (i.e. to no human king). This makes Zephaniah one of the most radical prophetic books, in its criticism of rulers in Israel or Judah. It also puts it close to Deuteronomy, in which Yahweh is king (Deut. 33:5), and the human king takes a minor role (Deut. 17:14–20).

THEOLOGICAL THEMES

GOD'S ELECTION OF ISRAEL, AND HIS KINGSHIP IN THE WORLD

The accusation of Judah is put in the context of Yahweh's judgement on the whole world. These two things are closely related. The relation between them goes back to the reason for Israel's 'election': to be a blessing to all the nations of the world (Gen. 12:1–3). In Old Testament thought, the fate of the whole world is bound up with Israel fulfilling its destiny as God's elect people. This is why, when Israel sins, the whole world is affected. The imagery of chaos in the created order expresses this fact. Zephaniah (like Micah) makes the connection right at the start (1:4–6).

The topic of creation is closely related to Yahweh's kingship. Creation and kingship are united in Zephaniah, first through *Adam*. In Genesis, 'Adam' can be a name for the first human being, and also the general noun meaning humanity. Sometimes it is hard to distinguish between these two senses, since the story about the first human being is really a story about the place of humanity in God's world, as a kind of *king*. Human beings have 'dominion' over the other creatures (Gen. 1:26; Ps. 8:3–8 [4–9]).

In Zeph. 1:3, in the passage about the undoing of creation, God threatens to 'sweep away' and to 'cut off' *Adam*; the threat occurs twice in the verse, showing that this is the most important point. The allusion to Genesis is clear because of the play on words (*'adam/'adamah*) noted above (Outline). Zephaniah has in mind humanity's responsibility to rule well over the earth (see De Roche 1980). The judgement on *Adam* in 1:3 is a judgement on all the nations to exercise good government. The failure of Israel and Judah has a central place in this. Its failure is the more serious because of its election-role as the one who should witness to the world about God.

But the bigger picture is put right in the foreground. With the human failure to rule well is contrasted the kingship of Yahweh. He will establish his rule in the world finally, ruling from Zion (Zeph. 3:15). Mason puts this well:

> (The Book of Zephaniah) passes sentence of death on the oppressive kingdoms of this world, and witnesses to the ultimate truth that they will become the kingdoms of God. (Mason 1994, p. 58)

MORE ON ELECTION: A 'REMNANT'

The idea of Israel's election is never far from the prophets' thought. They believed that their special relationship with Yahweh *ought* to be expressed in loyalty to him, and obedience to his commands. When Israel is unfaithful, this makes its election problematic, and its focus changes. After the fall of the northern kingdom, the election of Israel is carried on in the form of Judah. Yet Judah too is unfaithful. So the focus narrows to a 'remnant' which will be saved, and which will live up to the standards expected by Yahweh (3:12–13).

RELIGION AND ETHICS

Zephaniah criticizes Judah first for its false worship (1:2–6). This was also the main emphasis of Hosea, who preached over a century earlier in the northern kingdom. Its worship was syncretistic, that is, the people combined elements of different forms of belief (1:5). While polytheism was the norm in the ancient world, Yahweh's first commandment was that his people should have no other gods apart from him (Exod. 20:3).

But Zephaniah is also like Amos in his attacks on the pride of the powerful and their abuse of the weak and poor in society (1:9; 3:1–4). The complacency of ill-gotten wealth goes hand in hand with forgetfulness of God (1:12). The link between wealth and such

Think about
HUMILITY AND POVERTY

Compare NRSV's and NIV's translations of Ps. 10:12, 17. You will see that NRSV has 'meek' in v. 17, while NIV has 'oppressed'. Here, the two versions simply differ over a translation of *'anaw*, because the concepts of 'humble' and 'oppressed' are close.

This closeness is not just felt by modern translators, but is reflected in two very similar Hebrew words: *'ani*, 'poor, afflicted', and *'anaw*, 'humble'. (The two words look even more similar in Hebrew than they do when written in English letters. The difference is between the letters *yod* and *waw*, which were liable to be confused in copying Hebrew texts.) In certain cases a written form *'ani* has vowel pointing that indicates the word should be 'read' *'anaw*. (This is the phenomenon known as *qere*, that is, the form to be read, in contrast to the *kethib*, the form in the written text.) Psalm 10:12 is such a case, as is Ps. 9:12 [13]. Modern translations do not necessarily follow the Masoretic *qere*. NRSV's translation 'oppressed' in Ps. 10:12, and NIV's 'helpless', probably follow the written text.

The confusions between these terms can happen easily because of a natural similarity between the ideas of 'poverty' and 'humility'. Think about the relationship between the two. Do poverty and affliction make humble? Think too about the two forms of Jesus' beatitude on poverty in Matt. 5:3 and Luke 6:20. How important is the difference between them?

It is clear that Zephaniah is thinking of the virtue of humility in 2:3, because of his command to seek it, in parallel with righteousness.

forgetfulness is also seen by Deuteronomy (Deut. 8:11–20), but here it is made worse by injustice. The society is portrayed as deeply false (3:13), as we may suppose from Yahweh's declared intention that the restored remnant of Israel shall 'utter no lies, nor shall a deceitful tongue be found in their mouths' (3:13, cf. 3:9; see also Jer. 9:2–9 [1–8]).

Zephaniah touches on the major prophetic theme of 'justice'. Yahweh's justice and his right judgements contrast with the corruption of the rulers in Judah who should have been responsible for these things (3:1–5).

A special emphasis, however, is on *humility*. The importance of this is clear from 2:3, where the idea appears twice ('you humble of the land', 'seek . . . humility'). The idea is quite infrequent in the prophets (only elsewhere in Isa. 11:4; 29:19; 61:1; Amos 2:7), though a little more common in the Psalms (e.g. Ps. 9:12 [13]; 10:12, 17). There is a fine line in some of these texts between the virtue of humility and the condition of being oppressed or afflicted.

Zephaniah's ethics have implications for the way in which Judah is ruled. The rulers are severely criticized for their pride and their carelessness about justice. This is just the opposite of what God seeks in his people. True exercise of rule in society is humble, and protects the humble, who are also likely to be the oppressed.

THE DAY OF THE LORD: JUDGEMENT AND SALVATION

Zephaniah develops the concept of the Day of the LORD/Yahweh more than any other prophet. (Joel is the closest parallel.) His closeness to Amos is clear in 1:15 (see Outline). But (as with other prophets) there is a change in Zephaniah from judgement to

salvation, which comes to clear expression in the topic of the 'Day'. The change occurs between 3:8 and 3:9. Zephaniah 3:8 still refers to a 'day' on which Yahweh will vent his anger. But 3:9 suddenly speaks of a 'time' when he will turn the nations to himself. And 3:11 announces a 'day' of restoration for Judah. If the people of Amos's time had a false expectation that the 'Day of the LORD' would be one of salvation, Zephaniah shows how it will indeed be one. But here as elsewhere, it is only after an act of punishment, purging and restoration. And it brings with it the command to be faithful, as uncompromisingly as ever.

RHETORICAL INTENTION

We have seen that it is difficult to pin Zephaniah down to a specific time. This means that it also difficult to describe the book's rhetorical intention in one precise way. House's idea that the prophet is transformed in the course of the prophecy is helpful (Critical Interpretation), because it allows us to see the rhetorical force of the prophecy on different levels. The book addresses an audience with a message of salvation after judgement. This might seem like a happy ending, pure and simple. But the effect is more complex than that. This is because the vision for the renewed community is at the same time a command. The salvation is for 'a people humble and lowly' (3:17). The idea of a remnant also functions rhetorically, because it implies that the saved people might go on being reduced, according to their success or failure in establishing the obedient community.

The theology of God's grace is sometimes thought to contrast with one that calls people to repent. But there is no such opposition here. As Childs puts it; 'eschatology and ethics are not in tension' (Childs 1979, p. 461).

ZEPHANIAH IN THE CANON

Zephaniah has sometimes been thought a rather unoriginal prophet (House 1988, p. 9, citing J. M. P. Smith 1911). Another way of putting this is to say that the prophecy deliberately brings together a number of familiar theological themes. We have noticed similarities with several other prophecies. Childs again: 'The effect of the canonical process has been to structure the prophetic material within a theological understanding of the nature of God and his work.' He calls this gathering of materials a 'compendium' (Childs 1979, p. 460). The treatment of the 'day of the LORD' is the leading example of such a compendium in the book, and it constitutes Zephaniah's chief claim to an original addition to the prophetic canon.

However, two further canonical pointers may be suggested. The first is the dating of the prophecy in the time of Josiah. Though, as we have seen, we cannot be quite sure about a historical setting, the attribution of the book to Josiah's time is an important comment on the narratives of Josiah's reform in Kings and Chronicles, and also on its omission from Jeremiah. The reform, as we have seen, is not noticed in Zephaniah. But scholars have been unable to show that this is simply due to its having come before the reform. (A further problem with such a view is that the reform probably began in 628 BC, not with the discovery of the 'book of the law' in 621 BC. This is implied in 2 Chr. 34:3, and now held by a number of scholars (e.g. Nicholson 1967, pp. 7–12).) Zephaniah may show, therefore, that Josiah's

reform had no thoroughgoing effect. And this then may help us understand the relationship between Kings and Jeremiah on the same point.

The second pointer is in the context of the Book of the Twelve, where Zephaniah confirms the call of Habakkuk to wait patiently for the salvation of Judah. It also stands on the threshold of the prophecies of Zechariah and Haggai, closely associated with the restoration after the exile. House places Zephaniah at the bottom of a U-pattern in the Twelve, before the ascent in the final three books (Haggai–Malachi; House 1990, p. 151).

FURTHER READING

Items marked with * are considered suitable as first ports of call, while others are more complex, or relate to specific issues.

COMMENTARIES
*D. W. Baker *Nahum, Habakkuk and Zephaniah*. TOTC. Leicester: IVP, 1988.

A. Berlin *Zephaniah*. AB. New York: Doubleday, 1994.

O. P. Robertson *The Books of Nahum, Habakkuk and Zephaniah*. NICOT. Grand Rapids: Eerdmans, 1990.

R. L. Smith *Micah–Malachi*. WBC. Waco: Word Books, 1984.

*J. D. W. Watts *The Books of Joel, Obadiah, Jonah, Nahum, Habakkuk and Zephaniah*. CBC. Cambridge: CUP, 1975.

OTHER BOOKS AND ARTICLES
E. Ben Zvi *A Historical-Critical Study of the Book of Zephaniah*. BZAW 198. Giessen: Töpelmann, 1991.

B. S. Childs *Introduction to the Old Testament as Scripture*. London: SCM, 1979.

M. De Roche 'Zephaniah 1:2-3: The "Sweeping" of Creation' *VT* 30. 1980, pp. 104–09.

S. R. Driver *Introduction to the Literature of the Old Testament*. Edinburgh: T. & T. Clark, 1981.

W. L. Holladay 'Reading Zephaniah with a Concordance: Suggestions for a Redaction History' *JBL* 120. 2001, pp. 671–84.

P. R. House *The Unity of the Twelve*. Sheffield: Almond Press, 1990.

*P. R. House *Zephaniah: a Prophetic Drama*. JSOT Suppl. 69. Sheffield: JSOT Press, 1988.

J. P. Hyatt 'The Date and Background of Zephaniah' *JBL* 7. 1949, pp. 25–9.

A. S. Kapelrud *The Message of the Prophet Zephaniah: Morphology and Ideas*. Oslo: Universitetsforlaget, 1975.

*R. Mason *Zephaniah, Habakkuk, Joel*. OTG. Sheffield: Sheffield Academic Press, 1994.

E. W. Nicholson *Deuteronomy and Tradition*. Oxford: Blackwell, 1967.

J. M. P. Smith, W. H. Ward, J. A. Brewer *Micah, Zephaniah, Nahum, Habakkuk, Obadiah, Joel*. ICC. Edinburgh: T. & T. Clark, 1911.

D. L. Williams 'The Date of Zephaniah' *JBL* 82. 1963, pp. 77–88.

Chapter 15

HAGGAI

DATE AND DESTINATION

The Book of Haggai is one of the prophetic books (with Zechariah and Malachi) that can be dated clearly to the post-exilic period. These three books have in common a concern for the issues facing the people of Judah after the return of the exiles from Babylon, which began in 539 BC. They also share this setting, broadly, with Ezra, Nehemiah and the Books of Chronicles. This period, of course, encompasses several centuries, including the Persian period (539–333 BC) and the Greek (333–63 BC). Each book, therefore, has to be dated separately, and their respective purposes likewise.

However, there are obvious connections between Haggai, Zechariah and the account in Ezra 1—6 of the rebuilding of the Jerusalem temple in the years 520–516 BC. We learn in Ezra 5:1 that these two prophets ministered during that crucial time. The two prophetic books are also linked by a method of dating. (Note the shared pattern of dating in the two books: Hag. 1:1; 2:1; 2:10; 2:20; Zech. 1:1; 1:7; 7:1. See Baldwin 1972, for a table of all the dates in the two books; and see below, Critical Interpretation, for more on the links between them.) Haggai's criticism

of the people's loss of enthusiasm for the rebuilding should be read against the background of the account in Ezra 1—6, which tells of the difficulties put in the way of their attempts.

According to Ezra 3 the returned exiles had begun to rebuild the temple in the second year after the arrival of the first wave sent back by Cyrus, that is, in 538 BC (3:2–3, 8–9). This rebuilding was in one sense a completely new construction, since the former temple had been completely destroyed (2 Kgs 25:9). However, the site of that temple continued to be regarded as holy. During the exile groups of Jews who had not been taken to Babylon apparently continued to make offerings there (Jer. 41:4–5). And the returning exiles did the same, before a stone was laid; the author even refers to the place as 'the house of the LORD', though there was no building (Ezra 2:68). This illustrates the importance attached to the place, and explains the strength of the feeling that it was necessary to rebuild. The return to the historic land of promise should be followed by the re-establishment of the greatest symbol of God's promise.

The Book of Ezra also shows that the first attempt to rebuild was frustrated by local opposition (Ezra 4:4–5). The identity of those opponents is more a matter for the interpretation of Ezra than Haggai (though see the notes below on Hag. 2:10–14), but the opposition explains why, at the beginning of the reign of the Persian king Darius in 522 BC, the task begun sixteen years earlier had not been completed.

The occasion of the rebuilding may be specified further by reference to Ezra 5—6, which records how Darius was prevailed upon to search the imperial records to discover the decree of Cyrus, which had authorized and supported the temple project, and which Darius now implemented. A further issue concerns the elusive figure of Zerubbabel, one of the first returnees, who had led the early attempts to begin the work of rebuilding, along with the priest Joshua/Jeshua (Ezra 3:2). Haggai's language regarding this leader resembles that which was used for a king, especially the Davidic king (Hag. 2:21–23), with the 'signet-ring', and the 'shaking of the heavens and the earth' and 'overthrowing of kingdoms', recalling David's victories in war with Yahweh's help. Did Haggai, therefore, minister at a time when messianic hopes were nourished by the newly returned community, and was his message regarding the temple – symbol of the Davidic covenant – part of such a mission? This reconstruction is possible, and incidentally shows how complex is the relationship between the words we have received in the Book of Haggai and the historical events to which they relate.

However, we do not know enough to be sure quite how the book stands in relation to the course of events. Zerubbabel himself disappeared quietly from the record, and any messianic hopes attached to him died with him. We are not helped in this by any knowledge of the circumstances of Haggai's life. Had he been an exile in Babylon, and thus perhaps encouraged by the vision of Ezekiel? Or was he himself a Jerusalem priest, and thus (perhaps) motivated by the interests of temple and priesthood as institutions? There is no clear evidence (see further below on Rhetorical Intention).

The circumstances of the book may be reconstructed only this far, therefore: Haggai prophesied to the people of Judah in the reign of Darius of Persia, when the project to rebuild was in abeyance yet had received a new opportunity for fulfilment. The external constraints on building have been removed; only the attitude of the people themselves remains a problem. Whether Haggai's preaching is part of a messianic movement is not clear.

CRITICAL INTERPRETATION OF HAGGAI

Critical interpretation has often been concerned with the attempt to relate the texts in the book to historical events. It has been thought that Haggai reports the real beginning of the work on the temple, while Ezra 3—6 has recast events in favour of the first returnees. In that case the first appeal of Haggai, in 1:4, would mean that the temple still lay 'in ruins' exactly as it had since Nebuchadnezzar destroyed it nearly seventy years earlier. The work begun by Zerubbabel and Joshua in the sixth month of the second year of Darius (1:15) would be the laying of the foundations, referred to in 2:18. However, there is no actual account of the laying of the foundations before the continuation in 2:1–9, which assumes that the work is in progress, such that unfavourable comparisons can be made with the glory of the former temple.

It seems, then, that the work taken up in 1:14 is a return to work that had been begun at an earlier stage, as told in Ezra 3. It is not clear if that earlier work required the laying of foundations (Baldwin thinks not; 1972, pp. 52–53). Alternatively, some actual work may have been done before a formal ceremony of rededication (Petersen 1985, p.88–89).

A related issue concerns the interpretation of 2:10–14. This passage appears to intrude into the general argument of the prophecy, with its torah-dialogue on uncleanness. The dialogue culminates in the declaration that 'this people' is unclean (2:14), and discussion of it has focused on the identity of 'this people'. A classic opinion was that it meant the Samaritans, thus echoing the accounts in Ezra and Nehemiah of opposition from Samaria to the re-establishment of Jews in Jerusalem. The beginnings of the schism between Jew and Samaritan, well established in New Testament times, was thought to have its origins here in the exclusion of the latter from the worshipping community in Jerusalem.

However, this is unlikely on two counts. First, it is now recognized that the schism between Jews and Samaritans probably does not have its roots in the events of the first century after the return from Babylon, but later, in the Maccabean period (Coggins 1975, pp. 50–52, 68–72). Second, the continuation in 2:15–19 relates to the people of Jerusalem themselves. This might, of course, be a secondary application. But in the absence of a convincing alternative reading of 2:10–14 there are no grounds to suppose so.

On the final composition of Haggai and Zechariah 1—8 see the panel.

STRUCTURE AND OUTLINE

Haggai may be divided into four main sections, each introduced by a date formula (1:1; 2:1; 2:10; 2:20), giving the times when 'the word of the LORD came to Haggai' (cf. Zech. 1:1; 1:7; 7:1). Within that structure of four main groups of sayings of Yahweh, the prophecy may be further subdivided into units containing separate sayings of Yahweh, interspersed with short narratives. These

---

THE EDITING OF HAGGAI, ZECHARIAH 1—8 AND CHRONICLES

Similarities between Haggai and Chronicles have been pointed out by Mason. They include an emphasis on the presence of Yahweh; the ineffectiveness of human effort without his help; and points of rhetorical style (Mason 1990, pp. 189–90). Mason also sees differences between Haggai and Chronicles, however, since he thinks Haggai's eschatology is foreign to Chronicles (pp. 190–91). So while Haggai *may* have been edited in a 'chronistic milieu', he is also independent in some respects (in this he takes issue with Beuken 1967). It may be more accurate to say that Haggai was edited in a *temple* environment, and that his preaching influenced the kind of preaching that is later found in Chronicles (Mason 1990, pp. 191–95; see also Mason 1977).

Another approach to the editing of Haggai is to stress its similarity with Zechariah 1—8. Meyers and Meyers go so far as to say: 'Haggai and the first eight chapters of the canonical book of Zechariah belong together as a composite work' (1987, p. xliv). They think that this work was written down shortly after its message was proclaimed, and before the rededication of the temple in 515 BC, since that event is not mentioned in the books. Tollington agrees that this combined work was written at about this time, and suggests that Zechariah may have been its author (Tollington 1993, pp. 23, 33–34, 47).

typically take the form of a rhetorical dialogue, in which Yahweh puts questions to the people. The frequent allusions to a new saying of Yahweh give the sense of a conversation, in which we hear in the background the things the people are saying (1:2–6 is the best example). Yahweh generally gives the answers to the rhetorical questions himself, except in one case where answers are given by the priests (2:10–14). In a further case the narrative reports an event, namely the resumption of work on the temple project (1:14–15).

In the pattern of a rhetorical dialogue between Yahweh and his hearers, there are some similarities to Malachi. But the form of dialogue together with narrative insertions is unique to Haggai in the Old Testament. Haggai is spoken of in the third person, not only in the date formulae, but at other times (1:13; 2:13–14). This in itself is not new (Hosea 1; Amos 7:10–13). But here the editorial casting of the prophetic word into a framework seems particularly clear.

STRUCTURE
1:1–15   First exhortation to build the temple
2:1–9   Encouragement to leaders and people
2:10–19   Warning against unclean offerings
2:20–23   A messianic promise

OUTLINE
1:1–15: First exhortation to build the temple
1:1–6 Haggai's recorded prophecy begins in 520 BC, the second year of the Persian King Darius. The first day of the sixth month pinpoints the date to mid-August. The prophecy comes first to the two leaders, Zerubbabel and Joshua, governor and high priest. Though the post-exilic community no longer has a king the prophet still addresses those who wield responsibility. The message comes 'by the hand of Haggai', a usage that

stresses his instrumentality (cf. 2:1, and also the prophet as 'messenger', 1:13; cf. Mal. 1:1).

Verse 2 is introduced by a typical prophetic formula. 'This people' (1:2; rather than 'these people', NIV, NRSV) is a distancing formula (expressly not 'my people'; cf. Isa. 29:13). Yahweh refers to the community in Jerusalem and Judah, and their pretension to understand the times ('the time has not yet come'). His reply (vv. 3–4) is introduced with another prophetic formula, and is ironic (v. 4): they have discerned the times to their own short-term advantage. In becoming obsessed with their prosperity they have failed to see and grasp the significance of the new thing being done in Jerusalem since the restoration of exiles from Babylon. Yet another speech of Yahweh makes an exhortation ('Give careful thought to your ways' NIV), repeated in 1:7, which calls to serious self-examination. (NRSV's 'Consider how you have fared' is a less likely alternative.) Their failure to build the temple has consequences: if the people neglect the purpose of Yahweh in this respect, his purpose to establish a full relationship with them must fail. There is irony in this too; their best efforts to secure their own wealth result only in poverty.

1:7–11 If the previous section focused on the people's concern for their wealth, this one brings the neglect of the temple into sharp focus. With it is connected Yahweh's reputation ('that I may . . . be honoured'), which puts the significance of the rebuilding in the context of international recognition of Yahweh. The lack of prosperity is now couched in terms that remind of the covenantal curses (vv. 10–11, cf. Deut. 28:23–24). But the disruption caused by the people's covenantal failure has implications for the creation (v. 11c is reminiscent of Genesis 1).

1:12–15 We now see the effect of the prophecy on the people, beginning with Zerubbabel and Joshua (cf. 1:1). The 'remnant' of the people is a reference to the whole community, considered a remnant because it has survived the exile, in fulfilment of Isaiah's prophecy (Isa. 7:3; 10:21). Haggai is called the 'messenger of the LORD' (cf. on Mal. 1:1). The prophecy has its effect when Yahweh 'stirs up the spirit of' Zerubbabel, Joshua and all the (remnant of the) people. The date reference in 1:15, just twenty-three days from the time indicated in 1:1, brings ch. 1 full circle from the first introduction of Yahweh's word through Haggai there.

2:1–9: Encouragement to leaders and people

2:1–5 The second main block begins with a new word from Yahweh 'by the hand of Haggai' dated to early October 520 BC, almost a month after the work began. The recipients are again Zerubbabel, Joshua and all the 'remnant' (as in 1:12). The tone of the oracle now shifts to encouragement, with a threefold command to 'take courage' (v. 4).

Think about
ECHOES OF THE PAST

When Haggai encourages the people, he uses language that makes them think of what God did in the past. With vv. 4–5 compare Deut. 1:21, 29; 31:6; Josh. 1:6, 7, 9, 18, and also Exod. 3:12. What elements of those passages are present here? Note also the reference to the exodus from Egypt in v. 5. What effect do you think these echoes of the past are intended to have on the hearers?

What prompts this word is the unpromising look of the new temple in its early stages. The grief of those who could compare it with the old temple is also mentioned in Ezra 3:12. The reality, however, is greater than the appearance; Yahweh is in the work, and therefore his people will be brought into their inheritance.

2:6–9 A new word continues the encouraging tone with language that expresses Yahweh's power over all the earth, both the natural order and the nations. The rebuilding of the temple can happen because Yahweh can effect his will, even causing the nations to give up their wealth. There are echoes here of the foreign wealth that Solomon could command for the first construction (1 Kgs 5), and also of the provision of the Persian Kings Cyrus and Darius for the new one (Ezra 1:1; 6:4–8), which is portrayed as an act of Yahweh, who caused them to act in this way. The new temple will actually surpass the old. The term 'place' (v. 9) is a way of referring to Jerusalem as Yahweh's dwelling-place. And the establishment of 'peace' there (*shalom*, NIV, otherwise 'prosperity', NRSV) recalls King David's establishment of 'rest from enemies' and thus his independent rule (2 Sam. 7:1).

2:10–19: Warning against unclean offerings

2:10–14 A new oracle, on the twenty-fourth of the ninth month (in December), takes a step back from the underlying progression of the vision, in order to portray the difference between Judah as it had been, in its neglect of the temple, and the new blessing that has come as a result of its new devotion (vv. 15–19). 'This people', v. 14, therefore, refers to the people of Judah, just as it does in 1:2. The rhetorical dialogue between Haggai and the priests about causes of ritual uncleanness intends to characterize Judah as 'unclean'. The metaphor is appropriate in view of their neglect of the proper worship.

RHETORICAL INTENTION

In the preceding we have seen that the book of Haggai has been understood differently by different scholars. An identification of the theological themes in themselves still leaves the question of how they were made to serve the immediate purpose of the book. Is the temple to be viewed as a symbol of Yahweh's fulfilment of his promise, and thus the overthrow of enemies? Or has it been taken over by the 'hierocratic' party (in Hanson's terms), and is it therefore a symbol of acceptance of the Persian settlement, as promoted by those who held religious power in Judah? The task of interpretation is to try to match the themes to the situation. This is difficult, because even the broad outlines of the post-exilic situation are disputed, as is the setting of the book in its final form.

I have suggested, in the interpretation so far, that Haggai looked for further deliverance and restoration. His interest in the temple and the messianic hopes associated with Zerubbabel amounts to Davidic–Zion symbolism, with its power to express hope for a yet future fulfilment of the dynastic promise to David. Admittedly we read between the lines here. Coggins, noting the evidence concerning Zerubbabel, says: 'We should note that there is no direct suggestion that Zerubbabel will have "royal" or "messianic" status of a precisely defined kind; the people were under a Persian king' (Coggins 1996, pp. 35–36).

This, of course, is the debatable point; did the symbols drawn from the sphere of king and temple pose a challenge to the prevailing political situation, in which Judah was ruled by Persia? Or did they merely affirm in a general way that Yahweh was still with the community? The former seems more probable to me (because of the prominence of Zerubbabel, and especially the closing word to him). And therefore the book is best understood as being in the spirit of the prayer of Ezra in Neh. 9:32–36; it is even a step on the way to the apocalyptic vision of Daniel 7, with its succession of empires giving way finally to God's kingdom.

The message is by no means triumphalist, however. This is clear from the rhetorical style, by which the people are shaken out of complacency, in ways that leave no doubt that there is an open issue: will they be faithful and so enjoy the blessings of Yahweh? If there is promise here, it comes without the demand that the people discern the time and respond to it. Haggai continues from older prophecy in his sharp address to the people, calling them to recognize their failures, and their danger of falling from Yahweh's way. The phrase 'this people' (2:14) carries the warning that they could cease to be 'my people'. The rhetorical dialogue persuasively involves the listeners, drawing them into seeing things anew from Yahweh's perspective. The temple does symbolize Yahweh's commitment to them; but they must be as good as their ancestors and build it, as a sign of their response to their covenant calling.

HAGGAI IN THE CANON

How, finally, do we understand the hopes placed in Zerubbabel, in view of the fact that those particular hopes (evidently) came to nought? As a matter of historical interpretation one must admit that those hopes were disappointed. In Carroll's terms, 'prophecy failed' (1979, note pp. 157–58.)

Prophets, of course, were readers both of their times, and of the mind of God. And

'COGNITIVE DISSONANCE'

Carroll's term 'cognitive dissonance' is drawn from social psychology. It refers to the need for consistency between people's expectations (based on a whole range of factors) and their actual experience. 'Dissonance' occurs when there is a discrepancy between expectation and experience. Carroll thinks the prophets offer a good example of attempts to resolve dissonance. A particular kind of dissonance arose when prophecies were not fulfilled. Carroll uses Haggai and Zechariah as case studies of how unfulfilled prophecies could be appropriated in new ways in order to resolve the problem of dissonance.

For his analysis of 'cognitive dissonance', and its application to the prophets, see Carroll 1979, pp. 86–128 and, for Haggai and Zechariah, pp. 157–83.

with hindsight it seems that they were more likely to be right about the divine intentions than about the ways in which they would be fulfilled. As Ezekiel's temple was never built so Zerubbabel was never king in Judah. Yet in urging his fellow-Jews to build the temple he was nevertheless right in declaring that Yahweh would still be faithful to his chosen people. If prophets constantly made adjustments to their thinking about the divine salvation, this may not be clever manipulation so much as a conviction that he would be true to his promises.

In its setting among the Old Testament's prophetic books, Haggai reasserts the 'final' message of promise, that is, beyond judgement there is grace – a message enshrined within some of the larger books, but reiterated here to the community at a critical time. In its wider biblical setting Haggai points to the unlimited commitment of God to be with his people, to their need to trust

him in dark times, and to the call to a public obedience that demonstrates faith and subordinates the demands of self-interest.

FURTHER READING

Items marked with * are considered suitable as first ports of call, while others are more complex, or relate to specific issues.

COMMENTARIES
*J. G. Baldwin *Haggai, Zechariah, Malachi*. TOTC. Leicester: IVP, 1972.

C. L. Meyers and E. M. Meyers *Haggai, Zechariah 1—8*. AB. New York: Doubleday, 1987.

*D. L. Petersen *Haggai and Zechariah 1—8*. OTL. London: SCM, 1985.

P. Redditt *Haggai, Zechariah, Malachi*. NCB. London: Marshall Pickering; Grand Rapids: Eerdmans, 1995.

R. L. Smith *Micah–Malachi*. WBC. Waco TX: Word Books, 1984.

P. A. Verhoef *The Books of Haggai and Malachi*. NICOT. Grand Rapids: Eerdmans, 1987.

OTHER BOOKS AND ARTICLES
P. R. Ackroyd *Exile and Restoration: a Study of Hebrew Thought in the Sixth Century BC*. London: SCM, 1968.

W. A. M. Beuken *Haggai–Sacharja 1—8*. Assen: Van Gorcum, 1967.

R. P. Carroll *When Prophecy Failed: Reactions and Responses to Failure in the Old Testament Prophetic Traditions*. London: SCM, 1979.

*R. J. Coggins *Haggai, Zechariah, Malachi*. OTG. Sheffield: Sheffield Academic Press, 1987 repr. 1996.

R. J. Coggins *Samaritans and Jews*. Oxford: Blackwell, 1975.

P. D. Hanson *The Dawn of Apocalyptic: the Historical and Social Roots of Jewish Apocalyptic Eschatology*. Philadelphia: Fortress, 1979, revised edition.

R. A. Mason 'The Purpose of the "Editorial Framework" of the Book of Haggai' *VT* 27. 1977, pp. 413–21.

R. A. Mason *Preaching the Tradition: Homily and Hermeneutics After the Exile*. Cambridge: CUP, 1990.

Chapter 16

ZECHARIAH

DATE AND DESTINATION

The book of Zechariah is widely held to fall into two distinct parts (chs 1—8, 9—14), coming from different times. (We will say more about this under chs 9—14, and also in Critical Interpretation.) At this stage, we take each in turn.

ZECHARIAH 1—8
Clues to the time of the prophecy are given by several dates early in the reign of the

Persian King Darius I (522–486 BC): October 520 BC (1:1), 15 February 519 BC (1:7), 7 December 518 BC (7:1). These are very close to the dates in Haggai, and indeed the two books are linked by the method of dating (see Baldwin 1972, p. 29, for a table of all the dates in the two books; see also Haggai: Date and Destination). The period is around twenty years after the decree of King Cyrus, which allowed exiles to begin returning to Judah, and shortly before the rebuilding of the temple (516 BC), which was

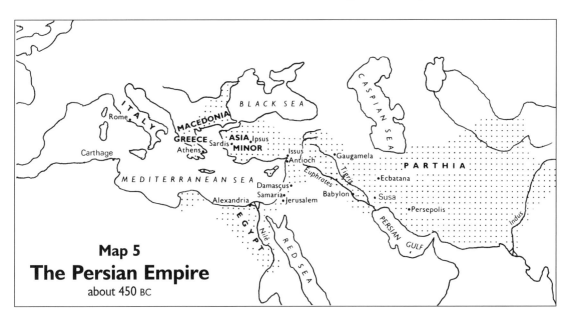

Map 5
The Persian Empire
about 450 BC

also the main issue in Haggai. Haggai and Zechariah are named in the Book of Ezra as the two prophets who encouraged the returned exiles to complete that rebuilding (Ezra 5:1–2). Their books have in common with Chronicles–Ezra–Nehemiah that they look back on the exile as a past event (2 Chr. 36:17–23; Ezra 1:1–4), and now look forward to what God is going to do in the new era of salvation. Zechariah himself may have been the 'son of Iddo' named in Neh. 12:16, and therefore of a priestly family. His name means 'Yahweh has remembered', and this chimes in well with his message that Yahweh is fulfilling his former promises.

The date in 1:7 seems to imply that all the visions came to Zechariah at one time. Taken by themselves they look as if they could have come at different times. For example, the first vision (1:7–11) is set at the end of the seventy years of exile (1:12), while the eighth (6:1–8) refers to the pouring out of the spirit on the exiles while still in exile. Some scholars have thought that the event or situation referred to within the dream or vision was a clue to the date of the vision itself. (Childs accepts the theory of Galling on this, though he is more interested, as always, in the interpretation of the text as such; Childs 1979, p. 477.) But this is not necessarily so. The situation of the one who had the visions could be quite different from the situations portrayed in them. It is not impossible that the visions might have been experienced as a unified sequence. (Petersen refers to research on dream-behaviour in this connection; 1985, pp. 111–12.)

This means, at least, that it will be more useful to focus on the way in which the visions function as a whole in the theology of the Book of Zechariah. Their effect is to show that God has fulfilled his former

promises, and they are a kind of review of those promises. The point of view of the visions as a whole is that the exile is in the past, and the time of salvation is near. (The fourth vision, 3:1–10, is a special case, to which we shall return in Critical Interpretation of Zechariah.)

The aim of chs 1—8 is to encourage the returned exiles to go on believing that God was at work in the community, and that he really was fulfilling the promises made by the prophets who had foretold the return from exile. His awareness of former prophecy is clear from the following:

i. Jeremiah's prophesied seventy-year exile (1:12; Jer. 25:11–12) is now in the past;

ii. 'the north' (2:6) is the place from which the destroying 'foe' first came, Jer. 4:6; 6:1;

iii. Zech. 1:6–12 has echoes of the salvation-promises in Isaiah 40—55;

iv. the 'measuring-line' of 1:16 recalls the same metaphor which plots the movement from judgement to salvation in Isa. 34:11, 17;

v. in Zech. 3:8 the phrase 'my servant, the Branch' (cf. 6:12) recalls the 'servant' in Isaiah 40—55 and also the promises of a king in Jer. 23:5; 33:15; Isa. 11:1;

vi. the vision-form itself has strong resemblances to Ezekiel (see Critical Interpretation of Zechariah). The motif of 'measuring Jerusalem' is shared with Ezekiel; Zech. 2:2 [6]; Ezek. 40:3.

The message has a note of caution too, because the 'former prophets' are also remembered as the ones who preached that Israel should obey God in truth (7:7, 8–10). Previous generations had refused to listen, and so were punished (7:11–14). All this is made a warning to the new generation, rather as the writers of Deuteronomy and the Historical Books made the past sins of Israel a basis for their exhortations to obey (e.g. Deuteronomy 32; 2 Kings 17; cf. also Ezekiel 20).

The first audience of Zechariah 1—8, then, was the people who had returned from Babylon, in the time between the beginning and the completion of re-building the temple (4:9). This is also suggested by Ezra 5:1–2. As Ezra implies, they may have been discouraged that the return had been hard, and not triumphant and glorious, as prophecies of return had suggested (Isaiah 40—55; Jeremiah 30—31; Ezek. 34:23–31). Zechariah's allusion to a 'day of small things' (4:10) could have this in mind.

It is possible that the people harboured 'messianic' hopes of a restored Davidic king, who would lead them into a time of victory and prosperity. This would be quite natural, in view of prophecies like Isa. 9:2–7 [1–6]; 11:1–9; Jer. 23:5–6; Ezek. 34:23–24. Royal messianic language is used in key texts in Zechariah (Zech. 3:8; 6:12–13, cf. Isa. 11:1; Jer. 23:5 – this is one of those echoes of former prophecies that we noticed above). It is often thought that Zerubbabel was the focus of these hopes. Zerubbabel was of royal descent, and it was he who had given a lead in rebuilding the temple, along with Joshua the priest (cf. Hag. 2:23, and see Haggai: Zerubbabel as messiah?). The Zechariah texts are difficult, however, and do not name Zerubbabel (though he is named in 4:7–10; see comment on the texts themselves). So if the royal messianism was a feature of Zechariah's preaching, it has been given a back seat in the shaping of the book.

We have already noticed the theory of Hanson, who regards Zechariah in chs 1—8

(with Haggai) as a conservative supporter of the priestly hierarchy in Jerusalem (1979, pp. 240–62; see Haggai: Theological Themes: The temple). Hanson thinks the voice of the visionary eschatological group, which he sees as marginalized in the community's religious life, is heard in Zechariah 9—14. But in chs 1—8 the prophet uses the visionary form in order to support the religious establishment against such eschatological expectation.

Hanson's interpretation of Zechariah 1—8 is probably over-subtle. It involves supposing that the author borrows the clothes of the opposition (i.e. symbolic visions). And it overstates the 'conservative', pro-Jerusalem stance of the visions. In fact Zechariah is in line with the expectations of earlier prophets about a restored Jerusalem. That is, it would be a place where Yahweh would be truly present (2:5 [9]); it would be inhabited by nations other than the Jews (Zech. 2:11 foresees nations joining the returning exiles to worship in Jerusalem, rather like Isa. 2:2–4); Yahweh's rule would extend over the whole earth [Zech.4:14; 5:3] cf. Ezekiel 38—39, Joel 3 [4]). (See also Coggins 1996, pp. 52–57, and Carroll 1979, for fuller critique.) So it is not certain that Zechariah 1—8 can be evidence for a division within the post-exilic community some time after the restoration.

ZECHARIAH 9—14

These chapters strike the reader immediately as different from chs 1—8, so much so that they are widely regarded as having a different origin and setting from those chapters. This latter part of the book is often called Deutero–Zechariah. The vision-form of chs 1—6 is absent, as are the time-indications (as in 1:1; 1:7; 7:1). The first-person narrative that held chs 1—8 together is limited here to 11:4–17. And the idea of the restoration of Jerusalem has receded. Differences of style and vocabulary have also been observed (Coggins 1996, p. 62).

The section falls into two further sub-sections, chs 9—11 and 12—14, each headed by the term 'An Oracle' (literally 'burden'; as in Nah. 1:1; Mal. 1:1, and in Isaiah's Oracles Against the Nations, Isa. 13:1 etc.). The contents of these sub-sections are different from each other. Chapters 9—11 are very like pre-exilic prophecy, because of:

 i. the references to both Israel and Judah (10:6);
 ii. the references to Assyria and Egypt (10:10–11), and other nations that were hostile to Israel and Judah in those times (Syria, Tyre, Philistia, 9:1–8);
 iii. the expectation of a king who would deliver from enemies and establish peace (9:9–10); this is similar to the messianic prophecies of Isa. 9:2–7 [1–6]; 11:1–9;
 iv. the poetic oracular form of 9:1—11:3.

In these chapters promises of salvation predominate (as in Isaiah 40—55), but there are notes of judgement too, in 10:2–3, and especially in 11:4–17. This passage tells of symbolic actions (like Jeremiah's breaking of pots, Jeremiah 18—19, or Isaiah's walking naked, Isa. 20:2; see Ezekiel: Prophetic symbolic actions).

Chapters 12—14 tell of the final victory of God, as the divine warrior (12:8), over the nations, and his vindication of Jerusalem. The images of this conflict are unnatural, and go beyond ordinary military victories (14:4). The universality and the extravagant imagery show that the reference is to an eschatological victory, not just an immediate deliverance from some crisis. Between the two main pictures of final conflict (12:1–9; 14) lies a section in which Jerusalem is portrayed as mourning in penitence, and being cleansed of sin (12:11—13:9). In this way the final victory goes hand in hand with a purification of Jerusalem, so that only a remnant will enjoy the fruits of the victory (14:2, 16).

Unlike chs 1—8, there is no clear indication of a particular setting for this diverse material. The former chapters seemed to want to encourage belief that God had delivered Judah, and to encourage the people to take certain steps towards establishing the community on the right lines. Chapters 9—14, with their need for cleansing and talk of a remnant, and their vision of apocalyptic victory, could address a rather more critical situation. This might have been the mid-fifth century BC, during the conflict between Persia and Greece, which could have affected the Judean community adversely (the theory of Meyers and Meyers 1993, pp. 26–28).

What this setting was is hard to identify. The fact that chs 9—14 are attached to chs 1—8 in itself suggests a post-exilic setting. The mention of Greece (Javan) in 9:13 may indicate this also, since most other references to it are in texts that are usually regarded as late (e.g. Gen. 10:2; Isa. 66:19; Ezek. 27:13; 1 Chr. 1:5; Dan. 8:21; 10:20; 11:2). Because of it, some scholars have thought Zechariah 9—14 came from as late as the Maccabean period (second century BC). But this allusion in itself is hardly decisive. It could in any case be a late gloss on an earlier text.

One further feature must be mentioned, however. Mason has pointed out that Zechariah 9—14 is different from older prophecy, because it consciously interprets it (e.g. 1977, p. 79). The clearest example is Zech. 13:5, which has an obvious echo of

Amos 7:14, but is used in a quite different way. Other examples are 12:2 (cf. Jer. 25:15–16); 11:4–17 (Ezek. 37:15–28). And we have already noticed ways in which chs 9—11 resemble pre-exilic prophecy.

If this observation is applied to other parts of the section, it is possible to read them as re-applications to contemporary events. For example, 9:1–8 may be a conscious re-application of an older saying, such as Ezekiel's oracle against Tyre in Ezekiel 28 (notice the common theme of pride). If Mason is right, chs 9—14 are close to Daniel 9, in which the author is aware of the prophetic books as a body of literature already in existence (Dan. 9:2). They would then be a kind of 'exegetical' form, and this could be seen as a development that took place well into the post-exilic period.

However, we cannot fix the date of chs 9—14 exactly. Formal features, like the ones we have just noticed, can take us so far. But there is no graph on which we can plot the development from pre-exilic prophetic forms to late ones. So even if it is true that Zechariah's view of prophecy is similar to that which we find in Daniel, we have no way of knowing how close in time to Daniel it must be placed. Indeed, we have already seen that there is conscious use of former prophecy in chs 1—8 also (note 7:7). This is actually one of the features that unites the parts of Zechariah rather than separating them.

CRITICAL INTERPRETATION OF ZECHARIAH

ZECHARIAH 1—8

We have met visions before in the prophets (Amos 7:19; 8:1–3; Isaiah 6; Jer. 1:11–19; 24; 1 Kgs 22:19–22). Some prophecies are even described as 'visions' (Isa. 1:1; Amos 1:1; Obad. 1:1). In Ezekiel it was prominent as a means of God's communication to the prophet (especially chs 8—11; 40—48). Prophetic visions come in several forms. The simplest are single images like Jeremiah's almond branch (Jer. 1:11–12) or Amos's basket of summer fruit (Amos 8:1–2), which receive brief explanations from God. A second sort is the vision of the heavenly throne and council (Isaiah 6 and 1 Kgs 22:19–22). In Ezekiel and Zechariah we find a more developed form, in which an angelic messenger leads the prophet through the visions. This feature is also shared with Daniel. Zechariah is closer to Daniel in one respect: that the angel goes beyond merely showing the visions. Instead, the prophet asks questions, and the angel gives explanations (Zech. 1:18–21 [2:1–4]; Dan. 10:15–21). This is one of the characteristics of 'apocalyptic' (see Daniel: Apocalyptic). (See also Niditch 1983, for the view that Zechariah comes at a transitional stage between pre-exilic prophetic vision and apocalyptic visions; cf. Coggins 1996, pp. 42–43, citing North 1972; and Collins 1984, p. 20).

Scholars sometimes suppose that Zechariah stands within a special 'vision'-tradition of prophecy. For example, Coggins contrasts Haggai, who is a speaker, with Zechariah, who is a see-er (1996, pp. 40–41; he qualifies this by saying the distinctions are not absolute). But Zechariah is not bound within such a tradition. We have noticed already that Zechariah looks back consciously on a range of prophecy, and this suggests he has some freedom in his choice of form. Therefore Zechariah cannot be used to chart a development in the vision-form. (In any case we have seen that the distinction often made between 'speaking' and 'seeing' as modes of prophecy is over-pressed; see

Amos: Outline: What do names tell us about the prophets?)

ZECHARIAH 1—8 AND 9—14

We have seen that these sections are often thought to have been originally independent of each other. One reason is the differences between them that we have already noticed (Date and Destination). Another is that Zechariah 1—8 is closely linked with Haggai, so much so that Haggai–Zechariah 1—8 have been regarded as originally a unified work (see Haggai: Critical Interpretation: The editing of Haggai, Zechariah 1-8 and Chronicles). Zechariah 9—14 will therefore have had its own history. Person (1993) has suggested that this work was composed in deuteronomistic circles. Meyers and Meyers qualify this heavily, pointing to the links between Zechariah 9—14 and a wide range of other biblical literature (Meyers and Meyers 1993, p. 39–45).

If Haggai–Zechariah 1—8 was originally a unified work, this must mean that at some point the two parts of it became separated, and Zechariah 1—8 joined, perhaps at a later stage, to chs 9—14 (Person 1993, p. 140, n. 1). When this might have happened depends on when Zechariah 9—14 is dated. The combination of chs 9—14 with Zechariah 1—8 could be attributed to the authors of chs 9—14 themselves, who may have seen themselves in a tradition going back to Zechariah (Meyers and Meyers 1993, pp. 27–28).

In spite of the differences between the two parts of the book of Zechariah, they have the following features in common (partly following Smith 1984, p. 242):

  i. eschatological and apocalyptic tendencies. The visions of chs 1—8 and the images of a great final conflict in chs 12—14 are both at home in the thought-world of apocalyptic. Chapters 9—14 can be seen as a development of chs 1—8 for this reason. An important argument for this was made by Gese in a German article (see Coggins 1996, pp. 65–66);
 ii. salvation of Jerusalem (1:12–16; 9:9–10; 12; 14);
iii. return of exiles (8:7; 10:9–12);
 iv. cleansing (3:1–9; 5:1–11; 12:10—13:2);
  v. salvation of the nations (2:18, 20–23; 9:10; 14:16–19);
 vi. the conscious use of older prophecy (as we have already seen).

To these may be added (with Childs):

 vii. a renewed paradisal fertility (8:12; 14:6, 8);
viii. a renewed covenant (8:8; 13:9);
 ix. the outpouring of the spirit (4:6; 12:10);
  x. a messiah who triumphs in humility (3:8; 4:6; 9:9–10) (Childs 1979, pp. 482–83).

Because of the uncertainty in dating each main section, it is impossible to be sure how the two came to belong together – or indeed that they really did have separate existences. (For an argument for unity, based on similarities of the sort noted above, see Baldwin 1972, pp. 60–70.)

STRUCTURE AND OUTLINE

STRUCTURE

On structure, little needs to be added to what has been said above. The basic division (chs 1—8, 9—14) may be refined slightly, as follows:

1:1–6	Israel's past sins, and Yahweh's judgement
1:7—6:8	Eight visions
6:9–15	Joshua crowned, but the 'Branch' is king

244

OUTLINE

1:1–6: Israel's past sins, and Yahweh's judgement

The unusual opening places Zechariah's first word in 520 BC (see also Date and Destination). The return from Babylon, begun in 539 BC, is well established, but still recent. Zechariah carefully places the returned community in relation to the former generations of Israel and Judah, who had rebelled against Yahweh and who had been punished by the exile. The language he uses contains allusions to the prophetic message. The leading idea is 'return', or 'repent'. Prophets had called for repentance (Jer. 4:1–2). When the judgement of exile became inevitable they knew that the way back after it would also be by repentance (Jer. 3:14; 31:18; cf. Deut. 30:1–5).

Zechariah is declaring that the sin, the

Digging deeper:
WHO 'REPENTED' (V. 6)?

I have suggested that the repentance in v. 6 means the repentance of the exiles, which was the requirement of restoration (according to Deut. 30:1–5). Verse 6b could be taken in different ways, however. Compare the interpretations in Meyers and Meyers 1987, p. 96; Baldwin 1972, pp. 91–92; Redditt 1995, pp. 50–51; Smith 1984, pp. 126–27. Notice how Meyers and Meyers' interpretation fits with their overall interpretation of Haggai–Zechariah 1—8. Notice how some external factor is often brought to bear on exegesis of individual texts.

punishment and the repentance needed for restoration (v. 6b) are in the past; the time has come for the restored community to live again in covenant with God according to his promises.

1:7—6:8: Eight Visions

1:7–17 The First Vision is dated to the twenty-fourth day of the eleventh month of Darius's second year (v. 7). The date applies to all the visions. This is three months after the first prophecy (1:1), but more importantly, it is exactly five months after Zerubbabel began work on the rebuilding of the temple (Hag. 1:15). This timing is important to our understanding of the visions, as the promises of salvation seem to be associated with the call to rebuild (cf. 4:9–10).

The vision has both the symbolism and the angelic messenger that we know from the apocalyptic visions of Daniel (Daniel 8; 10). The figures in the vision are the horses, the man riding the red horse (presumably the other horses have riders too, though this is not said), the angel who speaks with Zechariah (v. 9 = the 'angel of the LORD', v. 12), a man who is standing among the myrtle trees (v. 10). The confusion can be lessened if we suppose that these last three figures are the same person (Smith 1984, pp. 189–90).

The horses (or horsemen) who patrol the earth represent Yahweh's power over the whole world. (There may be four horses, if one of each colour is meant in v. 8, and because of the 'four winds of heaven' in the final vision, 6:5, but the number is not specified.) In the conversation between the angel and Yahweh, the angel asks, in a 'lament' form (v. 12), how long Judah's punishment must last, and refers to the seventy-year length of the exile foretold by

Jeremiah (Jer. 25:11–12). The point of this conversation is to show – like the opening verses of the chapter (1:1–6) – that the time of punishment for Judah is past, and that Yahweh now intends to put his promised salvation into effect.

Yahweh's 'compassion' (v. 16) is a feature of his salvation after exile (Deut. 30:3). His 'returning' to Judah recalls 1:3, and perhaps the vision of his return to the temple in Ezek. 43:1–5.

THE 'JEALOUS' GOD

God describes himself here as 'jealous' for Jerusalem (v. 14; again in 8:2). His 'jealousy' is his determined attachment to his chosen people. The idea also occurs in the Ten Commandments, that is, at the giving of the covenant with Israel in Moses' time; Exod. 20:5. In that key text, it is used to express his readiness to punish his own people if they break the covenant by worshipping other gods. The common factor between the Exodus and Zechariah texts is Israel's special belonging to him. Both the Exodus context and Zechariah's message as a whole have both effects of God's jealousy: to keep the people faithful, and to save them. See also Baldwin 1972, pp. 101–03.

1:18–21 [2:1–4] The Second Vision uses the image of 'horns', that we meet also in Daniel (Dan. 7:7–8; 8:5–10). It signifies the power and ferocity of conquerors (cf. also Deut. 33:17).

2:1–13 [5–17] The Third Vision. The measuring of Jerusalem for its rebuilding is a reference to Ezekiel (Ezek. 40:3). The promise of rebuilding is again revealed by an angel, this time in conversation with another angel (cf. Dan. 7:16). The image of an unwalled Jerusalem (2:4 [8]) is true to the facts in 519 BC, since the walls were not rebuilt until the middle of the next century by Nehemiah. Yahweh himself will be its walls (v. 5 [9], cf. Isa. 60:18). The command to return from 'the north' puts into reverse the scattering by a foe from the north (Jer. 4:6; 6:1). The command to flee Babylon also echoes Second Isaiah (cf. Isa. 49:8–12). The oppressor shall be punished in turn (v. 9 [14]), a common theme of older prophecy (Isa. 10:12–19; Jeremiah 50—51). Yahweh will again dwell among his people, and 'choose' Jerusalem. This picks up central themes from the Zion-theology (see Isaiah: Theological Themes). With the judgement on false interpretations of this now in the past, those themes can be reasserted (as was the case also in Jeremiah 30—33, especially 33:14–26, and Ezekiel 34—48).

3:1–10 The Fourth Vision. This vision has often been regarded as unoriginal in the sequence of visions, because it is so different from the others. The angel's role is only to show the scene (3:1), which concerns one of the leading figures of the restoration period, the high priest Joshua (cf. Hag. 2:2). However, the vision is still a vision of heaven. Zechariah sees the 'divine council', that is, the assembly around Yahweh in heaven, though Yahweh himself is not part of the vision. (For visions of God in heaven, see Isaiah 6; 1 Kgs 22:19–22; cf. Job 1.) The 'angel of Yahweh' presides, the 'Satan' (the Accuser) prosecutes, and Joshua is in the role of defendant (Petersen 1985, p. 191).

The changing of clothes is a feature of both the investiture of priests (Exodus 29) and on the Day of Atonement (Leviticus 16). So there is a correspondence between those events and this vision. However, the point of the vision is not to show the investiture of Joshua in his role as high priest (since he is

246

already named as such, v. 1), but to picture the ritual cleansing of the community symbolically in his cleansing. This is probably implied by the singling out of the 'turban' as the only item of high-priestly clothing that is actually named (cf. Exod. 28:36–38). This may be necessary because the normal temple rituals have not yet been re-established (Petersen 1985, pp. 199–201). Joshua seems to have access to the divine council itself (3:7).

The vision goes on to proclaim the coming of the messianic figure, who is called 'my servant' (cf. Isa. 42:1) and 'the Branch' (cf. Jer. 23:5), as a further sign of the age of salvation about to come (v. 8b). These hopes were probably pinned on Zerubbabel (cf. Hag. 2:23). The vision concludes with a further declaration of cleansing from sin (v. 9), and a paradisal picture (v. 10).

4:1–14 The Fifth Vision. Zechariah sees a lampstand with seven lamps, and two olive-trees beside it. The lampstand reminds of the lampstand in the tabernacle (Exod. 25:31–40), but is simpler. The angel explains the meaning of the lampstand by saying that Zerubbabel will indeed complete the temple that he has begun (vv. 8–10). In doing so he fulfils the role of the Davidic king (like Solomon). This seems to counter a sense of dismay, or even opposition (the 'great mountain') because of the poor progress, or the disappointing state, of the returned community. God is working by his spirit in it (vv. 6–7).

The olive-trees symbolize the supply of oil to the lamp. They are interpreted as 'two anointed ones (literally, "sons of oil") who stand by (or serve) the Lord of the whole earth' (4:14). This probably refers to leaders of the community, namely Joshua and

Zerubbabel. They stand, as it were, to the right and left of Yahweh himself, as if in the divine council. The picture establishes the dual human leadership of the community. The picture implies that the divine presence (the lamp) is fed by the human figures. Verse 12 looks like an addition, giving a different understanding (here the olive trees do not represent human figures, and the idea is of Yahweh supplying life to Israel).

5:1–4 The Sixth Vision. The flying scroll with written curses represents covenantal curses. The two sins picked out here may simply represent the whole range of possible breaches of covenant, or they may have been particular problems in the community at the time. The overriding point is, however, that above and beyond the human authorities of Joshua and Zerubbabel lies the authority of Yahweh, who finally establishes justice and order by his power over the whole earth.

5:5–11 The Seventh Vision. The 'ephah' in the vision is a kind of measure. It is not necessarily a 'basket', as some translations have it, trying to envisage how it could be big enough for a woman to be in it. In the world of the visions the pictures need not be rational. There seems to be no special reason why the evil should be taken away by a woman or women. The picture symbolizes the guilt and wickedness of Judah, which is being sent away to the land of 'Shinar' (the area of Babylon). This contributes to the purification of the land. There is also a balance in it. As exiles return from Babylon to the land, so the evil in the community is exported there, perhaps also signifying that Babylon was now under God's judgement.

6:1–8 The Eighth Vision. The final vision has similarities with the first, but also important differences (Petersen sets these out; 1985, p. 269). The horse-drawn chariots are coming out from God's presence (represented by the two mountains), to patrol the whole earth. The colours of the horses are given no significance here (but see Rev. 6:1–8). The vision declares that God's spirit is at rest 'in the north country'. This seems to contrast with 1:11–12. Justice has now been established in the whole earth.

6:9–15: Joshua crowned, but the 'Branch' is king

The real topic of this passage is the relationship between Joshua, the high priest, and Zerubbabel, 'the Branch'. The crowning of Joshua is probably not the act that makes him high priest, but is a symbolic action to put him in his place in relation to 'the Branch'. ('Crown' in v. 11 is literally 'crowns'. It is usually changed to smooth the sense of the verse, but the plural perhaps refers to crowns for both Joshua and Zerubbabel. Petersen translates: 'make crowns, and set (one) on the head of Joshua'; p. 272.) It is the Branch (not the priest) who will build the temple (as in 4:9). He will be king, and a priest by his side. The crown in v. 14 (again literally plural) is to be kept as a memorial. Zerubbabel will be helped to build the temple by returning exiles.

7:1—8:23: Covenant renewed – and call to true obedience

7:1–14 We turn from visions back to the narrative line begun at 1:1, with a date (7 December 518 BC) two years after Zechariah's ministry began. A delegation comes to Jerusalem to seek an authoritative answer from the priests at the temple about certain fasts (v. 5). These were presumably observed in lamentation for the destroyed temple (the 'seventy years' is a reference to the period of exile; cf. 1:12). As the seventy-year period may now be regarded as over, the question about the need for the fasts has arisen.

The delegation may have come from Babylon. This involves reading v. 2, not as NRSV, NIV ('the people of Bethel sent'), but 'Bethel-Sharezer sent Regem-melech and his men' (cf. Baldwin 1972, p. 142–43; and, slightly differently, Petersen 1985, p. 281). This means the delegation has come from Jews who are still in Babylon.

Zechariah responds to the delegation with two oracles criticizing false fasting and insisting on true obedience. And he explains that the exile had come because of such disobedience. The thought of these verses is like Isa. 58:1–9a, and also recalls the opening passage in the prophecy (1:1–6).

8:1–23 The sayings given to Zechariah in this chapter turn from past judgement to the future salvation of Jerusalem (again rather like the turn that happens in ch. 1, between vv. 1–6 and the visions that follow). Verses 1–14 have been seen as 'sermons', based on other sayings of Zechariah himself (Tollington 1993, pp. 27–30). Yahweh speaks of his 'jealousy' for Zion, and this is the reason why he will save it (v. 1, cf. 1:14–17, and see note there). Jerusalem will be filled with people of all ages (vv. 4–8), though this may still seem impossible to the few who have returned (cf. Jer. 32:17).

The community will not merely survive, but be blessed, because Yahweh has now decided to save rather than punish (vv. 9–14). Even so, he still requires obedience (vv. 14–17). The question of fasting is now answered: the fasts shall be times of rejoicing (vv. 18–19). A final passage foresees people not only of Judah but of other nations coming to worship at Jerusalem (vv. 20–23).

9:1—11:17: A coming king, and salvation for Israel and Judah

9:1–8 In the second major part of the book, the theme of the salvation of Judah continues. Zech. 9:1—11:17 as a whole is headed by the title 'A Burden' (see Date and Destination). This opening passage has the form of an Oracle against Nations, in this case Syria, Tyre and Philistia. Yahweh will bring down the pride of Tyre (cf. Ezekiel 28). Philistia, after judgement, unexpectedly receives a promise, for it will become 'a remnant for our God', 'like a clan in Judah' (v. 7). This is part of Yahweh's purpose to restore his temple (v. 8).

9:9–10 After the conquest of enemies (vv. 1–8), this best-known part of Zechariah 9—14 pictures the victorious coming of a king to Jerusalem. His victory in war and making peace draws on the themes of the Zion-theology. As in the final vision (6:1–8), war is now past, at his command, and the time of peace has come for the whole world. The royal language has echoes of Isa. 9:2–7 [1–6]; 11:1–9. The idea of universal peace is similar to Isa. 2:2–4; Mic. 4:1–4, and also Ps. 72:8. The humility of the king is unusual, but recalls the Suffering Servant (Isa. 52:13—53:12). There is no revelling in victory here (contrast Ps. 72:9), but only the end of war.

9:11–17 The lens shifts back to victory over enemies, with the language of the Divine Warrior and Holy War. The salvation of the people (called variously 'Judah', 'Ephraim', 'Zion') comes by victory. The named enemy is now Greece (v. 13), the power in the region from the late fourth century.

The 'blood of my covenant with you' (literally 'the blood of your covenant') refers to the blood-sacrifices that accompanied the making of covenant (Exod. 24:5–8). But it also hints at the blood spilt in victory, because of v. 15. Note the use of the term in Heb. 10:29.

10:1—11:3 A number of familiar prophetic themes come together here. The passage begins with a call to seek Yahweh and not other gods, with a warning against false religion and leaders (10:1–2). It continues with a promise of restoration: reliable leaders replace the false ones (vv. 3–5; cf. Jer. 3:15). Judah and Joseph/Ephraim will be saved by God's compassion (vv. 6–7; cf. Hos. 11:8–9). Exiles will be gathered in from various nations, as in a new exodus (vv. 8–12, cf. Isa. 43:2). God's judgement comes against all pride (11:1–3, cf. Isa. 2).

11:4–17 After these words of assurance comes a prophetic symbolic action (cf. Isaiah 20; Jer. 13:1–11). Zechariah is to behave like a shepherd to the people, because their actual shepherds have shown no compassion. He makes – then breaks – two staffs (Pleasant or Favour, and Unity), signifying a covenant with all peoples and the unity of the northern and southern kingdoms of Israel. The people reject the shepherd, paying him off with thirty shekels of silver. God then tells Zechariah to throw this 'to the potter' (or 'into the treasury'; the confusion arises because these two words sound similar – Matthew 27:6–9 combines both possibilities). The 'potter' could equally be a shaper of metals, and therefore the point may be that the silver will be used for making an image. This again illustrates the people's disobedience. Finally Zechariah acts again as a shepherd, now a bad one. If the people reject good leaders they will be saddled with bad ones.

The sign recalls Ezekiel's staff that symbolized the unity of Israel and Judah

(Ezek. 37:15–28). But this oracle is one of judgement. Its exact setting is unclear (as are the 'three shepherds' whom Zechariah disposed of, v. 8; Baldwin 1972, pp. 181–83).

12:1—14:21: Battle for Jerusalem, and pilgrimage by the nations

12:1–14 Following the word of judgement in ch. 11, the first theme of this chapter is God's victory over the enemies of Judah and Jerusalem (vv. 1–9). It uses the familiar idea of the 'day of the LORD' to speak of this victory (like Joel 3:1–3, 14–15 [4:1–3, 14–15]).

The focus then turns back to Judah, and its repentance for its sin (vv. 10–14). The sin itself is the subject of v. 10. This verse is translated in different ways by both ancient and modern versions, because it is difficult in both its structure and its thought (contrast NIV: 'they will look on me, the one they have pierced', cf. Smith 1984, p. 276; and NRSV: 'they look on the one they have pierced'). A further option is: 'they will look to me concerning the one they have stabbed' (Meyers and Meyers 1993, p. 307; cf. Baldwin 1972, pp. 190–92). Though John 19:37 applies this verse to Jesus' crucifixion the reference in Zechariah is to some event in the prophet's time, or Israel's history (cf. Baldwin 1972, p. 191). It may have been a murder or execution of some figure in a conflict over the leadership or direction of the post-exilic community. It has also been identified with King Josiah (Person 1993, p. 131). Or again, it may be general and metaphorical. Meyers and Meyers think it refers to the rejection of true prophets by the kings and officials over generations (1993, pp. 339, 358).

The chapter seems to have a view of leadership in the post-exilic community in which the old privileges of the Davidic house are balanced by new and more 'democratic' forms. This has been seen as indebted to a 'deuteronomic' influence (Person 1993; cf. Meyers and Meyers 1993, pp. 356–57). The act of mourning is compared to some ritual involving the god Hadad-Rimmon, and its intensity is compared to the mourning for a firstborn son (vv. 10c–11). The mourners themselves represent the Davidic and priestly establishment (vv. 12–14; Baldwin 1972, p. 194).

13:1–9 The cleansing of Judah and Jerusalem from wickedness (13:1) recalls a theme of the visions (3:1–10; 5:5–11). The idea is continued with a saying about idolatry (v. 2a), then a passage about prophecy (vv. 2b–6; cf. 10:2–3a on false leaders). The passage is often taken to refer to false prophets, rather than all prophets, since they come in the same context as idolatry and the unclean spirit (Baldwin 1972, p, 196; Meyers and Meyers 1993, p. 400; Coggins 1996, p. 70). The execution of prophets who led Israelites to worship other gods (v. 3) was required by Deuteronomy 13. Verse 5 has an echo of Amos 7:14, but here it refers to false prophets who now deny that they ever acted as prophets. The wounds they try to hide (v. 6) came from self-mutilation while prophesying (cf. 1 Kgs 18:28). The phrase 'On that day' is important, however. In the eschatological period, there will be no more need for prophets, and therefore all who claim to be so are bound to be false (see also Theological Themes: Knowing God's will).

Verses 7–9 are sometimes attached to ch. 11, because of the theme of the false shepherd whom Yahweh strikes, and the effect of this on the people. Here, however, these things happen so that the people might be refined, and a remnant restored (Jer. 6:29–30; Ezek. 22:20–22; cf. Isa. 1:21–26).

14:1–21 The final chapter once again presents the sequence of Judah and Jerusalem defeated (vv. 1–2) then redeemed when their enemies are defeated in a great final battle (vv. 3–5; as in Ezekiel 38—39; Joel 3 [4]). The whole picture is another variation of the 'Day of the LORD' (v. 1). Yahweh as Divine Warrior is pictured graphically, appearing on the Mt of Olives, to the east of Jerusalem and Mt Zion (v. 4). This odd picture of the dividing of the mountain is to allow the people in Jerusalem to escape from the enemies who have taken it (Baldwin 1972, p. 201).

Various images are used to point to a great redemption, in which Yahweh is king of the whole earth, and Judah is at the centre of his kingdom (vv. 6–11). This is expressed by several allusions to other Old Testament passages about creation and redemption (v. 6, cf. Gen. 8:22; Isa. 60:19–20; v. 8, cf. Ezek. 47:1–12; v. 9, cf. Deut. 6:4, Ps. 93:1; v. 10, cf. Isa. 40:4).

There follows an eschatological portrayal of Jerusalem's salvation in the great final conflict. Here images of war mix with images of plague (vv. 12–15). (Verse 14 probably means that Judah fights 'at' Jerusalem, not 'against' it, with NIV, NRSV.) The survivors among the nations will join Judah in worship for the Feast of Booths, associated with the reading of the Torah. So familiar prophetic passages are in view here (Isa. 2:2–4; Mic. 4:1–4). In a twist on these visions, however, a threat is now extended to those who refuse to do so (vv. 16–19). And finally the holiness that once belonged to temple and priests is extended to Judah and Jerusalem generally (vv. 20–21).

THEOLOGICAL THEMES

BETWEEN SALVATION AND SALVATION

A theological reading of Zechariah depends on its position in time soon after the return from exile. Pre-exilic prophets had warned of the judgement that was still to come, and also gave glimpses of a life after it. Zechariah (like Haggai) now looks back on the judgement of the exile, from within the community that has been restored to Judah and Jerusalem.

Zechariah's prophecies affirm that God has indeed acted to deliver his people. The end of the 'seventy years' is a key turning-point for the people (1:12–17). However, Zechariah is 'between' past and future. This 'betweenness' is illustrated by the plan to rebuild the temple, which has been begun but not completed (4:9). The unfinished temple is quite central to the thinking in the book. It is a kind of symbol that tells much about the community itself. It has been saved, yet the working out of salvation remains before it as a challenge.

The challenge is nothing less than to become the true covenant community. That is why the book opens with a reminder that preceding generations had been called to repent and obey God's commandments (1:2–6). It comes again in 7:8–14. The restoration from Babylon was not the end of the story. The post-exilic people were still called into a faithful relationship with Yahweh. The other side of this call to faithfulness is God's promises of cleansing or purification. The cleansing of the community is symbolized in the vision of the cleansing of Joshua (3:1–5). And the second part of the book speaks directly of the purification of the people (Zech. 13:1).

The call to obedience was not easy, perhaps not even clear. It was one thing to know there must be no return to idolatry, but quite another to understand how this new community should be organized and led. Was Zerubbabel really the messianic king? What kind of authority should the high priest have? Or indeed the future king (12:7–8)? It seems as if there was uncertainty and debate about these things in the post-exilic community. Part of the call to obedience was to work out God's will about the practical business of organizing the community's life.

If the people were unsure, it was because they were 'between' the deliverance from exile (past) and a fuller realization of salvation. This was symbolized, as we saw, by the half-completed temple. But there was a larger scale of salvation too. The temple would be completed only a couple of years on from Zechariah's visions. But the promises of restoration would only be properly fulfilled in a farther future. The Book of Zechariah always has one eye on the circumstances of the community of Zechariah's day and another on an 'eschatological' salvation, in which Israel and Judah and people from all the nations would be saved.

The final salvation involves conflict (Zechariah 12; 14). As in other books (Joel 3 [4]), this is portrayed as a battle for

---

KNOWING GOD'S WILL: DID PROPHECY CEASE AFTER THE EXILE?

After the exile, the older prophets who had warned of God's judgement were viewed in a new way. After all, so it seemed, their prophecies had come true, in both exile and restoration. It seems that their written words were now preserved and listened to in a more systematic way than before (see above, Date and Destination; Zechariah 9—14). We become aware of the beginning of a 'canon' of prophetic books.

So was there room for more prophecy? Obviously it did not cease immediately after the exile, since we have the books of Haggai, Zechariah and Malachi. But there are signs that it tailed off. Was this because of opposition to it as an institution?

Some think that Zech. 13:2–6 means that prophecy as an institution has fallen into disrepute (Coggins 1996, p. 22; Blenkinsopp 1984, p. 263). An alternative is to suppose that the prophets mentioned here are false prophets (see Outline). But the key phrase is probably 'On that day' (v. 2). This means that the passage refers to the 'eschatological' time, when there will be no more need for prophecy. This could fit in with the New Covenant prophecy in Jer.

31:33–34, which foresees that there will be no more need for teachers, since each individual will know God directly (Person 1993, pp. 197–98, and n. 59). In that case it would not rule out prophecy in the post-exilic community.

However, we have seen that both parts of Zechariah (1—8, 9—14) re-interpret older prophecy. The prophetic office has changed since Hosea and Amos, simply because of the memory of older prophets. 'Prophetic' knowledge of God, therefore, has now to reckon with 'scripture'. One view of this would be to suppose that prophets simply changed from being proclaimers to interpreters, like preachers who preach on 'texts'. (If the author of 13:2–6 is opposing all 'prophets' in his own day, then he can hardly be a prophet in the traditional sense himself.) This is the view taken by Blenkinsopp (1984, pp. 256–67). Perhaps, however, prophets and their hearers had to try to work out how the authoritative words of the past, now regarded as 'scripture', related to 'new' revelation – a problem that is still felt by some modern faith communities.

Jerusalem. Yet the final vision is also inclusive, for there is not only a remnant of Judah (13:7–9; 14:2), but also a remnant from the nations, who will worship at Jerusalem (14:16; cf. Isa. 2:2–4). In this way, the hope of salvation is lifted out of the immediate context, and the idea of worship at Jerusalem becomes a metaphor for the turning of all nations to Yahweh. The image in the book's last paragraph – in which cooking-pots throughout Judah are as holy as the ones dedicated to the temple-service (14:20–21) – is another instance of this.

Think about
BETWEEN SALVATION AND SALVATION

Zechariah works out how the covenant applies in the present, but also has an eschatological vision (Tollington 1993, pp. 29–30). It looked back on salvation (from Babylon) and also forward to salvation (of all nations in the end-time). Do you see a parallel with the story of salvation in the New Testament? How does this apply to issues that face Christians? Do they simply wait for the fuller salvation to come? Or should they expect to encounter hard issues in the Church's life in the 'between'-times? And how should they handle these? Consider one or more of the following examples from the New Testament; Acts 15; Romans 13; 1 Corinthians 8.

MESSIAH

The expectations of a Davidic king well illustrate the 'two horizons' of hope in Zechariah. In the visions it seems as if Zerubbabel carries the hopes of the restoration of the Davidic monarchy. Chapters 3, 4 and 6 portray the balanced leadership roles of Joshua and Zerubbabel, and it seems that in those places Zerubbabel is in the role of the 'branch', the well-known messianic title (Jer. 23:5). Yet Zerubbabel drops out of sight in the book, and also in history. Instead, the messianic theme returns with the famous announcement of a king coming to Jerusalem riding a donkey. This king comes following victory, putting an end to war over Jerusalem and the land of Israel. His kingship will not just be over Judah, but 'from sea to sea and from the River to the ends of the earth' (9:9–10). The formula is based on the description of the extent of the promised land of Israel (Deut. 11:24), but transforms it into the universal, eschatological peace, which will be enjoyed by all nations. In the context of chs 9—14, this messianic vision belongs together with the 'day of the LORD' images of chs 12 and 14.

RHETORICAL INTENTION

The basis of Zechariah's kind of persuasion is the fact that previous prophecy has come to pass. The hearers of its oracles, or readers of the book, know that in the past God warned the people by prophets, they failed to listen, he judged them, then he saved them. That is why the book opens as it does. The example of the previous generations is given, with the exhortation: do not be like them (1:2–6).

This then applies to the entire communication in the book. Salvation and judgement both remain as models illustrated by the past, but possible in the present and future. The visions serve two rhetorical purposes: first, to declare that a new time of salvation really has come, and second, to encourage the people to action. The vision form is a powerful way of saying that all that is happening to Judah has the force of God's decree behind it. At the same time, the visions reveal that all is not finished (the people need to go on being cleansed by the atonement rituals that the high priest presides over; 3:1–10; and they need to go on having the faith and courage to rebuild the temple; 4:9–10). The visions also instruct and exhort. They are a carefully conceived part of the prophetic message, going hand in hand with the more traditional style of prophetic exhortation in chs 7—8 (Tollington 1993, pp. 120–21).

In chs 7—8, Zechariah illustrates the re-use of prophetic oracles. The question about fasting is met by a reminder that the 'former prophets' had exposed the hypocrisy of fasting in the past (7:6–7). And in ch. 8, the formula 'thus says the LORD', is repeated frequently. This may mean that a number of separate oracles have been carefully collected here, into a written sequence. This could have been done by Zechariah himself (so Tollington 1993, pp. 27–30). The effect of it is to drive home the message, by insistent repetition. It is a message of salvation. However, it too slips in notes of exhortation: 'Let your hands be strong' (vv. 9, 13); 'Do not be afraid' (vv. 13, 15c); 'therefore love truth and peace' (v. 19c); and note the exhortations of vv. 16–17. Here, the authority of prophecy, together with the reality of salvation already achieved, is made the basis of an exhortation to live according to God's commands.

In chs 9—14 a mixture of types of saying combines to produce a vision of future salvation. The traditional Oracles Against the Nations form (9:1–8) is combined with a messianic oracle (9:9–10) to promise a new salvation (9:11–17). Traditional topics in prophecy (e.g. the 'shepherd', 11:4–17; the 'Day of the LORD') are woven into a message that comments on current matters (12:7–8), warns about possible unfaithfulness (13:2–6), and repeats promises of future salvation (12, 14). Underlying the diverse material in these chapters there is a controlled use of known prophetic forms in a powerful exhortation. The rhetorical effect of this material often does not lie on the surface. For example, the sayings in 12:7–13 have the form of predictions of what God will do. But they have the effect of commanding a certain attitude (a) about the relative roles of David and the people of Judah, and b) to the case in 12:10, which requires repentance. In general, the prospect of the final deliverance of Jerusalem is again a basis for the call to the community to remain faithful.

ZECHARIAH IN THE CANON

Zechariah occupies an important near-climactic place in the Book of the Twelve, and thus in the Christian canon of the Old Testament. This impression of special significance is strengthened by the fact that it is also one of the longest books in the Twelve. With its emphasis on salvation, it strikes a different balance from the opening books of the Twelve (Hosea to Micah). It helps tell the 'story' of judgement-to-salvation that underlies the Twelve. Indeed that story is re-told within Zechariah itself.

Zechariah marks a distinct move in prophecy towards eschatology. We saw that it was sometimes thought to represent a stage on the way from prophecy to apocalyptic. Canonically, it allows the eschatological tendency to gather momentum as the Old Testament canon (in its Christian form) moves towards its conclusion. The eschatological orientation has two canonical aspects that may be noted.

First, Zechariah takes the old traditions of the promised land and transforms them into a hope for all the nations. The eschatological germ lies deep within Israel's traditions. Deuteronomy (which on the surface does not look eschatological at all) contains the basic ingredients of this, because it sets Israel before the promised land. Canonically it has the effect of putting Israel always in that position, about to inherit the promise (see Person 1993, pp. 180–82). Zechariah puts Israel (in its remnant form of the returned Jewish exiles) once again before the possibility of land. It has this in common with Isaiah 40—55, for example. Indeed it re-uses Second Isaiah's imagery of new exodus into land (10:10–11; cf. Isa. 43:2–3). Deuteronomy's vision is expanded, however, since the nations now find a place in the eschatological order. And the language applied to the promised land is re-applied to the whole earth (Zech. 9:10).

The second canonical aspect of Zechariah's eschatology is that it opens the Old Testament story on to the New Testament.

Think about
ZECHARIAH 9—14 IN THE PASSION-NARRATIVES

Zechariah 9:9–10 is only one of a number of echoes of Zechariah 9—14 in the Gospels' passion-narratives:

- Zech. 9:9–10   Matt. 21:4–5; John 12:15
- Zech. 11:12–13   Matt. 26:15; 27:9
- Zech. 12:3   Matt. 21:44*
- Zech. 12:10   John 19:37
- Zech. 13:7   Matt. 26:31; Mark 14:27

Why do the expressions of messianic hope in Zechariah 9—14 lend themselves particularly to the passion-narratives? Look at the distribution of the passages from Zechariah 9—14 in the Gospel accounts. Notice that only one text is shared by Matthew and John. What does this tell us about why they found this section of Zechariah so compelling for the passion-narratives in particular? What is the background in Zechariah to the idea of a humble king (recall that hopes regarding Zerubbabel have disappeared)? (See Redditt 1995, p. 104.)

The parallels to Matt. 21:1–9 in Mark and Luke do not cite the Zechariah text. Does this mean they have not been influenced by it?

Notice, in contrast to the use of Zechariah 9—14 in the passion-narratives, that Matthew turns mainly to Daniel for his visions of the coming of Christ in power (Matthew 24). (See, however, Matt. 24:31, Zech. 2:6; 9:14; and Zech. 14:5; Matt. 25:31.)

For a treatment of the New Testament's messianic interpretation of Zechariah 9—14, see Duguid 1995.

*This verse is not printed in all English versions (e.g. RSV), as it is missing in some ancient texts. See marginal note in NRSV.

Its idea of a universal salvation is an obvious preparation for the New Testament. But this is also open to a Christological interpretation, for two reasons. First, its symbolic language invites re-application by the New Testament. Thus the vision of Yahweh coming to the Mt of Olives in the great final victory over the nations (14:4) probably lies behind the saying at the Ascension of Christ (from the Mt of Olives) that he would come again as he went (Acts 1:11).

The second reason why Zechariah lends itself to Christological interpretation is its messianism. The expectation of a messianic king within Zechariah itself (as we saw, Theological Themes: Messiah) was pointedly lifted out of its immediate setting (hopes for Zerubbabel) and re-applied to a future time (9:9–10). So it is not surprising that the vision of the king coming in victory in that text should re-appear in Matt. 21:4–5; John 12:15.

The idea of the temple takes several metaphorical shapes in the New Testament. But among them is the idea that God is building his temple the church, with Christ as the cornerstone (Eph. 2:21–22). The same typology of past saving event, call to faithfulness in the present, and prospect of completion in the future applies in this New Testament view. Zechariah and the author of Ephesians (and the New Testament more broadly) share a belief in a past and coming salvation which puts the believer at a mid-point between them, and which demands his/her obedience as part of the way to the ultimate fulfilment.

FURTHER READING

Items marked with * are considered suitable as first ports of call, while others are more complex, or relate to specific issues.

COMMENTARIES

*J. G. Baldwin *Haggai, Zechariah, Malachi*. TOTC. London; IVP, 1972.

*R. Mason *The Books of Haggai, Zechariah and Malachi*. CBC. Cambridge: CUP, 1977.

C. L. Meyers and E. M. Meyers *Haggai, Zechariah 1—8*. AB. New York: Doubleday, 1987.

C. L. Meyers and E. M. Meyers *Zechariah 9—14*. AB. New York: Doubleday, 1993.

D. L. Petersen *Haggai and Zechariah 1—8*. OTL. London: SCM, 1985.

P. L. Redditt *Haggai, Zechariah, Malachi*. NCB. London: Marshall Pickering; Grand Rapids: Eerdmans, 1995.

R. L. Smith *Micah–Malachi*. WBC. Waco: Word Books, 1984.

OTHER BOOKS AND ARTICLES

P. R. Ackroyd *Exile and Restoration*. London: SCM, 1968.

J. Blenkinsopp *A History of Prophecy in Israel*. London: SPCK, 1984.

R. P. Carroll 'Twilight of Prophecy or Dawn of Apocalyptic?' *JSOT* 14. 1979, pp. 3–35.

B. S. Childs *Introduction to the Old Testament as Scripture*. London: SCM, 1979.

*R. J. Coggins *Haggai, Zechariah, Malachi*. OTG. Sheffield: JSOT Press, 1987, repr. 1996.

*J. J. Collins *Daniel with an Introduction to Apocalyptic Literature*. FOTL 20. Grand Rapids: Eerdmans, 1984.

I. M. Duguid 'Messianic Themes in Zechariah 9-11' in P. E. Satterthwaite, R. S. Hess and G. J. Wenham eds *The Lord's Anointed: Interpretation of Old Testament Messianic Texts*. Carlisle: Paternoster, 1995, pp. 265–80.

P. D. Hanson *The Dawn of Apocalyptic: the Historical and Social Roots of Jewish Apocalyptic Eschatology*. Philadelphia: Fortress, 1979 rev. edn.

R. Mason 'The Relation of Zechariah 9—14 to proto-Zechariah' *ZAW* 88. 1976, pp. 226–39.

S. Niditch *The Symbolic Vision in Biblical Tradition*. HSM 30. Chico, Calif.: Scholars Press, 1983.

R. North 'Prophecy to Apocalyptic via Zechariah' *SVT* 22. 1972, pp. 47–71.

R. F. Person *Second Zechariah and the Deuteronomic School*. JSOT Suppl. 167. Sheffield: JSOT Press, 1993.

J. E. Tollington *Tradition and Innovation in Haggai and Zechariah 1—8*. JSOT Suppl. 150. Sheffield: JSOT Press, 1993.

Chapter 17

MALACHI

DATE AND DESTINATION

The heading of the book tells us nothing about its date or circumstances, or about the prophet. It is not even clear if 'Malachi' is really a name. This is for two reasons: it appears nowhere else in the Old Testament as a name; and it can be translated simply as 'my messenger'. The same word appears in 3:1, where it is always translated 'my messenger'. The Greek Old Testament (LXX) took it as 'his messenger/angel', and the Jewish Targum thought the 'messenger' might have been Ezra (Verhoef 1987, p. 154). However, there is strong support among recent commentators for taking 'Malachi' as a proper name (Hill 1998, p. 135; Verhoef 1987, p. 156; and Baldwin 1972, pp. 211–12). The form 'my messenger' in 1:1 does not strictly fit as an ordinary word (one would expect 'his messenger' in the context). It is more natural, therefore, to think that a proper name is meant. The *point* of the name, however, is indeed that this prophet is Yahweh's 'messenger'.

The heading 'An oracle' is like the headings at Zech. 9:1; 12:1, which reminds us that these last books of the Old Testament have links between them (see Malachi in the Canon).

Malachi belongs, like Haggai and Zechariah, in the post-exilic, Persian period in Judah. It is set after the temple was finally rebuilt in 516 BC, as is clear from 1:10; 3:1, 8. The word 'governor' (1:8) is used most frequently in the Old Testament for the Persian provincial governors (e.g. Ezra 8:36; Neh. 2:7, 9; Esth. 3:12; Hag. 1:1, 14). Its background is the same general situation of religious decline that Ezra and Nehemiah found in the mid- to late fifth century BC. Some have thought that Malachi must come before these, since we know that they carried out religious reforms (see Verhoef 1987, p. 157). However, we also know that reforms imposed by leaders did not always penetrate or last. (This is clear from 2 Kings 22—25, and indeed from Nehemiah 13.) So we cannot be sure when exactly Malachi worked. Hill dates Malachi around 500 BC, partly on linguistic grounds (Hill 1998, pp. 82–83). Verhoef favours a time after 433 BC, that is, between Nehemiah's two visits to Judah (1987, pp. 158, 160). Coggins is more cautious (1996, pp. 74–75). And note Glazier-McDonald 1987 (p. 5): 'Malachi offers no reference points for concrete dating.'

All we can say with confidence is that Malachi should be dated in the Persian period after the building of the temple, that is, between 516 and 330 BC. The sort of situation addressed can only be deduced by a reading of the book.

Digging deeper:
MALACHI AND NEHEMIAH

Compare the problems faced by these two leaders. Nehemiah 13:6–31 records several examples of the people's failure to keep faith with Yahweh, which are echoed in Malachi. Find what the two books have in common, and one concern of Nehemiah's not echoed in Malachi. Then compare Verhoef 1987, pp. 161–62.

CRITICAL INTERPRETATION OF MALACHI

Malachi is widely agreed to be a unity. It is structured in a dialogue form, which suggests it is a coherent work. Scholars sometimes find 'deuteronomistic' glosses (e.g. 'my special possession', 3:17, cf. Deut. 7:6). And the last three verses (4:4–6 [3:22–24]) are often held to be appendices from a separate author or authors. However, Glazier-McDonald argues that these verses also may belong integrally to the book (1987, pp. 243–70).

STRUCTURE AND OUTLINE

The structure is generally agreed. The book is in the form of dialogues, or 'disputations', between Yahweh and members of the community. The form is not unique to Malachi (cf. Mic. 2:6–11), but only Malachi is structured entirely around it. This has been called 'an oral debate' (Glazier-McDonald 1987, p. 2) or 'six disputational oracles' (Hill

1998, p. 41). These oracles are 1:2–5; 1:6—2:9; 2:10–16; 2:17—3:5; 3:6–12; 3:13—4:3 [3:21]. Following the oracles the book closes with words about Moses and Elijah (4:4–6 [3:22–24]).

STRUCTURE

The structure of the book, then, is as follows:

1:1–5	God's love for Israel
1:6—2:9	Bringing offerings and keeping covenant
2:10–16	Covenant and marriage
2:17—3:5	A refining judgement on Judah
3:6–12	Bringing the full tithe
3:13—4:3 [3:21]	The 'sun of righteousness'
4:4–6 [3:22–24]	Moses and Elijah

OUTLINE
1:1–5: God's love for Israel
The first 'debate' sets one of the great themes of the book, God's love for Israel. The illustration of Jacob and Esau shows that it is God's love in *choosing* Israel that is meant. This refers to the beginning of the Old Testament's story, in which God chose Abraham (Gen. 12:1–3), then his descendants, to be the people through whom he would bring his blessing to the world. In this story, God chose Isaac's younger son Jacob in preference to the older son Esau (Gen. 25:19—27:46). For Yahweh to 'love' his people is very close to his 'choosing' them, especially in Deuteronomy (Deut. 7:7–8).

Edom was the people descended from Esau (Gen. 36:1). It was Judah's nearest neighbour to the south-east, and a traditional enemy. It may be mentioned here because of some attack or invasion by Edomites during the Persian period. Or it may be another case of Edom standing representatively for the enemies of God and his people (as in Isaiah 34; see Hill 1998, pp. 77–78; Coggins 1996, p. 75).

The point of the dispute is given in 1:5; 'Great is the LORD beyond the borders of Israel' (as most translations have it). That is, God is powerful to put into effect his love for Israel, even overcoming their enemies on their own soil. (Hill has '. . . *over* the territory of Israel', 1998, p. xl, putting a different slant on it.)

1:6—2:9: Bringing offerings and keeping covenant
1:6–14 The right response to Yahweh's love for Israel was for them to love him in return (Deut. 6:5; 10:12). The love of son for father and servant for master (1:6) are ways of expressing the covenantal relationship (see Theological Themes). This word of Yahweh is directed against the priests especially, and the bringing of blemished animals was forbidden by Israel's law (1:8, cf. Lev. 22:2–25; Deut. 15:21). They would not dishonour the Persian governor as they are dishonouring God. Yahweh's rejection of this false sacrifice (1:10) is like the older prophets' condemnation of meaningless worship (e.g. Amos 5:21–25).

The failure of the priests is depicted as deep-seated contempt for God (1:13). The offerer of the poor sacrifice does not escape blame either (1:14). This contempt is the opposite of the reverence, or 'fear', due to Yahweh as the 'great king' (another term from the covenantal realm of ideas).

The contempt shown by priests and people is contrasted with honour shown to Yahweh by non-Jews. In 1:11, Yahweh's name is honoured throughout the world (i.e. 'from the rising of the sun to its setting', cf. Ps. 50:1). The text is remarkable because it teaches that true worship is (or will be) offered by priests in other places than the temple in Jerusalem, and outside the chosen land of Israel. Possible interpretations are as follows:

i. It teaches that non-Yahwistic worship was actually acceptable to Yahweh if done sincerely. It would especially refer to non-Israelite religion that was tending towards monotheism, like some Persian religion (Lindblom 1962, p. 406). This would be significantly different from other universalistic prophetic texts (like Isa. 2:2–4), for these teach that the nations will in the end worship Yahweh in Jerusalem.

ii. It refers to Jews in exile among other nations, and perhaps proselytes (converts to Judaism; Blenkinsopp 1984, pp. 240–41).

iii. The thought is metaphorical or a rhetorical exaggeration (Smith 1984, pp. 314–15. Mason's view is close to this also; 1990, pp. 295–96, n. 25).

iv. It looks forward to the messianic age, when all divisions between Jew and Gentile, and between 'holy land' and the wide world will be broken down (Gal. 3:28–29; and see Glazier-McDonald 1987, pp. 60–61; Verhoef 1987, pp. 229–32; Baldwin 1972, pp. 227–30). The last of these is probably to be preferred (see below, Theological Themes). Malachi 1:14 has a similar thought, though it need only mean that the nations show respect to Yahweh, not necessarily worship him.

2:1–9 The 'command' given to the priests is not specified in v. 1, but from v. 4 may be taken to mean the same as the 'covenant with Levi'. That is, the special duty of the priests to teach, to lead in the worship of Yahweh and honour his name (v. 2). In performing this duty, the priest was God's 'messenger' (2:7), the first use of this term in its general sense in the book. The priests were failing in their duty, however. The curses with which they are threatened affect

A 'COVENANT WITH LEVI'?

There is no Old Testament record of the making of a 'covenant with Levi'. Malachi 2:4 and Jer. 33:21 suppose that a 'covenant with Levi' existed from ancient times. 'Levi' and 'Levites' in these texts refer to the whole tribe of Levi (cf. Deut. 18:1). That is, they do not use the term 'Levites' in the narrower sense of the non-Aaronites who were given subordinate duties to the Aaronite priests according to Num. 3:1–10. Malachi is often said to follow Deuteronomy in its concept of the priesthood, rather than the Priestly parts of the Pentateuch.

(On the difference between P and Deuteronomy on this topic, a standard treatment is Emerton ('Priests and Levites in Deuteronomy', VT 12. 1962, pp. 129–38). I have taken a different view (*Law and Theology in Deuteronomy*. JSOT Suppl. 33. Sheffield: JSOT Press, 1984, pp. 124–53). For a short but helpful note, see Wright (*Deuteronomy*. NIBC. Peabody, Mass.: Hendrickson, 1996, pp. 220–21).)

What might this covenant refer to, then, in the stories of Israel's beginnings? Deuteronomy 10:8–9 recalls a time during Israel's wilderness wanderings when the tribe was 'set aside' for priestly duties. Deuteronomy 33:8–11 tells that Moses assigned to Levi the Urim and Thummim, the priestly method of enquiring of God, as well as the priestly roles of teaching and offering sacrifice. Here too it seems to be assumed that Levi's priestly role is already known. Finally Exod. 32:26–29 tells of the zeal of the Levites at the time of the golden calf incident at Mt Sinai, and how they 'ordained themselves for the service of the LORD'. Yet it is not clear that this is the same as the 'covenant with Levi'. So there is no event we can point to in which a covenant with Levi was made. Jeremiah and Malachi simply use this concept of covenant to describe the long-standing special role of the Levitical tribe as priests.

their priestly role directly: their 'blessing' of the people (v. 2, cf. Deut. 10:8c) will be turned to cursing, they will be made ceremonially unclean (v. 3, cf. Exod. 29:14; Lev. 4:11–12), they will be put out of God's presence, and their descendants also disqualified from the priesthood.

The fault of the priests was in failing to give true teaching ('torah') to the people, and so causing them to disobey Yahweh (vv. 6–9).

2:10–16: Covenant and marriage

The argument in this section is that the people of Judah are being faithless to Yahweh by being faithless in the realm of marriage. The prophet appeals rhetorically to what he takes the people to believe: that they have the same 'father' (Yahweh), who also created them (2:10). (Some think the 'father' is the forefather Abraham; Baldwin

1972, p. 237. But the parallel of 'father' and 'creator' suggests it refers to God; cf. Deut. 32:6; Isa. 64:8, and Smith 1984, p. 321.) Should they then be divided? Two kinds of offence are in view: marriage to foreign women, who worship foreign gods (v. 11b), and divorce between marriage partners who were Yahweh-worshippers. In both cases the offence is made worse because the people continue to worship as if there was nothing wrong.

The first offender is to be 'cut off' from the people, so that he will have no descendants of mixed religion (v. 12). ('Cut off' is sometimes taken in a stronger or a milder sense. Hill thinks it means in effect that the offender would be killed, referring to the phrase in Pentateuchal texts where this seems to be implied, e.g. Lev. 7:20–27; Hill 1998, pp. 233–34. Baldwin 1972, p. 239, takes it in the milder sense, simply as a prayer that the offender would have no offspring.)

Marriage between two worshippers of Yahweh, however, is seen as a covenant (v. 14; see Hugenberger 1994, pp. 27–30). This emphasizes the strong obligation to the partner in marriage. Verse 16 also voices the strongest opposition of God to divorce in the Old Testament. (The Hebrew text shows signs of having been changed in its copying, perhaps to reconcile 2:16 with Deut. 24:1–4, which permitted divorce. But translations rightly restore it to mean that Yahweh hates divorce.)

2:17—3:5: A refining judgement on Judah

In another dialogue form, people are accused of saying that Yahweh is unjust (2:17). This idea was sometimes expressed in genuine doubt (e.g. Ps. 73:3–14). Here it appears more like cynical unbelief, as it 'wearies' God, and comes in the context of other accusations of disobedience and carelessness. In answer, God says that he will suddenly come to his temple, preceded by his messenger. He will come in refining judgement, first on the priests (3:3), but also on all who are faithless in religion or wicked in their dealings with others (3:5; cf. Deut. 18:9–14 for the prohibition of 'sorcerers').

The 'messenger', or 'messenger of the covenant', reminds of Malachi himself (see Date and Destination). But the word has its general sense here (though it refers to a different person than 2:7). The idea of a messenger preparing the way for Yahweh to come was found in Isaiah 40—55 (Isa. 40:3; 57:14; 62:10). The 'messenger' in those passages came to a people already prepared to receive God as king. The present community does not yet fit that description (Childs 1979, p. 493).

3:6–12: Bringing the full tithe

The dialogue opens with God affirming that he has stayed with his people in spite of their persistent unfaithfulness (3:6–7). Repentance has always been an option for his people as a way back. Typically in these dialogues, Malachi's hearers appear reluctant to comprehend this. Their refusal to bring the full tithes is like their refusal to offer unblemished sacrifices (1:8). The tithe requirement was part of the religious duty of every Israelite (cf. Deut. 14:22–29; Num. 18:21–24). What God says about tithing reminds of the logic of Deuteronomy, which taught that when the people gave their offerings they would have more, not less, for God would bless them (notice the final clause in Deut. 14:29). This is not a mechanical process; rather, it is the way of faith as opposed to ordinary calculation. The calculation that holds back the full gift reckons without the fact that God is the giver of all prosperity. The language of blessing here is taken from the deuteronomic covenantal blessings (Deut. 28:12, cf. vv. 38–39).

3:13—4:3 [3:21]: The 'sun of righteousness'

The final disputation involves people who reject obedience to God out of hand, because it is, apparently, of no use. Instead of a response to them as at other times, there is a narrative passage, which tells how God will make a distinction between the righteous and the wicked. This is Malachi's version of the 'remnant' idea that we have met frequently (Isa. 1:27–31; Joel 2:32 [3:5]; Zech. 13:7–9). Their names will be written in a book and unfailingly remembered (Exod. 32:32; Ps. 69:28 [29]. It is this remnant that will count as the 'special possession' of Yahweh, the name he had once given to Israel as a whole (Exod. 19:5; Deut. 7:6).

Think about
SHOULD CHRISTIANS TITHE?

Some churches today insist that the Bible teaches that all Christians should give a tithe of their income to the work of the church. In interpreting the Old Testament's tithe requirement we need to understand its purpose in the world of the Old Testament itself, and also its canonical context. The following statements may serve as discussion starters.

● Tithes were part of Israel's sacrificial system, and went for the upkeep of priests and temple service; therefore they cannot be directly carried over into the practice of the Christian church.

● Jesus nowhere required tithing, and was even critical of fussy attention to it. He looked instead for a heartfelt desire to do God's will. In this he was like the prophets (Matt. 23:23–24; cf. Hos. 6:6).

● Part of the purpose of the tithe was to help care for the weak and poor in society. This role is partly taken by modern taxation systems. There is a historic connection between the biblical tithe and modern taxation.

● Attempts to apply the tithe law directly today meet problems of interpretation and practice. How exactly does one calculate the tithe in relation to income and other wealth? The demand for a tithe sounds fair on the face of it, but actually falls unfairly, being a hardship for the poor, or the family struggling on one modest income, while being a light burden for the well off.

Consequently, in my view, Christians are not under any compulsion to give a 'tithe'. If they feel the need to do so, they will still have to work out in conscience what exactly that means. The Christian obligation to give is a matter of conscience, led by the Gospel command to give oneself totally. The New Testament has examples of tremendous self-denial (Mark 12:41–44; Acts 4:36–37). Its rule is that each should give generously, and as they were able (2 Cor. 8:2–3; Acts 11:29).

On the 'day' when he comes (cf. the 'day of the Lord' in other prophets: Zeph. 1:7–16; Zech. 12:1—13:6), he will make this judgement. His salvation of the faithful will be like the rising of a 'sun of righteousness', a beautiful metaphor which means that God will fill the whole world with salvation and righteousness (cf. Ps. 50:1–6; Ps. 19:1–6 [2–7]; Hab. 2:14).

4:4–6 [3:22–24]: Moses and Elijah
The book finishes with two sayings unlike anything that has preceded. Malachi 4:4 [3:22] is the most 'deuteronomic' text in the book. Moses is present at the close of the (Christian) Old Testament canon as he was (almost) at the beginning. The passage rounds off the prophetic canon as much as it does Malachi. It insists that the Mosaic laws are still operative in the post-exilic time. The community (which counts as 'Israel') is bound by 'torah'. This must now be read, however, in the light of the whole prophetic message.

The book closes with a surprising word about Elijah, who is apparently in the role of the 'messenger' of 3:1. Elijah may stand for prophets as Moses stands for 'torah'. His mysterious end – he did not die but was taken to heaven in a chariot of fire (2 Kgs 2:11) – may mean that he can come mysteriously again. His role will be the prophetic role of bringing people to repentance before the great day of judgement. The New Testament sees a parallel with John the Baptist (Mark 9:4–5; Matt. 11:14 – but John 1:21 has a different angle).

The note of warning continues to the last breath in the prophetic corpus. The very last word is the most ominous imaginable, *herem* (4:6 [3:24]), that is, 'devotion to destruction', the terrible phrase used to describe the fate of the nations of the promised land that God decided to give to Israel (Deut. 2:34). The purpose of 'Elijah' will be to bring people to repentance in order to avoid this fate.

THEOLOGICAL THEMES

COVENANT WITH YAHWEH

The covenant made at Mt Sinai between Yahweh and Israel underlies the whole argument of the prophecy. It is expressly mentioned in 2:10 and 3:1. In 2:10 'the covenant of our ancestors/forefathers' points to the Sinai generation. The phrase is also like Jer. 31:32, where it refers to the 'old' covenant as opposed to the New Covenant. Malachi may imply by this allusion that the situation in his time is like that in Jeremiah's time, when the covenant had been broken, and the New Covenant had not yet come (so Hill 1998, p. 225).

The theme of covenant is much deeper than the occurrences of the term itself. The language of Deuteronomy, the Old Testament's leading 'covenantal' book, pervades Malachi. This language includes faithfulness, love, fear, servant, election, righteousness (*sedaqah*), wickedness (*rish'ah*), 'devotion to destruction' (*herem*), 'treasured possession' (*segullah*) (Coggins 1996, p. 76; Hill 1998, p. 42). Deuteronomy also provides the background to the idea of bringing offerings to the sanctuary to

honour Yahweh's 'name', tithes to the storehouse, and unblemished animals in sacrifice (Mal. 1:7–8; 3:10; Deut. 12:5–6; 14:28–29; 15:21). The dependence on Deuteronomy is not exclusive, however, as there is priestly terminology too.

The book opens with an argument based on Yahweh's election, or 'love' of Israel (1:2–6; Deut. 7:6). The loyalty owed to him in return is likened to that of a 'son' and a 'servant' (1:6), both Deuteronomic metaphors (Deut. 10:12; 14:1; 1:31; cf. also Mal. 3:17). The election theme returns at the end, when Yahweh says he will make the faithful remnant his 'special/treasured possession' (*segullah*), and again uses the metaphors of 'son' and 'servant' (3:17).

The covenant theme has a strongly personal aspect. Writers often notice how the person of God is at the centre of the prophecy. No other prophecy opens with such a direct, personal, emotive saying of God 91:2). And as Verhoef puts it: 'God is the all-important subject of Malachi's dialogues' (1987, p. 181). The relationship between God and people is expressed in a variety of emotional language.

> **Digging deeper:**
> **GOD'S AFFECTIONS**
>
> Consider how God is portrayed in Malachi. One way to do this is to search the book for the attitudes and emotions that are attributed to him, beginning with 1:2–3: 'I loved . . . I hated . . .'

The covenant in Malachi is conditional, like the Mosaic one. Israel itself has been 're-invented' in his vision, not as the historic people, but as those who prove faithful to

Yahweh. The 'treasured possession' has been redefined in this way too. But even then nothing is final. The ending of the book makes it clear that the need for obedience continues.

PARTICULAR COVENANTS

The covenant with Yahweh is the umbrella under which the whole life of the people with him and with each other is played out. Relationships and specific responsibilities become 'covenantal'. This applies first to the priests, the tribe of Levi, whose calling is described as a special covenant with Yahweh (2:4, 5, 8), as it was in Jer. 33:21. Then it applies to marriage (2:14), which is conceived as a covenant between the partners. This extension of the idea was intended to reinforce the need for loyalty in the marriage relationship. The marriage covenant is closely related to the covenant between all members of the community and God. This is clear in Yahweh's declaration of strong hostility to divorce (2:16), and the implication tha tmarriage has a crucial role in perpetuating the covenant people (2:15). This is not to be understood crudely in the sense of procreation, still less of ethnic purity, however. Rather,

Think about
'COVENANTS'

Malachi uses the idea of 'covenant' creatively in the ways we have seen. The Methodist Church has found it helpful as a vehicle for periodic re-commitment to God. Do you think it can usefully be applied to situations and obligations today? How might it be used in the life of a congregation, and of an individual? Does it help to make a connection between commitments in personal or professional relationships and one's fundamental commitment to God?

there is a connection of kind and quality between the two loyalties, so that the one depends on the other (Hill 1998, p. 247).

FORM AND SPIRIT IN WORSHIP

As with Haggai, it may strike us as odd to find a prophet calling people to formal worship in the temple. If our image of the prophet comes from Jeremiah, for example (Jer. 7:1–15), this will be strange. The return to the forms and routines of worship in the post-exilic prophets, however, comes from the situation. The prophetic call is now to live as might be expected of a restored community. As in Zechariah, that community is 'between' salvation and salvation.

In the meantime, Malachi says something about worship itself. While he penetrates to the heart, the seat of thought and desire, he also affirms the close connection between this 'spiritual' life and its expression in gift and obedience in the regular worship of the community. Priests are prominent here, not because of a campaign against sacrifice and priesthood, because they have a calling to lead the people in performing their duty to God. Malachi's emphasis should not surprise us in the light of Old Testament emphases in general. Even the pre-exilic prophets were not aiming to separate the inseparable: they knew too of the powerful bond between heart and action (see on Jeremiah 30—33). It is important that, in this prophetic book, which addresses a patient, ongoing life of a community awaiting the action of God, this aspect of Old Testament religion should be reaffirmed.

ESCHATOLOGY

Malachi has in common with other prophets that he foresees an age in the future when nations will join with Jews in worshipping Yahweh (Isa. 2:2–4; 42:1–7; Jer. 3:17; Zeph. 3:9–10; Zech. 8:20–22; 14:16). Usually these

DIVORCE

Malachi makes a rather uncompromising contribution to the question of divorce in biblical ethics. The categorical words of God: 'I hate divorce' are in line with the more stringent formulations of Jesus' words in the New Testament (Mark 10:5–12). There is also a biblical strain that permits divorce in certain circumstances. Deut. 24:1–4 presupposes that it was allowed in Moses' day. Jesus actually tightens up on Moses in Matt. 19:3–9 (cf. 5:31–32), with an argument based on God's intention for human beings at creation. But this saying ends with the famous 'Matthean exception', which permits divorce for adultery. (This is the usual interpretation of Matthew's term *porneia*. For a discussion of this and other interpretations, see Hagner 1993, pp. 124–25.)

The question whether the 'Matthean exception' gives permission for divorce and remarriage in the cases it refers to has given rise to a huge literature on the subject. Heth and Wenham (1997) give a broad review of this literature, and of the range of interpretations that have been adopted by Christians. Their position, which they think challenges the 'evangelical consensus', is that Jesus absolutely prohibited divorce *and* remarriage (e.g. p. 198). Grenz, also taking a strong interpretation of Jesus' words, nevertheless addresses pastoral issues surrounding divorce and remarriage; 1998, pp. 117–45.

This issue, because of its hermeneutical, theological and pastoral dimensions, is a salutary case study in biblical interpretation.

eschatological visions have some connection with Jerusalem. In some cases this is not a close link (e.g. Hab. 2:14, cf. Isa. 9:11). But in Malachi a new note is introduced by the perspective in 1:11, where the connection with Jerusalem seems to broken. For the eschatological interpretation of this passage, see above (outline). This should not be exaggerated, as Malachi's message as a whole is orientated towards the community centred on Jerusalem. (For example, 2:10 should not be misread as supporting the idea of the brotherhood of all humanity; Baldwin 1972, p. 237.) In some respects his vision of the future is also linked to the destiny of that people (in its distinction between the righteous and the wicked, 4:1–2 [3:19]; in the insistence that Moses' laws would continue to be valid, 4:4 [3:22]; and in the idea of Elijah coming to preach repentance and turn away the curse from the land; 4:5–6 [3:23–24]). Even so, it is appropriate that the final book of the prophetic corpus, and of the Christian form of the Old Testament canon, should take a step towards a kind of universalism.

RHETORICAL INTENTION

The disputation form is the most important rhetorical feature of Malachi's speech. At the simplest level, this shows an essential aspect of rhetoric. That is, it begins with what the hearers accept and agree with, and leads them from there to where the speaker wants to take them. An example is the argument about bringing defective animals for sacrifice (1:6–8). Malachi's hearers would agree that they would not try cheating the governor out of due taxes; how much less should they cheat God!

The disputation form probably goes deeper than this. For even the things that Malachi attributes to the people might have the effect of searching their hearts. It may be that the dispute form actually helps the hearers articulate what is going on in their minds and hearts. As usual, we try to imagine what Malachi's audience was like largely from what he says to them, since we only know very general things (that they were the people of Judah some time after the rebuilding of the temple). Perhaps the main thing that Malachi had to address was their discouragement. He shows them by his way of arguing that discouragement easily turns into loss of faith and even cynicism. (See also Hill 1998, pp. 40–41, citing Hendrix 1987.)

The 'covenant'-language also has rhetorical force. It is not that Malachi is simply to be classed as a 'deuteronomist', because he so readily turns to the language and ideas of Deuteronomy. Rather, the covenant language is deliberately used as part of his strategy to convince the people that the right option is faith. This is the force of Yahweh's opening ('deuteronomic') words; 'I have loved you' (1:2). The simple directness of this, together with the questioning response, tells as much as anything about the rhetorical intention of the book. It affirms Yahweh's faithfulness to his ancient love, exposes the people's lack of faith as the cause of their malaise. At the same time it encourages them by exhortation, and with forceful reminders that God's love needs to be met with obedience. As the prophecy began with 'love', it ends with 'herem' ('devotion to destruction'), its very opposite. There could be no more powerful invitation to faithfulness.

Malachi uses a large number of literary and rhetorical devices (see Hill 1998, pp. 38–39, for an extensive list, e.g. alliteration, 2:10–14; anthropomorphism, 3:3, 5, 10; hyperbole [exaggeration], 4:1 [3:19], 'neither root nor branch'; rhetorical question, 1:2).

MALACHI IN THE CANON

Malachi brings to a close the Book of the Twelve, the prophetic corpus and the Christian canon of the Old Testament. Its canonical function is somewhat heightened by this placement. In terms of the Twelve, it maintains the movement from emphasis on judgement to emphasis on salvation. This is qualified – like Haggai and Zechariah – by the people's frustration at hopes not quite fulfilled. In its broader background are the tremendous expressions of such hopes in Isaiah (40—55), Jeremiah (30—33) and Ezekiel (34—48). In its Old Testament context, Malachi insists one last time on the goodness of God, who created and elected Israel, and called them into relationship with him, in righteousness and truth. The perspective on the Old Testament as a whole is clear from the last three verses, which have echoes of the Law (Moses) and the prophets (Elijah), two of the three divisions of the Hebrew canon. Law and Prophets combine to show the people how to live in covenant with God who has chosen/loved them, and to call them again to faithfulness in doing it.

The appearance of Moses in this prominent final position in the Old Testament may be surprising, if we think that the path from Old Testament to New Testament is a movement away from law. However, that concept of the Bible is too simplistic. The issue is always *how* to respond to God's law not *whether* to do so. Moses is accompanied here by Elijah, and this tells us that our reading of law must always be informed by the spirit of the prophets, who teach that God loves mercy and not sacrifice (Hos. 6:6). In the same spirit Jesus also teaches that the law does not pass away (Matt. 5:17–20).

The return of Elijah, a new idea in prophecy, puts the well-known prophetic topic of the Day of the LORD in a slightly different light (4:5 [3:23]). Though the 'Day' is 'terrible', and inevitably will bring judgement, Elijah will come to prepare people for it, and this shows that God's intention is to save.

In its context of Old and New Testaments together, Malachi allows the former to end on a note of expectation. The last three books of the Twelve are, as we have seen, between salvation and salvation. The story continues in the Christian canon with the Gospel of Christ. Elijah makes an unmistakable bridge, when John the Baptist is identified with him in at least some of the Gospels (Mark 9:4–5; Matt. 11:14).

FURTHER READING

Items marked with * are considered suitable as first ports of call, while others are more complex, or relate to specific issues.

COMMENTARIES

*J. G. Baldwin *Haggai, Zechariah, Malachi*. TOTC. Leicester: IVP, 1972.

A. E. Hill *Malachi*. AB. New York: Doubleday, 1998.

W. C. Kaiser *Malachi: God's Unchanging Love*. Grand Rapids: Baker, 1984.

*R. L. Smith *Micah–Malachi*. WBC. Waco TX: Word Books, 1984.

P. A. Verhoef *The Books of Haggai and Malachi*. NICOT. Grand Rapids: Eerdmans, 1987.

OTHER BOOKS AND ARTICLES

J. Blenkinsopp *A History of Prophecy in Israel*. London: SPCK, 1984.

B. S. Childs *Introduction to the Old Testament as Scripture*. London: SCM, 1979.

*R. J. Coggins *Haggai, Zechariah, Malachi*. OTG. Sheffield: Sheffield Academic Press, 1987 repr. 1996.

B. Glazier-McDonald *Malachi: the Divine Messenger*. SBL Diss 98. Atlanta: Scholars Press, 1987.

S. Grenz *Sexual Ethics: a Biblical Perspective*. Louisville: Westminster John Knox, 1997; Carlisle: Paternoster, 1998.

D. Hagner *Matthew 1—13*. WBC. Dallas: Word Books, 1993.

J. D. Hendrix '"You say": Confrontational Dialogue in Malachi' *RevExp* 84. 1987, pp. 465–77.

W. Heth and G. J. Wenham *Jesus and Divorce. Towards an Evangelical Understanding of New Testament Teaching*. Carlisle: Paternoster, 1997, second edition.

G. P. Hugenberger *Marriage as a Covenant: a Study of Biblical Law and Ethics Concerning Marriage, Developed From the Perspective of Malachi*. VT Suppl. 52. Leiden: Brill, 1994.

J. Lindblom *Prophecy in Ancient Israel*. Philadelphia: Fortress, 1962.

R. A. Mason *Preaching the Tradition; Homily and Hermeneutics After the Exile*. Cambridge: CUP, 1990.

INDEX